Book of Britain's
Walks

D1419289

AA

Left: Ashton Cleave, Exmoor

Previous page, clockwise from top
left: Marloes Peninsula, Pembrokeshire;
Mosedale Bridge, Cumbria; high on
Mam Tor, Peak District; Moles Chamber,
Exmoor

Produced by AA Publishing

© The Automobile Association 1999
Reprinted Jan 2002

Published by AA Publishing (a trading name
of Automobile Association Developments
Limited, whose registered office is Millstream,
Maidenhead Road, Windsor SL4 5GD; registered
number 1878835)

Ordnance Survey® This product includes mapping data
licensed from Ordnance Survey® with
the permission of the Controller of Her Majesty's
Stationery Office. © Crown copyright 2002. All rights
reserved. Licence number 399221

Visit the AA Publishing Web site at
www.theaa.co.uk.

Hardback ISBN 0 7495 2242 9
Softback ISBN 0 7495 3031 6
A CIP catalogue record for this book is available
from the British Library.

Colour separation by Leo Reprographic Ltd.,
Hong Kong

Printed and bound by Fratelli Spada SpA, Italy

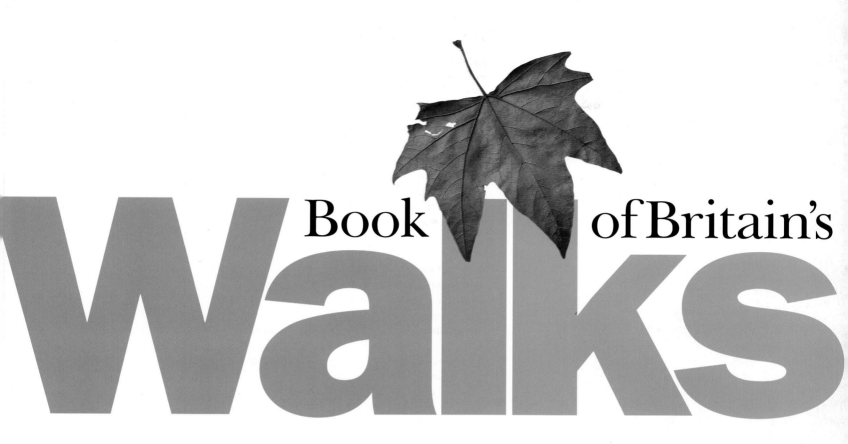

Book of Britain's Walks

The Walks

Introduction

Roly Smith *chairman, Outdoor Writers' Guild*

Why walk?

Walking is the number one outdoor activity in Britain, with many more participants than angling, golf or even watching football. According to the official figures, as many as 15 million people regularly take a walk of 2 miles or more every month, either individually, in families, or in organised groups or clubs.

That's a staggering 180 million rambles a year – over 40 times the number of anglers' outings and seven times the total annual football attendances in Britain each season. So we can safely say that Britain is a nation of walkers. Or, to be more strictly accurate, we are a nation of ramblers, and the use of that gentler, more ambulatory and very British term is significant.

Above: a feast of wild flowers on the Welsh coast

In America, walkers are known as hikers or backpackers, and in continental Europe excursionists or wanderers, signifying a much more worthy and serious enterprise. Rambling, on the other hand, means to wander where you fancy, to generally rove about, sometimes with no particular destination in mind.

This book is aimed at those ramblers who want to find out more, to seek out the relatively undiscovered corners, and delve behind the usual tourist board clichés so often glibly trotted out to describe this country. There is no doubt that the best way to see and really experience Britain is on foot. Fleeting coach- or car-bound tourists can only expect to receive a sanitised view. It is left to the

Below: chalky downland in the Vale of Pewsey

walker to really explore the warp and weft of the land, to seek out its real character, and to meet the people who have shaped it over so many generations.

But what is the attraction? There are many reasons, of course, apart from the sheer physical and mental pleasure of getting away from it all. Hippocrates is credited with first coming up with the maxim that walking is the best medicine. And in a famous essay on walking published in 1913, the great English historian George Macaulay Trevelyan claimed that when his mind or body was out of sorts, he knew he only had to call in his two doctors - his left leg and his right.

It is now generally accepted that walking has great therapeutic properties, both mentally and physically. Unlike more vigorous exercise such as running or jogging, which put unnatural strains on joints and muscles, with walking you are always in control and can set your pace according to your own personal levels of fitness and commitment. You can ramble, in fact. It is also widely recognised that regular, brisk walking reduces blood pressure, harmful cholesterol levels and also stress.

Where to walk

Apart from its health-giving qualities, another aspect that makes walking so attractive a prospect in Britain is the wonderfully varied and outstandingly beautiful scenery with which our islands are blessed. There are few other countries in the world where, during the course of a day's walk, you can pass from airy coastal cliffs, sand dunes, through lovely riverside meadows and woods to towering crag-bound lakes and mountains. But it remains perfectly possible in places like the English Lake District, Wales or Scotland. In this book there are many walks to these spectacular natural showplaces, from the awesome rift of Hell's Mouth on the wild north Cornish coast to the ice-carved splendour of the Cuillin Hills on the Isle of Skye and the hidden Lost Valley of Coire Gabhail in Glencoe. In between are the apparent wildernesses of Hampshire's lovely New Forest and the forbidding moorland wastes of Cross Fell in the North Pennines and the Kinder plateau in Derbyshire.

Britain is a land rich in history and folklore. Some sites visited in these pages still hold on to their age-old secrets. For example, no one can be sure why and by whom the uninhibited Cerne Abbas Giant was carved on a Dorset hillside, or what strange ceremonies were enacted around Long Meg and her enigmatic 'Daughters' in Cumbria.

Humans have so shaped the land over the 10,000 years of their history that there are few places left which can truly be termed wilderness. Only the steepest mountain crags or coastal cliffs have not felt the influence of their hand in one way or another. Even the wide, barren moorlands of the north of England, Wales and Scotland - which many people would regard as wildernesses - are only that way because they have been cleared of woodland and used for grazing by generations of farmers and graziers since the Stone Age.

The whole British landscape has been described as a palimpsest - a living manuscript which has been written on over and over again. With a little help such as that given by the expert authors of this volume, it can also be read like a book. And the first thing that a landscape historian discovers, as Professor W G Hoskins pointed out nearly 50 years ago, is that everything is older than you think.

Those dimpled depressions in a clearing of the conifers in Norfolk's Breckland mark the neolithic flint mines which were among the first industrial sites in Britain. That insignificant mound on a Peak District hilltop may be the last resting place of a Bronze Age prince, buried with all the riches associated with his position, some 4,000 years ago. And those strange corrugations which mark so many Midland pastures, or the step-like lynchets on the steepest slopes of the southern chalk downlands, show where every available piece of land had to be cultivated to counter the very real threat of starvation in the early medieval period.

Other sites give hints of a violent past, such as the sylvan Severn-side water meadows round Tewkesbury, where the fate of the Crown was decided in a series of medieval battles, and the Elizabethan defences of Berwick-upon-Tweed, for so long a bulwark against the Scots. A network of ancient trackways crosses our countryside, from the prehistoric Ridgeway across the Wessex downs to the paved packhorse routes of the Pennines, these once important arteries of commerce and industry now offering quiet highways rich in history for the observant walker.

Many other areas remain treasured havens for wildlife, and the nature walks in this book introduce you to a few of the most special. Stroll among the ancient beechwoods of the Cotswolds, try to spot an adder or a rare natterjack toad in the New Forest, or listen to the ravens cawing around the summit of Cader Idris: you may be surprised at the diversity that still survives in Britain today.

The scenery of the British Isles, whether spectacular or gentle, wild or welcoming, has often inspired great human artistic achievements, and walks are described that lead you in the footsteps of great writers, painters and poets who have been influenced by ever-changing scenery or the timeless sense of.

Practicalities

There are 140,000 miles (225,300km) of public rights of way in England and Wales, and in most mountain areas and Scotland there is a de facto right of access above the enclosed foothills. In some hill areas, particularly in the Peak District, access agreements are in force which allow the walker the virtually unlimited right to roam, and the Government has announced that it intends to introduce this right to all mountains, moorlands and uncultivated land in due course.

Elsewhere, it is the law of the land that you should stick to those rights of way which, it should be noted, have the same status in law as a public highway like the M1 motorway. Therefore, if you find one that is blocked, you have the right to clear it to allow your free passage, although we do not reccomend that you argue or try to force a way. It is better to report the blockage to the responsible authority, (usually the county council or unitary authority highways department). If you stray from a right of way, technically you will be trespassing, but unless you do damage you cannot be prosecuted, despite what some signs still say. All the routes in this book have been rigorously checked and are either on rights of way or on well-established, legal paths.

When out in the country, you should respect the life of the people who live and work there, especially the farmers, who have to such a large extent created the landscapes we know and love today. The Country Code was a commonsense set of principles which is probably best encapsulated by the maxim: 'Take only photographs, leave only footprints'.

Dogs

For many dog owners, a walk in the country would not be complete without their animal companion. Dogs are allowed on all the walks in this book, but courtesy and responsibility to other countryside users is always a necessity. Keep your dog on a lead and under control at all times.

Walking in Safety

Finally, a word should be said about equipment and safety. The most important single item of equipment required for country walking is a good pair of boots or sturdy walking shoes. Boots give better support to your ankles, especially in rough or hill country, and your feet need to be kept warm and dry in all conditions.

Britain's climate is nothing if not unpredictable, so warm and waterproof clothing is the next essential, but you don't need to spend a fortune on an Everest-specification jacket for strolling in the Cotswolds. There are many efficient and breathable alternatives which need not

Above: autumn in the Stretton Hills

cost the earth. Waterproof trousers or gaiters are also a good idea, and as up to 40 per cent of body heat is lost through the head, a warm hat is essential. Some of the mountain walks in this book should not be attempted in winter conditions unless you have previous experience and the technical knowledge of winter walking techniques.

None of the walks described in this book will take you more than a day, but you will need a rucksack to hold extra clothing, food and a drink for the longer walks. Look for one with about a 20-35-litre capacity, with plenty of stormproof pockets for your map, compass (a good idea on any hill walk), camera and other bits and pieces.

If you get into trouble, fall or are injured on a country walk, particularly in the hills, the rule is to send someone for help and alert the emergency services by ringing 999. They will ascertain the extent of the injury and whether it is appropriate for the mountain rescue service to be called, for an evacuation of the casualty. A careful note should be made of your exact location, and ideally, someone should stay with the injured party, keeping the person warm and dry until help comes.

Below: a dusting of snow on Skiddaw

Above all, enjoy your walking. After all, 15 million people can't be wrong!

Maps Each walk is shown on an illustrated map. Many of these will stand up to being used alone to navigate your way around the walk, and the Pocket Book of Directions and Maps is specially designed for you to use in this way. However, some detail is lost because of the restrictions imposed by scale. Particularly in the upland areas, we recommend that you use them in conjunction with a more detailed map, produced for walkers by, for example, Ordnance Survey or Harvey Map Services. In poor visibility, you should not attempt the walks in upland areas unless you are familiar with bad weather navigation in the hills.

Using the illustrated maps is simple, just read off the numbered instructions around the edge. Remember the countryside and especially towns, are changing all the time, and with the seasons, so features mentioned as landmarks may alter or disappear.

Information Each walk has a coloured panel giving information about the distance, total ascent, terrain, gradients, conditions under foot and where to park a vehicle. All the walks are suitable for motorists who wish to return to their cars at the end. There is also information here about any special conditions which apply to the walk, for example restricted access or access/entrance fees. The parking suggestions given have been chosen to minimise the impact of leaving cars parked in the countryside. They do not imply that motorists have a guaranteed right to park in the places suggested. Please park your vehicle with due consideration for other traffic and countryside users, especially agricultural access. Refreshment places mentioned in the text are suggestions by field researchers for their convenience to the route. Listing does not imply that they are AA inspected or recognised, though they may coincidentally carry an AA classification.

Below: trees and hedges mark the field boundaries in the Kent landscape

Grading The walks have been graded simply to give an indication of their relative difficulty. Easier walks, such as those around towns, or with little total ascent and over shorter distances have one boot. The hardest walks, either because they include a lot of ascent, greater distances, or are in mountainous or otherwise difficult terrain, are given three boots. Moderate walks have two boots. These gradings are relative to each other and for guidance only.

Access All the walks in this book are on rights of way, permissive paths or on routes where de facto access for walkers is accepted. On routes in England and Wales which are not on legal rights of way, but where access for walkers is allowed by local agreements, no implication of a right of way is intended.

Safety Although each walk here has been researched with a view to minimising the risk to the walkers who follow its route, no walk in the countryside can be considered to be completely free from risk. Walking in the outdoors will always involve a degree of common sense and judgement to ensure that it is as safe as possible.

- Be particularly careful on cliff paths and in mountainous terrain, where the consequences of any slip can be very serious.
- Remember to check tidal conditions before walking on the seashore.
- Some sections of route are by or cross busy roads, take care here and remember traffic is a danger even on minor country lanes.
- Be careful around farm machinery and livestock, especially if you have children with you.
- Be aware of the consequences of changes in the weather and know the weather forecast for the day of your walk.

Southwest England

Southwest England

The southwest of England tapers into a long and remarkably varied peninsula, stretching from the rural heart of England to the broken cliffs and coves of the Lizard and Land's End (the southernmost and westernmost points of mainland Britain respectively). Tiny fishing coves and hidden smugglers' haunts contrast with bustling seaside resorts such as Newquay and Penzance, and the rolling farmland of central Devon.

Previous page: the cliffs at Land's End, Cornwall

Right: for many readers, Thomas Hardy defined the landscape of Dorset

Below: sheep grazing on Porlock Hill, Devon

Despite the extensive granite uplands rising inland, you're never far from the sea, the Atlantic crashing down on the north coast and the gentler waters of the English Channel lapping the south coast. The proximity of the ocean means this corner of England gets its fair share of mist and rain – Dartmoor in particular has a reputation for being a foggy place – but the warming effects of the Gulf Stream also give the region more hours of sunshine than almost anywhere else in England: the area around Torquay in Devon is not known as the 'English Riviera' for nothing.

The Southwest has two national parks: the wild and extensive upland blanket bogs of Dartmoor and the coastal cliffs and rolling heaths of Exmoor. Protected Areas of Outstanding Natural Beauty encompass large stretches of the Cornish coast, Bodmin Moor, parts of Devon and Dorset, as well as the Quantock Hills and North Wessex Downs. There are also lengths of designated Heritage Coast with dramatic landscape and rich history. There's a wealth of natural history to explore in the uncultivated land of the Cotswold escarpment, or the rugged, recessed gorges of the Mendips. It's worth seeking out these little worlds, though in some cases, where the need to protect is greatest, access may be limited.

This is an area rich in legend. Untouched by the Romans, Cornwall was a last bastion of Celtic culture in England when the rest of the country had become Anglo-Saxon. This is the legendary homeland of King Arthur, who was born, tradition has it, at dramatically sited Tintagel, now a ruin. The wildness of the coastal scenery makes this easy to understand. With a little imagination you can stand at Land's End and gaze out to the shattered remnants of lost Lyonesse of Arthurian legend, but it is more likely to be the Isles of Scilly, shimmering in the sea. Further east the hills of the Dorset and Wessex Downs are scored by ancient earthworks and decorated with chalk figures, including a veritable herd of white horses and the enigmatic Cerne Abbas Giant. In the fields below, mysterious crop circles continue to appear, though

now their mischievous human provenance seems to have been proven.

As the land diminishes ever westwards, vowels in local speech become longer and the structure of the dialect hints that this was once a place apart, with a rich tradition all of its own. In the rolling downs of Devon and Dorset there are echoes of Alfred's Kingdom of Wessex, though the latter is a name now more commonly associated with Thomas Hardy. The literary tradition is strong in the Southwest, and Hardy's novels contain some of the best descriptions of the English countryside ever put to paper. In *Tess of the D'Urbervilles* (1891) there are eloquent descriptions even of the way people walked through the countryside, their gait and movement captured in painstaking detail. Other literary works lead you through Exmoor in search of Lorna Doone and Tarka the Otter, or almost anywhere in Cornwall after Daphne du Maurier's characters.

An area's eventful past can turn a simple walk there into a real journey of discovery, and if the clashing steel and musket fire of summer re-enactments are anything to go by, interest in the old battle sites has never been stronger. We tend to think of England as a peaceful land, but it has suffered bloody internal conflicts and a debilitating civil war. Even in more recent times, the need to train a modern army in a country where space is precious has led to some drastic moves; the evacuation of an entire village and farm landscape around Tyneham in Dorset and the continued occupation of vast tracts of northern Dartmoor by the army bear witness to this. And as the Cold War fades into memory a number of secret bunkers have opened up, including Bolt Head in south Devon, a disturbing sign of how seriously the threat of nuclear war was taken well into the 1980s.

For those whom only the most spectacular walks can satisfy, the Southwest is blessed with a continuous coastal path from Minehead to Poole Harbour – the South-West

Coast Path, no mere seaside stroll but one of the most varied and interesting walks in Britain. Trodden by excisemen and smugglers over the centuries, this path takes in a succession of rugged cliffs and coves. The granite buttresses around Zennor and Land's End are awesome, the gaping declivity of Hell's Mouth, breathtaking. Inland, the landscape may be less dramatic but the views are no less spectacular – the Quantock Hills, for instance, may be small in stature, but they rise from a low-lying landscape and offer sweeping views across the countryside.

At the opposite end of the scale, attractive and historic towns offer the walker a fascinating urban landscape to discover. Largely ignored by the Industrial Revolution, many West Country towns – such as Cheltenham, Bath and Tewkesbury – retain their Georgian elegance. Smaller and less overrun by tourists than Bath,

Above: the weathered rocks of Combstone Tor, Dartmoor

Best of the Rest

Lyme Regis and Dorset Coast Meryl Streep brought the image of the Cobb in Lyme Regis to cinema screens all over the world. The Dorset seaside town is the setting for John Fowles' international bestseller *The French Lieutenant's Woman,* and was used extensively in the film version. From Lyme walks extend along the beautiful coast in both directions, with nearby Golden Cap, the highest point on the south coast, a notable highlight.

Tintagel The north Cornish coast is rich in Arthurian legend, and at Tintagel the dramatic cliffs are surmounted by the brooding ruins of a plausible Camelot. Whether or not the British hero really lived in the castle here will seem irrelevant as you explore the rugged coastline, traced by the excellent South-West Way.

Forest of Dean A remote corner of Gloucestershire, nestling up to the Welsh border, it became rich through the exploitation of its mineral wealth. Now time has healed its industrial scars, leaving a legacy of excellent footpaths and bridleways through beautiful forest and, at Symond's Yat, a breathtaking view of the River Severn meandering through a wooded gorge.

Bath The Romans understood the importance of Bath's therapeutic waters, but it took the commercial savvy and aesthetic brilliance of the Georgians to create this upmarket watering hole of the 18th century. There are famous tourist sights in Bath, such as the Roman Baths and the Pump Room, but it is a walk around the lesser known parts which will bring the true history of the city to life. The squalor of the servants' living quarters and the expedient shortcuts in construction are shown up by a walk around the passages and alleys of this great World Heritage Site.

Slaughters For many the Cotswolds are epitomised by the chocolate-box images of Upper and Lower Slaughter. But away from the tourist coaches a network of excellent paths connect these idyllic settlements and gives the walker a unique view of this most English of landscapes.

The Somerset Coal Canal Hidden in the deep valleys which connect with the Avon near Bath is a lost industrial relic, a testament to a time when the Industrial Revolution touched every remote corner. To extricate coal from the now vanished Somerset coalfield for industrialising Bristol, a branch was built from the great Kennet and Avon waterway up the Cam valley to Paulton. Geology made the coal hard won, and the railways soon slashed the price of heavy transport. A walk along the canal's remnants now is a fascinating reminder of a bygone pioneering spirit.

Left: Badgworthy Water in the Doone Valley, Devon

Below: the rolling country around Painswick Beacon, Gloucestershire

Tewkesbury in particular is a charming place to explore, dominated by its great Norman abbey, and with Georgian façades and medieval timbered buildings still much in evidence. Alternatively, wander round the steep, cobbled streets of the old wool town of Frome, or explore the picture-postcard Cotswold villages.

There is no shortage of footpaths and trackways available to explore this southwestern corner of England.

Our most ancient forebears trod along the crest of the downs when Britain was a wild and wooded place. In early Christian times, when Cornwall was the 'Land of the Saints', missionaries were accustomed to using the peninsula as a stepping stone between mainland Europe and Ireland. Tinners and tourists, drovers and drivers, wool-carriers and walkers, all have left, and continue to leave, their mark.

Above: the curious pinnacle of the Devil's Chimney on Leckhampton Hill, Gloucestershire

Dorset Heaths of Thomas Hardy

WALK
1

The countryside he loved so well is explored in a walk from Hardy's birthplace to the spot where his heart – literally – lies

Top right: Hardy's cottage at Higher Bockhampton

Above: Thomas Hardy at Max Gate in the early 1920s

Below: a patchwork of fields in Blackmore Vale, from Bulbarrow Hill

Thomas Hardy's beloved Egdon Heath survives only in patches of heather and gorse, encroached on all sides by forestry and farming. Hedgerows, harbouring abundant bird and insect life, have been diminished by barbed wire or electric fencing; tarmac networks and petrol fumes enshroud the dirt roads and horse-drawn traffic. But the contours of the land remain, the sweeping prospect of field and meadow and the meandering River Frome in the valley. There are stretches of ancient hedgerow, churches and riverbanks that Hardy knew well, buildings that he designed as well as those he loved.

The cottage at Higher Bockhampton, where Hardy was born, was built by his great-grandfather. The author made it the Dewy's home in *Under the Greenwood Tree*, and in the lane here, the letter from a London magazine commissioning *Far from the Madding Crowd* was dropped and almost failed to reach him. From here, too, Hardy walked across Egdon Heath to visit his relatives in Puddletown. The path remains but the heath is hidden by trees. A favourite boyhood haunt on the heath was the Rainbarrow, a Bronze Age burial mound, from where he could see Dorchester. Hardy remembered bonfires there with his father, and Clym and Eustacia preached there in *The Return of the Native*. The view is

breathtaking over the Great Valley of the Dairies, and you can imagine the heath stretching towards Puddletown.

In the Frome basin below lies Lower Lewell Farm, the model for Talbothays Dairy where Tess worked. The 17th-century farmhouse still stands, although extended and altered. Further along the road, Talbothays Lodge, where Hardy's brother and sisters lived, was designed by Hardy and built by his brother. Hardy visited most Sundays by bicycle or on foot from his home at Max Gate, passing the church at West Stafford, where Tess and Angel were wed.

Hardy was a faithful visitor of family and friends, and after the death of his friend William Barnes, he visited his grave at Came church. The path over the hill to Max Gate is the one Hardy would have taken and Came Rectory, where Barnes lived, is a short detour from the route. Max Gate was the house which Hardy designed, where he wrote *Tess of the d'Urbervilles*, *Jude the Obscure* and most of his great poetry, where he entertained the literary giants of his time and where he died in 1928.

His ashes were buried in Westminster Abbey, but his heart lies at Stinsford church, alongside his family. This is the Mellstock church of *Under the Greenwood Tree*, and it lies at the heart of Hardy's story, his rootedness in Wessex, his sense of family, his connection with the church. Like Tess, he trudged the heaths, riverbanks, towns and byways of Dorset; he knew it and loved it.

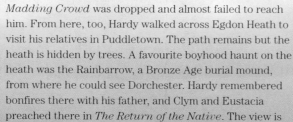

Dorset Heaths of Thomas Hardy

Explore the rolling, varied landscape which the writer knew and loved

Distance: 9 miles (14.4km)
Total ascent: 165ft (50m)
Paths: good but muddy in wet weather
Terrain: heathland, woodland, open roads and fields
Ascents: very few and gradual
Refreshments: Wise Man Inn, West Stafford (half way round the walk)
Park: Hardy's Cottage car park (National Trust), Higher Bockhampton, ½ mile from A35, NE of Dorchester

1 From the car park head for Hardy's Cottage, signed via a woodland path. From there take the path, signposted Puddletown, to a path junction. Continue to the next junction and turn right, continuing until the path descends steeply. The Rainbarrow is through a break in the hedge to the right.

2 Continue down the steep path, ignoring all other paths, until it turns left to the bottom of the hill. Take the small track through the bushes, ignoring the stile to the right, continuing over two stiles then left across the field. Cross the road to the track opposite.

8 Go through the farmyard and follow the footpath sign. Cross 3 fields, over stiles, through gates and past a house, turning left onto a farm track. Continue across a minor road, eventually turning left at a crossroads. The path forks right, then turns left and leads down to the car park.

7 Over a bridge turn right, following the waymarkers, through a kissing-gate, across a field and a bridge. Continue over another bridge, turn left and then right to Stinsford. Retrace your steps to the river and continue to Lower Bockhampton. Cross the bridge and turn left, signposted Thorncombe Wood.

6 Cross to Max Gate. Continue across the bridge, turning right before the roundabout and right again towards a gate marked Louds. Turn left before this, into Smokey Hole Lane. Cross a railway bridge down to a road. Turn right, right again then left for Stinsford.

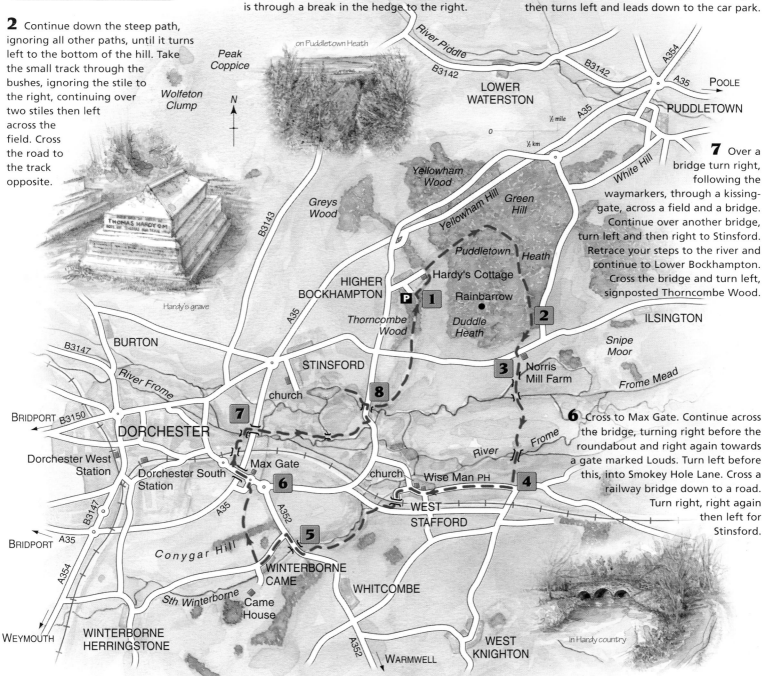

3 Continue along the farm track until a junction; bear left then right following the blue waymarkers. Follow this track across the field and cross the bridge over the river. Follow the blue waymarker through a gate and continue to the end of the track. Turn right at the gate, then go over the field to cross the wooden bridge and stile. Walk with the fence to the left, over another stile, across the field and through the gate to reach the end of the track.

4 Continue to the junction with the road, then turn right to West Stafford. Turn left at the church along Rectory Lane. Follow the blue waymarkers, under the railway bridge, across the road and over a stile. Continue through several gates until you reach a gate to the main road.

5 Turn right and then left through gates beside a lodge. Continue to the crossroads at Came and turn right towards Dorchester. At the top, where the road curves, go straight ahead. Cross the stile, following signs for Max Gate, exiting at a roundabout.

Purbeck's Ghost Village

The poignant remains of Tyneham are the focus for this fascinating exploration of the Dorset coast

WALK 2

Top right: the distinctive concrete telephone box at Tyneham

Below: cliffs tower above Worbarrow Bay

Inset: the church and roofless houses of Tyneham

The residents of Tyneham village received notice to quit their homes on 16th November 1943. The week before Christmas they were gone. They willingly made the sacrifice for the war effort, believing that peacetime would return them to their homes. More than 50 years later Tyneham remains a firing range for the army, despite a determined campaign to return it to civilian ownership. However, access is permitted to the general public on a limited basis at holidays and most weekends. The walk through Tyneham is clearly marked and warnings abound to stay within the designated paths for fear of coming across unexploded shells.

The village centres on the church, the school and Post Office Row. A concrete telephone box sits in front, containing an old-fashioned phone and a black box with buttons A and B to press. Of the now roofless houses, little remains but the fireplaces, from Victorian cast-iron ranges and bread ovens to the latest 'modern' red brick. There are exhibitions in the church and school with leaflets giving a guided tour of this long-forsaken little time warp. The route from Rectory Cottage to Laundry Cottage, by woodland paths to the duck pond and on to Gardener's Cottage and Tyneham Farm, poignantly recreates the simple community, so rudely shattered that November day. The greatest vandalism was perhaps visited on

Tyneham House, outside the village and not accessible to walkers, which was built in the 14th century, had been continuously lived in and extended by the same family until 1943 and has now been razed to the ground. The most impressive historic site is Flower's Barrow, a vast Iron Age fort on the cliffs above the village. It is an unparalleled vantage point for the switchback of cliffs, the sea and the patchwork of fields inland. No enemy could have breached this ancient fastness from land or sea undetected, although the sheer cliffs would have deterred invaders from the sea.

The sea provided a livelihood for the village of Worbarrow, where there are remains of several cottages and a bungalow as you descend to the beach where the coastguard station and the fishermen's cottages clustered. Fishing and smuggling were the trades that sustained them. Many tales are told of the battles between the smugglers and the forces of law and order, in which the local gentry colluded with the smugglers. The fishing was mainly for lobster, which they sold to fishmongers from Wareham or carried to Weymouth.

By the 1940s, however, the fishing industry was already in decline and the village school had closed in 1932. Although it was a bitter sacrifice for the people who lost their homes, there have been gains from the dereliction of Tyneham. The birds and wildlife here are more abundant and varied than elsewhere, where intensive farming methods have destroyed natural habitats and food supplies. Free of mechanised ploughing, the land still reveals the medieval strips and Celtic field systems of days gone by. Without the clearance, Tyneham would almost certainly have become another picturesque little seaside holiday village with cafés, souvenir shops and traffic jams in the narrow lanes, instead of a unique and fascinating glimpse of the past.

Purbeck's Ghost Village

Lost in time, the Dorset village of Tyneham is preserved amid the army ranges

1 Turn right from the car park, towards Tyneham village. The town trail is short but interesting. Each of the buildings has a marker and a leaflet available from the church explains what they were. The church and schoolroom contain an exhibition of the village history.

2 From the water fountain in front of the church take the road to the right past a marker pointing to Flower's Barrow and Whiteway car park. Follow the yellow waymarkers, passing behind the church and going through a kissing gate, and continue uphill.

7 Return to the path and, following the yellow markers, ascend Gad Cliff and proceed along the coastal path. Cross a stile and, at the sign pointing left to Tyneham, head downhill following the markers. This will return you to the car park.

6 Continue over the wooden bridge and turn left up a stone track, going right at the yellow marker, up the steps to arrive at a cairn. From here take the track up Worbarrow Tout for a superb view over the bay and the switchback cliffs.

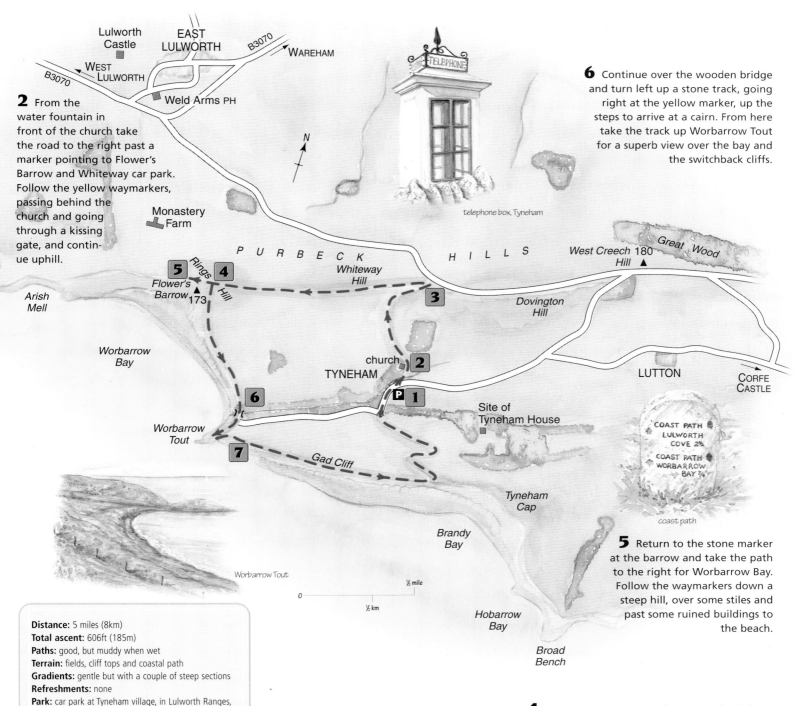

telephone box, Tyneham

coast path

Worbarrow Tout

Distance: 5 miles (8km)
Total ascent: 606ft (185m)
Paths: good, but muddy when wet
Terrain: fields, cliff tops and coastal path
Gradients: gentle but with a couple of steep sections
Refreshments: none
Park: car park at Tyneham village, in Lulworth Ranges, between Corfe Castle and West Lulworth
Note: this walk is on the Lulworth Army Ranges and access is strictly controlled. They are open most weekends and in holiday periods, but for up-to-date information, call the Range Office on 01929 462721 ext. 4819

3 At the flagpole at the top take the path to the left, cross a stile and head uphill past a trig point. Continue on the path downhill, until the road curves to the right. Veer left onto a track at the yellow marker.

4 Continue along the track, over a stile, following yellow waymarkers. When you reach an area with picnic tables, you are in the middle of Flower's Barrow. A stone marker points the way to Lulworth Cove. Continue on this path to the outer rings of this prehistoric fortification for a superb view along the coast.

5 Return to the stone marker at the barrow and take the path to the right for Worbarrow Bay. Follow the waymarkers down a steep hill, over some stiles and past some ruined buildings to the beach.

The Mystery of the Cerne Abbas Giant

From one of Dorset's most picturesque towns it is just a short walk to one of Britain's most mysterious figures

WALK 3

Right: attractive half-timbered buildings line the streets in Cerne Abbas

Below: the mighty figure at Cerne Abbas dominates the surrounding countryside

About 1,400 years ago St Augustine came to Dorset as a missionary from Rome. He walked up the valley of the river we now call the Cerne and preached to the Celtic folk of a hamlet beneath a spur of the valley ridge. Unimpressed, they tied cows' tails to his cloak, pelted him with mud and sent him on his way. The saint stumbled to the base of the spur and stopped at a spring to clean himself of his humiliation. He washed, looked skyward and saw God.

It would be all too prosaic to record that what the saint actually saw was the chalk-cut figure above Cerne Abbas. But the story does not say that, and it is not even certain that it was there when Augustine came this way. Neither is it certain whom it represents: the figure is a mystery.

The figure is 180ft (55m) tall and holds a club 120ft (37m) long. It is outlined by trenches cut into the chalk, each trench being 2ft (60cm) wide and deep. The figure is strikingly masculine, though, as archaeologist Jacquetta Hawkes noted, that particular part of its anatomy is 'the source of so much interest and so little open comment'.

The first record of the figure was published in the 'Gentleman's Magazine' of 1764. Since most experts agree a cutting date of 1,800 to 2,000 years ago, one may ask why it took 1,600 years for someone to consider it worthy of comment. The recent history of the figure suggests that if it is not maintained, its trenches periodically scoured, it disappears beneath the grass. The drawing of 1764 shows a navel as well as the existing features and this has now disappeared completely. For at least 500 years a Christian monastery sat beneath the Giant's feet. On the evidence of the navel, the monks must have scoured the figure many times, showing surprising respect for a pagan monument.

It is now generally agreed that the figure was cut either just before or just after the Roman invasion (AD 43). Evidence for pre-Roman construction lies in similarities with other known Celtic works, suggesting it represents the god Nodons. But it might also be Hercules, the Greco-Roman hero depicted with a club and a cloak thrown over an arm, the hand of which holds a bow. Could these later objects have been lost over the years, like the navel?

Our walk approaches the figure from Cerne Abbas, but from the hillside, close to the chalk man's feet, the view is disappointing, the figure foreshortened and difficult to make out. From further along the valley, descending towards Minterne Parva, the figure disappears before being revealed, dominating the valley (and the last section of the walk) like a charging giant. A local legend maintains that the figure represents a real giant who once preyed on local sheep. Townsfolk killed him as he slept and then marked his outline to prove his size to future sceptics.

The Mystery of the Cerne Abbas Giant

*High on a Dorset hillside a strange figure is carved
in the chalk*

WALK 3

1 In Cerne Abbas, make your way to the church, which stands in Abbey Street and walk along the street with the church to your right. To your left is an elegant row of timbered houses complete with overhangs.

2 Go past the village pond, to the right. Ahead now is beautiful Abbey Farm.

8 Cross the main road with care, bearing right and then left along the minor road towards the village, soon reaching the Kettle Bridge picnic site where there is alternative parking. Turn left (signed for the village centre), then follow the sign for the Pottery. Before crossing the bridge, turn right along a path with the river on your left. After about 200yds (182m) turn left over a footbridge and follow the path into the village.

7 Just beyond a white gate marked 'Private', go left along a field path, heading towards the modern barns, regaining the road and following it to its junction with the main road.

6 Turn left and follow the road, with great care, for 220yds (200m), then turn right along the road for Up Cerne. Follow this narrow, but quiet, road through beautiful Up Cerne, reaching the village 'square'. Continue uphill: there is a fine view of the Manor House from here.

5 Go through the gate and across the field beyond to reach another gate. Go through and maintain direction, passing several waymarkers to reach a gate. Cross the field beyond to reach a track, following it to a crossing of tracks. Turn left (signed for the main road) and follow the track (which becomes metalled) through Minterne Parva to the main road (A352).

4 Now follow a clear path beneath the Giant – which lies beyond the fence on your right. When the fence ends, continue along the obvious path, eventually crossing a stile and then maintaining direction to reach a waymarker near a barn. Go to the right past the barn, and follow the hedge on the left for about 380yds (346m) to reach a gate, also on the left.

3 Just beyond the pond, go right, under an arch and diagonally across the cemetery – the site of Cerne Abbey. Leave the cemetery through another arched gateway and cross the field diagonally beyond – the abbey ruins are to your left. Go over a stile to reach the base of Giant Hill.

Distance: 5 miles (8km)
Total ascent: 575ft (175m)
Paths: waymarked paths and minor roads
Terrain: fields and country lanes; very sticky and slippery mud after rain
Gradients: gradual
Refreshments: several possibilities in Cerne Abbas; on the A352 at Godmanstone, the Smith Arms is claimed to be Britain's smallest pub
Park: limited parking available in Cerne Abbas, and also at the viewpoint of the figure beside the A352

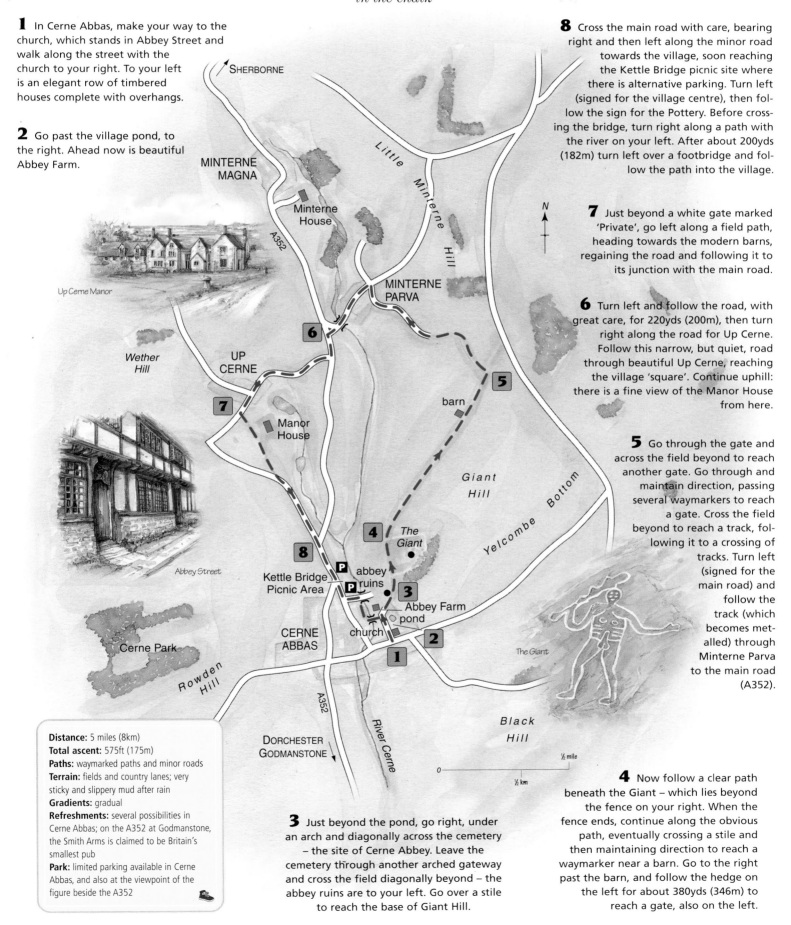

SHERBORNE

MINTERNE MAGNA

Minterne House

Little Minterne Hill

MINTERNE PARVA

Up Cerne Manor

Wether Hill

UP CERNE

Manor House

barn

Giant Hill

Yelcombe Bottom

Abbey Street

The Giant

Kettle Bridge Picnic Area

abbey ruins

Abbey Farm pond

church

CERNE ABBAS

The Giant

Cerne Park

Rowden Hill

Black Hill

DORCHESTER
GODMANSTONE

River Cerne

A352

N

½ mile
0
½ km

Among the Tors of Dartmoor

WALK

4

Granite created by volcanic activity almost 300 million years ago underlies the magnificent wilderness of Dartmoor

Top right: hardy sheep graze these moors

The granite of Dartmoor, Britain's southernmost national park, forms a thin, acidic soil which supports a limited range of plants and encourages the formation of peat bogs, which define the moor in popular imagination. The 16th-century traveller William Camden wrote of 'squalida montana Dartmore', a phrase which seems even more descriptive for not being translated. Then Sabine Baring-Gould, in his *Book of Dartmoor*, published in 1900, recorded the view of a Plymouth tailor: '…only unwhole-some-minded individuals can love Dartmoor.' When Arthur Conan Doyle set *The Hound of the Baskervilles* on Dartmoor, with, as its centrepiece, the fearsome Grimpen Mire (almost certainly modelled on Foxtor Mires in the southern half of Dartmoor), Dartmoor's reputation as a place of leg-swallowing bogs, of interest only to fools, was firmly established.

Inset: Hound Tor, one of the many granite tors on Dartmoor

But while Dartmoor certainly deserves its reputation, in part at least, it is also, in the right conditions, a magical place, the last true wilderness in southern England (High Willhays, Dartmoor's tallest peak, is the highest point in England south of the Herefordshire Black Mountains) and one of the very finest in Britain. Large tracts of the northern moors are controlled by the army, who find its inhospitable environment perfect for survival training. Less harsh, the southern moors are more accessible to walkers.

This walk starts at the most famous of Dartmoor's tors, Haytor. Tors are exposed outcrops of granite moulded into fantastic shapes by centuries of wind, rain and frost. The views from up here are marvellous: on a fine day you can see the cultivated lowlands of Devon to the east, the coast and Teign estuary to the south, and the boulder-strewn moorland of Dartmoor to the north and west.

Below: rocky outcrops and moorland are typical of the Dartmoor landscape

From Haytor the walk heads across the moor to visit the nearby granite quarries. They were opened in the early 19th century, the stone being carried on a tramway which used granite rails – they lasted much longer than the iron version and the raw material was readily available.

The quarries have been silent for years, the largest now fenced off as the water which fills them makes them both an attraction and a danger. But the water-filled pits also add another habitat to wild Dartmoor, as they are a breeding ground for dragonflies and damselflies. Of these the walker is most likely to see common and southern hawkers, large dragonflies with vivid green and blue spotted bodies, and the black darter. Plant lovers may be somewhat disappointed, as the acidic water supports a limited range of plants. The most unusual is shoreweed, with its yellow, heart-shaped flowers.

The returning walk crosses rough moor. Though there are no bogs on this stretch, the typical moorland vegetation – heather and tough grass – will test the legs. The final climb is to the second Haytor granite outcrop, this one set, unusually, in the hillside. Called Low Man, it is a favourite with rock climbers.

Among the Tors of Dartmoor

A spectacular walk among the granite tors of this last southern wilderness

1 From the car park, cross the road and head up the wide grassy path to reach Haytor. Despite the forbidding face first reached, the tor can be easily climbed up a series of big steps at the back.

2 Walk past the rock mass, with it on your right, and pause. Ahead is an area of western Dartmoor, one of the most accessible, but beautiful, sections of the moor. In the distance, slightly left, is Hound Tor, with Greator Rocks to its right. Beyond Haytor Down, which spreads out in front of you, is the wooded valley of the River Bovey. Down and right (northeast) you will see the remains of Haytor Quarry. To continue the walk, aim for the quarry's perimeter fence and pick up the rough track just to the right.

3 After skirting the right hand edge of the quarry bear left to follow the clear granite tramway. Go past the quarry entrance and continue on the tramway as it bears right across a stone embankment to a T-junction. Turn left and follow the tramway to bear right at a fork. After a few paces take one of the many paths that head off right across open moorland towards Smallacombe Rocks.

4 There are excellent views of the surrounding moor from the rocks. Turning to face Haytor, lower and to the right you will see a quarry set in the back of Holwell Tor. Take the path from Smallacombe Rocks which heads just to the left of the quarry. This will take you back to the tramway.

7 The walk can be extended, in fine style, by heading onwards from Holwell Tor south across the moor to Saddle Tor, then turning left across the wide and low ridge back to Haytor.

6 From Holwell Tor take a direct line across the moor – there is a rough and indistict path – heading for Low Man, the cliff to the right of Haytor. From Haytor reverse the outward route back to the start.

5 Turn right along the tramway, passing a ruined building and the main quarry, then continuing round the back of the quarry, crossing a ruined bridge. Just over the bridge, head left up to the top of Holwell Tor.

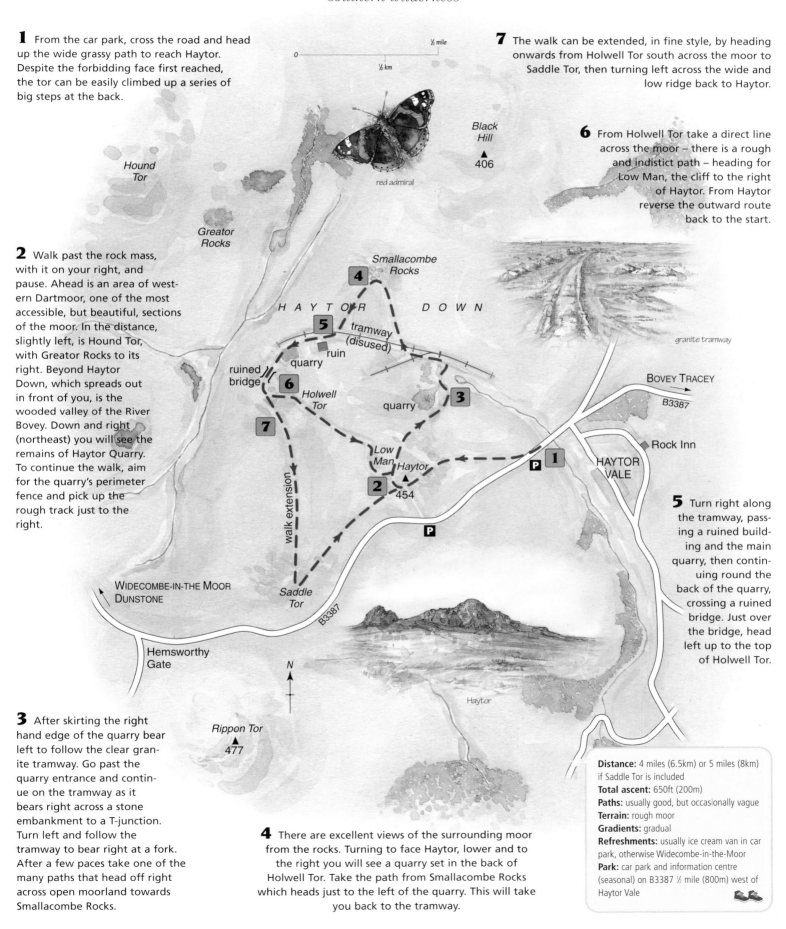

red admiral

granite tramway

Distance: 4 miles (6.5km) or 5 miles (8km) if Saddle Tor is included
Total ascent: 650ft (200m)
Paths: usually good, but occasionally vague
Terrain: rough moor
Gradients: gradual
Refreshments: usually ice cream van in car park, otherwise Widecombe-in-the-Moor
Park: car park and information centre (seasonal) on B3387 ½ mile (800m) west of Haytor Vale

Bolt Head's Wartime Secrets

Set on the strategic heights of the Bolt peninsula, an old RAF site with a proud past rests in relative obscurity

WALK
5

The majestic 400-foot (137m) rampart of the Bolt peninsula runs for 5 miles (8km) along the south Devon coast. Composed of hard mica schist, more resistant to erosion than the surrounding slates, it has remained relatively untouched by the ocean's assault and, with its commanding views both inland and seaward, has served as a natural fortress and lookout for thousands of years. Iron Age man recognised the Bolt's inherent security and built a fort at Bolt Tail. Ever since, the headland and its plateau-like hinterland have been used in times of war.

In 1588 cliff-top lookouts anxiously scanned the horizon for the Spanish Armada. At the beginning of the 19th century, 'Boney' (Napoleon Bonaparte) was the name on the watchers' lips. And from 1940, through the ensuing war years, the Bolt's most intense military occupation, the dark cloud of Nazi occupation lay only 130 miles (210km) away across the Channel.

Yet as you head out from Bolberry Down across the great hogsback of West Cliff, your senses are dominated by sea and rock. Inland is a telltale radio antenna, but out here on the exposed ridge, nature holds sway. The oranges and greys of lichens encrusting the serrated schist walls, the shortcropped grass and the rocky pinnacles on the skyline as you slog up the steep ascent from Soar Mill Cove, push thoughts of human efforts into the background. Not until you are out on the flat, breezy plateau of the Warren does mortal history intrude again. The distinctive pyramid-capped tower of the Lloyd's Signal Station, used in the past to inform agents and owners about ships' movements, is a reminder of the importance of the Bolt in trade as well as war.

Perched on the very edge of the cliff at Bolt Head itself is the ruined coastguard lookout, site of many a cold, lonely and eye-straining vigil, but by the first years of World War II the watchers had another tool – radar. After the harvest in 1940, the eastern part of the Bolt was requisitioned, hedges cleared, and RAF Bolt Head established. From its two runways, directed by the radar of the highly secret Ground Control Interceptor station (GCI), Spitfires flew escort duty and harried German bombers while Lysanders ferried agents into occupied France.

RAF Bolt Head closed in 1947, although the radar station operated until the mid-1950s. When it, too, closed down, the site was used for a nuclear bunker – a Regional Seat of Government (RSG) – a vast underground complex to which the authorities and the military would have retreated had the Cold War ever heated up. Never used in anger, the grim concrete structure of the RSG still stands behind its double barbed-wire fence half a mile (800m) from East Soar Farm.

Below: the rugged Devon coastline

Below right: recruitment posters of the period stressed the heroic potential

SERVE IN THE WAAF WITH THE MEN WHO FLY

Bolt Head's Wartime Secrets

*From prehistoric times to the Cold War this South Devon
headland has kept watch over the sea*

1 From the boulders at the end of the car park, follow the coast path with the sea on your right for about ½ mile (800m) to where the track drops down and then cuts back inland to the floor of a steep valley.

2 Continue down the valley and over a footbridge spanning a stream. Ascend steeply along the path right, skirting the pinnacled ridge to seaward. After a stile, descend into a small valley, cross a footbridge and ascend straight to just before the ridge. Turn inland onto the plateau of The Warren.

3 Follow the clifftop for 1 mile (1.6km) to a wall and stile. At the next wall take the right-hand stile, signed for Bolt Head. Continue up over the open top of Bolt Head, bearing right to a wall and stile.

4 Descend rightwards via a small valley to the headland with its ruined lookout.

5 Return to the stile and continue downhill with the wall on your left. Turn left over a stile (signed Soar Mill Cove) and just before the next wall turn right (signed South Sands) down to a stile.

8 Cross the road via two stiles and bear right, then left around the barn to take a path beside a bramble hedge for ¼ mile (400m) to a stile in the corner of the field. Cross this, turn left along the tree-lined Jacob's Lane for ½ mile (800m) to the road and follow this left past radio masts to the car park.

7 Follow the road to the white cottages, going straight on to where the Soar Mill road joins from the left. 100yds (91m) on, at Rew Cross, take the footpath which strikes left over fields to Southdown Farm.

6 Cross the stream and take the lane to a stone barn. Go through the gate, uphill for 50yds (46m) and right, through another gate, to a fingerpost. Turn left, up the valley to East Soar Farm, left through a gate, then through the farm gate to follow the farm track past the farmhouse and the nuclear bunker with its radio mast, to East Soar car park.

> **Distance:** 7 miles (11.3km)
> **Total ascent:** 700ft (215m)
> **Paths:** cliff and field paths, farm tracks, short stretch of metalled road; mostly good but occasionally muddy
> **Terrain:** cliff top, open grassland
> **Gradients:** two steep ascents on cliff path
> **Refreshments:** Port Light Hotel, Bolberry Down (limited winter opening)
> **Park:** Bolberry Down car park, seaward of the Port Light Hotel and reached by following signs from the A381 at Malborough

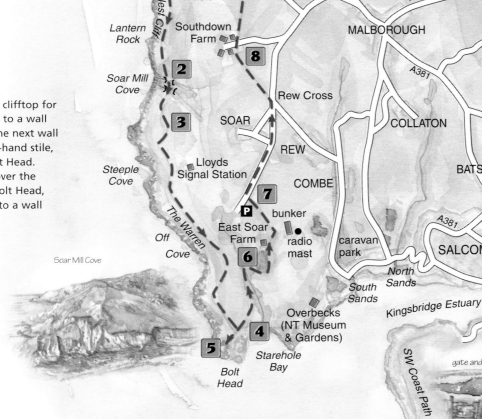

Smugglers' Tales from the Helford River

'Free traders' once flourished along the Cornish coast, and you can follow the paths worn by their resolute pursuers

WALK

6

Below: enchanting Frenchman's Creek is best explored on foot

Bottom: a quiet moment on the Helford River

The South-west Coast Path, running for 273 miles (440km) around the coast of Devon and Cornwall, owes much of its existence to the patient, tramping feet of customs men who, armed with spyglass and pistol, made nightly forays along the coast in search of smugglers. Cornwall's remote coves and creeks were a favoured haunt of smugglers for hundreds of years, but the trade was not merely 'brandy for the parson, baccy for the clerk.' Almost anything liable for duty was likely to be spirited into and out of the county. In Elizabethan times, for instance, 75 per cent of the tin exported from Cornwall was smuggled, and there was a thriving trade in wool and salt.

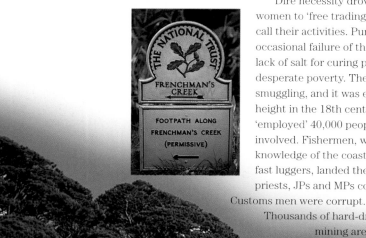

Dire necessity drove Cornishmen and women to 'free trading', as they preferred to call their activities. Punitive taxation and the occasional failure of the pilchard fishery or lack of salt for curing pilchards resulted in desperate poverty. The only way out was smuggling, and it was estimated that, at its height in the 18th century, smuggling 'employed' 40,000 people. Everybody was involved. Fishermen, with their intimate knowledge of the coast and skill in handling fast luggers, landed the cargoes; the gentry, priests, JPs and MPs connived and many Customs men were corrupt.

Thousands of hard-drinking men in the mining areas inland provided a ready market, and by the 1770s something like 100,000 gallons (455,000 litres) a year of brandy – 'Cousin Jackie' – were being smuggled.

Either side of Dennis Head runs a smugglers' coast. To the north lie Swanpool Beach and the River Fal and its tributaries, while to the south the rugged and remote coast of the Lizard has plenty of secret landing sites. Inland from Dennis Head is the peaceful estuary of the Helford River. Despite the early presence of the Gweek Customs House at the head of the estuary, the river's wooded coves and creeks provided ideal cover for landing contraband. Bosahan Cove, Frenchman's Creek (where Daphne du Maurier based the novel) and Gillan Creek remain relatively inaccessible today, and 200 years ago, on a foggy night and with a fair tide, the smugglers could carry on their business with only a small chance of being caught. Nevertheless, seizures did occur. In September 1762 some 27,579 pounds (12,510kg) of tea and 9,000 gallons (41,000 litres) of brandy were impounded.

For the Exchequer, which had to foot the bill for the American War of Independence and later the Napoleonic wars, the loss of potential revenue through smuggling was grievous. After 1815 a huge effort was made to eradicate the illicit trade. A heavy coastal blockade was enforced, and the abolition of salt duties in 1825 – combined with the rise of the temperance movement – meant that, by 1835, trade was a fraction of what it had been.

Today the Helford River is home to flotillas of yachts. The sounds of muffled oars, whispered commands and the gentle whinny of the pony as she is laden with a cask of brandy for the rectory have been replaced by the flat chug of the diesel engine.

Smugglers' Tales from the Helford River

Following the tracks of excise men and 'free traders' around this idyllic Cornish inlet

Distance: 7 miles (11km)
Total ascent: 900ft (275m)
Paths: can be very muddy in places, particularly in winter
Terrain: fields, farm tracks, coast path
Gradients: undulating; several steep sections
Refreshments: Shipwright's, Helford
Park: by the church in St Anthony-in-Meneage, 8 miles (12.9km) from Helston

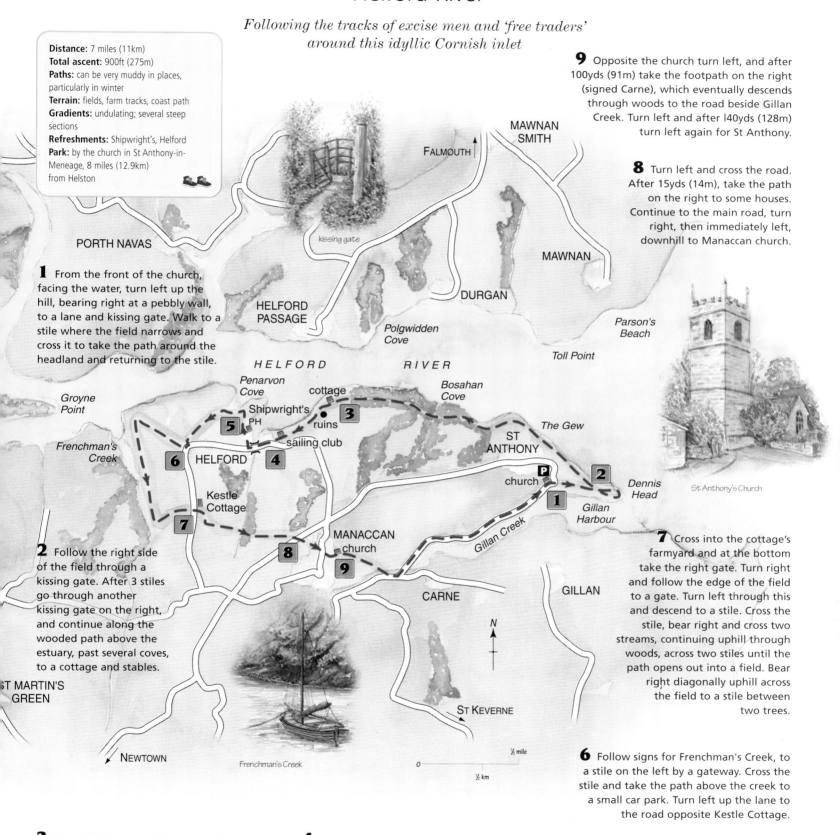

kissing gate

St Anthony's Church

Frenchman's Creek

½ mile
0
½ km

N

1 From the front of the church, facing the water, turn left up the hill, bearing right at a pebbly wall, to a lane and kissing gate. Walk to a stile where the field narrows and cross it to take the path around the headland and returning to the stile.

2 Follow the right side of the field through a kissing gate. After 3 stiles go through another kissing gate on the right, and continue along the wooded path above the estuary, past several coves, to a cottage and stables.

3 Bear right between the ruins and the cottage and then left up a track. Fork downhill at the top of the track and turn left up some steps just before a white cottage. Continue past the sailing club and a kissing gate on the right and go through another one straight ahead.

4 Turn left, then immediately right, to follow the road down through the village to a footbridge. Cross this, turn right and continue to the Shipwright's pub. Go left up the hill out of the pub car park, ignoring the path on the right to the ferry, and after 100yds (91m), turn right at a footpath sign.

5 Take the footpath to Penarvon Cove. Cross the beach and take the track left and uphill, away from the cottages. Join the road and after another 120yds (110m) turn right at a cattle grid.

6 Follow signs for Frenchman's Creek, to a stile on the left by a gateway. Cross the stile and take the path above the creek to a small car park. Turn left up the lane to the road opposite Kestle Cottage.

7 Cross into the cottage's farmyard and at the bottom take the right gate. Turn right and follow the edge of the field to a gate. Turn left through this and descend to a stile. Cross the stile, bear right and cross two streams, continuing uphill through woods, across two stiles until the path opens out into a field. Bear right diagonally uphill across the field to a stile between two trees.

8 Turn left and cross the road. After 15yds (14m), take the path on the right to some houses. Continue to the main road, turn right, then immediately left, downhill to Manaccan church.

9 Opposite the church turn left, and after 100yds (91m) take the footpath on the right (signed Carne), which eventually descends through woods to the road beside Gillan Creek. Turn left and after 140yds (128m) turn left again for St Anthony.

Zennor and the Spectacular Coast Path

WALK

7

Storm-tumbled cliffs, haunted by wheeling gulls, guard Penwith's wild and beautiful Atlantic shoreline

Below: sunset at Zennor church

Penwith forms the very toe of Cornwall kicking out into the Atlantic. It is a granite landscape, rising to over 800 feet (244m) at Trendrine Hill. A mile (1.6km) west of Trendrine, below the moors that sweep down to the coastal plain, lies the village of Zennor, a Cornish jewe l set in a granite crown. Zennor's 14th-century church and pub, its barns, farms and homes hide in a fold of the hills to escape the westerly wind that is a constant of this treeless landscape.

Less than a mile to the north, the Atlantic is maintaining its interminable assault on the cliffs, but leave Zennor and head out over the patchwork of Stone Age fields and the sea is more sensed than seen. This ancient plain, once a beach before the land rose thousands of years ago, is dotted with farms and homesteads which, like Zennor, hide in valleys or shelter behind stands of gnarled, hardy hawthorns: Tremedda, Tregerthen, Wicca, Treveal. Squat, powerful houses and barns with russet stone walls and lichened slates, all as old as the Cornish tongue in which they are named, and all as much a part of the land as the granite and the buzzards. After Treveal there is a descent into the stream valley

Below: the coast path follows the Cornish headlands

which leads to River Cove, a deep, narrow valley with a dense growth of trees. But even here, out of the wind, the trees raise their heads no more than a few feet.

Out on the coast path, you enter a world of sea and rock. Offshore is the reef of the Carracks, around which the sea boils on even the calmest day, and ahead, the great mass of Mussel Point. The climb to the summit of the point gives little indication of what is to unfold but, on breasting the last rise, the view to the west is breathtaking.

Below is the wide sweep of Wicca Pool with the prominent granite thumb of Wicca Pillar. Beyond, Porthzennor Cove lies beneath the blunt rampart of Zennor Head. The jutting fortress of Gurnard's Head stands proud and isolated while the last land visible before the Atlantic is Pendeen Watch with its lighthouse.

Down in the bay, the rocky shelf of Gala Rocks provides a feeding spot at low tide for thousands of seabirds, while Porthzennor Cove is a popular spot for seal-watching. Squadrons of gannets, huge and luminous, patrol offshore, occasionally diving, Stuka-like, for fish. And on a lucky day, with a large sky and the sea the kind of azure seen only in Penwith, there may be a school of dolphins or even a pod of cruising pilot whales – memories to sustain you on the long ascent to the summit of Zennor Head and a last sight of Gurnard's Head and Pendeen, before turning inland to meander back to Zennor.

WALK 7

Zennor and the
Spectacular Coast Path

*Traverse the Cornish coast's front line, defiantly
facing the mighty Atlantic Ocean*

Distance: 5½ miles (9km)
Total ascent: 800ft (244m)
Paths: mostly good but can be very muddy, particularly between Tregerthen and Wicca
Terrain: fields, farm tracks, coast path
Gradients: steep in places on the coast path
Refreshments: Tinners Arms and Old Chapel Café, Zennor
Park: car park, Zennor, on B3306 betweeen St Ives and St Just

8 Head back inland, rising slightly, to a stile. Follow the narrow path for 50yds (46m), to where it meets the road above a white house. Take the road back to Zennor and the car park.

1 Turn left out of the car park and head up the hill. Immediately after the church turn right by some railings and take the footpath over the fields, crossing several stiles, to Tremedda Farm.

2 Cross the farm track via two stiles, continue across open fields to the hamlet of Tregerthen and cross another track. Follow the narrow, muddy track through thickets until it opens out to fields which lead to Wicca Farm.

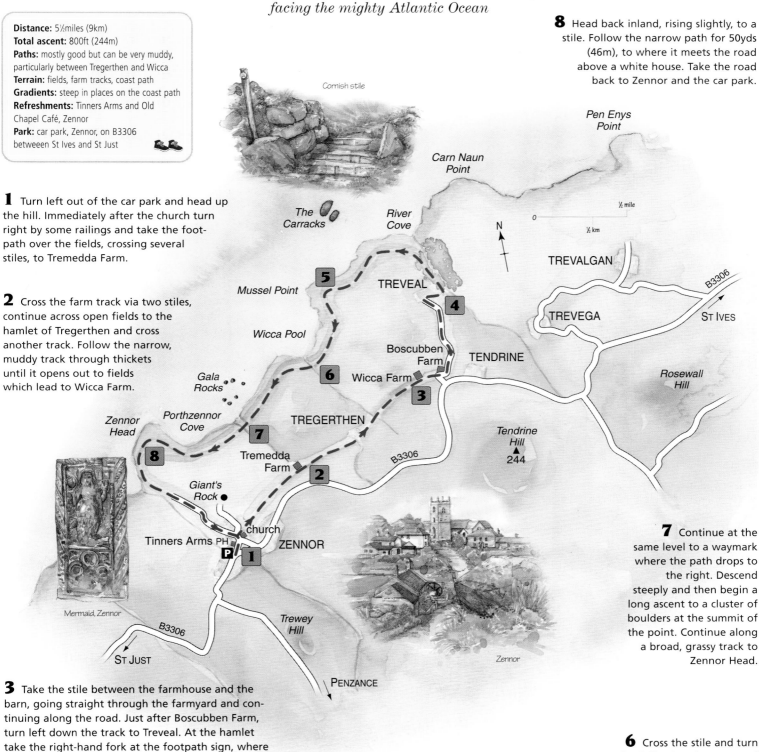

Cornish stile

Mermaid, Zennor

7 Continue at the same level to a waymark where the path drops to the right. Descend steeply and then begin a long ascent to a cluster of boulders at the summit of the point. Continue along a broad, grassy track to Zennor Head.

3 Take the stile between the farmhouse and the barn, going straight through the farmyard and continuing along the road. Just after Boscubben Farm, turn left down the track to Treveal. At the hamlet take the right-hand fork at the footpath sign, where the track turns back on itself and leads down to a cattle grid.

4 Take the path signed River Cove down the wooded valley to the stream, where the path starts to rise and then descends to the coast. Veer left and follow the coast path, which eventually rises steeply to some prominent rocks at the summit of Mussel Point.

5 Continue round the point and follow the path across the open, grassy hillside. After a prominent boulder on the right the path drops steeply into a small valley. Cross the stream on stepping stones to a stile.

6 Cross the stile and turn right, following the coast and descending slightly before ascending to a small point. The path then zigzags steeply down, almost to sea level. Continue along a flatter section for ½ mile (800m), then bear inland and uphill steeply, over one stream and on to another.

Hell's Mouth and the North Cornwall Coast

Indented with countless coves, this treacherous coast presents thrilling – and sobering – views from its exposed cliffs

Right: herring gulls wheel above the cliffs

Below: the lighthouse on Godrevy Island, just off shore

Inset below: the jagged rocks at Hell's Mouth have caused many a shipwreck

Between Bideford in north Devon and Penzance on the south-west peninsula lies a fearsome stretch of coastline some 150 miles (240km) long. Exposed to the full might of 3,000 miles of Atlantic Ocean to the west, the coast has only two safe harbours, Padstow and St Ives. Small wonder that around the Cornish coast have grown stories of wrecks and wreckers.

The golden arc of Hayle Sands extends for 3 miles (5km) along the eastern shore of St Ives Bay before merging almost imperceptibly – or so it seems as you walk the coast path – into the slate headland of Godrevy Point. The gentle, open grassland beneath your feet belies the hardness of the rock, but offshore the lighthouse perched on Godrevy Island hints that many a hull has been ripped open by dark fangs lurking beneath the surface. It was built in 1859 after public outcry at the loss of the British and Irish Steam Packet Company's 700-ton steamer, the *Nile*, and all aboard her in 1854. This light, along with those at Pendeen Watch and Trevose Head, still warns shipping of the proximity of a cruel coast.

This cruelty becomes more apparent as the cliffs build in height between Godrevy Point and the Knavocks. Fulmars, jackdaws and the odd raven wheel above vast, crumbling walls of shale and slate, which drop 150 feet (46m) into the boulder-strewn bed of Kynance Cove.

From the trig point on the Knavocks, the highest point of the walk, the view is panoramic. Across St Ives Bay are the hills of Penwith, with the stern cliffs of Carn Naun Point the last visible land before the Atlantic horizon. In the opposite direction a seemingly endless wall of cliff, broken only by the occasional beach, weaves and dodges its way north-east before fading away at the blue-grey smudge of Trevose Head 30 miles (48km) distant. East, above the old mining town of Camborne, lies the hill of Carn Brea (740 feet/225m) with its monument.

For nearly a mile (1.6km) there is respite for those troubled by the great drops to their left, but at North Cliff the path meets the cliff top with a vengeance. From here on, although easy, the walking is always exposed. Across the top of Hudder Down your gaze is inexorably, if sometimes reluctantly, drawn to the orange and black cliffs below, and to the line of black sharks' teeth in the bay, waiting to snap at the keels of unwary mariners.

Despite its name, Hell's Mouth is not quite so threatening; perhaps the fence at the cliff edge softens the impact of its magnificent lichen-clad pinnacles. Beyond Hell's Mouth, however, lies a final surprise. Below a yawning, quartz-streaked, black wall are the remains of a 2,500-ton timber carrier, the Panamanian *Secil Japan*, which went down en route from Lisbon to Liverpool on 13 March 1989. All but one of her 12 crew were rescued, but her decaying hull, its rusting and twisted plates barely recognisable, testifies to the treachery of the north Cornwall coast.

Hell's Mouth and the North Cornwall Coast

On the rollercoaster of headlands and clifftops around Godrevy Point

Distance: 5½ miles (8.8km)
Total ascent: 700ft (213m)
Paths: mostly good but can be muddy; short stretch of metalled road
Terrain: cliff top, open grassland
Gradients: two steep ascents on cliff path
Refreshments: café and Sand Sifters Hotel, Godrevy car park; Hell's Mouth café
Park: Godrevy National Trust car park, reached from the B3301, 2½ miles (4km) north of Hayle. Do not park adjacent to the café

1 Turn left out of the car park and walk up the road to the coast of St Ives Bay.

2 Follow the cliff-top road for ½ mile (800m), passing Godrevy Farm. St Ives is visible on the opposite side of the bay. Just before the toilets (seasonal only) on your right, bear left across open, springy turf to a stile.

9 Take the B3301 right, back past Hell's Mouth, up the hill to the North Cliff National Trust car park. Descend into the Red River valley with St Ives Bay ahead. At the stone bridge turn right and back to the car park.

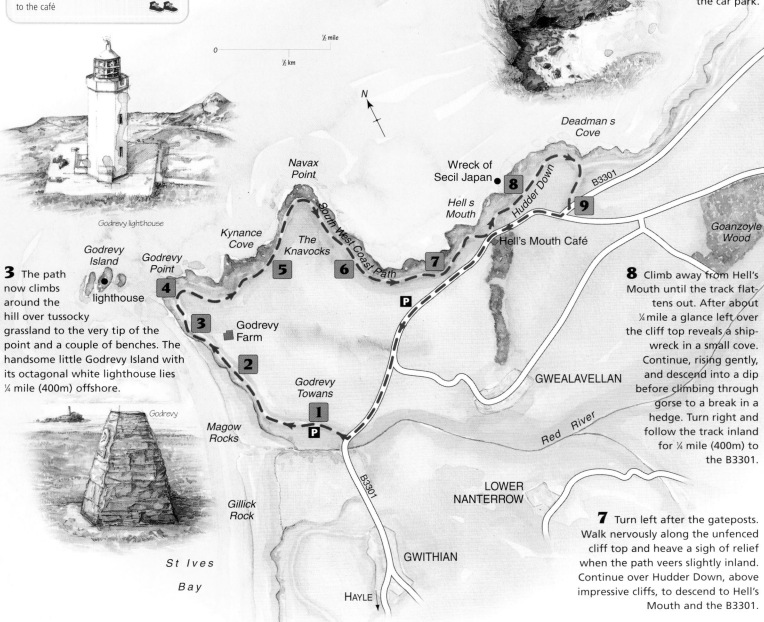

3 The path now climbs around the hill over tussocky grassland to the very tip of the point and a couple of benches. The handsome little Godrevy Island with its octagonal white lighthouse lies ¼ mile (400m) offshore.

Godrevy lighthouse

Godrevy

8 Climb away from Hell's Mouth until the track flattens out. After about ¼ mile a glance left over the cliff top reveals a shipwreck in a small cove. Continue, rising gently, and descend into a dip before climbing through gorse to a break in a hedge. Turn right and follow the track inland for ¼ mile (400m) to the B3301.

7 Turn left after the gateposts. Walk nervously along the unfenced cliff top and heave a sigh of relief when the path veers slightly inland. Continue over Hudder Down, above impressive cliffs, to descend to Hell's Mouth and the B3301.

4 Continue round the cliff top, with magnificent views up the coast. On a clear day you can see the faint outline of Trevose Head, nearly 30 miles (48km) up the coast. Follow the path over some very impressive (unfenced) cliffs for ¾ mile (1.2km), to a kissing gate.

5 Take the track, rising gently, over the downland of The Knavocks to the highest point of the bleak headland and a trig point. Continue, descending slightly, through an area of gorse to two stiles.

6 Cross a field to another stile and turn left along the lane, which becomes a narrow path after 100yds (91m). Follow the path through thickets to two granite gateposts.

The Rocky Coast beyond Woolacombe

Spines of slate break through the quiet, heathy headlands away from the bustling beach resort of Woolacombe

Top right: the stonechat favours coastal regions

Woolacombe, a hamlet in Mortehoe parish, grew mostly in the 20th century. Facing the Atlantic, it was too exposed for fishing or the Victorian holidaymaker, but its breakers attract today's neoprene-clad surfers, even in winter. Trees and hedges lean with prevailing south-westerly winds, but frost is rare, and in sheltered places are found tender plants such as black iris from the Mediterranean. Also introduced are the succulent hottentot fig and silver ragwort, now equally at home in gardens and on cliffs. Tamarisk and escallonia have spread from windbreaks. Amidst these exotics is the exotic-looking but native tree mallow or lavatera.

The acres of sand on Woolacombe beach show few signs of life, but away from the shoreline shelled creatures burrow. In Victorian times local women would rake the beaches for their unbroken shells to sell to visitors. Common shells cast ashore include razor, necklace, carpet, rayed trough, common and Venus cockles and variegated scallop. More than 50 species have been found at Barricane Beach. Most sought after amongst visitors are the cowries and lace shells, or wentletraps. Offshore, rare cup corals and sea fans can be found and, in rock pools,

the leopard-spotted goby, a shy fish found only on the North Devon coast. Today the area is part of a Voluntary Marine Conservation Area, which encourages education and exploration without collection of live specimens.

Charles Kingsley wrote: 'Wild folk are these here, gatherers of shellfish and laver and merciless to wrecked vessels.' Off Morte Point lies Morte Stone, where a strong tide race runs, resulting in many

Above: looking north from Woolacombe to Morte Point

Right: the rocky cove at Mortehoe

shipwrecks, fragments of which are often uncovered. Until the mid-19th century, wreckers lured ships on to the rocks on dark, stormy nights. A wreck was regarded as a gift from the sea and was defined as 'anything from which no living creature came ashore alive.' There was thus no incentive to save lives, and the name Morte has been linked with such grim death. Tradition has it that Grunta Beach derives its name from the wreck of a shipload of pigs. Bull Point Lighthouse was originally built in 1879 to protect shipping from the 'cruel Morte slates'. In 1972 it too succumbed to the sea, resulting in a modern, automated replacement.

The shining, silver-grey Morte slates protrude in spines along the headlands and shore, disturbed by veins of quartz during earth movements. Milky white or flushed with pink, these latter form resistant ridges. Hard quartz blocks used by prehistoric people as standing stones remain dotted around the area. There was once a cromlech on Morte Point consisting of a large rock slab perched across two others, but the top stone became dislodged and tumbled downhill.

Thrift, sea campion, kidney vetch and rock samphire grow on the cliffs (the acid-tasting samphire was once gathered for food). Amongst the grassy coastal downs grow patches of heath resplendently coloured with common gorse, ling and bell heather in late summer. This provides habitat for stonechats and warblers whilst buzzards and kestrels hover overhead. Little combes running to the sea hold daffodils, primroses and bluebells and shelter finches, larks, pipits and warblers during migration. It is this wealth of natural detail beside the dramatic coastline that rewards the careful observer.

The Rocky Coast beyond Woolacombe

The North Devon coast becomes spikier as the sands give way to clifftop paths

1 From either car park turn left, following the South West Coast Path alongside the road to Mortehoe. It's possible to walk nearer to the sea in places but you must return to the road before the bend at the foot of the hill up to Mortehoe.

6 At the end of the caravan site drive, find a path descending through the trees and crossing the stream at the bottom. Ascend to the path junction and turn right and over a stile by a National Trust sign. The path descends the valley side for nearly a mile (1.6km). Just before the bottom there is a small gate at a sharp bend in the path. Take the gate and follow the road straight down to the coast road. Turn left to return to the start.

2 Follow the coast path signs to cut out the bend in the road and follow the road a short distance up the hill towards Mortehoe. About 300yds (273m) up the hill turn left. Follow the coast path signs for the next 3 miles (4.8km). The path keeps close to the coast all around Morte Point, down into a little valley below Mortehoe and another behind the beach at Rockham and up to Bull Point lighthouse.

5 Turn right down the road towards Mortehoe and take the first field gateway on the left. Keep straight ahead with the bank on your right and cross a stile onto a drive in a caravan site. Turn left, following the drive to a footpath by a stream. Cross the stream at the bottom and go up to the junction with a footpath. Bear right along the path and take the first turning left. Keep straight ahead between the caravans.

3 At the entrance to the lighthouse compound turn right up the tarmac drive. However, it's worth continuing on the coast path to the seat on the hillock above the lighthouse for the view along the coast to Ilfracombe and returning to the drive. The drive ascends 1 mile (1.6km) to the edge of the village at Mortehoe.

4 Pass through the signed gateway at the end of the drive and take the second footpath signposted to the left, passing through a thicket alongside a house. Take the stile into the field, carrying straight on across the middle of the field and coming out by a stile onto a bend in a tarmac drive. Keep right, going up the drive past the golf course and from the bend onto a road at the top.

Map labels

Rockham Bay
Rockham Bay
Morte Point
Morte Bay
Bull Point
lighthouse
combe
combe
South West Coast Path
South West Coast Path
South West Coast Path
MORTEHOE
Ship Aground PH
golf course
caravan park
tourist information centre
WOOLACOMBE
Red Barn PH
B3343
Woolacombe Sand
Woolacombe
BRAUNTON
Lee Bay
ILFRACOMBE
HIGHER WARCOMBE
Borough Valley
war memorial, Woolacombe
Fortescue Arms PH
ILFRACOMBE
B3343
N
½ mile
0   ½ km

Distance: 6 miles (9.6km)
Total ascent: 650ft (200m)
Paths: generally good; grass slippery when wet
Terrain: coastal grass and heathland, fields
Gradients: gradual and fairly short
Refreshments: Woolacombe
Park: either of two car parks by beach in Woolacombe village; can be busy in summer, but there is plenty of other parking

High Moors above the River Exe

Nineteenth-century efforts to tame the wilderness of Exmoor are revealed in a landscape characterised by twisted, wind-blown hedges

Top right: the path slices through Moles Chamber, a dangerous bog in days gone by

Right: bare trees on the high moorland of Exmoor Forest

Above: these gentle hills are part of Exmoor's varied landscape

Exmoor can be viewed as concentric rings: an outer ring of patchy heaths and fields and, inside that, a ring of heathery commons with a bull's-eye of grass moorland which is Exmoor Forest. This was not a forest of trees but, from Norman times, an area under forest laws which protected what was royal property. No monarchs visited their Exmoor property. To them it was merely a source of income from annual rents.

Failing to prove of value for forestry, the 20,000-acre (8,100ha) estate was divided up in the early 19th century between all those who had an interest in it. John Knight, a wealthy Midlands industrialist, set about buying out the interests, including the king's half. He and his son Frederic spent their fortune trying to tame the wilderness and play the part of country squire. Their legacy lies in the beech-topped hedge banks, isolated farmhouses, and hardy northern stock grazing the moors, and in Pinkworthy Pond, John's enigmatic folly.

Beech grows higher here than elsewhere in Britain. Russet-coloured leaves cling to the young twigs until pushed out by their downy, sap-green replacements in spring. This made them useful shelter for stock in fields newly reclaimed from the moor. Some have been left to grow straggly in times of recession, and the earth has been washed from their roots, their gnarled silhouettes adding atmosphere to many an Exmoor skyline.

That which the Knights did not touch was left as in Saxon times, and the hand of ancient man lies everywhere. The route follows a prehistoric track fording the River Barle. Some say that it is the Bronze Age equivalent of the M5, running from the Midlands to Cornwall. Its name, Harepath, suggests its later use as a Saxon military road. Where the path became rutted, another was made alongside, leaving a series of parallel grooves in the hillside. It crosses Moles Chamber, once a dangerous bog where a farmer named Mole was said to have sunk to his death with his horse. In a nearby fence is the Sloley Stone, an 18th-century boundary marker between two Devon manors. From here to Woodbarrow many smaller stones, called merestones, mark the forest and county boundary.

As you gain altitude the beeches lean and straggle more with the wind, petering out at about 1,400 feet (427m). You are left in a lonely, wild, wet landscape of big skies. Rushes spike the black surface of peaty pools, and deer sedge forms springy mats between. It is worth the short detour to the top of the ridge at Chains Barrow. Here heath spotted orchid tinges the moor mauve in June and the unbroken plateau appears limitless.

WALK

10

High Moors above the River Exe

*Never tamed by human industry, The Chains retain the
wildness that impressed Exmoor's earliest settlers*

1 From the lay-by walk along road towards Simonsbath for 350yds (319m). Turn right down drive signed to Mole's Chamber (follow blue waymarked signs all the way to Wood Barrow). Follow bridleway off the drive at point where it becomes private, and go through gate at bend after bridge. After next gate take smaller path straight ahead, keeping slightly right and following top of steep valley side, gradually descending to stream. Follow path through gate at Mole's Chamber.

6 Take gate signed to B3358 or detour 300yds (273m) for view from Chains Barrow and return. Follow line of posts all the way to bottom of field. Go through gate and follow bank on left down to road and start.

5 Go through gate and follow bank over dam and upwards 1 mile (1.6km).

2 Go through gate near road at Sloley Stone, then sharp back right along bridleway. Keep following track through gates and over fields to gateway in corner of field.

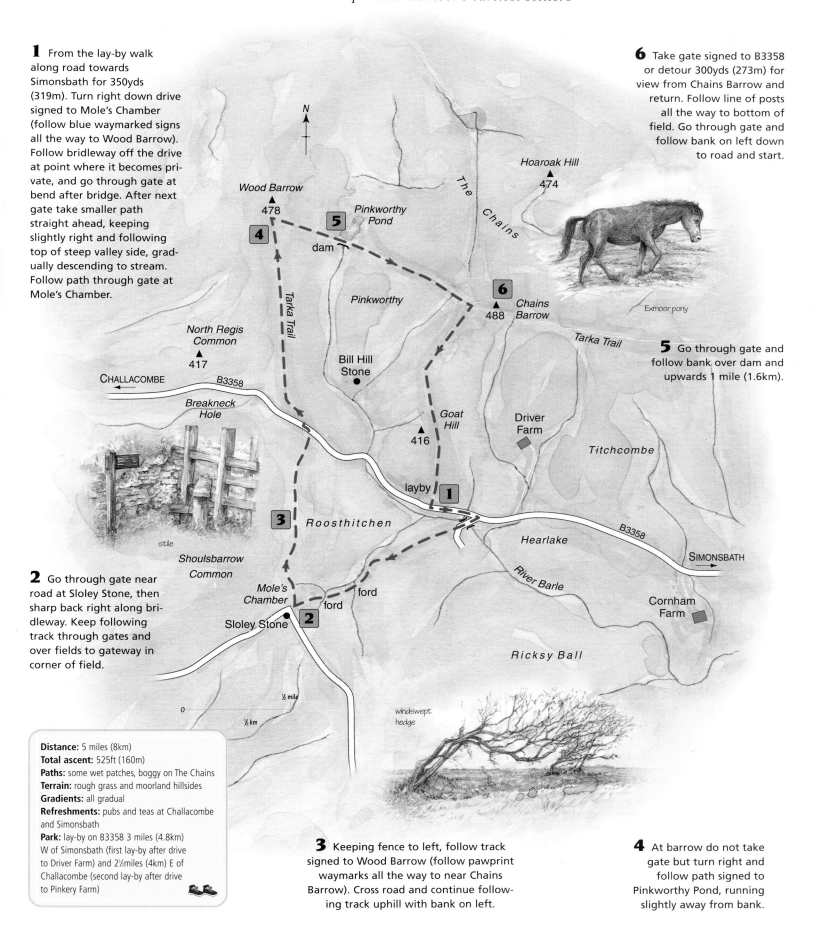

Distance: 5 miles (8km)
Total ascent: 525ft (160m)
Paths: some wet patches, boggy on The Chains
Terrain: rough grass and moorland hillsides
Gradients: all gradual
Refreshments: pubs and teas at Challacombe and Simonsbath
Park: lay-by on B3358 3 miles (4.8km) W of Simonsbath (first lay-by after drive to Driver Farm) and 2½miles (4km) E of Challacombe (second lay-by after drive to Pinkery Farm)

3 Keeping fence to left, follow track signed to Wood Barrow (follow pawprint waymarks all the way to near Chains Barrow). Cross road and continue following track uphill with bank on left.

4 At barrow do not take gate but turn right and follow path signed to Pinkworthy Pond, running slightly away from bank.

In Search of Lorna Doone on Exmoor

Track down the real places amid the hills and vales of Exmoor linked with a classic tale of adventure

WALK
11

For many, their only knowledge of Exmoor is from a 19th-century novel, R D Blackmore's *Lorna Doone*. At the heart of the novel is a great story which has been adapted for both large and small screen. Exmoor is wild yet gentle, open yet cosy. Blackmore described its rounded hills as like the folds of the palm of a woman's hand. Between the hills are hidden combes which change with every turn and where one can sense that there is still something to be discovered. According to legend, one such fold of the land hid a band of 17th-century outlaws: the Doones.

Blackmore's book became popular after the engagement of Princess Louise to the Marquis of Lorne, who was reputed to have been descended from the Doones. Debate about whether it is a great or merely popular novel then began. If you have not read the book, read it after this walk, not before. Whilst Blackmore was vague in his geography, his descriptions of what Thomas Hardy described as 'little phases of nature' were wonderfully accurate. Likened by the poet Gerard Manley

Hopkins to brush strokes, they painted a vivid picture of Exmoor without being true to any particular location. Get to know Exmoor first, then judge Blackmore's prose.

Choose a fine day for this walk or you could be lost in mist. It starts high on the windswept ridge between Doone Country and the Bristol Channel and on the boundary between Devon and Somerset. The coastal heath is a gaudy mass of pink, purple and yellow in August.

Yenworthy was the scene of a raid where a Doone was shot. The farm at Oare House is one possible site for Plovers Barrows, home of the story's hero, Jan Ridd. Oare church was the scene of the marriage between Jan and Lorna, and subsequent dramatic events. Beside it is Oare Manor, home of the real-life Snowe family woven into the novel. At Hoccombe Water are grassy hummocks, all that remain of a medieval settlement reputedly reinhabited by Doones. At Lank Combe is a waterslide, possibly the meeting place of Jan and Lorna, above which lies a hidden valley most like the Doone Valley of the novel. Blackmore was inspired by local legends, real characters, places and events, but most is fiction. Don't try to match novel with reality, just absorb the romantic atmosphere of Exmoor.

Above: sheltered Malmsmead, close to Doone country

Top right: a myriad of colours on Yenworthy Common

Below: Lank Combe waterslide

In Search of Lorna Doone on Exmoor

R D Blackmore's heroine lived among these charming combes and peaceful moors

1 Cross the road from the car park entrance and take the bridleway along the heath, signed to Broomstreet Farm.

2 Turn right up the drive past Yenworthy Lodge. Cross the road, take the stile and follow a yellow waymarked path down to Oare. Skirt through trees around a farm at Oare House then turn left onto a road, over a bridge and up to Oare church. Turn left, then take the gate to left of churchyard, signed to Larkbarrow. Follow the blue waymarks straight up over fields, keeping the field perimeter on your right.

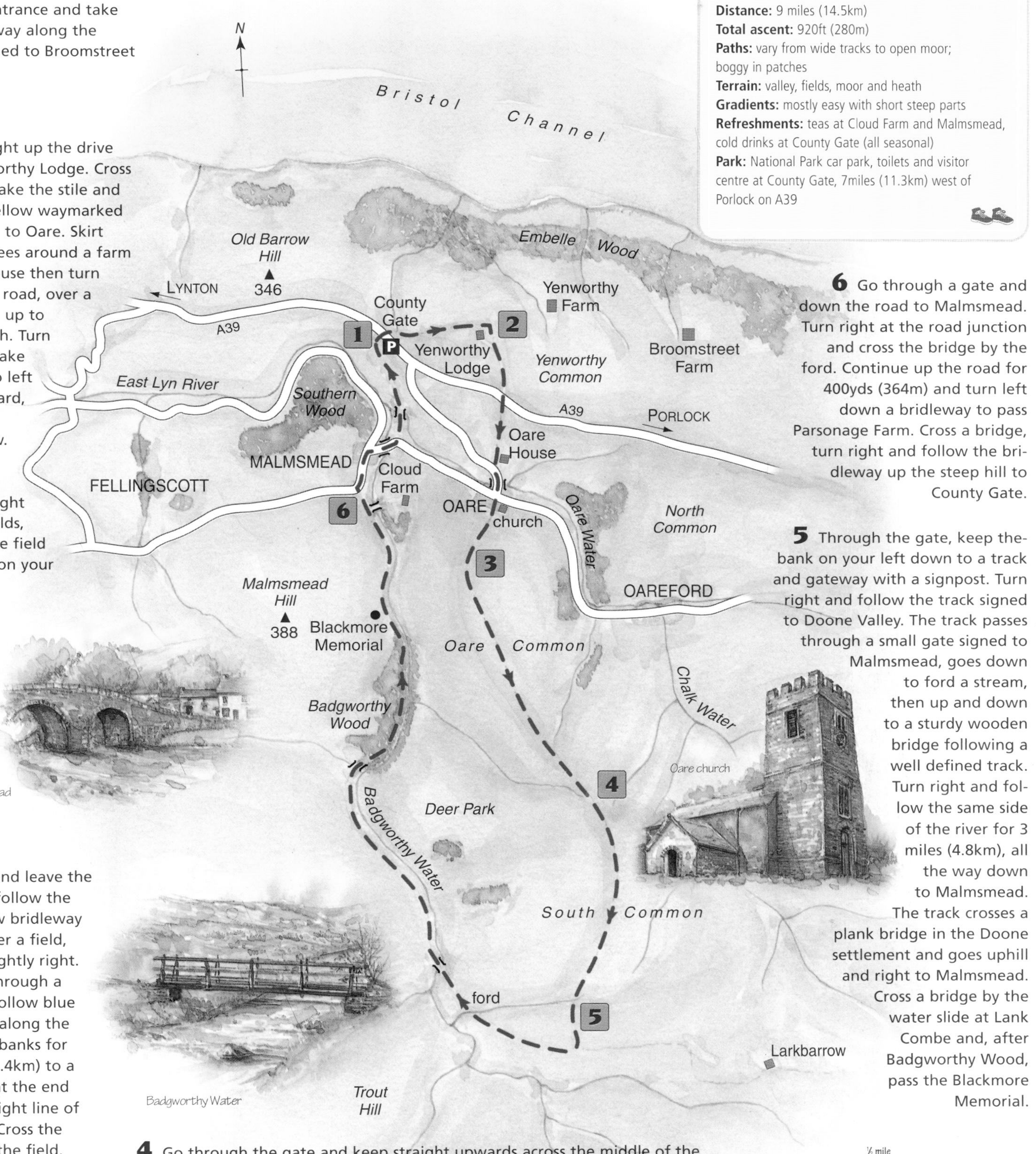

Distance: 9 miles (14.5km)
Total ascent: 920ft (280m)
Paths: vary from wide tracks to open moor; boggy in patches
Terrain: valley, fields, moor and heath
Gradients: mostly easy with short steep parts
Refreshments: teas at Cloud Farm and Malmsmead, cold drinks at County Gate (all seasonal)
Park: National Park car park, toilets and visitor centre at County Gate, 7miles (11.3km) west of Porlock on A39

6 Go through a gate and down the road to Malmsmead. Turn right at the road junction and cross the bridge by the ford. Continue up the road for 400yds (364m) and turn left down a bridleway to pass Parsonage Farm. Cross a bridge, turn right and follow the bridleway up the steep hill to County Gate.

5 Through the gate, keep the bank on your left down to a track and gateway with a signpost. Turn right and follow the track signed to Doone Valley. The track passes through a small gate signed to Malmsmead, goes down to ford a stream, then up and down to a sturdy wooden bridge following a well defined track. Turn right and follow the same side of the river for 3 miles (4.8km), all the way down to Malmsmead. The track crosses a plank bridge in the Doone settlement and goes uphill and right to Malmsmead. Cross a bridge by the water slide at Lank Combe and, after Badgworthy Wood, pass the Blackmore Memorial.

Malmsmead

Badgworthy Water

3 At a bend leave the track and follow the Larkbarrow bridleway sign up over a field, bearing slightly right. Turn left through a gate and follow blue waymarks along the fence and banks for 1½ miles (2.4km) to a waymark at the end of the straight line of the bank. Cross the middle of the field, bearing slightly left to a gate in the fence.

4 Go through the gate and keep straight upwards across the middle of the next field and over the top to a gate through a low bank onto the moor, still following Larkbarrow bridleway signs. Cross the moor straight ahead and bearing slightly left. Keep straight on and do not be misled by numerous tracks. In ½ mile (800m) you should have rounded the head of a small combe and come to a gate in a bank with a bridleway sign.

Map labels: Bristol Channel, N, Old Barrow Hill ▲ 346, LYNTON, A39, East Lyn River, Southern Wood, MALMSMEAD, FELLINGSCOTT, Malmsmead Hill ▲ 388, Blackmore Memorial, Badgworthy Wood, Badgworthy Water, Trout Hill, County Gate, Yenworthy Lodge, Yenworthy Farm, Yenworthy Common, Broomstreet Farm, A39, PORLOCK, Oare House, OARE, church, Oare Water, North Common, OAREFORD, Oare Common, Chalk Water, Oare church, Deer Park, South Common, ford, Larkbarrow, Cloud Farm, Embelle Wood, ½ mile, 0, ½ km

Spectacular Views from the Quantock Hills

The panoramas are superb on this varied walk through the wooded valleys and open heights of the Quantocks

WALK
12

Top right: a plaque marks Coleridge's cottage in Nether Stowey

Above: red deer thrive in the Quantocks

Quantocks means the 'headland of the waters', and Holford lies at the junction of streams running down beautiful Quantock combes. These were well known to the poet Samuel Taylor Coleridge, who lived near by at Nether Stowey. William Wordsworth and his sister, Dorothy, came to visit him in 1797 and admired the scenery. Dorothy recorded their jaunts in her diary and described how they 'pryed into the recesses' of Holford Glen. Wordsworth envied the way Coleridge's mind had become 'habituated to the vast'. Soon he returned to rent the Queen Anne mansion at Alfoxton for a year. Both the scenery and the company inspired the poets to write and this walk would have been very familiar to them. Dorothy wrote:

'Wherever we turn we have woods, smooth downs, and valleys with small brooks running down them through green meadows… The hills that cradle these valleys are either covered with fern or bilberries or oak woods… Walks extend for miles over the hill-tops; the great beauty of which is their wild simplicity.'

The walk from Alfoxton follows one of the poets' walks up Longstone Hill. Near by you cannot but notice the nuclear power station at Hinkley Point, but then gaze beyond the mouth of the Parrett to Brent Knoll and Burnham-on-Sea. Northwards you can see to Weston-super-Mare, the islands of Steepholm and Flatholm, and across the Bristol Channel to Barry, weather permitting. From Bicknoller Post you may see westwards over Williton to Minehead and Dunster, and as you climb Thorncombe Hill the view of Exmoor opens out, with Dunkery on the horizon. At Hurley Beacon the view extends to the south, along the ridge of the Brendon Hills to Willet Hill with its tower and beyond to the Blackdowns. The ridgeway you follow is reputed to have been used by Bronze Age people carrying Welsh and Irish gold across the southwest peninsula en route to the Mediterranean. At Crowcombe Park Gate it meets the Harepath, an equally old route running the length of the peninsula and reputedly a Saxon military route. All round are the

remains of prehistoric settlements and burial mounds, including the flint weapons of Stone Age hunters. Possibly they were following the red deer and wild ponies which still abound here.

The woods at the head of Holford Glen are 'ancient woodland' dating back at least to medieval times. They run over Dowsborough, covering the large Iron Age fort on its summit, and the view today as you approach Lady's Combe is very much as it was in the Stone Age. Much of the heathland was formed after clearance of the woodland by Bronze Age people. The remaining fragments of woodland were much valued and the trees coppiced for charcoal and tan bark. The wheel of the old tannery, now Combe House Hotel, can be seen at the end of the glen. The straggly sessile oaks grow several spindly trunks from each cut 'stool' or stump. Larger English oaks, which were pollarded (cut higher up the trunk) to keep growing branches away from browsing deer, are festooned with lichens and ferns. The glen now partly belongs to the League Against Cruel Sports, to protect it from deer-hunting, a controversial subject. The old dog pound at the beginning of the walk has a grim connection with hunting. It was erected to keep dogs away from the kennels at Alfoxton, where a huntsman was killed by his own hounds whilst trying to silence them for barking at stray dogs.

Right: the view from Hurley Beacon

Spectacular Views from the Quantock Hills

Last of the southwest moorlands, the Quantocks boast fine views over Somerset and the Bristol Channel

Distance: 7 miles (11.3km)
Total ascent: 820ft (250m)
Paths: mostly good but muddy after rain; shallow stream to ford in Holford Combe
Terrain: mostly open heath or wooded valley
Gradients: gradual, but one short, steep downhill section
Refreshments: Plough Inn, Holford, and teas in village in season
Park: car park in old quarry by bowling green at Holford, on minor road between Holford village and Alfoxton Park

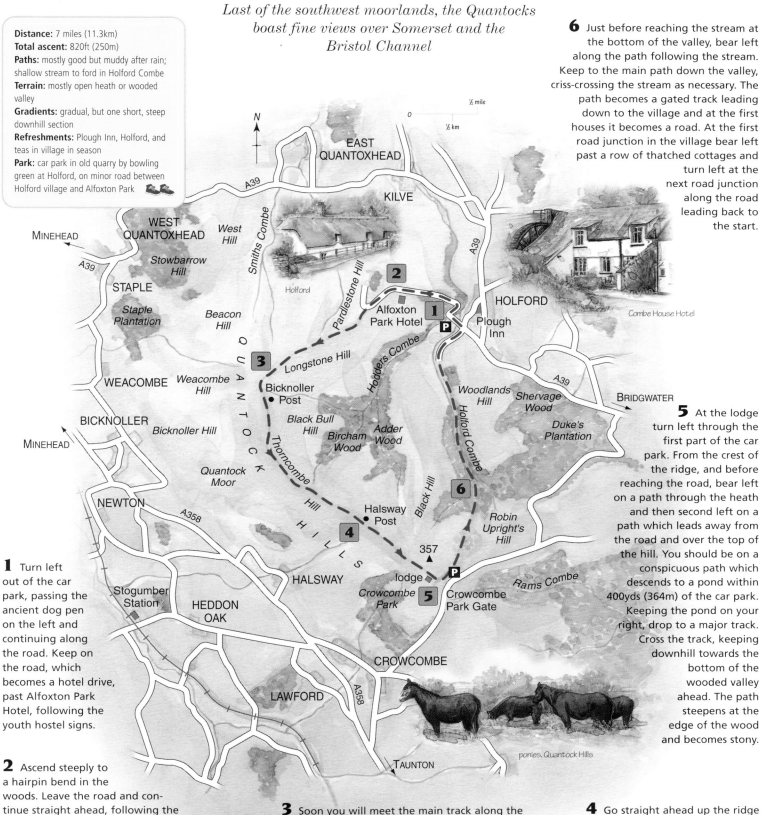

Combe House Hotel

ponies, Quantock Hills

6 Just before reaching the stream at the bottom of the valley, bear left along the path following the stream. Keep to the main path down the valley, criss-crossing the stream as necessary. The path becomes a gated track leading down to the village and at the first houses it becomes a road. At the first road junction in the village bear left past a row of thatched cottages and turn left at the next road junction along the road leading back to the start.

5 At the lodge turn left through the first part of the car park. From the crest of the ridge, and before reaching the road, bear left on a path through the heath and then second left on a path which leads away from the road and over the top of the hill. You should be on a conspicuous path which descends to a pond within 400yds (364m) of the car park. Keeping the pond on your right, drop to a major track. Cross the track, keeping downhill towards the bottom of the wooded valley ahead. The path steepens at the edge of the wood and becomes stony.

1 Turn left out of the car park, passing the ancient dog pen on the left and continuing along the road. Keep on the road, which becomes a hotel drive, past Alfoxton Park Hotel, following the youth hostel signs.

2 Ascend steeply to a hairpin bend in the woods. Leave the road and continue straight ahead, following the path up the bottom of the valley. Emerging from the trees at a crossing of tracks on the heath, keep straight ahead, bearing slightly right and gradually uphill, following the sign for West Quantoxhead. Keep uphill on the main track. At the top of the hill turn left, descending slightly.

3 Soon you will meet the main track along the Quantock ridge at Bicknoller Post. Bear left along this track. You can follow the higher track over Thorncombe Hill or the lower one along the left-hand side of it, but continue ahead along the ridge. Keep slightly to the left along the top of the hill to join the main track, which drops to a tall post and crossing of tracks at Halsway Post.

4 Go straight ahead up the ridge with a fence on your right. Keep on the main track over the hill and down to a dip in the ridge and lodge at Crowcombe Park Gate.

The Other Sides to Cheddar Gorge

The remarkable plant life of this famous landmark is celebrated on a spectacular circuit from Cheddar

WALK

13

Right: the common rockrose, one of the many plants which can be seen in the area

It took 2 million years to form Cheddar Gorge and about 200 for commercial tourism to spoil it. However, it is still both spectacular and beautiful and holds a wealth of interest. The gorge is cut in carboniferous limestone, 280–345 million years old. It was shaped during the Ice Age, and the sequence of stalactite deposits in its caves has provided evidence of the changing climate over the last 350,000 years. Within the caves have also been found the bones of mammoth, bison, cave lion and cave man.

It was once thought that the gorge was one huge collapsed cave, but current theory has it that it was cut by a river swollen with meltwater from snow during the Ice Age. The ground remained frozen, preventing seepage of water through the porous rock. Today's river runs underground, emerging as 18 separate springs through the rocks at the bottom of the gorge. They have been dammed to form ponds which once powered water mills, and since the 1920s have supplied water for Bristol and beyond.

The climb up the edge of the gorge is repaid by several points where you can rest and admire the view, including Pavey's Tower, which looks out over Cheddar and the Somerset Levels. The greatest sheer drop is about 395 feet (120m) and the best view of the gorge is probably towards the end of the walk. Its sides are cloaked in yew, ash and rare whitebeams, and grassy areas provide the only British habitat for the Cheddar pink and Cheddar bedstraw, plus another 17 nationally scarce plants and 29 resident species of butterfly. The best time to visit is in June, when the pinks are in flower.

The walk passes through several nature reserves and Sites of Special Scientific Interest. At Black Rock there are four reserves, under different ownership but all managed by Somerset Wildlife Trust. At Velvet Bottom and Ubley Warren there has been lead mining since prehistoric times, and here in the flat-bottomed valley formed by

old settling ponds is a mix of lime-loving and lead-tolerant flora. Acid-loving flora grows on patches of loess, a soil created by Ice Age wind-blown deposits. The limestone supports rockrose, salad burnet and bee orchids, whilst lead-tolerant plants include spring sandwort and alpine pennycress.

Medieval lead mining produced hummocky ground described locally as 'gruffy'. The more visible signs of mining are mostly Victorian. The Romans came to mine lead, leaving remains of a fort and settlement near Ubley Warren, and the route passes an earthwork described as an amphitheatre. Black Down, the highest point of the Mendips at 1,067 feet (325m), is capped with barrows. Its sandy soils are in contrast to the limestone and produce heaths. On a clear day sweeping views take in the mountains of south Wales and the hills of the Forest of Dean, Cotswolds, Blackdowns, Quantocks and Exmoor, and the Mendip ridge.

Below: the bee orchid flourishes in the nature reserves

Right: the road winds below the steep limestone cliffs of Cheddar Gorge

The Other Sides to Cheddar Gorge

A fine circuit of nature proves there is more to Cheddar than cheese and tourists

1 From car park turn right towards the Gorge. Cross the bridge and take the next road on the right, keeping uphill. Just before the brow of the hill turn left up behind cottages. At the end of the lane follow the bridleway up to the left. Keep following the Gorge Walk waymarks along the edge of the gorge for 1¼ miles (2km). The path ascends to the top of a ridge and descends through woodland to the road at the head of the Gorge.

2 Cross the road and take the gate and track ahead into Black Rock reserve. Follow the main track up the bottom of the valley for ⅔ mile (1km). After the National Trust sign turn right over a wall and follow the waymarks up the bottom of the valley for another mile (1.6km).

6 Cross a stile from fields into a scrubby area. Bear left, then right, to pick up the Gorge Walk waymarks. Keep dowhill with the Gorge on your left. It is worth the detour down a steep flight of steps to a viewpoint. Returning, the path steepens to descend through woods to a track. Turn left down the track, then right and down the road through the Gorge to return to the start.

5 Turn right along the road and take the next turn to the left, down a farm drive. Keep right of Charterhouse and Piney Sleight Farms, then follow the yellow waymarks ahead across fields, keeping close to the walls on your right.

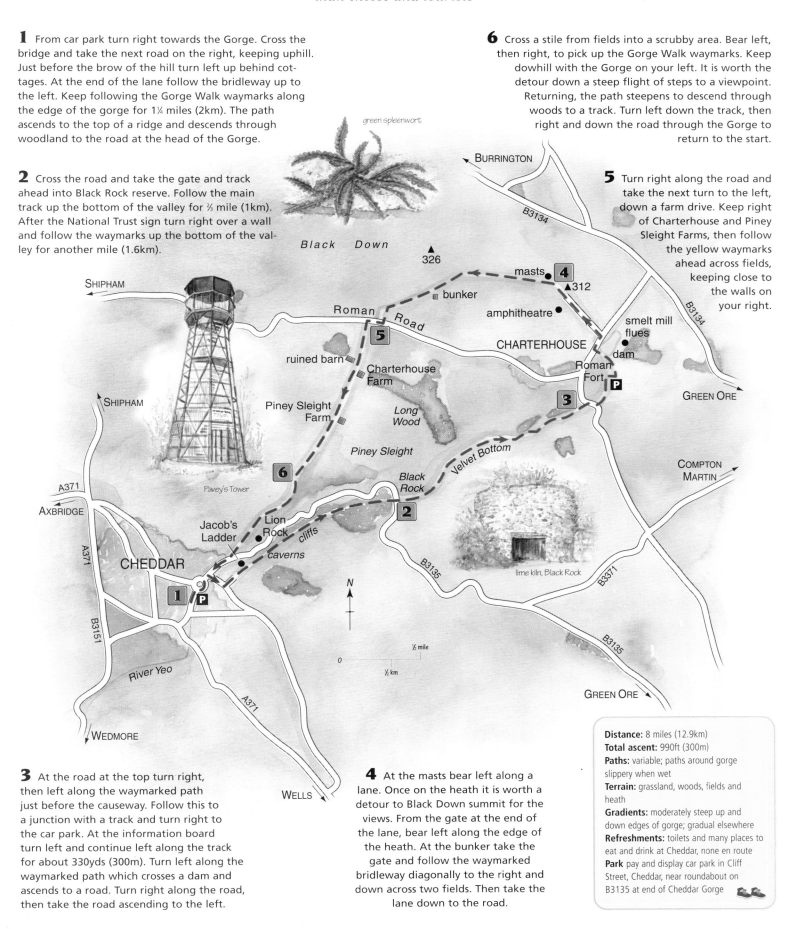

green spleenwort

Black Down

▲ 326

masts **4** ▲ 312

bunker

amphitheatre

CHARTERHOUSE

smelt mill flues

dam

Roman Fort **P**

GREEN ORE

BURRINGTON

B3134

B3134

Roman Road **5**

ruined barn

Charterhouse Farm

Piney Sleight Farm

Long Wood

Piney Sleight

Velvet Bottom

COMPTON MARTIN

Black Rock **2**

lime kiln, Black Rock

B3135

B3371

SHIPHAM

SHIPHAM

Pavey's Tower

6

A371

AXBRIDGE

A371

B3151

CHEDDAR

Jacob's Ladder

Lion Rock

cliffs

caverns

1 **P**

River Yeo

A371

WEDMORE

WELLS

N

0   ½ mile
    ½ km

GREEN ORE

3 At the road at the top turn right, then left along the waymarked path just before the causeway. Follow this to a junction with a track and turn right to the car park. At the information board turn left and continue left along the track for about 330yds (300m). Turn left along the waymarked path which crosses a dam and ascends to a road. Turn right along the road, then take the road ascending to the left.

4 At the masts bear left along a lane. Once on the heath it is worth a detour to Black Down summit for the views. From the gate at the end of the lane, bear left along the edge of the heath. At the bunker take the gate and follow the waymarked bridleway diagonally to the right and down across two fields. Then take the lane down to the road.

Distance: 8 miles (12.9km)
Total ascent: 990ft (300m)
Paths: variable; paths around gorge slippery when wet
Terrain: grassland, woods, fields and heath
Gradients: moderately steep up and down edges of gorge; gradual elsewhere
Refreshments: toilets and many places to eat and drink at Cheddar, none en route
Park pay and display car park in Cliff Street, Cheddar, near roundabout on B3135 at end of Cheddar Gorge

Lansdown – a Civil War Battle for Bath

A walk on the last of the high Cotswolds threads its way through a battlefield to a well-known viewpoint

WALK
14

Top right: the monument to Sir Bevil Grenville is near the start of the walk

Below: Langridge hides in Bath's Cotswold hinterland

In 1642 England was a country divided in its loyalties. King Charles I had lost the trust of many and was in open conflict with much of his Parliament. Although the first battle of the Civil War, on 23 October at Edgehill in Warwickshire, proved inconclusive, the monarch's fortunes started to rise at that point. By the summer of 1643 the King controlled almost all of England, his armies winning a series of battles. Never again would his position be as good as it was then, when victory seemed to be within his grasp.

As part of a continuing strategy of rooting out Parliamentarian forces prior to a concerted advance on London, a Royalist force advanced on Bath in early July. Facing it was Sir William Waller, who had brought his army south to counter the Royalist threat and had installed himself in Bath. Waller did not want a siege of the city, and neither did he want a battle on the flat lands to the west, where his army would likely be wiped out by the superior Royalist army. He therefore set up a position on the steep edge of Lansdown to the north of Bath. Today a road crosses the down, passing Bath racecourse on its way to the city. On each side of the line of the road Waller built earthworks behind which he set his cannons, hoping to force the Royalists into attacking uphill. He then, curiously, led his men to the foot of the hill where the battle started. Some believe this was a ruse, Waller's men making an early retreat and fleeing up the slope, pursued by the Royalists whose force then lost its shape. When Waller's cannons fired over the heads of his retreating men, the Royalists sustained heavy casualties and their pursuit ground to a halt.

The day seemed lost, but Sir Bevil Grenville rallied his Cornishmen and led them in a charge up the slope, while other Royalist bands led a flanking attack up the steep edge of Hanging Hill and across what is now a golf course. Finally the Cornishmen reached the scarp edge, forcing Waller's men to turn and flee to a new position some 450yds (400m) back along Lansdown, behind a stone wall. The wall is long gone, but we cross its line as we walk beside the golf course. In the final moments of the charge, Grenville was unhorsed and attacked as he lay on the ground. His men, exhausted by the battle and demoralised by their leader's wounding, did not pursue the Roundheads, instead taking up a position at the scarp edge. Sir Bevil was taken to Cold Ashton Manor, a little way to the north, where he died during the night.

All night the Royalists watched the flickering fires of the Roundheads' camp. Then, at first light, they advanced on the wall, only to find that under cover of darkness Waller had retreated to Bath, leaving the burning fires as a decoy. Troops on both sides were exhausted, and while neither could claim a clear victory, the Royalists' failure to win was a psychological defeat which presaged the irreversible decline of the English monarch's power.

Our walk starts near a monument to Sir Bevil Grenville (erected on the spot where, tradition says, he fell), following the Cotswold Way along the scarp edge to reach Prospect Stile, a local viewpoint. The walk crosses Bath racecourse, and then the ground over which Waller's men retreated to Bath under cover of night, before descending to the lovely church of St Mary Magdalene at Langridge.

The final section of the walk follows the steep hill up which the Cornishmen charged, an area still called The Battlefields: Waller's artillery occupied the ground crossed on this last lap.

Lansdown – a Civil War Battle for Bath

Where Sir Beville Grenville led his Cornishmen in a heroic charge

1 From lay-by cross road and follow well-waymarked Cotswold Way, joining private road to fire brigade building.

2 Turn right with Way just before brigade complex, then, soon, left along field path. Follow Way to trig point on Hanging Hill, seen over wall. Turn left over stile and step left to walk past trig point, continuing with hedge on right. Cross stile to reach golf course, bearing left to follow bridleway along left edge. Turn right, as signed, to follow Cotswold Way across course and then left along bridleway between wood on right, and course's northern edge, on left.

3 Leave course through gate, soon turning left off descending track, with Cotswold Way to stile. Walk parallel with fence on left, and follow it sharp left then on, across Little Down hill fort, exiting across section of ditch. Turn right and follow edge of hill, with race course starting stalls on left, to panorama dial at Prospect Stile.

8 Eventually, Cotswold Way joins from right. Carry on through gate and after 100yds (91m) go right, uphill to wall and Cotswold Way signpost. Go over stile and walk with wall on right to scarp edge where much of the Battle of Lansdown was fought, before bearing left to monument. Lay-by is 100yds (91m) further along track.

7 Continue past church, passing house on right, to Tynings Cottage (on left). Turn left just before cottage, climbing steep lane. Go over crest and descend to barn on right. Turn left up signed bridleway, maintaining direction where it narrows.

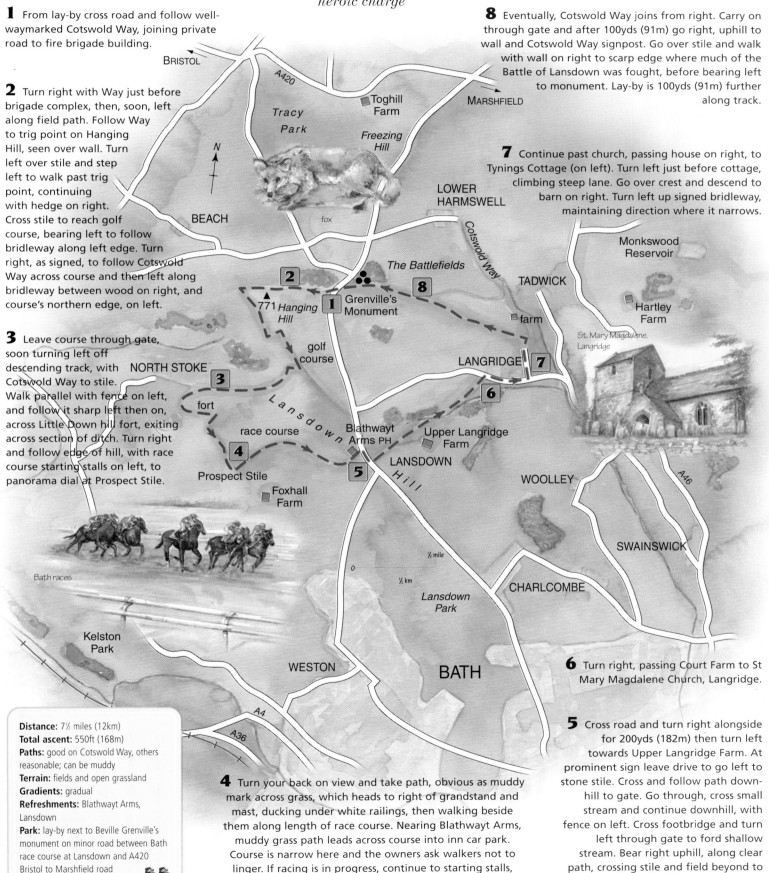

6 Turn right, passing Court Farm to St Mary Magdalene Church, Langridge.

5 Cross road and turn right alongside for 200yds (182m) then turn left towards Upper Langridge Farm. At prominent sign leave drive to go left to stone stile. Cross and follow path downhill to gate. Go through, cross small stream and continue downhill, with fence on left. Cross footbridge and turn left through gate to ford shallow stream. Bear right uphill, along clear path, crossing stile and field beyond to gate onto road.

4 Turn your back on view and take path, obvious as muddy mark across grass, which heads to right of grandstand and mast, ducking under white railings, then walking beside them along length of race course. Nearing Blathwayt Arms, muddy grass path leads across course into inn car park. Course is narrow here and the owners ask walkers not to linger. If racing is in progress, continue to starting stalls, going around behind them and returning to inn car park.

Distance: 7½ miles (12km)
Total ascent: 550ft (168m)
Paths: good on Cotswold Way, others reasonable; can be muddy
Terrain: fields and open grassland
Gradients: gradual
Refreshments: Blathwayt Arms, Lansdown
Park: lay-by next to Beville Grenville's monument on minor road between Bath race course at Lansdown and A420 Bristol to Marshfield road

Frome's Medieval Highlights

Enjoy a walking tour of one of Somerset's most charming historical towns, once a hub of the woollen trade

WALK
15

Right: architectural detail on the Blue House depicts an almswoman

Below: the Blue House is one of Frome's most interesting buildings

Right: Catherine Hill is lined with fine 17th-century houses

I n Saxon times Frome was an important place. St Aldhelm, famous as the Abbot of Malmesbury and first Bishop of Sherborne in Dorset, built a monastic house here, and Athelstan, King of Wessex, held a royal council in the town. Later another Wessex king, Edred, died in the town. After the Norman Conquest, however, Frome began to decline in importance, the new rulers of England not refounding the monastery.

By the 14th century Frome had re-established itself, becoming a centre for the making of cloth, which was coloured using locally-made natural dyes, including woad. At first the industry was cottage-based, but eventually factories were built in the town to increase efficiency. Cloth maintained the town's prosperity for several centuries: although the industry was in decline by the 1800s, the last mill did not close until the 1960s.

The town's tourist information office occupies the Round Tower, an 18th-century wool-drying building situated close to the River Frome. The walk starts with an exploration of the heart of the old town, where a number of interesting buildings testify to the prosperity which wool brought. The Town Museum is housed in a curious triangular building, the gift of a rich clothier to the town in 1868. Built as a 'Literacy Institute', the building now displays a collection covering local archaeology as well as illustrating the town's history.

The walk next passes the Blue House, built in 1728 on an island formed by two arms of the River Frome. The two wings were almshouses for old women, while the central section was a charity school for poor boys. These early uses are reflected in the statues on the central façade, which depict an almswoman and a boy. Cheap Street is one of Frome's most appealing streets, lined with fine houses mostly dating from the 17th century (though the last but one on the left dates from the early 16th century) and with a narrow water channel running down its centre for the whole of its length.

Frome's church, dedicated to St John, almost certainly stands on the site of St Aldhelm's monastery. Inside are some interesting monuments, while in the churchyard, on the east side of the church, is the dignified tomb of

Thomas Ken, the Bishop of Bath and Wells, forced to resign for refusing the oath of allegiance to William III.

The walk follows Gentle Street beside the church. This is one of Frome's most charming streets: towards the top stood the Wagon and Horses Inn from where, in the 17th century, a coach called the *Flying Wagon* left on its two-day journey to London. Catherine Hill is Gentle Street's main rival for Frome's best street. The steep street, lined with fine 17th-century houses, is named after St Catherine's Chapel, built in the 13th century, which stood near the top until the 16th century. To the right, halfway down the street, is Sheppard's Barton, a group of weavers' workshops and cottages dating from the 18th century.

Frome's Medieval Highlights

Discover the faded charm and surprising medieval wealth of this once great Somerset town

Distance: 4½ miles (7.2km)
Total ascent: 200ft (61m)
Paths: town streets and good paths
Terrain: town streets and fields
Gradients: gradual, though the ascent of Gentle Street belies its name
Refreshments: numerous opportunities in Frome
Park: car park beside the tourist information centre

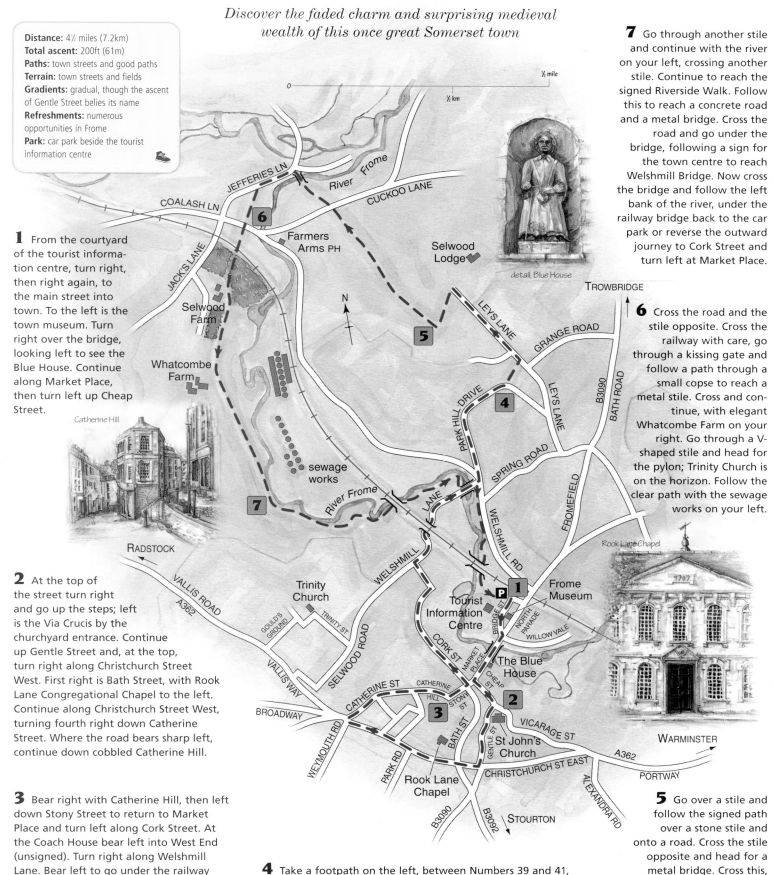

Catherine Hill

detail, Blue House

7 Go through another stile and continue with the river on your left, crossing another stile. Continue to reach the signed Riverside Walk. Follow this to reach a concrete road and a metal bridge. Cross the road and go under the bridge, following a sign for the town centre to reach Welshmill Bridge. Now cross the bridge and follow the left bank of the river, under the railway bridge back to the car park or reverse the outward journey to Cork Street and turn left at Market Place.

6 Cross the road and the stile opposite. Cross the railway with care, go through a kissing gate and follow a path through a small copse to reach a metal stile. Cross and continue, with elegant Whatcombe Farm on your right. Go through a V-shaped stile and head for the pylon; Trinity Church is on the horizon. Follow the clear path with the sewage works on your left.

1 From the courtyard of the tourist information centre, turn right, then right again, to the main street into town. To the left is the town museum. Turn right over the bridge, looking left to see the Blue House. Continue along Market Place, then turn left up Cheap Street.

2 At the top of the street turn right and go up the steps; left is the Via Crucis by the churchyard entrance. Continue up Gentle Street and, at the top, turn right along Christchurch Street West. First right is Bath Street, with Rook Lane Congregational Chapel to the left. Continue along Christchurch Street West, turning fourth right down Catherine Street. Where the road bears sharp left, continue down cobbled Catherine Hill.

3 Bear right with Catherine Hill, then left down Stony Street to return to Market Place and turn left along Cork Street. At the Coach House bear left into West End (unsigned). Turn right along Welshmill Lane. Bear left to go under the railway bridge and continue along Welshmill Lane, crossing the River Frome. Cross into Park Hill Drive, following it around to the right.

4 Take a footpath on the left, between Numbers 39 and 41, maintaining direction along Packsaddle Way for a few steps before turning left into Leys Lane. Continue to reach a gate for Selwood Lodge. Follow the drive beyond, but where it bears right, go left over a stile and follow the hedge on the right.

5 Go over a stile and follow the signed path over a stone stile and onto a road. Cross the stile opposite and head for a metal bridge. Cross this, reaching a lane soon after. Turn left for 100yds (91m) then turn left along a signed path across a field to a road.

Old Ways on the Wiltshire Downs

The grassy hilltops of the Downs are a walker's delight, carved with mysterious figures and steeped in ancient history

WALK
16

Top right: the Alton Barnes White Horse

Above: looking down on Alton Priors from Walker's Hill

Below: Knap Hill on Pewsey Downs

Squeezed between Devizes and the Vale of Pewsey to the south and Swindon and the M4 to the north, the Wiltshire Downs have been described as a walker's paradise – a place of mystery and legend offering constant reminders of the lost world of prehistoric Britain. By tracing a lonely course over wind-battered summits and across broad expanses of breath-taking downland you are literally following in the footsteps of our early ancestors. William Golding wrote, in *From a Moving Target*, 'the Romans seem modern compared with the nameless tribes, nations and empires that rose and fell here before Claudius Caesar conquered the land.' It is hard to believe today, but this entire region was once one of the most populated areas in the country, inhabited by the people of the late Stone Age and Bronze Age.

The walk begins at the Saxon church in Alton Barnes, but have a look at the village and its neighbour, Alton Priors, before you leave. Alton is Anglo Saxon for 'farm or village by the springs', and they can be seen very clearly, bubbling away on the bed of a pretty little stream in the vicinity of Alton Priors' Church of All Saints. The church, which contains a 12th-century chancel arch and wide nave, is delightfully situated in the middle of a meadow. The stone paths here were probably laid to help prevent those people travelling on foot between Alton Barnes and Alton Priors from becoming submerged in the damp marshy ground.

The walk climbs high above the two villages, passing through the 400-acre (160ha) herb-rich Pewsey Downs Nature Reserve to reach a pillow mound, a medieval rabbit warren joining several prehistoric barrows. It is at this early stage of the route that you begin to explore a great chain of hills rising up to form a formidable wall of defence – natural rather than man-made. Very soon another landmark looms into view, as the path cuts right across the top of the Alton Barnes White Horse, first cut in 1812, one of several chalk figures to be found on the Marlborough Downs; however, the carving is best appreciated from some distance away.

Beyond the White Horse the walk follows a stretch of the Wansdyke, a bank and ditch probably built by the Britons as a defence against possible Saxon attack. Looking at what remains of the Wansdyke today, a low, crumbling, grassy bank, it is hard to believe this was once a vital frontier. Away to the north, blending into the distant landscape, is Silbury Hill, the largest man-made mound in prehistoric Europe. Built 4,600 years ago, its true purpose still remains a mystery. Ahead now lies Tan Hill, which, at 961ft (293m), is the highest point in Wiltshire.

Turning its back on the spectacular scarp scenery now, the walk heads south into the low-lying clay country of the Vale of Pewsey, described by William Cobbett as 'my land of promise'. Near the village of All Cannings you join the towpath of the Kennet and Avon Canal for the final leg of the walk, following the waterway to the old wharf at Honeystreet, just south of Alton Barnes. Finally completed in 1810, the 87-mile (140km) canal was built to establish a direct link between London and Bristol, though it was abandoned for 40 years following the nationalisation of the railway network in 1948. Returning to your start point, it is sometimes difficult to comprehend the scale of historical changes which this peaceful vale has witnessed.

Old Ways on the Wiltshire Downs

Prehistoric pathways, Saxon defences and a Georgian canal towpath span this quiet corner of Wiltshire

Distance: 8 miles (12.9km)
Total ascent: 519ft (158m)
Paths: mainly good; lower paths and towpath can be very wet
Terrain: downland, linear earthwork, gentle farmland, canal towpath
Gradients: one lengthy climb, though not steep
Refreshments: Kings Arms, All Cannings; Barge Inn, Honey Street
Park: on roadside by Alton Barnes church, in Vale of Pewsey between Devizes and Marlborough

1 From Alton Barnes church, go through the turnstile to follow the paved path towards Alton Priors church. Keep left of the tower, go through a kissing gate and turnstile and follow the road between houses. Cross over at the next road junction, follow the Ridgeway up to the next road and turn right. Turn left through a gate into Pewsey Downs National Nature Reserve, up the grassy track parallel to the road. Approaching a fence, bear left up to the summit of Walker's Hill.

6 Continue past the next bridge at Stanton St Bernard, and the Barge Inn at Honey Street, to the next bridge. Go up to the road and follow it into Alton Barnes. The turning for the church is on the right.

5 Cross to All Cannings Cross Farm and continue, keeping a fence on the left. Keep in line with power cables and follow the track to meet a bridleway. Turn left and walk to the canal. Drop down to the towpath and, keeping the waterway on the left, follow it to the next road bridge.

2 With round barrows on left, go down to cross the ditch and follow the path towards the White Horse. Continue above the chalk carving, through a gate and on to a fence on the right. Follow the fence, making for a gate round the far side of the woodland. Follow the track across open downland to a gate. Continue ahead with a fence on the right to the next gate. Go through it and, with a fence on the right, drop down the field to a gate and stile.

3 Turn left and follow the track down to the Wansdyke at the foot of the hill. Keep the ditch on the right and follow the linear earthwork in a westerly direction for about 1½ miles (2.4km).

4 At a fence by a gate and bridleway sign turn left, with the fence on the right and head south over Tan Hill. At the summit make for a stile in the field corner. Head down to the next stile and gate, then turn left and drop down to the field corner. Cross a stile and turn immediately right. Keep the fence on your right and follow the path to the next gate and stile. Don't cross it, but turn left and follow the path along the foot of the escarpment. Turn right at the fence corner and follow the path to a stile in the right-hand boundary; step over and join a path south through trees. Follow it to a grassy track running to the road.

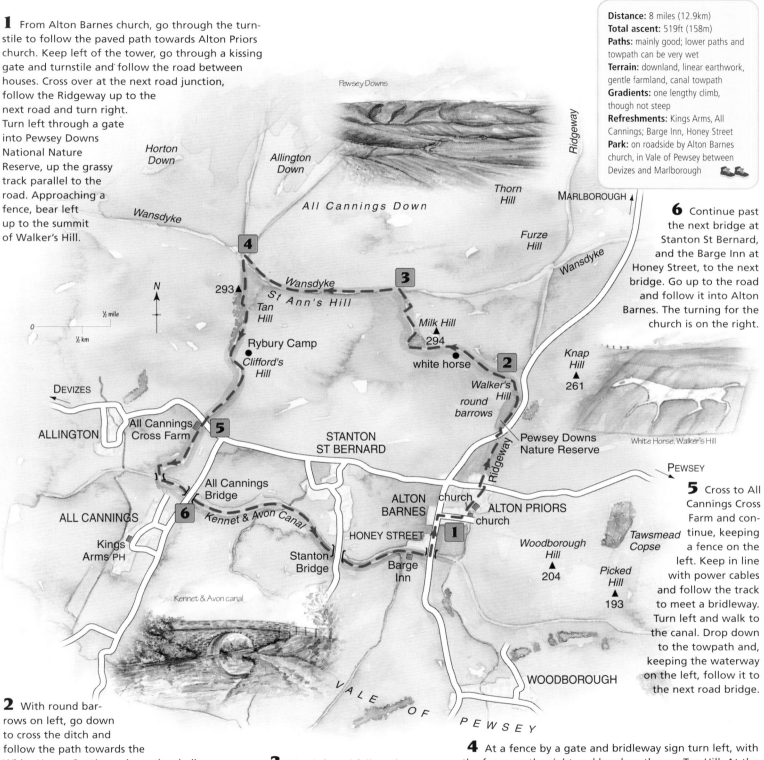

Pewsey Downs

Horton Down

Allington Down

Ridgeway

All Cannings Down

Thorn Hill

MARLBOROUGH

Wansdyke

Furze Hill

Wansdyke

4

293 ▲

Wansdyke

St Ann's Hill

Tan Hill

3

Milk Hill
▲
294

Knap Hill
▲
261

Rybury Camp
● *Clifford's Hill*

white horse
●

2

DEVIZES

Walker's Hill
round barrows

White Horse, Walker's Hill

ALLINGTON

All Cannings Cross Farm

5

STANTON ST BERNARD

Pewsey Downs Nature Reserve

Ridgeway

PEWSEY

All Cannings Bridge

6

Kennet & Avon Canal

ALL CANNINGS

Kings Arms PH

Stanton Bridge

ALTON BARNES

church

ALTON PRIORS
church

HONEY STREET

1

Barge Inn

Woodborough Hill
▲
204

Tawsmead Copse

Picked Hill
▲
193

Kennet & Avon canal

WOODBOROUGH

V A L E   O F   P E W S E Y

N

0   ½ mile
    ½ km

Uley Bury and Hetty Pegler's Tump

Two mysterious and ancient sites along the Cotswold Way evoke a strong sense of wonder

WALK

17

Right: Owlpen Manor is at the heart of a seemingly timeless village scene

Above: the intriguing entrance hole to Hetty Pegler's Tump

Below: the commanding view across to Downham Hill from Uley Bury hill fort

Not many short walks link up such a number of pleasures as this one. Taking in breathtaking views as you walk the Cotswold Way, you arrive at one of Britain's best-preserved neolithic tombs, have the opportunity to visit an excellent village pub, then finish by dipping down into a delightful secret valley. But first, travel back two and a half millennia as you stroll around the ramparts of the giant hill fort of Uley Bury.

How did the local Dobunni tribesmen find the perseverance and the manpower to build the huge defences that dominate the hilltop above Uley? The circumference of Uley Bury hill fort is all of a mile (1.6km), and the loftiest of the great earth banks is well over 40 ft (12m) high. The fort was built around 500 BC, and for at least 500 years the Dobunni held it. Excavations have brought to light one of their gold coins, along with some Roman money. Perhaps the two cultures clashed bloodily on the hilltop, or maybe they came to some more peaceful accommodation involving trade and social contact.

Walking here is a pleasure at any time of year for the view, which rolls out west across the broad plain of the River Severn – seen as a silvery ribbon far below – to the

distant hills of Wales. In summer the grassy slopes of the hill fort are spattered with bugle, scabious, tormentil and other bright little plants.

The Cotswold Way footpath leads you north through the trees along the spine of Gloucestershire's great limestone escarpment. Views are wonderful all the way to Hetty Pegler's Tump, a grassy mound lying just off the B4066. When the Dobunni built Uley Bury, this cleverly constructed chambered tomb must already have been well over 2,000 years old.

You crawl in through a low doorway and along a short passage walled and roofed with golden oolitic limestone. Four semicircular side chambers open off this passage, each one a burial place for cremated bones. Sitting here in the dark, or by the glow of a torch, hemmed in by the weight and solemnity of cold stone, you can speculate on the thoughts and motives of the tomb builders, far more remote from us in time and culture than the gold-working, fort-building Dobunni.

A mile (1.6km) away in the charming Cotswold village of Nympsfield, the Rose and Crown prides itself on the excellence of its cooking. It's a shame, though, that Heg Peg Dump is absent from the menu, for that mysterious delicacy has its place in local folklore:

Nympsfield is a pretty place
Built upon a tump,
And what the people live upon
Is Heg Peg Dump.

Down in the valley below, sealed in by wooded ridges, Owlpen lies secure in its own little world. Ancient stone manor house, church, barns, cottages and mill buildings make up a picture of untroubled and timeless peace, a gem in a green setting whose beauty will stay with you long after your walk is over.

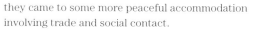

Uley Bury and Hetty Pegler's Tump

*Strange earthworks abound on this walk through
the Cotswold fringe*

1 In Uley take the path to the right of the church; before the churchyard wall ends, bear right up a path which leads to a stile into a steeply rising grassy field.

2 Climb the slope, aiming diagonally left, up to a stile into the woods. Follow the path up through the woods to another stile. Cross the stile and bear left to walk around the ramparts of Uley Bury hill fort, a 1-mile (1.6km) circuit. Keep high up when you get to the second side of the fort.

3 After completing three sides of the circuit, keep ahead through the trees for 200yds (182m) to join the well-waymarked Cotswold Way below a lay-by on the B4066. Follow the Cotswold Way through Coaley Wood for 1 mile (1.6km) and on reaching a junction of path, bridleway and road end, take a sharp right, ascending to meet the B4066.

7 Descend on a path through the trees, and leave the wood in the valley bottom. Keep the wood edge close on your left for 1 mile (1.6km), descending over a stile to join a farm track to the road at Dingle Farm. Turn left here to view Owlpen Manor and church; turn right to return to Uley.

6 From the Rose and Crown turn right to pass the church. In 100yds (91m) turn right at a footpath sign to cross a field, a track and then a road. Cross the following field, descending half right into the trees.

5 After exploring inside and outside the chambered tomb, retrace your steps along the B4066 to where it meets the Cotswold Way and turn right along a side road, signposted Nympsfield. Take the first lane on your left and, in 300yds (273m), bear right into Nympsfield to find the Rose and Crown pub.

4 Turn right along the grass verge of the road. In ⅓ mile (535m), turn right off the road on a signposted track to Hetty Pegler's Tump, a green grassy mound lying by the edge of the wood.

Distance: 6 miles (9.6km)
Total ascent: 425ft (130m)
Paths: mostly good; can be slippery after rain
Terrain: hilly, wooded countryside
Gradients: one particularly steep climb
Refreshments: Old Crown, Uley; Rose and Crown, Nympsfield
Park: Uley Church, on the B4066, 2 miles (3.2km) east of Dursley
Note: take a torch for Hetty Pegler's Tump

Birdlip and the Cotswolds

Passing through venerable beech woods and returning across the high wold, the walk follows part of the Cotswold escarpment

WALK
18

Top right: the beech wood is home to many birds including the jay

Right: an isolated copse of birches

Below: Birdlip Hill is perhaps named from 'bird's leap' because of the steepness of the scarp slope below it

On Barrow Wake, near the start of the walk, an interesting memorial to local geologist Peter Hopkins illustrates the rock types that underlie local features and those, further away, that can be seen from the viewpoint. The geology is important here – the oolitic limestone beneath the Cotswolds grew a rich grass that fed the sheep that created the wealth of the area. It also supported sturdy beech trees, and while the high, grassy wolds are almost gone now, you will pass through some of the best remaining beech woods as you follow the walk.

The walk follows the Cotswold Way National Trail along the Cotswold's scarp edge to Birdlip Hill (topped by The Peak). The hill is clothed by the first of the beech woods, the trees tall and thick-trunked. In spring some areas of the wood are carpeted in bluebells, others with the white-flowered, pungent ransoms, which belong to the garlic family. The wood is home to a great number of species: you may spot all manner of tits, woodpeckers, finches and thrushes. Look out for the quick slate-blue flash of a sparrowhawk, hovering kestrels or buzzards working the updrafts of air created by the sharply rising scarp slope.

Beyond Birdlip the walk crosses a section of high wold. Here Cotswold sheep – often called the Cotswold lions – once outnumbered people, growing fleeces that made the area the richest in England (and England one of the richest countries in Europe) in medieval times. Now the land has been enclosed and Cotswold sheep can only be seen in farms specialising in rare

breeds, but the enclosing hedges are a haven for wildlife. In spring you will hear the distinctive two-note crow of male pheasants anxious to find a mate. The flamboyant, colourful males are easy to spot, but the dowdier brown females are more elusive – not necessarily a disadvantage in fox country. Groups of shy little roe deer also live on the hills, although whether you manage to see one is a matter of luck: some walkers have rounded a hedge to find three or four deer just yards away, while others have walked the wolds for years and never caught a glimpse of one.

For its final leg, the walk rejoins the Cotswold Way. After passing an eerily empty military camp the Way continues through Short Wood, one of the finest remaining sections of beech wood, with magnificent trees, their vast canopies of leaves creating a patchwork of sunlight on the woodland floor in which wood sorrel and violets thrive. Beyond the wood is Crickley Hill, an Iron Age hillfort which has been extensively excavated and has given its name to a country park.

Birdlip and the Cotswolds

A walk through woodland and farmland shows the Cotswold escarpment at its best

1 From the panorama board and memorial in the car park bear left along the Cotswold Way to a stile into beech woodland. There is a fine view to the right, but it is even better if the short detour is taken to The Peak. From here return to the Cotswold Way and follow it through the wood. After passing a high bank on the left a distinct path goes off left.

2 Turn left, bearing left at a fork to a gate. Follow the wall on the right across the field beyond to reach a road (the B4070). Cross the road, footbridge and way-marked stile and cross the field beyond to another stile (don't cross). Turn left along field edge to a stile on to the A417.

3 Cross with care and go over the stile opposite. Follow the hedge on the right to a waymarker post. Continue along the hedge on the right (beyond the gap), pass another waymarker and turn left in the corner to continue beside a hedge. Follow hedge sharp right along a wide track. After 30yds (27m) turn left, walking with a hedge on your right and turning left with it, then following a wall on the right to its end. Here step right, around the wall end, and turn left beside a hedge.

4 Follow the hedge to where it turns left and turn left along a broad, grassy swathe to a gate. Follow the lane beyond between houses to reach a road by the masts. Turn right and follow the road, but where it goes right, continue ahead, soon forking left along a metalled lane. Where the lane bears right at a mast and transformer, bear left along a track, following it downhill between deer fences to reach a road. Bear left for a few steps to the main road.

5 Cross and take the road opposite, following it past the golf club, to the right, and the National Star Centre, to the left. Between the two the Cotswold Way joins from the right. At the next cross-roads go straight across, following the Cotswold Way. When the road descends, go left up steps and follow the Cotswold Way, crossing two stiles before descending into Short Wood. Stay close to the right edge, emerging close to a car park at Crickley Hill Country Park. Follow the Way through the car park, passing the visitor centre and interpretive panels. Follow the Way across the hill fort to reach a wall, turning left to walk with it.

6 Go through a gate, through the ramparts of the fort and a wood to reach the A417 by the Air Balloon Inn. Cross the road and follow the road-side path uphill. Bear right, away from the road, but where the Cotswold Way turns right, continue along the path to return to the start.

> **Distance:** 7½ miles (12km)
> **Total ascent:** 400 ft (120m)
> **Paths:** Waymarked section of the Cotswold Way on good paths, together with reasonable field paths
> **Terrain:** fields and open grassland
> **Gradients:** gradual
> **Refreshments:** The Air Balloon Inn
> **Park:** Barrow Wake viewpoint car park on A417 near the Air Balloon Inn

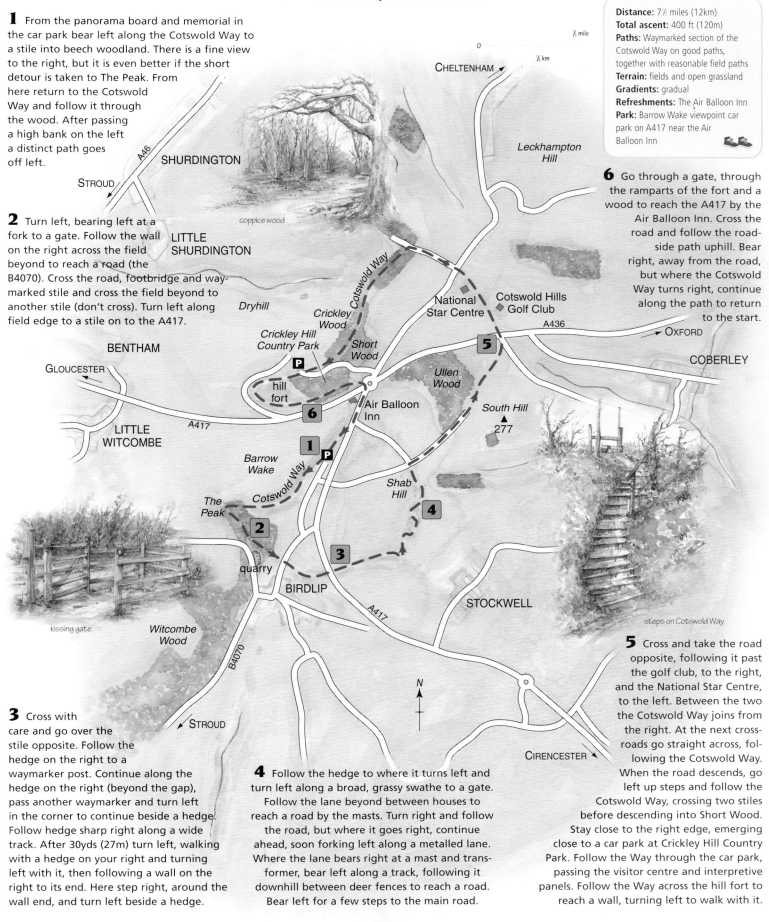

coppice wood

kissing gate

steps on Cotswold Way

CHELTENHAM

Leckhampton Hill

SHURDINGTON

STROUD

A46

LITTLE SHURDINGTON

Dryhill

BENTHAM

GLOUCESTER

A417

LITTLE WITCOMBE

Crickley Wood

Crickley Hill Country Park

hill fort

Cotswold Way

Short Wood

National Star Centre

Cotswold Hills Golf Club

A436

OXFORD

COBERLEY

Ullen Wood

Air Balloon Inn

South Hill
▲ 277

Barrow Wake

The Peak

Cotswold Way

quarry

Shab Hill

BIRDLIP

A417

STROUD

B4070

Witcombe Wood

STOCKWELL

CIRENCESTER

½ mile
0
½ km

N

Turmoil at Tewkesbury

A peaceful town became a bloody battleground that was the scene of a decisive victory in the Wars of the Roses

Top right: detail from the Western Door of Tewkesbury Abbey

Below: the Battle of Tewkesbury

Below: magnificent Norman Tewkesbury Abbey

Tewkesbury is a rare survival of a medieval town, its timber-framed structures tightly packed along the narrow, winding alleys leading off the main street. Its abbey is one of the finest Norman buildings in the country. On 4 May 1471 this glorious church witnessed a desperate episode in the War of the Roses, when some of the Lancastrian forces were trapped within its walls; their armour, beaten out into iron plates, lines the door of the sacristy in the south choir aisle. In the centre of the choir is the tomb of the Lancastrian King Henry VI's 18-year-old son Edward, Prince of Wales, who was killed as he fled the field of battle. Above him on the vault glows a circle of suns, badge of the victorious Yorkists.

The Battle of Tewkesbury was crucial to both the sides in the second of three wars known collectively as the Wars of the Roses. The red rose Lancastrians, led by Queen Margaret, wife of the weak King Henry VI, were determined to remove the white rose Yorkist King Edward IV from his throne once and for all, after the roller-coaster fortunes that both sides had suffered for 25 years.

As you begin the walk along Lower Lode Lane, you pass through the battle lines of the doomed, hastily assembled Lancastrians. Here were the troops of Margaret's right-hand man, the Duke of Somerset. Edward, Prince of Wales, was with his force to the east, and beyond him the troops commanded by theEarl of Devon.

As you turn left you enter Bloody Meadow where some of the fiercest fighting took place. Here many of the fleeing Lancastrians, hoping to escape across the river, were caught and killed. Going through the golf course into Tewkesbury Park, you cross the Yorkist lines – 400 yards (365m) south of the Lancastrians. Here was the Duke of Gloucester, brother of Edward IV (and later king himself as Richard III). The king's force was beside him, with men commanded by Lord Hastings to the east of them. From the hill on which the clubhouse now stands, 200 Yorkist spearmen descended to wreak havoc on Somerset's forces.

There is dispute about where the main battle was fought. Holme Hill beside Lower Lode Lane may have been the Lancastrian's main stand, or it may have been further east in the area called Gaston, southeast of the abbey. But the outcome was not in doubt. King Edward's army of 3,500 defeated Margaret's larger force. The victorious Edward was soon able to return to London and order the execution of Henry VI. Margaret was imprisoned, and Edward was secure on his throne until his death in 1483.

Reminders of a more peaceful England are visible as you pass through quiet fields towards Deerhurst. The Saxon church of St Mary dates back in part to AD 804; don't miss the 10th-century stone angel outside on the east end. Across the road is Odda's Chapel, now structurally part of Abbot's Court farmhouse. It was founded in 1056 by Odda, friend of King Edward the Confessor. From here the massive tower of the abbey, dominating Tewkesbury, points your way back to town along the River Severn.

Turmoil at Tewkesbury

A walk across the Bloody Meadow from Tewkesbury recalls its bitter role in the Wars of the Roses

1 From the Abbey Lawns car park go through the gate, along the north of the abbey and leave by the main gateway, turning left. Pass the long-stay car park then turn right along Lower Lode Lane. Go left at the Battle Trail sign (crossed swords).

2 Go over a stile to the right and follow the hedge to a plinth commemorating the battle. Turn right along the lane, through the golf club gates and along the drive, veering left along the signed footpath, and following further waymarks to reach a stile.

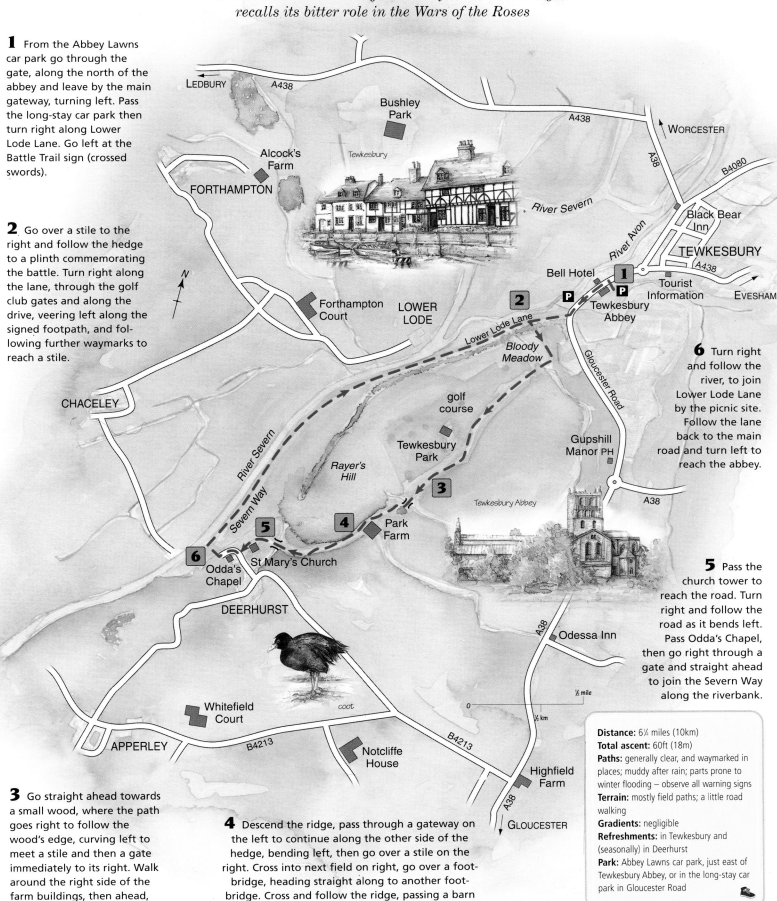

6 Turn right and follow the river, to join Lower Lode Lane by the picnic site. Follow the lane back to the main road and turn left to reach the abbey.

5 Pass the church tower to reach the road. Turn right and follow the road as it bends left. Pass Odda's Chapel, then go right through a gate and straight ahead to join the Severn Way along the riverbank.

3 Go straight ahead towards a small wood, where the path goes right to follow the wood's edge, curving left to meet a stile and then a gate immediately to its right. Walk around the right side of the farm buildings, then ahead, with a hedge on the left.

4 Descend the ridge, pass through a gateway on the left to continue along the other side of the hedge, bending left, then go over a stile on the right. Cross into next field on right, go over a footbridge, heading straight along to another footbridge. Cross and follow the ridge, passing a barn to enter St Mary's churchyard.

Distance: 6¼ miles (10km)
Total ascent: 60ft (18m)
Paths: generally clear, and waymarked in places; muddy after rain; parts prone to winter flooding – observe all warning signs
Terrain: mostly field paths; a little road walking
Gradients: negligible
Refreshments: in Tewkesbury and (seasonally) in Deerhurst
Park: Abbey Lawns car park, just east of Tewkesbury Abbey, or in the long-stay car park in Gloucester Road

Southeast England

Southeast England

OLIVER CROMWELL

There is an air of busy industriousness in the southeast of England. Road and rail routes hum with activity, and even the sky is seldom free from aircraft.

Previous page: symbol of England, the whitecliffs at Cuckmere Haven, East Sussex

Right: Civil War leader Oliver Cromwell was a farmer from East Anglia

Below: poppies at the edge of a barley field in the 'breadbasket of England'

All the conurbations, and especially London, are in a constant state of motion. Amid the hustle and bustle there are green oases of peace and calm to discover, an immensely long and complex history to unravel, ancient ways to travel, mysteries to ponder – and the best way to see it all is on foot. It's a gentle, rolling landscape with no towering heights, essentially agricultural but well wooded in places, threaded by a fine assortment of paths and tracks. Substantial areas of rolling downs and coast have been designated as Areas of Outstanding Natural Beauty, and there is a network of long distance walks.

If one geographical feature has shaped Britain's history more than any other, it is the English Channel. A mere 5,000 years ago, the Channel made Britain into an island, a place apart from the rest of Europe, but the journey towards becoming an island nation has been a bloody one. Not only had the early Britons to fend for themselves, but wave upon wave of invaders had to be accommodated and assimilated. In their turn came Celts, Romans, Saxons, Vikings and Normans, missionaries, mercenaries and refugees. They all fought their battles and left their mark on the landscape for you to discover.

The white cliffs of Dover, the Seven Sisters and other chalk cliffs form England's southern bulwark. The eastern coast is altogether gentler and lower-lying, often crumbling into the sea. Sand and shingle are constantly on the move, a characteristic well illustrated at the curious bank of Orford Ness. Between the eastern and southern coasts, the River Thames has a broad and busy estuary. Following the river inland, you could walk the streets of London for an quintessentially urban experience, or trace the river upstream to Cookham, the inspiration for Kenneth Grahame's *The Wind in the Willows*. This fascinating river with its lazy meanders can be followed through Oxford all the way to its source at Thames Head.

Between the Thames and the English Channel the landscape rises and falls according to the underlying geology, forming ridges such as the North Downs, Weald and South Downs. The North Downs were traversed by Chaucer's pilgrims, and today you can follow their footsteps along the ancient Pilgrim's Way or the more modern North Downs Way. Either way, as you drift from Sussex to Kent, there are apple orchards and hop gardens to delight the eye. The region is rich in maritime history and the historic streets of the Medway towns and channel ports can engross the inquisitive walker for many hours.

Left: beautiful old timbering at Coggeshall, Essex

If you continue round the coast to Beachy Head, the South Downs Way offers a fine route inland. Away from the high downs you could enjoy a tour of little towns and villages, maybe walk in the footsteps of the bohemian intellectuals of the Bloomsbury Set at Alciston, or explore the Arun valley, a wilderness wetland nature reserve known affectionately as the 'Sussex Carmargue'. By the time you reach the ancient royal capital of Winchester you are in Hampshire and within easy reach of the bountiful walking opportunities of the New Forest. Despite its name, this is an ancient forest, and if you are there in the right

Above: Leeds Castle, Kent – the epitome of elegant living

Below: Looking over the South Downs from Ditchling Beacon

mood, at the right time, you could be in one of the world's great wild woods. Deer, wild ponies and abundant adders are additional delights. Just offshore, the Isle of Wight offers a splendid network of well-marked paths and trails. Though of limited compass, there are spectacular cliffs, gentle downs and lush woodlands.

North of the Thames and London the only high ground is formed by the chalk escarpment of the Chilterns, famous for their well-established beech woods. You can traverse a stretch of the ancient Icknield Way along their foot or climb to Ivinghoe Beacon, Combe Hill or other notable heights to enjoy the view. While the landscape may look monotonously agricultural and flatter than the uplands to the north and west, it repays careful exploration, especially in terms of its historic interest and hidden secrets.

The tiny old county of Huntingdonshire might be overlooked were it not for the fact that the only commoner ever to rule Britain was from those parts. Love him or hate him, the yeoman farmer Oliver Cromwell occupied the

nation's top job for over five years. It's possible to drive across Suffolk and Norfolk and be aware only of the vast prairie-like fields, but take a walk through the landscape and you will be astounded by its variety and complexity. The ancient underground warren of Grime's Graves and the lingering remains of huge, isolated airfields are just two intriguing stories waiting to be told. What was East Anglia like for the scores of American servicemen posted to its windswept countryside?

Maybe you're just looking for a quiet rural retreat, a place to enjoy an easy walk and perhaps a sense of timelessness. That can be felt on some of the open heaths and barren coasts of East Anglia. It can also be felt when gazing across one of the artist John Constable's favourite scenes, such as Flatford Mill, or wandering round a quaint medieval village like Coggeshall in Essex. For some people, just to stand beside a huge field of wheat as it billows and rustles in the breeze under the vast East Anglian sky is enough to transport them to a higher plane. It's strange how a field can sometimes create the same feeling as sitting on a lonely shore.

There are those who would say that the Southeast is buried beneath main roads and motorways, but others would see an opportunity for easy access. For example, one person might consider the Devil's Punch Bowl ruined by the A3 running through it, while somebody else might consider that same highway a handy access point to, say, the Greensand Way or the various nature trails that traverse the area. The Southeast is indeed a busy and densely populated area, but there are enough paths and tracks to get you away from the roads. As you tread in the footsteps of packmen and pilgrims, warriors and wayfarers, you occasionally catch a brief glimpse of a landscape that cannot have altered much despite centuries of change, a landscape that keenly remembers

Best of the Rest

Dover During World War II the white cliffs of Dover came to symbolise the free world, beyond the yoke of Nazi occupation. This is a fascinating landscape, deeply pitted with the scars of its strategic importance. A walk out on the high cliffs is the perfect foil to an exploration of this historic town, and of the defences dubbed 'Hellfire Corner' for their proximity to German guns across the Channel.

Beacon Hill North Hampshire's landscape of gently rolling hills and crystal clear rivers tops out in a fine ridge of downland, mirroring the Ridgeway on the opposite side of the Kennet Valley. At Beacon Hill, above Highclere near Newbury, the views become far reaching and spectacular. The strategic vantage point was not lost on the local Iron Age population, who built a mighty hill fort here.

Coombe Hill The Chiltern Hills stretch north from the Thames in a delightful arc of beechwoods and rolling downs. At Coombe Hill they reach a high point, and from nearby Wendover a fine walk connects this vantage point with the prime ministerial grandeur of Chequers and the prehistoric mystery of Cymbeline's Mount.

Thames Path From the Thames Barrier to its Cotswold source, the Thames Path follows England's greatest river. Around Kew and Richmond, London's more opulent suburbs show their back-garden style and hundreds of pleasure craft line the banks. This is a gentle side to the metropolis and a fine way to enjoy some of its most famous sights.

Essex marshes This small corner of Essex from Burnham to Bradwell-on-Sea is closer in spirit to the deserted shores of Suffolk than the brashness of Southend-on-Sea. The tiny village of Bradwell-on-Sea, at a tactful distance from the nearby nuclear power station, has an intriguing history. The site was settled by the Romans, and later by the Saxons – an ancient barn near by has been found to be a Saxon church, part of what must have been impressive fortifications built on the edge of the sea.

Norfolk Coast Lashed by the North Sea and prey to ungovernable tides, the Norfolk coastline seems wilder and more remote than most – and a birdwatcher's paradise. The perfect way to explore it is on the Norfolk Coast Path, from Hunstanton to Cromer, which threads its way through dunes and salt-marshes, and takes in the stately home and park of Holkham.

Suffolk Coast The Suffolk coast, cut off from the rest of the country by the road and rail lines running 5 miles (8km) inland, is one of the most isolated and unspoilt stretches of coast in the country. The variety of habitats – patches of forest, ancient heathland and vast reedbeds as well as seaside sand and shingle – means that nature-lovers can see a great diversity of wildlife, and pleasant seaside towns like Southwold and Aldeburgh (famous for its music festival) are good start and end points for walks.

Epping Forest The 6,000 surviving acres of this once mighty forest make a wonderful day out for the family, and only a tube ride away from central London. Go blackberrying or mushrooming in early autumn, pick up a hiking leaflet at the visitors' centre and choose a walk through stands of ancient pollarded oak, beech and hornbeam, or simply relax with a picnic on a patch of grassy heath.

Left: boats hauled high and dry at Hastings, East Sussex

Constable's Suffolk Landscapes

A contemplative walk in the Stour Valley reveals the artist's favourite haunts amongst willow-lined riverbanks and green pastures

WALK

20

Top right: the young John Constable

Below: Flatford Mill was the inspiration for many of Constable's paintings

To the young John Constable, the daily walk from his house in East Bergholt to the Reverend Thomas Grimwood's Grammar School in Dedham, along the Essex and Suffolk border, was a source of constant delight and inspiration. 'I associate my "careless boyhood" with all that lies on the banks of the Stour. Those scenes made me a painter', he wrote in later life. Golding Constable, a prosperous miller, failed to persuade his son to join the successful family business. The Constables owned not only Flatford Mill but also Dedham Mill, bought complete with granary, wharfs, barges and a cottage, in addition to a windmill and roundhouse in East Bergholt. This was a busy stretch of the River Stour, with trade links to the coast and on to London, with barges built at Flatford.

Retracing the steps of one of Britain's best-loved landscape artists, you can sense the same serenity he experienced 200 years ago. His works also reflect the family occupations, such as *Flatford Mill on the Stour* (1817) and *Boatbuilding near Flatford Mill* (1815). They may well have an ethereal quality, but they also depict contemporary life with working bargemen, boatbuilders and farm labourers.

As you pass alongside the river, keep a sharp eye open for bird life which can be seen both in and out of the water. Large numbers of geese settle on the fields to crop the grass. Cattle are never far away, as portrayed in Constable's paintings, including *Summer Evening* (1811)

and *Dedham Vale* (1811). All this conjures up an idyllic life in the countryside, as was the fashion in art at the time, but which bore little relation to real life. Still, to us walking in these pastures and along the riverbank there is a pervasive tranquillity reminiscent of a bygone age, an antidote to the rush of modern life. The scene has changed little over two centuries, and although busy in summer, the Flatford Mill Centre has been well preserved, with little in the way of intrusive modern facilities.

In East Bergholt you may find time to visit the church where Constable's parents and Willy Lott, owner of the cottage in Constable's most famous painting, *The Haywain* (1821), are buried. Stop and look at the unusual and curious 16th-century wooden bell cage in the churchyard, believed to have been constructed to accommodate the huge, hand-rung bells when funds ran out for the building of a conventional bell tower. Past the church is the site of the house where Constable was born and lived, now disappointingly gone. But his studio still exists, a small cottage just down the street to the left of the village stores.

Returning to Dedham you follow the route used by Constable on that daily trip to school. Descending from East Bergholt, you rejoin the riverbank which winds towards Dedham Mill. Glancing to your left you will catch glimpses of the tower of Dedham church which features so prominently in many of Constable's works.

Constable's Suffolk Landscapes

From 'Dedham Vale' to 'The Haywain', the Suffolk countryside was a constant theme in the artist's work

WALK 20

1 Turn left out of the car park and up to T-junction. The church and old grammar school are opposite. Turn left and where the road bends sharp right, take the path signed Flatford, diagonally to the left. Keep right at the farm.

2 Follow the path and take the river route to Flatford, over a small dyke then across a field to the river. Keep right of the bridge and continue alongside the river. Turn left over a stile before the bridge at Flatford. Go over the river and past Bridge Cottage (teashop). Turn right, past Flatford Mill and Willy Lott's Cottage.

3 Follow a yellow waymark forward at Flatford Mill then left at the car park and take the public footpath to the right. At a double finger post take the Stour Valley path left. Cross the stile and keep by the fence, to the right side of a pylon, to a stile. Continue, crossing over two more stiles.

4 Continue to a double stile. Go straight over the field and continue by a hedge. Go over a stile then take the lane on left. Continue uphill about 600yds (546m) to road and turn left. After 40yds (36m) take the very narrow public footpath to left.

5 Proceed to an open field and go straight over to a waymark. Go through the wood, past houses to a gate. Cross over the lane, through a field and over a stile. Continue to the left of next field, towards a farm. Go down the hill and turn right into a lane, then up hill to East Bergholt.

6 Turn left at the crossroads and follow the road for ¾ mile (1.2km) to the church, turning right. Continue past the Constable birthplace plaque on the fence to the right. Turn left at the no-through road by a shop to see his studio, on the left.

7 Retrace your steps to the war memorial opposite the church. Take the no through road right. After 300yds (273m) take a footpath to right, signed private road. Continue down the track, past a cottage, keeping left, then right to a bridge. Go over bridge.

8 After 75yds (68m) take right fork, signed to Dedham. Follow a narrow path to agate and cross a field with the river to left. Follow the path across a field to a road. Turn left, over the bridge, past the mill and back to the car park on the left.

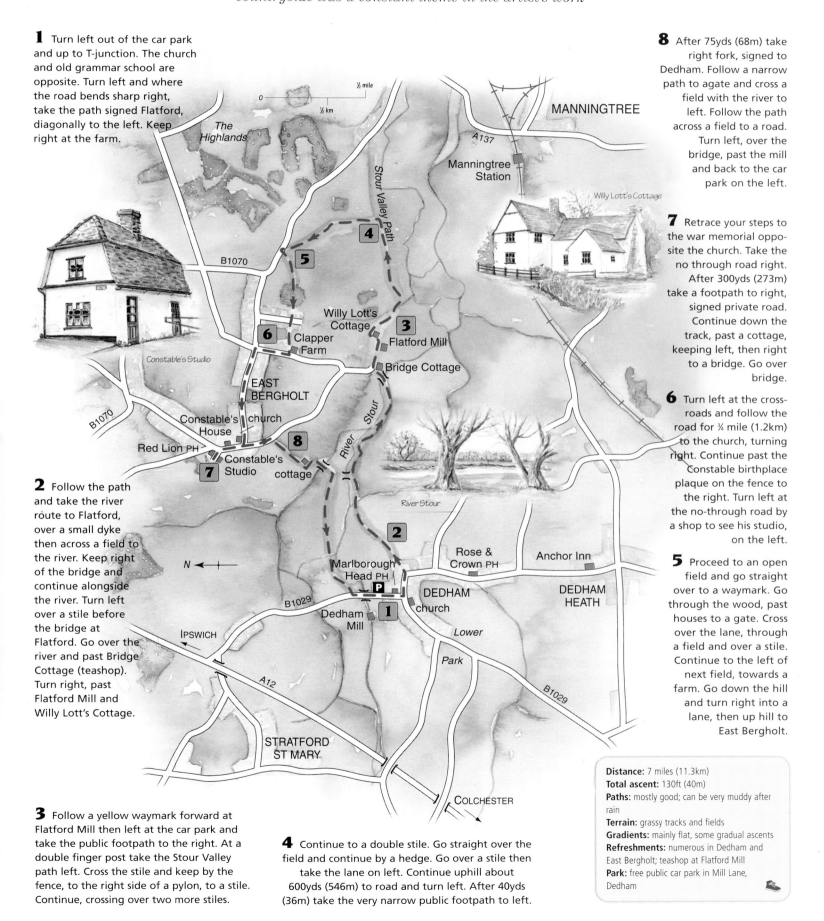

Distance: 7 miles (11.3km)
Total ascent: 130ft (40m)
Paths: mostly good; can be very muddy after rain
Terrain: grassy tracks and fields
Gradients: mainly flat, some gradual ascents
Refreshments: numerous in Dedham and East Bergholt; teashop at Flatford Mill
Park: free public car park in Mill Lane, Dedham

Atomic Secrets of Orford Ness

Wildlife has thrived on this remote shingle spit, cut off from the world in the interests of national security

WALK
21

Up until 1995 you could not legally set foot on Orford Ness, a great shingle spit that runs parallel to a lonely stretch of the Suffolk coast. Since World War I the Ministry of Defence had owned it, using and abusing it as they tested every kind of weaponry – including nuclear devices minus only their fissile material.

The Armament and Experimental Flight of the Royal Flying Corps had been the first to arrive, researching machine-gun technology, bombing and aerial combat techniques during World War I. Between the wars Robert Watson-Watt experimented with radar here, capturing the first ever radar images. During World War II the Ness became a bombing and firing range. In the 1950s and 1960s, great pagoda-roofed laboratories arose,

Above: wild flowers soften the wasteland around the radar tower

Right: deserted atomic weapons testing bunkers lurk in the shingle

inside which the Atomic Weapons Research Establishment tested the casings and internal workings of atomic bombs for their reaction to heat, cold, vibration and shocks. Weirdest of all the Orford Ness installations was Cobra Mist, a top-secret system involving a gigantic fan-shaped net of aerials which monitored the flight of rockets and bombing planes far behind the Iron Curtain. If only a certain mysterious hum hadn't distorted all its signals …

When the AWRE ceased work on Orford Ness in 1971, their legacy was a mass of unexploded ordnance, dozens of ugly, semi-derelict buildings and a network of concrete roads. What they had also left behind them was 5 miles (8km) of coastline wholly untouched by 20th-century development, where wildlife was thriving in ways that made the shingle spit unique and precious. That was why – after the old bombs and bullets and the rest of the MoD mess had been cleared away – the National Trust bought Orford Ness in 1993, and has since opened it to the general public.

Some of the old military buildings have been retained and now house displays. In the former Telephone Exchange you can learn about the history of the site and about the wildlife of the marshes, muds and shingle. The Bomb Ballistic Building contains a display on the testing of bombs, while in the Black Beacon displays explain the activities of the coastguard and lighthouses, as well as what went on in the 'pagodas' such as Lab 1, where nuclear devices (containing no fissile material, we are told) were tested in conditions of the utmost secrecy. From the Black Beacon you can stroll across to Lab 1 and enjoy a peek inside this strange 'hush-hush' building.

But the chief glory of Orford Ness is the wonderfully rich wildlife of the shingle and marshes. Birds include greenshank, barn owls, marsh harriers and twites, along with 16,000 pairs of gulls and a nesting colony of little terns. On the storm-heaped shingle ridges grow rare lichens, sea pea, yellow-horned poppy, sea campion. Rabbits, hares, foxes and feral cats live here undisturbed.

Best of all, there is a sense of peace, of walking in a place cut off from the outside world, where salt wind, slippery shingle and the hiss of waves are all that matter.

Atomic Secrets of Orford Ness

This remote shingle spit on the Suffolk coast was once the scene of historic military experiments

1 From Orford Quay take the National Trust ferry to Orford Ness jetty. The Red Trail leads off up the road for ½ mile (800m) to a T-junction. Immediately on your right is the Old Telephone Exchange display building.

6 From Lab 1 return to the Black Beacon, and bear left to reach the Bailey bridge and the road back to the jetty.

5 The Blue Trail leaves the Red Trail at the Black Beacon and heads out south-west along the shingle for ⅓ mile (535m) to reach Lab 1 where non-fissile experiments were carried out on Britain's first nuclear weaponry.

2 Leaving the display, turn right to pass the NT offices and workshops. In ½ mile (800m) bear right across a Bailey bridge over Stony Ditch. Bear immediately left, aiming for the lighthouse, to reach the Bomb Ballistic Building (display).

3 From the Bomb Ballistic Building, walk forward along the clear path through the shingle ridges to reach the lighthouse. Turn right and follow the path across the shingle and parallel with the shore, to the skeletal-looking Police Tower.

4 At the Police Tower turn right and walk inland to arrive at the Black Beacon (displays and upper-storey viewpoint over the entire shingle spit and surrounding countryside).

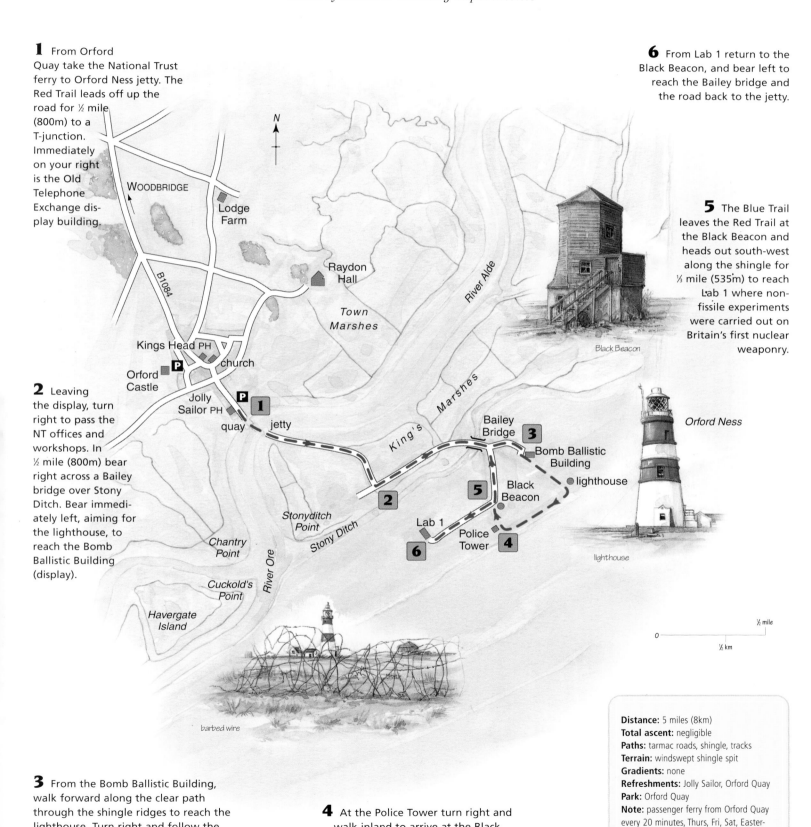

WOODBRIDGE

Lodge Farm

B1084

Raydon Hall

Town Marshes

River Alde

Black Beacon

Kings Head PH

church

Orford Castle

Jolly Sailor PH

1

quay   jetty

King's Marshes

Bailey Bridge **3**

Bomb Ballistic Building

Orford Ness

lighthouse

2

5

Black Beacon

lighthouse

Stonyditch Point

Stony Ditch

Lab 1

6

Police Tower **4**

Chantry Point

Cuckold's Point

River Ore

Havergate Island

barbed wire

½ mile

0

½ km

Distance: 5 miles (8km)
Total ascent: negligible
Paths: tarmac roads, shingle, tracks
Terrain: windswept shingle spit
Gradients: none
Refreshments: Jolly Sailor, Orford Quay
Park: Orford Quay
Note: passenger ferry from Orford Quay every 20 minutes, Thurs, Fri, Sat, Easter-end Oct. To visit in winter, call (01394) 450900. This is National Trust land and an entrance fee is payable

Village Ways in Coggeshall

A town-and-country walk combining handsome historic buildings with wide open spaces and ancient woodland

WALK

22

Below: Church Street flourished with the wool trade

Bottom: Paycocke's is one of Coggeshall's best known medieval houses

Coggeshall is a delight to explore, with medieval half-timbered houses and carved beams wherever you look, seemingly unchanged for centuries. During the Dark Ages simple huts were built on the old Roman road which passes through the centre of the village but Coggeshall didn't really become established until the arrival of the monks who founded a Cistercian abbey in 1140. Initially under the monks' direction, the wool trade flourished and, with an influx of European immigrants and refugees, Coggeshall reached the peak of its prosperity in the 16th and 17th centuries. This is reflected in buildings such as the venerable Woolpack inn and Paycocke's, a magnificent wool merchant's house built around 1500 – take your time to admire the five oriol windows and the elaborate carving on the overhanging timbers. Sadly, with the arrival of industrial machinery in the early 19th century, the wool trade moved to northern England. Coggeshall, however, rallied with a flourishing silk and lace trade, the latter thriving until well into the 20th century. Nowadays seed production is big business, and the village has a reputation for antique shops and good restaurants, bringing it right up to date.

Just outside the village are the ruins of the abbey and the site of the mill where, in the 12th century, the monks diverted the River Blackwater to provide a dependable head of water. Religion played an important part in the economic growth of Coggeshall. Protestant Huguenot refugees erected the present mill building as a silk mill in the 17th century. It was converted for grinding corn in the mid-19th century and is now the only working mill on the Blackwater. Beyond the farmyard is the gatehouse chapel of St Nicholas, now part of the parish of St Peter-ad-Vincula in the village. The chapel was used as a cowshed for over 300 years but was restored as a place of worship at the end of the 1800s. Despite the lack of heating or electricity, services are still held occasionally. From here a section of the Essex Way leads past the spectacular 12th-century Grange Barn, one of the oldest tithe barns in Europe and noted for its superb timber frame.

On leaving the village you head through tranquil open country, studded with pockets of woodland. Here you'll be walking under the vast open skies that have long attracted artists to East Anglia. Emerging from the woods you reach Marks Hall Estate. The house was demolished in 1949, although restored outbuildings remain and you can see the lakes, reportedly dug by Cromwell's men during the Siege of Colchester in 1648. The estate boasts a fine arboretum, and a visitor centre. Returning to the village through Tilkey, there are more fine buildings which typify the architectural wealth of this historic village.

Village Ways in Coggeshall

Exploring an Essex village which has retained its medieval charm

1 Leave the car park by the clock tower. Cross the road diagonally and turn left into Church Street. Continue to Woolpack Inn and church on the left. Cross road opposite the end of the church and take marked Essex Way path on the right.

2 Continue past the school into the recreation ground to the left-hand corner and turn left into East Street. Follow a footpath then cross over and take the Essex Way to right at the end of houses. Follow hedge to a stile and continue by fence following Essex Way towards farmyard.

3 Turn right and pass a mill on the left, through the farmyard with abbey ruins on right. Continue past the chapel to T-junction (Grange Barn opposite). Turn right down the hill. Beyond a bridge, turn left then shortly left again into West Street. (Paycocke's is on left). Cross over, taking the path by an old school.

Distance: 8½ miles (13.7km)
Total ascent: 100ft (30m)
Paths: good, some can be very muddy after rain
Terrain: pavements, fields, woodland tracks
Gradients: few, very gradual
Refreshments: numerous in village; Compasses, Pattiswick; teashop, Marks Hall
Park: public car park, Stoneham Street, Coggeshall

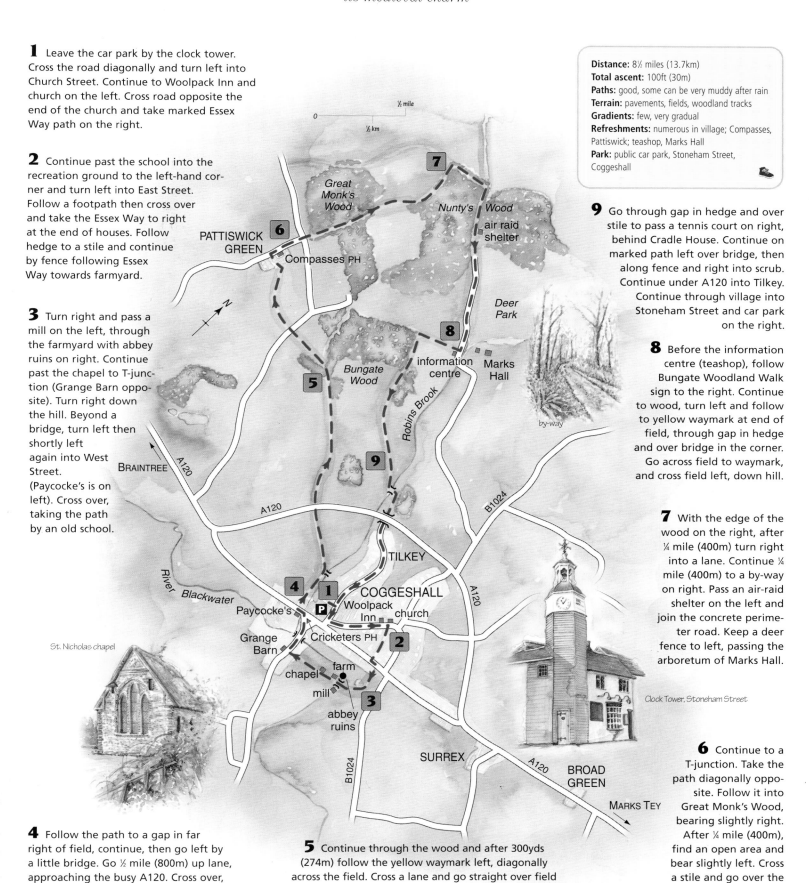

9 Go through gap in hedge and over stile to pass a tennis court on right, behind Cradle House. Continue on marked path left over bridge, then along fence and right into scrub. Continue under A120 into Tilkey. Continue through village into Stoneham Street and car park on the right.

8 Before the information centre (teashop), follow Bungate Woodland Walk sign to the right. Continue to wood, turn left and follow to yellow waymark at end of field, through gap in hedge and over bridge in the corner. Go across field to waymark, and cross field left, down hill.

7 With the edge of the wood on the right, after ¼ mile (400m) turn right into a lane. Continue ¼ mile (400m) to a by-way on right. Pass an air-raid shelter on the left and join the concrete perimeter road. Keep a deer fence to left, passing the arboretum of Marks Hall.

Clock Tower, Stoneham Street

6 Continue to a T-junction. Take the path diagonally opposite. Follow it into Great Monk's Wood, bearing slightly right. After ¼ mile (400m), find an open area and bear slightly left. Cross a stile and go over the field towards Nunty's Wood.

4 Follow the path to a gap in far right of field, continue, then go left by a little bridge. Go ½ mile (800m) up lane, approaching the busy A120. Cross over, taking no-through road. Continue ¾ mile (1.2km) to Bungate Wood.

5 Continue through the wood and after 300yds (274m) follow the yellow waymark left, diagonally across the field. Cross a lane and go straight over field by pylon. Follow to waymark and go along hedge. Turn left, then right into lane, passing the Compasses pub.

Historic Medway Towns

Follow the river to explore the birthplace of the Royal Navy and the town which inspired Charles Dickens

WALK
23

Right: a warship's figurehead surveys Chatham's Historic Dockyard Museum

Below: Rochester Castle's Norman keep rises up above the city and river

Chatham's maritime heritage can be felt almost as soon as you start this walk. It is subtle but significant: in the names of streets, the models of ships in people's windows, the almshouses built for 'mariners and ship-wrights' in 1594. There are places where it seems as if someone has tried to sweep all this history away – but the past is too strong and soon reasserts itself.

Military and maritime relics lie along Dock Road. You pass Fort Amerhurst, a Napoleonic complex of under-ground tunnels built to protect the Royal Naval Dockyard from attack, then a gateway above which sits a coat of arms, erected on the 50th anniversary of D-Day to commemorate Chatham Dockyard's role in support of Operation Overlord – the Allied invasion of occupied Europe.

Eventually you reach Chatham's most famous spot, the Historic Dockyard, which is considered to be the birth-place of the British navy. Henry VIII used to winter his ships on the Medway, and his successor, Elizabeth I, later established a dockyard at Chatham. Nowadays the river is quiet and it is hard to believe that many of the ships that defeated the Spanish Armada sailed from these docks. It was here too that Drake, and later Nelson, learned their seamanship.

Passing the Medway Tunnel you soon come to a quiet area known as St Mary's Island, where modern residential development mingles with decaying industry. Here, incon-gruous against the houses, is the brooding black hulk of the submarine HMS *Ocelot*, the last warship built for the Royal Navy at Chatham. Made for stealth and silence, it now sits uneasily on the quayside, as if uncomfortable with the attention it attracts.

Although much of historic Chatham may have disap-peared, Rochester still retains a quaint charm. The little High Street would certainly be recognised by Dickens – possibly even by Henry VIII, who met his fourth wife Anne of Cleves here for the first time and was famously disap-pointed. Dickens loved the town and it featured a lot in his work. Restoration House for instance, a forbidding brick building, became Satis House in *Great Expectations*. Today its iron gate still keeps the outside world at bay just as it did for mad Miss Havisham.

The walk now takes you past Rochester Cathedral, which was founded in AD 604. A Benedictine monastery once stood on this spot, and its monks are thought to be responsible for some ancient graffiti in the crypt. Immedi-ately opposite is the magnificent milky castle, its walls – 12 feet (3.7 m) thick in places – built by the Normans on the remains of an earlier Roman fort. Cool and aloof in the morning, it mellows to a gentle shade of buttermilk under the setting sun.

Dickensian associations dominate the High Street, but there are other points of interest too, such as the Guildhall, erected in the 17th century by the deliciously named Admiral Sir Cloudesley Shovell. This is a surprising oasis of history where even the traffic noise is muffled by the abundance of fascinating stories to be told.

Historic Medway Towns

A rich and varied past is all around you on the historic streets of Rochester and Chatham

WALK 23

> **Distance:** 5½ miles (8.8 km)
> **Total ascent:** 100ft (30m)
> **Paths:** good
> **Terrain:** city streets
> **Gradients:** gentle
> **Refreshments:** available throughout
> **Park:** Rochester Station

1 From Rochester Station turn left, go under the rail bridge and walk right, down to the main road. Turn left along Medway Street, follow the road round, then turn left again up Dock Road, signposted to Historic Dockyard.

2 Keep walking up this busy road. Go straight on at the roundabout, then left into the Historic Dockyard. After exploring the dockyard come out and turn left. Go over the roundabout, then past the Medway Tunnel. Cross the road at the next roundabout and walk up to the submarine Ocelot.

3 Follow the road back into town. At the clock, cross over to the Pentagon Shopping Centre. Turn right up a pedestrianised street, then go right along a quiet part of Chatham High Street. Keep going straight ahead, back to Rochester Station.

4 Pass the station, walk up to the main road, cross over and walk down the pedestrianised High Street. Just after Eastgate House turn left, up Crow Lane. Cross over at Restoration House and follow the sign for Centenary Walk, which leads over a small park.

5 Turn right at the end, go down the hill, then left at the bottom. Pass the cathedral, cross the road and turn left round the castle, following Centenary Walk signs. Pass Satis House, turn right at the river, then right again by the bridge.

6 Walk right along the High Street, exploring the small alleys and passageways. Cross the road at the end and walk back to the station.

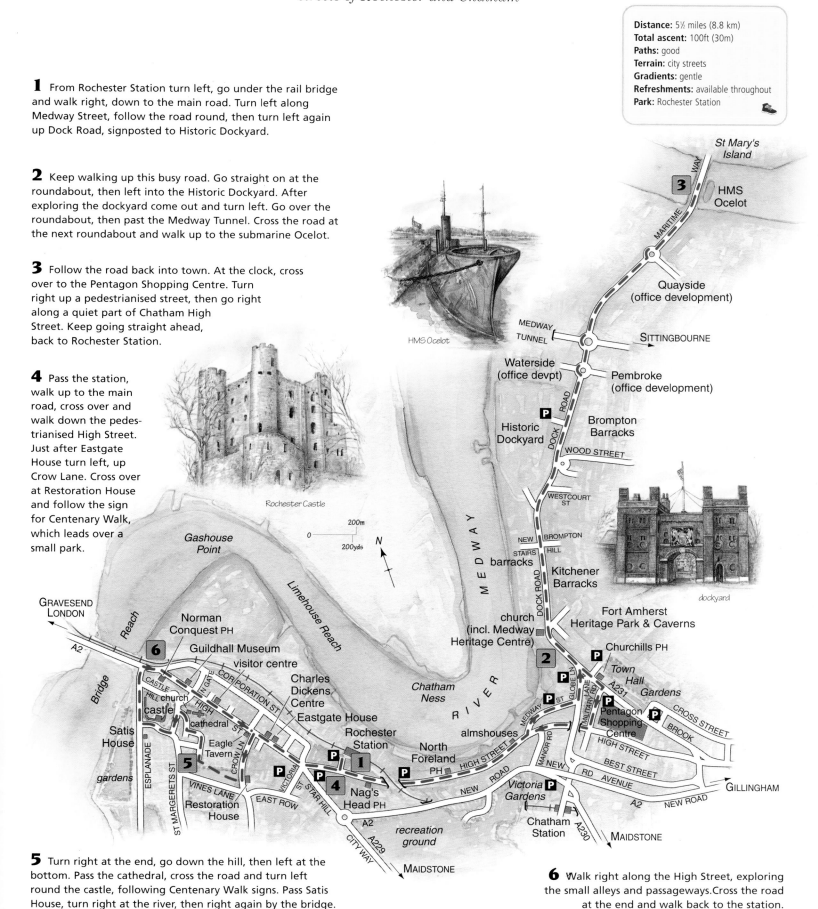

HMS Ocelot

Rochester Castle

dockyard

Following the Pilgrims through Kent

An ancient pilgrims' path winds through the rolling Kentish countryside from the village of Hollingbourne

WALK 24

Top right: pilgrims on the road to Canterbury

Above: half-timbering in Hollingbourne village

Below: a tranquil sweep of chalky downland

The Pilgrims' Way is one of the oldest trackways in the land. It was almost certainly used by prehistoric man as a trading route linking the Straits of Dover – and thereby mainland Europe – to England's West Country with its rich mineral resources. Later it seems likely that it was used by pilgrims travelling from Winchester (the old capital of Wessex) to Canterbury and the shrine of St Thomas à Becket. Incidentally, this was not the route followed by Chaucer's pilgrims as they went to 'Caunterbury with ful devout corage' – they started out from Southwark in south London and travelled along the more northerly Roman Watling Street, which is the A2 today.

Setting off from the straggling village of Hollingbourne you cannot but reflect on the thousands of travellers who have passed through the village before you. Passing the old manor house, once the home of a branch of the Culpepper family, the famous herbalists, you soon come to one of the most distinctive features of the Kentish landscape – an oast house. These buildings, with their warm red, circular roofs, were used to dry the hops that once covered thousands of acres of countryside. Laced high above the ground in a delicate latticework, the hops were picked by people from the East End of London who frequently used harvest time as their family holiday.

Soon you are on the Pilgrims' Way itself, which clings to the southern slope of the hills. Its route allowed travellers to avoid exposure to the elements on the chalky downs above, and the stickiness of the heavy clay soil in the vale below.

Canterbury became a pilgrimage site after Thomas à Beckett, then Archbishop of Canterbury, was murdered in his own cathedral. This was the culmination of a bitter dispute with the King, Henry III. Furious that Thomas would not give in to his demands for greater power over the church, the King famously asked his courtiers to 'rid me of this turbulent priest'.

From the Pilgrims' Way the route branches across country where, if there has been heavy rain, you soon understand the problems the glutinous clay soil might have caused poorly shod pilgrims. You now pass a number of manor houses, a common sight in this area. For centuries land in Kent was inherited according to the Jute law of *gavelkind*, whereby on a man's death his land would be divided equally among his heirs. The Normans recognised this law and did not impose their own system – with the result that Kent has fewer grand estates than other counties, but plenty of substantial manor houses.

Eventually you come on to the North Downs Way, where you are rewarded with glorious views of undulating countryside. This long-distance trail coincides with the Pilgrims' Way for much of its length. As you make your way back into Hollingbourne you should realise that your footprints have joined the millions of others along these ancient tracks.

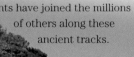

Following the Pilgrims through Kent

At Hollingbourne, medieval pilgrims bound for Canterbury found hospitality in a pleasing village

1 From the street opposite the manor house walk up the road by the house. Turn right where the path forks. You will pass a converted oast house. Follow the byway sign. At the electricity sub-station, go right and up to the Pilgrims' Way.

6 Cross Broad Street then go up steps following North Downs Way signs, over a stile, then down steps into a wood. At the T-junction, turn left then right and go through a metal barrier. Coming out onto open land, turn left and go through three gates and follow the path across fields and through trees back down to Hollingbourne.

5 Go up a steep hill, then down and over two stiles. Follow North Downs Way as it bends, left then right near the farm, then go over two more stiles and through the wood. In a field follow the path to the top corner and go over a stile then right to the road.

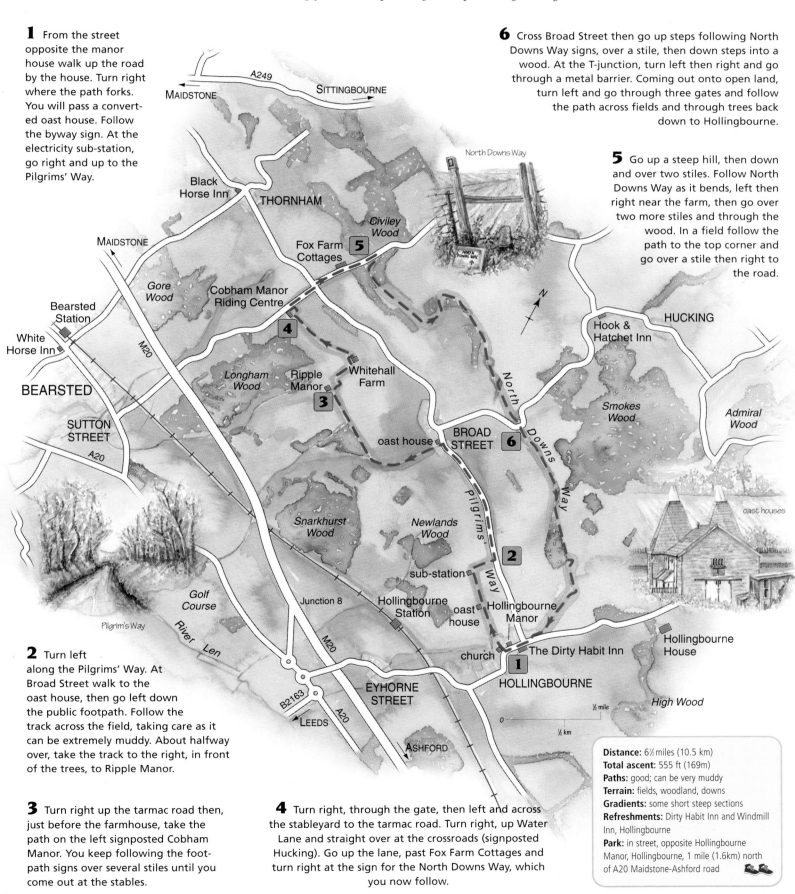

2 Turn left along the Pilgrims' Way. At Broad Street walk to the oast house, then go left down the public footpath. Follow the track across the field, taking care as it can be extremely muddy. About halfway over, take the track to the right, in front of the trees, to Ripple Manor.

3 Turn right up the tarmac road then, just before the farmhouse, take the path on the left signposted Cobham Manor. You keep following the footpath signs over several stiles until you come out at the stables.

4 Turn right, through the gate, then left and across the stableyard to the tarmac road. Turn right, up Water Lane and straight over at the crossroads (signposted Hucking). Go up the lane, past Fox Farm Cottages and turn right at the sign for the North Downs Way, which you now follow.

Distance: 6½ miles (10.5 km)
Total ascent: 555 ft (169m)
Paths: good; can be very muddy
Terrain: fields, woodland, downs
Gradients: some short steep sections
Refreshments: Dirty Habit Inn and Windmill Inn, Hollingbourne
Park: in street, opposite Hollingbourne Manor, Hollingbourne, 1 mile (1.6km) north of A20 Maidstone-Ashford road

'Mad Jack's' Brightling Follies

Follow the trail of a celebrated eccentric who left his – several – marks on the Sussex Weald

WALK
25

Top right: the Obelisk stands alone on the hill, screened by a bank of wild flowers

Below: the path to the conical Sugar Loaf

Inset below: 'Mad Jack's' distinctive mausoleum in Brightling churchyard

Born into one of the wealthiest and most influential families in Sussex, John (Jack) Fuller (1757–1834) inherited Brightling Park on his 20th birthday. Not surprisingly, he became wilful and autocratic, embarking on a colourful political career in 1801 to air his extravagant views. A large, outspoken man, who wore a pigtail and hair powder, he drank three bottles of port a day, refused a peerage, travelled from London in a carriage with footmen armed with pistols and swords, and revelled in impossible wagers. After swearing at the Speaker of the House of Commons in 1810, Fuller became disillusioned with politics and turned his attention to the arts and sciences, becoming a renowned patron of the arts and an active promoter of scientific research. He also spent time and energy building unusual monuments and follies around Brightling.

Two of Fuller's early buildings are the Observatory and the Obelisk (Brightling Needle). Here far reaching views extend over the Sussex High Weald into Kent and across to the Pevensey Marshes. The Observatory, now a private residence, may have been built to satisfy Fuller's amateur enthusiasm for science, but it was well equipped with sophisticated instruments. The classic story tells how Fuller's servants used the telescope to look out for his homebound carriage, so that food, drink and his slippers would be ready on his arrival.

The Obelisk, standing on private land 200 yards (70m) from the road, was probably erected to celebrate Wellington's victory over Napoleon in 1815.

The Sugar Loaf is a cone-shaped folly built after a wager Fuller had with some friends. He claimed he could see the spire of Dallington church from his estate, but on drawing the curtains back in the morning he saw nothing but rolling woods and fields. To save face and win his bet, he hurriedly had a duplicate spire ('nothing more than stones held together by mud') erected in one night on the edge of his land.

In the middle of Brightling Park, landscaped by Capability Brown, stands the Grecian-style Rotunda Temple. Stories embellished over the years suggest it was used to hide smuggled wares, to store Fuller's wine, or as a venue for gambling sessions, or the entertainment of his lady friends. On the edge of the park is the two-storey Tower, supposedly erected so that Fuller could see Bodiam Castle, which he later purchased to save it from demolition.

Fuller's final 'folly' was a sandstone pyramid mausoleum, erected 24 years before his death after he agreed with the rector to build a new inn down the road (the one opposite the church was too popular a distraction for his parishioners) in return for a space in the churchyard. For years it was believed that he had been interred seated, dressed for dinner wearing a top hat and holding a bottle of claret. It was later discovered that his mode of burial was uncharacteristically conventional.

'Mad Jack's' Brightling Follies

*A tour of the charming landmarks built by
'Mad Jack' Fuller, a Sussex eccentric*

1 From crossroads follow Willingford Lane (signed Burwash Weald) with Obelisk on left. Pass Barn Farm right and take bridleway left along concrete track. At junction, just beyond cottage, turn left over a stile and follow left-hand edge of field to another stile.

2 Bear half-right downhill to bridge and stile. Head straight uphill, then down to stile and descend to cross bridge. Climb steps and stile, then head uphill to gate and turn right at junction, following hedge to stile. Proceed to stile on edge of woodland, turning left at fingerpost on path parallel with woodland. Shortly, turn right at junction.

3 Cross forest track and descend through gorse. Ignore path on left and continue down sunken bridleway to cross stream. Follow path left to track and turn sharp left on bridleway, passing two posts. Ascend for ¼ mile (400m), past two houses.

4 Follow lane uphill. Disregard first footpath left and take second arrowed path, beyond two houses. Go through gate, pass right of pond to fingerpost by hedge ahead. Keep straight on path towards Sugar Loaf. Cross double stile and bear half-left to gap in hedge near end of houses.

8 Ignore arrowed path right through trees and keep to ha-ha. Proceed at end through small copse and large gate into field. Turn left along field edge to gate and follow path signed The Sugar Loaf through woodland to forest drive. Bear right and keep right by Forestry Commission board to lane. Turn right, then left at junction (signed Burwash), and follow lane back to start.

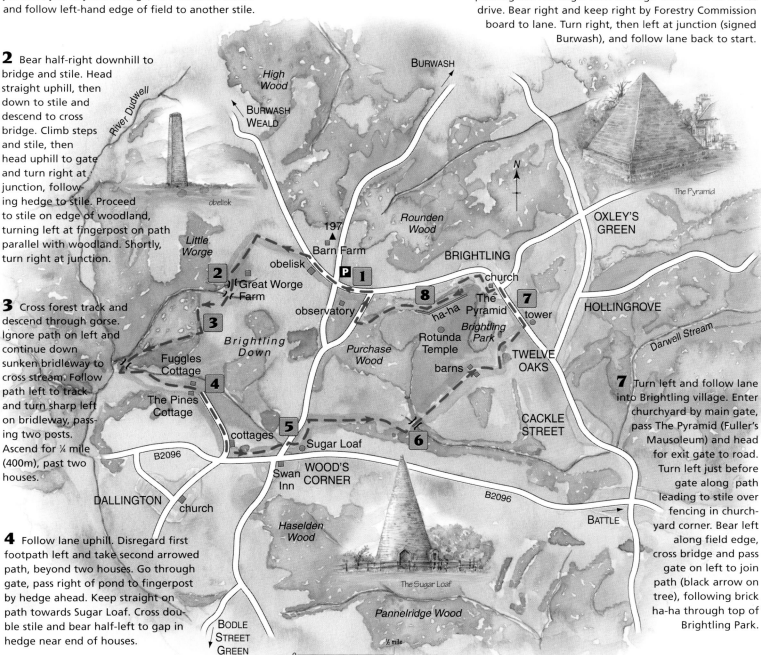

Distance: 6 miles (9.7km)
Total ascent: 650ft (198m)
Paths: good; muddy after rain
Terrain: fields, woodland, open parkland
Gradients: gradual
Refreshments: Swan Inn, Wood's Corner
Park: on verge near Fuller's Obelisk and Observatory on Brightling Down, between Wood's Corner and Burwash, 1 mile (1.6km) north of B2096 at Wood's Corner

5 Turn left along road to entrance to salvage yard. To view Sugar Loaf, enter yard (yellow arrow), pass gates to first yard and follow markers uphill along fenced path to gate. Return to yard entrance and follow white arrows on right into Purchase Wood. Ignore path to Brightling, left, and keep ahead on path (signed The Tower), eventually merging with gravel track. ½ mile (800m) into woodland look for arrowed post left for The Tower.

7 Turn left and follow lane into Brightling village. Enter churchyard by main gate, pass The Pyramid (Fuller's Mausoleum) and head for exit gate to road. Turn left just before gate along path leading to stile over fencing in churchyard corner. Bear left along field edge, cross bridge and pass gate on left to join path (black arrow on tree), following brick ha-ha through top of Brightling Park.

6 Descend into wood, cross bridge and pass through gate into Brightling Park. Proceed through gate ahead and follow path through edge of woodland to gate. Keep left along field edge (The Temple clearly visible to left - no access), eventually reaching gate by barns. Turn right on track and keep left at junction to follow track to lane. Turn right to view The Tower.

A Wealth of Wildlife in the Arun Valley

A ramble through the water meadows of Amberley Wild Brooks to the South Downs reveals why this area is known as the Sussex Camargue

WALK 26

Top right: a grey heron waits, motionless, for its prey

Above: the colourful plumage of a male pintail

Right: looking out over Pulborough Brooks

The Arun, rising in St Leonard's Forest near Crawley, is Sussex's longest river. With its tributary, the Rother, it drains a very large area of the western Weald. The river is fast-flowing and, with the added effect of being tidal up to Pulborough, it floods the Arun Valley extensively in winter.

Covering some 3900 acres (1583 ha) between Arundel and Stopham, the Arun Valley floodplain – managed for centuries as flood meadows, grazed with livestock and cut for hay, and for the supply of water to the ditch network – is one of the most biologically diverse wetlands in the UK. A number of sympathetically managed areas – Pulborough Brooks Nature Reserve (RSPB), Amberley Wild Brooks, Coldwaltham Brooks, Wildfowl and Wetlands Trust (Arundel) – have been designated as Sites of Special Scientific Interest for their diversity of other habitats, including woodland, scrub, hedgerows and dry, permanent pasture.

Before setting off on this walk, do go to the fascinating visitor centre at the Pulborough Brooks Reserve for up-to-date information on local birds. The reserve has a nature trail with viewing hides.

The walk, however, concentrates on exploring Amberley Wild Brooks, an area of water meadows, scrub and marsh. The route follows the Wey-South Path across the reserve but there is an 'open-access' area for all to wander at will. In summer, cattle-grazing and hay-cutting provide a mosaic of different grass heights on the low-lying fields by the river, providing perfect nesting sites for waders, snipe and lapwings. Migrant warblers and, perhaps, nightingales can be spotted in the denser, scrubby areas of

marsh, while nuthatches and woodpeckers are resident in the woodland on the eastern flank of the reserve. The ditches support fresh-water plants such as flowering flag irises, kingcups and flowering rushes, and marsh lovers like bladderwort and arrowhead. An impressive variety of butterflies and dragonflies also thrives here.

The colder months offer the chance to view wintering wildfowl on the flooded meadows. You may see Bewick swans and dabbling ducks including teal, shoveler and pintail on the pools, and wigeon grazing on the short grass, along with snipe, lapwing and, if you're lucky, a few white-fronted geese. Look out for herons hunting eels in the ditches, hovering kestrels, a barn owl silently patrolling the brooks, and wintering fieldfares and redwings as you squelch your way towards Amberley.

Having strolled through the village, with its pretty brick and flint thatched cottages, 11th-century church and impressive castle, you walk beside the Arun before beginning a long and, in places, steep climb to the top of the South Downs. Your reward, if you take the time to pause on the breezy South Downs Way, is a magnificent panorama across rolling downland and, more importantly, north across the broad expanse of the Arun floodplain. It is from this lofty vantage point, especially in winter, that you can really appreciate the impressive natural beauty and ecological importance of the flooded watermeadows. Among the many who have admired the quiet beauty of Amberley Wild Brooks was composer John Ireland, who lived nearby and named a fine piano piece after it.

A Wealth of Wildlife in the Arun Valley

A walk across the wetlands of the Arun Valley and up onto the Down reveals why this area is affectionately known as the Sussex Camargue

1 From the car park turn right across the bridge and over the stile (Wey-South Path) immediately right. Walk along the river bank, pass through a gate and bear right on reaching a track. Bear sharp left beyond Limekiln house and follow the track through farm buildings, ignoring the path right by metal barns. At a fork bear right and descend past Hayles Barn.

2 Turn left along the field edge to a gate in the corner. Turn right following Wey-South Path marker to go through a gate and across a bridge on the left. Turn right beside the ditch and soon cross the wooden bridge into Amberley Wild Brooks. Keep to the path, heading south through marshland, over a stile to open pasture and on to another stile, joining the track to Amberley village. Turn right at the lane then right again at the T-junction towards the church. Drop down to pass Rock Cottage and follow the track beneath the walls of Amberley Castle.

3 Bear right at a gate and follow the path to the railway line. Cross via stiles and remain on the path towards Bury Church. Climb a stile and bear left to cross a bridge over a dyke. Keep ahead, cross a further bridge and water meadow to join the raised path beside the River Arun. Turn left and follow the river bank, bearing left to a gate beyond the footbridge over the river. Now on the South Downs Way (SDW), soon follow the fenced path right to reach the B2139.

6 Turn left and continue to a T-junction at Greatham. Turn left and follow the road for just over ½ mile (800m) back to the car park.

5 Turn left, then right in 50 yds (46m) to join narrow Rackham Street. Walk through Rackham, passing the lane to Amberley and soon taking the path left by houses to a gate. Pass a house and skirt woodland to a junction of paths by a footbridge. Bear right along the edge of woodland, ignore the path on your right and keep left, eventually passing through woods to a metalled lane.

4 Turn right and, shortly, cross the road, soon to reach a metalled lane. Turn left with SDW marker and gradually ascend the South Downs. Keep right at the junction, pass High Down house, then bear left up a steep stony track to a gate. Continue ascending on SDW, then at the crossing of bridleways at the top of Rackham Hill, turn left and descend on a winding path through woods to the B2139.

PULBOROUGH

HARDHAM

½ mile

0

½ km

Hardham
Priory

COLDWALTHAM

N

Greatham Bridge

WIGGONHOLT

A283

A29

1

P

River Arun

GREATHAM   church

*Pulborough
Brooks Nature
Reserve (RSPB)*

Limekiln

Hayles Barn

B2138

WATERSFIELD

2

*Northpark
Wood*

Greatham   *Common*

6

A29

*Amberley
Wild
Brooks*

River Arun

RACKHAM

5   STORRINGTON

BURY
church

3

castle   church

AMBERLEY   B2139

Black
Horse PH

*Rackham
Hill*

4

A29

South Downs Way

farm

Downs   Way

South

HOUGHTON

Bridge   Amberley
Inn   Station

ARUNDEL

B2139

NORTH STOKE

stile, Amberley

Distance: 8½ miles (13.7km)
Total ascent: 600ft (183m)
Paths: mostly good; Amberley Wild Brooks can be very boggy in winter, with sections underwater after heavy rain
Terrain: marsh, open grassland, woodland, open downland
Gradients: few, gradual, but two steep sections up and one down
Refreshments: Black Horse, Amberley; Pulborough Brooks RSPB Reserve
Park: car park at Greatham Bridge ¾ mile (1.2km) east off the A29 at Coldwaltham

Up and Down on the Seven Sisters

The open Downs and chalk cliffs of this famous landmark offer a rich contrast to the woods and tiny hamlets inland

WALK 27

Top right: a lychgate frames Friston's ancient church

Below: pleasing meanders in the Cuckmere River

Bottom: the Seven Sisters sweep eastwards from Exceat

In the summer over 45 different species of tiny wild flowers grow on the downland turf, and there are skylarks, wheatears and stonechats, and the lovely chalkhill blue butterfly.

The walk begins at Exceat (pronounced 'Exseet') at the mouth of the Cuckmere River, the only river in Sussex not to have had a port built at its mouth. Exceat was once a flourishing village and a centre for landing smuggled goods, but by the end of the 14th century, because of the Black Death and raiders from France, only two houses remained. The area is now part of the Seven Sisters Country Park owned by East Sussex County Council.

Across the road from the car park, and up a grassy hill, is the 2000-acre (810 ha) Friston Forest, with beech and pine trees, wide rides and picnic glades. Planted about a hundred years ago to protect the quality of the water supply to Eastbourne and surrounding areas, it is a beautiful place to walk at any time of the year. Steps lead down to the almost hidden flint-built hamlet of Westdean,

where the manorial rights are said to have been held by King Alfred. Today there is a pretty pond, a circular flint dovecote in the garden of the manor house, a tiny church, and a rectory claimed to be the oldest inhabited one in the country.

The porch door of the early Norman church at Friston is dedicated to the composer Frank Bridge, and Benjamin Britten's first

teacher. Inside, medieval graffitti is the result, it says, of visits of a certain class possessed of a knife and itching fingers. The pond opposite may have existed since prehistoric times, and in 1974 it became one of the first in England to be registered as an ancient monument. In the 17th century three large stones were taken from the bottom of it and placed near the church's Tapsell Gate. The gate is a reproduction of one designed in the early 19th century by John Tapsell, a Sussex blacksmith. Coffin bearers could rest their burden here as a procession was forming.

Following the path between church and pond you come to Crowlink, another secluded hamlet, where Edith Nesbit, author of *The Railway Children,* lived. In the last century, when erosion had not bitten so deeply into the chalk cliffs, the area was a famous landing place for smuggled goods. Crowlink gin, stored in the cellars of Crowlink House, had such a fine reputation that it was known in London as 'Genuine Crowlink'.

From here the path widens out to the Downs, almost in the middle of the Seven Sisters as they stretch between Birling Gap and Cuckmere Haven. The grass is smooth and clipped by Downland sheep, and beneath the white vertical chalk cliffs you can hear the roar of the the sea pounding on the shingle. Heading west from Crowlink you join the third of the Sisters, Brass Point, 160 feet (50m) high.

This is a superb, if testing part of the walk – up and down, up and down – with magnificent views of the other Sisters until the final descent over Haven Brow into Cuckmere Haven. A century ago, the cliffs at the estuary here were 200 feet (61m) further out to sea; from there, it was said, King Alfred's ships once sailed. Today, the sheltered waters of the river as it winds inland provide a haven for swans, mallards, herons, geese and kittiwakes.

Up and Down on the Seven Sisters

White cliffs epitomise the South Coast and there is no better place to walk on them than the Seven Sisters

WALK 27

2 Take the road on the right of the pond, signposted Friston and Jevington, and continue on into Friston Forest. Follow the ride between the trees until it curves left. Do not follow this, but take the wide fork straight ahead and continue until this meets a narrow track.

1 From the car park cross the road, and with the visitor centre on your left, walk up the grassy hill, on the South Downs Way, to a flint wall at the top. Climb over the wall, turn slightly to the right and take the Friston Forest Forestry Commision signpost. The path soon leads steeply to steps down to Westdean Pond.

Distance: 7 miles (11.3km)
Total ascent: 250ft (76m)
Path: wide forest rides; good field paths
Terrain: forest, fields, downland
Gradients: some steep sections on Seven Sisters
Refreshments: Seven Sisters Restaurant and Tea Rooms, Exceat
Park: car park at Exceat, on A259 opposite Seven Sisters Country Park Visitor Centre

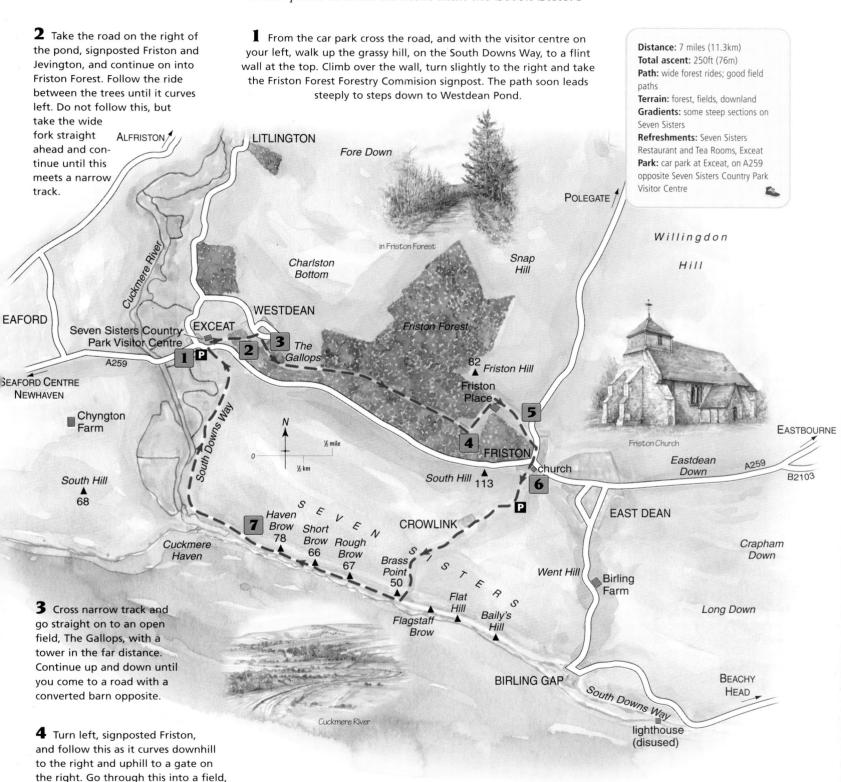

3 Cross narrow track and go straight on to an open field, The Gallops, with a tower in the far distance. Continue up and down until you come to a road with a converted barn opposite.

4 Turn left, signposted Friston, and follow this as it curves downhill to the right and uphill to a gate on the right. Go through this into a field, with an electric fence on your right, and walk to the gate at the far end.

5 Walk diagonally across the next field. Climb over the stile at the end, up some steps onto a minor road which leads to the A259 at Friston church and pond. Cross the road.

6 Follow the no-through road next to the church, past the National Trust car park, and down the tarmac path to the hamlet of Crowlink. Walk through a gate to a grassy path and follow this until the Downs open up. Bear right up the hillside to tackle Brass Point l60ft (50m), Rough Brow 216ft (67m), Short Brow, 2l4ft (66m), and the last Sister before Cuckmere Haven, Haven Brow (also, the highest at 253ft/78m).

7 At a signpost follow the South Downs Way down to Cuckmere Haven, with a wire fence on your left. Turn right along a concrete path which leads back alongside the river to Exceat car park.

Lewes – Birthplace of the English Parliament

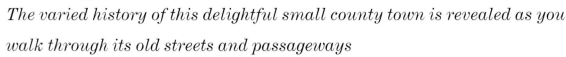

The varied history of this delightful small county town is revealed as you walk through its old streets and passageways

Top right: detailed tile-hanging epitomises Lewes's charm

Right: the 15th-century bookshop on the High Street

Below: the Barbican guards the medieval core of the town

The best way to see Lewes for the first time is to climb to the top of the 11th-century castle built by William de Warenne in 1068, look down, and there it all is: a jumble of red roofs and narrow streets, medieval spires and turrets, small houses and neat gardens. Through the water meadows around it, the River Ouse meanders to Newhaven seven miles away, and beyond sprawl the South Downs with Offham Hill to the west. It was here in 1264 that Simon de Montfort and his barons defeated Henry III in a battle which led to the first English parliament meeting at Westminster.

Built in a gap in the South Downs, Lewes (the name comes from the old English 'hlaew', meaning hill) has been strategically important since Saxon times and was known for its shipbuilding until the river silted up and became un-navigable. Today, Lewes is a small town of sudden, round-the-corner surprises and twisting medieval passages (twittens) that wind between chunks of the old

Town Wall. Walking along the main street that stretches spine-like through the centre, you are following the line of an ancient causeway and there's a marvellous mixture of buildings along it: beamed Tudor, elegant Georgian, bow-fronted windows, gabled roofs and pale colour-washed walls.

South of the town are the ruins of an 11th century priory that was bigger than Chichester Cathedral until destroyed by Henry VIII. Medieval knights jousted on what is now a 300-year-old bowling green, and George IV, when Prince Regent, is said to have driven his coach-and-four down the steeply cobbled Keere Street. In Pipe Passage (the town sentry's walk in the Middle Ages) clay pipes are still sometimes found.

Lewes is a town of small shops and a particular haven for antiques enthusiasts. There are art and craft galleries to browse in, and beautiful gardens to sit in. A former brewery has been converted into craft workshops, ship-building premises into specialist food shops with a café overlooking the river. The town has over 20 pubs, a brewery, and many restaurants and cafes to choose from. At the White Hart, a 16th-century coaching inn, Thomas Paine led political discussions before going off to fight in the American War of Independence, and William Cobbett, visiting Lewes on his 'Rural Rides', harangued the farmers. Shelleys Hotel can trace its history back to 1526 and was once owned by the poet's aunts.

Anne of Cleves never lived in the 16th century timber-framed house that bears her name – it was part of her divorce settlement from Henry VIII, and is now a museum with a collection of iron and stone work, medieval furniture and relics from Lewes' sometimes turbulent past. Barbican House, home to the Sussex Archaeological Society, has a museum, bookshop, and a mini-theatre with a model of Lewes, where you can watch a 20-minute *son et lumiere* of the town's history from the 10th to the 19th century.

The biggest night of the year in Lewes is November 5, when huge crowds come to see the largest Bonfire Night festivities in the country. With torchlit processions and spectacular costumes, bands and firework displays, the celebrations continue into the night.

Lewes – Birthplace of the English Parliament

Walking through the ancient streets of this Sussex county town

Distance: 7 miles (11.3km)
Total ascent: 100ft (30m)
Paths: good, mostly paved; some muddy sections
Terrain: town streets and riverside
Gradients: moderate
Refreshments: wide choice
Park: car park at railway station

1 With your back to Lewes railway station, turn left. Turn first left into Mountfield Road and almost immediately right into narrow path. Continue to end of path and turn right alongside playing fields. Bear right by brick lock-up workshops through to priory ruins. Follow grass path with ruins on right to tennis club on left.

2 Leave priory grounds, turn right at Priory Cottage on corner into Cockshut Road and follow this under low-arched bridge to Southover High Street. Turn left. Anne of Cleves House is a little way along on right. Retrace steps back along Southover High Street with Southover parish church on right, to King's Head and turn left.

3 At corner of Eastport Lane (right) is entrance to Southover Grange gardens. Explore gardens but return to this point. On leaving gardens, turn right. Walk past 16th-century Southover Grange, continue up steep, cobbled Keere Street to 15th-century bookshop at top. Turn right into High Street. Follow High Street to Castlegate on left and walk to castle.

4 Turn left up through 14th-century Barbican arch, continue past 300-year-old bowling green to Battle of Lewes memorial plaque on left under trees. Go down steps (on right, if facing plaque), down Castle Banks, and cross road into Abinger Place. Continue to end. Fork left at church (St John sub Castro), down to The Pells, an L-shaped canal.

5 Continue along path (canal on left) to white, railed bridge. Turn left just before bridge, and walk along river path. Ignore first rail bridge and at third stile, just past a small concrete building, turn left. Cross another stile, walk under railway bridge into meadow, with stream on left.

6 At end of field, cross stile next to five-bar gate, turn left along woodland path. At converted barn (on right) keep left, continue through council estate, past school and after bollards, fork left to narrow path. Follow it over railway bridge to The Pells. Return to Abinger Place and go left after church into Lancaster Street and right up Sun Street.

7 At top, turn left. Cross road almost immediately into Fisher Street. Continue to end and turn left into High Street. Walk past war memorial, down to pedestrian precinct. Continue over river into Cliffe High Street.

8 At T-junction, retrace steps back to end of precinct, turn left into Friars Walk which becomes Lansdown Place. Turn left at the crossroads into Station Road and back to station.

Keere Street

Lewes Castle

Anne of Cleves House

The South Downs and the Bloomsbury Set

WALK
29

In the early 20th century a group of artists and intellectuals made their home in this lovely rural setting

Views of the sea, wide fields and small villages are all within walking distance of Charleston Farmhouse, the Sussex home for many years of Bloomsbury Group artists Vanessa Bell and Duncan Grant, and Vanessa's husband, the art critic Clive Bell. The house was found for Vanessa in 1916 by her sister, Virginia Woolf, who lived nearby, and it soon became a centre for writers, poets, musicians and artists – Lytton Strachey, E M Forster, T S Eliot, Bertrand Russell and Benjamin Britten among them. After Duncan Grant's death in l978 the house was restored and is now open on certain days to the public who come from all over the world to see it, fascinated by the Bloomsbury Group for their artistic work and free life-styles. The house provides a portrait of an era in British decorative art, for Vanessa Bell and Duncan Grant covered the walls and furniture with their paintings. In the dining room the table around which the Woolfs, Lytton Strachey and many others sat and talked, was decorated by Vanessa, the cane chairs were made by Roger Fry, and the curtains designed by Duncan Grant.

The Bloomsbury Group's work can also be seen in the 12th century church in the nearby village of Berwick. In 1942, during World War II, many church windows had been destroyed by bombs and the Bishop of Chichester felt artists should be allowed to paint on church walls rather than design windows. The idea was a controversial one in Berwick – not all locals welcomed the idea – but a compromise was reached and the paintings put on to panels enabling the artists (Vanessa and Quentin Bell, Duncan Grant, Angelica Garnett) to work in their own homes. The barn in the nativity scene is at Tilton (the

Above: Berwick's church nestles in the Downs

Right: Duncan Grant's portrait of Vanessa Bell

Below: the tithe barn at Alciston

nearby summer home of economist Maynard Keynes and his ballerina wife Lydia Lupokova), the models for the soldier, sailor and airman over the chancel arch were local people, and the two disciples in the altarpiece were Australian Air Force men, quartered in Sussex during the war.

The walk begins at Berwick and soon, as the chalky Downland paths wind upwards, there are magnificent views of the sea and the wide unspoilt valley of the Weald, dotted with farmhouses. In the distance, Arlington Reservoir, an 150 acre (60ha) nature reserve and a haven for wildfowl, sparkles blue on a summer's day. Ahead is the 718ft (220m) high Firle Beacon, with its neolithic and Bronze Age barrow, and Firle Place (nearby but not on the route) home of the Gage family since the l5th century. The first English greengage is said to have been grown here.

The view coming down the side of Firle Beacon along a well-marked grassy path is breathtaking, with curving fields and small copses, the sun, on a summer afternoon, casting long shadows over the hillside. The walk then descends to Alciston, once known as the Forgotten Village after its population fled at the time of the Black Death. This interesting hamlet has a 13th-century church, a farmhouse once lived in by monks, a duck pond, a tithe barn 170ft (52m) long, said to the longest in England, and a pretty main street with thatched and timbered cottages.

From Alciston church the route leads across the fields back to Berwick in a lovely spire-to-spire walk, a striking contrast in landscape between London's Bloomsbury area from which the group took its name, and the Bloomsbury they created in the Sussex countryside.

The South Downs and the Bloomsbury Set

A fine downland walk introduces the landscape which inspired a Bohemian generation

1 From the main street walk past the Cricketers Arms to the end of the village and take the walled path signposted to the church. Continue past the church to a field where you turn right. Walk past a silage pit and at a T-junction turn left onto a farm track.

2 With a barn on your right, turn left into a tree-lined path. Continue up the hill, past a house, to meet a pebbled track. At crossroads, turn right towards Firle Beacon, about 4 miles (6.4km) away. At the end of this path, take the far left track with wonderful views over to Alfriston and the Cuckmere Valley, up to a ridge on the South Downs Way.

7 Continue past barn on right and brick and hung-tile cottages on left, until fork in the road. Turn left and take road back to Berwick's main street.

6 Climb stile and go straight on along the edge of a field (signposted for Berwick). Go through a break in the hedge on the right and turn left into next field. Continue along the edge of it, turning left at the end and walking alongside a hedge, then turn right, following path between two fields which leads to a farm track. Bear left.

5 Cross this road and follow the path between two houses. Take the first track on left down to Alciston. At the church turn right up public footpath to the porch door. Climb over stile on left and walk alongside flint wall on right to another stile.

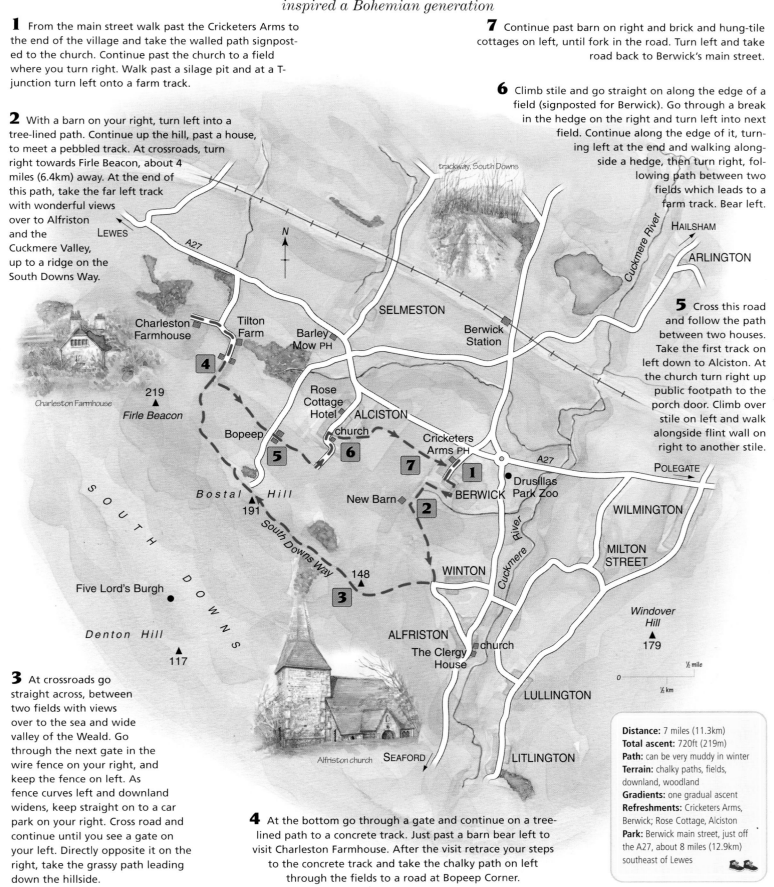

trackway, South Downs

Charleston Farmhouse

LEWES

A27

N

SELMESTON

Berwick Station

Cuckmere River

HAILSHAM

ARLINGTON

Charleston Farmhouse

Tilton Farm

Barley Mow PH

219 ▲ *Firle Beacon*

Rose Cottage Hotel

ALCISTON

Bopeep

5

church

6

7

Cricketers Arms PH

1

POLEGATE

A27

Bostal Hill
191 ▲

New Barn

2

BERWICK

Drusillas Park Zoo

Cuckmere River

WILMINGTON

MILTON STREET

Five Lord's Burgh ●

South Downs Way

148 ▲

WINTON

Windover Hill
179 ▲

SOUTH DOWNS

3

Denton Hill
117 ▲

ALFRISTON

The Clergy House

church

LULLINGTON

½ mile

0

½ km

SEAFORD

Alfriston church

LITLINGTON

3 At crossroads go straight across, between two fields with views over to the sea and wide valley of the Weald. Go through the next gate in the wire fence on your right, and keep the fence on left. As fence curves left and downland widens, keep straight on to a car park on your right. Cross road and continue until you see a gate on your left. Directly opposite it on the right, take the grassy path leading down the hillside.

4 At the bottom go through a gate and continue on a tree-lined path to a concrete track. Just past a barn bear left to visit Charleston Farmhouse. After the visit retrace your steps to the concrete track and take the chalky path on left through the fields to a road at Bopeep Corner.

Distance: 7 miles (11.3km)
Total ascent: 720ft (219m)
Path: can be very muddy in winter
Terrain: chalky paths, fields, downland, woodland
Gradients: one gradual ascent
Refreshments: Cricketers Arms, Berwick; Rose Cottage, Alciston
Park: Berwick main street, just off the A27, about 8 miles (12.9km) southeast of Lewes

The New Forest –
a Royal Hunting Ground

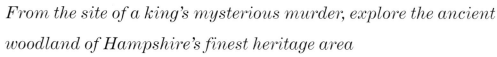

From the site of a king's mysterious murder, explore the ancient woodland of Hampshire's finest heritage area

WALK

30

Top right: the Rufus Stone marks the site of King William's death

Below: ancient beeches in the New Forest

Bottom: there are many attractive open spaces in the Forest

The great thing about walking in the New Forest is that every time you go there it seems to offer something new and surprising. Beneath the surface, away from the roads and villages, the campsites and the car parks, there are 145 square miles (375sq km) of ancient, unspoilt woodlands, peaceful glades and wide-open heather expanses to savour and enjoy. Stretching for 20 miles (32km)from the south coast to the Wiltshire border, and the largest remaining medieval forest in Western Europe, this enchanting corner of the country provides a rare, much-needed haven of tranquillity in the crowded, densely populated southern half of Britain.

William the Conqueror established the New Forest as his deer park and royal hunting preserve more than 900 years ago. Contrary to the popular belief that he laid the entire region to waste, William endorsed its status by ordering more afforestation, extending its boundaries and introducing a strict code of law. The New Forest is a natural habitat for many animals. Apart from the legendary ponies, there are donkeys and wild deer, grazing cattle and foxes.

The New Forest is still administered by the Verderers who sit in open court every two months in the Verderers Hall in Lyndhurst, the Forest capital. Their duties are largely political and judicial – concerning rights of common, conservation issues and the implementation of local bylaws. Lyndhurst is also home to the New Forest Museum and Visitor Centre where you can learn all about the region – its culture, history and heritage, as well as its role in the modern world as a living, working community.

The walk starts at Rufus Stone, one of the New Forest's most famous attractions. The memorial stone, erected in 1841, marks the spot where William Rufus, successor to William the Conqueror, was accidentally killed by an arrow shot by the nobleman Sir Walter Tyrrell while out hunting in Canterton Glen in the summer of 1100. Sir Walter had supposedly meant to kill a stag, but his arrow glanced off and struck Rufus, the most hated of kings. According to some sources, the shooting was not an accident, though nothing has ever been proved.

From this historic landmark the walk heads through dense woodland where it is possible to conjure up images of how this unique, magical place might have looked in William's day. Parts of the New Forest consist of enclosures dating back to the 15th century and they still play an important role in timber production. Elsewhere the landscape is characterised by ancient and ornamental woodland, mostly beech and old oak. Beyond Brook you skirt Bignell Wood, where Sir Arthur Conan Doyle, creator of Sherlock Holmes, lived in his latter years. He is buried at nearby Minstead.

Back at the memorial stone you can pause to savour the delights of this vast, wooded landscape. Silent, undisturbed and undiscovered, this is where the real New Forest weaves its own distinctive brand of magic.

The New Forest – a Royal Hunting Ground

In Hampshire's special Heritage Area a king once died in mysterious circumstances

1 With Rufus Stone opposite, turn right and walk along to Sir Walter Tyrrell Inn. Veer left at 'Except for Access' sign and cross turf, keeping to right-hand half of open grassy area. Cross several little streams and make for obvious gap in trees. Negotiate shallow ford here and follow indistinct path ahead. Cross winter ford and simple water meadow bridge spanning gully. Keep left when path forks just beyond bridge and follow it through trees to join concrete track leading to Long Beech Caravan Park. Pass several barriers to reach water tower.

2 Pass concrete track immediately beyond tower and continue for about 50 yds (46m) to barrier. Veer right here and make for some wooden posts. Follow path between bracken and gorse bushes and head for corner of King's Garn Gutter Inclosure. Continue on path, keeping inclosure boundary fence on right. Avoid gate in fence and look for Janesmoor Pond up ahead. Make for next corner of inclosure and turn right.

3 Follow path down between inclosures descending gently into glade. Head for track, avoid gates on left and right and go straight on over track to wood. Cross over stream (King's Garn Gutter) and follow path through trees to emerge on edge of golf course. Keep to track beside greens and fairways and when it peters out, continue over grass, keeping tight to woodland on left. Walk behind two greens before heading out across open ground, dotted with gorse bushes and fringed by woodland on left, towards car park on far side.

4 Cricket ground is to right between trees. Cross grass, keeping building on right, and continue along wooded edge of golf course. Curve left to another green on right, and join clear track running up slope to left. Walk across car park and continue to road. Turn left and head for Brook. Follow road through village, pass The Bell Inn and The Green Dragon and avoid footpath on left just beyond.

5 Pass Canterton Lodge and veer right into Canterton Lane. Follow road over several streams and note large white house up on left bank. Continue ahead when lane becomes stony underfoot and pass bridleway on right. On left now is Bignell Wood. Follow track as it swings right to Greys Farm.

6 Pass between wooden posts and veer left off track, following path to gap in trees ahead. On reaching clearing immediately beyond them, turn right at junction by manhole cover and follow path across stream, up gentle slope and back to car park.

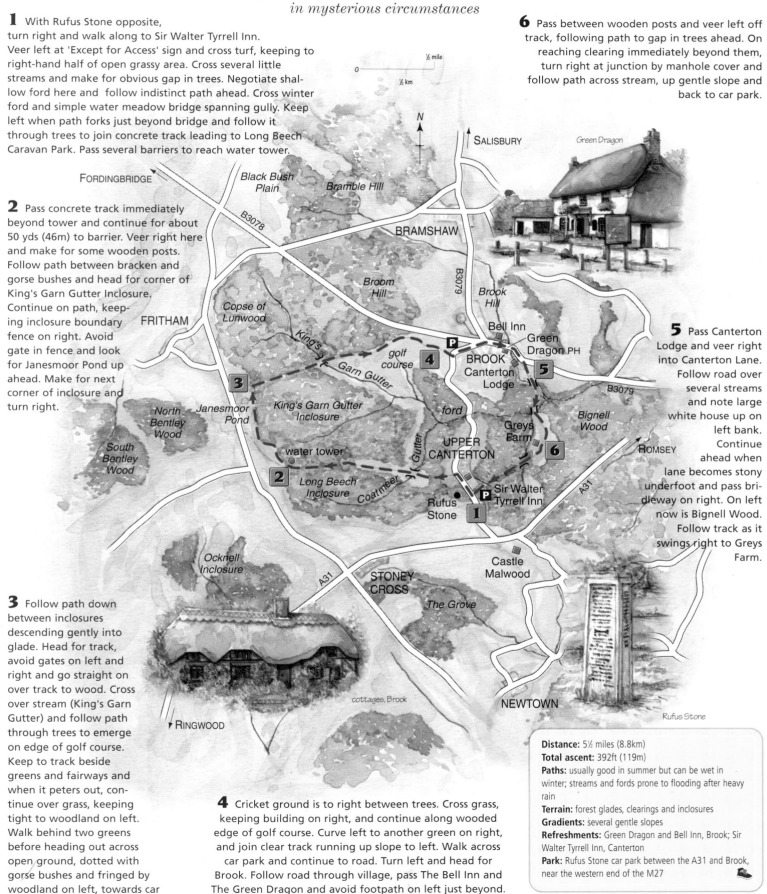

Distance: 5½ miles (8.8km)
Total ascent: 392ft (119m)
Paths: usually good in summer but can be wet in winter; streams and fords prone to flooding after heavy rain
Terrain: forest glades, clearings and inclosures
Gradients: several gentle slopes
Refreshments: Green Dragon and Bell Inn, Brook; Sir Walter Tyrrell Inn, Canterton
Park: Rufus Stone car park between the A31 and Brook, near the western end of the M27

Coast to Coast on the Isle of Wight

The subtle change in wildlife between tidal salt-water and fresh-water habitats is explored in this marshy ramble

WALK
31

Above: Yarmouth's tide mill made good use of the Solent's complex tidal flows

Top right: swans prefer the fresh water end of the marshes

Below: the Yar Valley marshes are a haven for wildlife

With its stone quays, old houses, castle remains and boat-filled harbour, Yarmouth is the picturesque starting point for this varied and fascinating nature walk. With the opening of the Newport, Yarmouth and Freshwater Railway in 1889, Yarmouth became a popular destination for travellers arriving by train from London via the Lymington ferry. The railway fell under the Beeching axe in 1953, and the former line was converted into a splendid, level footpath and cycleway crossing the western 'neck' of the island and connecting with the Freshwater Way and Tennyson Trail. Your route heads south from Yarmouth past the old tide mill, built in 1793 to harness the tidal flow of the Yar Estuary. Joining the route of the old railway line, you pass close to the tidal salt marshes south of Yarmouth. Keep your binoculars at the ready if you're here at low tide, when a vast expanse of saltings and mudflats is exposed. Most of the common waders will be seen, and you'll delight in the spine-tingling, bubbling trill of the curlew and watch fascinated as it uses its delicate, down-curved beak to probe the mudflats for morsels. The bright red legs of the shy but appropriately-nicknamed 'warden of the marshes' – the redshank – will also be seen, elegantly striding across the mud but taking flight at the slightest disturbance.

If you are doing the walk in winter, huge flocks of black-necked Brent geese, which have returned from their breeding grounds in the high Arctic, will fill the mudflats and neighbouring flood meadows. They feed almost exclusively on the eel grass which grows in the muddy shallows between the high and low water marks. Occasionally the snowy white of a wintering egret is seen here.

In summer, these saltmarshes are rainbow-bright with the pink cushions of thrift, purple sea-lavender and the fleshy-leaved spikes of golden samphire, but as you reach the sluice valve of the Causeway, the vegetation changes to the fresh-water plants of the Afton Marsh Nature Reserve, which is followed by the West Yar Nature Trail. Fed by lime-rich water from the stream issuing from the chalk of Afton Down, this incredibly rich habitat supports a wide variety of aquatic wildlife, with the bright, waxy yellow blooms of the marsh marigold perhaps being the most striking. The electric blue, iridescent flash of the kingfisher – after which the halcyon days of summer were named – is matched by the whirring wings and darting flight of the numerous dragonflies and damselflies that hover above the still wetlands.

The thickets of trees that line the Freshwater Way back to Yarmouth are alive with birdsong in summer, and include the seductive cooing of the cuckoo and the incomparable, melodic song of the inconspicuous nightingale, which can fill the heavy, sultry air if you are lucky enough to be on the trail at dusk.

Coast to Coast on the Isle of Wight

*Connecting tidal and fresh water nature reserves on the
western side of this lovely island*

1 From The Square in Yarmouth head towards the church and walk along St James Street to cross the A3054 into Mill Road. At the sharp left bend, follow the arrowed path ahead (signed Freshwater) towards the old tide mill. Ignore the footpath left, walk beside the mudflats and turn right along the old railway. Remain on this path for 1½ miles (2.4km) to the causeway at Freshwater.

2 Turn left, away from the river, and follow the lane to the B3399. Turn left and cross almost immediately into Manor Road. In a few paces bear left (Freshwater Way) and gently ascend across grassland towards Afton Down. Go straight at a junction beside the golf course, soon to follow the gravel track right to the clubhouse. Go through the gate, pass in front of the building and walk down the access track, keeping left, to the A3055. Turn right, downhill, into Freshwater Bay.

3 Walk past the car park and turn right into Coastguard Lane, opposite Albion Tavern. Keep ahead at the end, along a path skirting the edge of marsh and eventually reaching a road. Turn right, then, just before the river bridge, turn left into Afton Marshes Nature Reserve.

6 Climb the stile to the right of the metal gate, pass through a copse to a stile and bear left, uphill, along the field edge. Enter the field on your left and keep to the path along the right-hand edge to a stile on the edge of woodland. Soon drop down through the wood to a track and turn left, following it to the A3054. Turn right along the pavement, back into Yarmouth.

5 Take the waymarked path (Freshwater Way) between a cottage and the churchyard. Cross a stile and proceed along the farm road. At the farmyard entrance cross the double stile on the left and bear right along the field edge, skirting a barn to a stile. On reaching a track and the main entrance to Kings Manor Farm, cross the stile ahead beside double gates and follow a wide track to a gate and junction of paths.

4 Cross the footbridge, bear right towards Yarmouth and join the nature trail, following the left-hand path beside the stream, through the reserve to the A3055. Turn left and almost immediately cross over to join footpath F61 along the old railway. In ½ mile, (800m) reach The Causeway and turn left, following the lane to Freshwater church and the Red Lion.

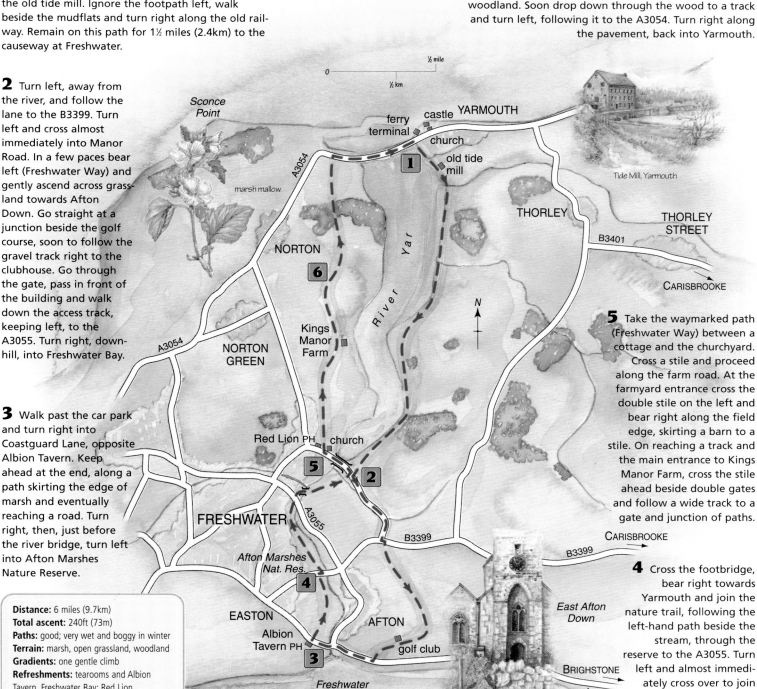

Tide Mill, Yarmouth

All Saints, Freshwater

Distance: 6 miles (9.7km)
Total ascent: 240ft (73m)
Paths: good; very wet and boggy in winter
Terrain: marsh, open grassland, woodland
Gradients: one gentle climb
Refreshments: tearooms and Albion Tavern, Freshwater Bay; Red Lion, Freshwater; various pubs and tearooms, Yarmouth
Park: car park by A3054, near Lymington to Yarmouth ferry terminal, or leave your car at Lymington Pier and take the ferry to Yarmouth

Chobham Common – Last of the Surrey Heaths

Discover a curious oasis of open, broomy heathland which flourishes unexpectedly in the Surrey commuter belt

WALK

32

Top right: a monument marks the place of Queen Victoria's first inspection of troops on the Surrey heaths in 1853

Below: the wild desolation of Chobham Common is a surprise after the cosy little town

There is something curiously indefinable about Chobham Common. In places it has an eerie, hostile feel to it, evoking a strange sense of foreboding. A walk across it, with a little imagination, can transport you back to a time when highwaymen and footpads lurked unseen in the shadows and few people ventured this way in safety. The spirit of Chobham Common and its sense of wilderness remain with you as you explore these tracts of lonely heath, but in places there are sudden and unwelcome reminders of our modern world: the M3, dividing the Common into two distinct halves, and to the north the grim, featureless buildings of an MoD research establishment. Enclosed by high perimeter fences and overlooking miles of exposed, open country, it would not seem out of place in an episode of *The X Files*.

However, Chobham Common has in fact strong links with science fiction classics. In H G Wells's book, *The War of the Worlds*, Martians land near Chobham, Chertsey and Woking, and, constructing mighty killing machines, advance on London, destroying everything in their path. Wells clearly considered this inhospitable landscape a perfect setting for their terrifying invasion.

Moments after you start out along the shallow valley of Albury Bottom, the wide-open spaces and miles of bracken and heather can be seen stretching to the horizon, stimulating a wonderful sense of distance and perspective. Extending to over 1,500 acres (600ha) of open heathland, woodland and wetland, Chobham Common is the largest national nature reserve in the south-east of England as well as being one of the finest remaining examples of

lowland heath. Since the Industrial Revolution most of our heaths have disappeared, leaving the few surviving fragments to act as increasingly precious refuges for rare heathland wildlife. Over 300 species of wild flowers can be seen on Chobham Common, including orchids and rare marsh gentians. Foxes, deer and sand lizards basking on sunny sandy tracks might also be spotted.

But Chobham Common is not just the preserve of rare plants and wildlife. Go there on a fine Sunday morning and the place is a hive of human activity. Walkers and horse riders thread their way across the heathland paths and tracks, and model aircraft enthusiasts concentrate on controlling their treasured machines which gyrate above them. From the southeast corner of the Common, as you head through dense woodland and across farmland to the village of Burrowhill, look for the old pump on the village green. Suitably refreshed at one of the two inns, head back for the Common, the mellow hues of its bracken, gorse and heather staining the landscape as far as the eye can see.

As you pass under the M3 and the roar of traffic fades, a stark monument looms into view. Queen Victoria reviewed 8,129 of her troops on Chobham Common in June 1853, and 400 parishioners erected this simple granite memorial, shaped like a plain Celtic wheel-cross, shortly after her death in 1901. Gently undulating, the final leg of the walk takes you right across Chobham Common. With the M3 ahead, the MoD buildings on your left and far-reaching views of the timeless heath on your right, the walk reaches its conclusion with a very special blend of ancient and modern.

WALK 32

Chobham Common – Last of the Surrey Heaths

The ever present gorse marks this heath apart from the sprawl of Surrey's commuterland

Distance: 7 miles (11.3km)
Total ascent: 245ft (75m)
Paths: mostly good; can become waterlogged after heavy rain
Terrain: heath, common, woodland, fields, several stretches of road
Gradients: gentle
Refreshments: Four Horseshoes and Cricketers Inn, Burrowhill
Park: Longcross car park, just off the B386, western end of Longcross village

7 Follow path across common to MOD perimeter road. Turn right and walk to roundabout. Cross and take exit to Longcross. Follow road over M3, pass Chobham turning and return to car park.

6 Follow track to B386, cross and descend into hollow. Ascend, then turn right at bridleway post and follow path across heath. At next junction, with railway visible ahead, turn right.

5 Follow track to road; cross to path ahead. Ascend between trees and gorse, and when path levels out, turn right on bridleway. Bear left just before car park and follow path descending to tunnel under M3.

1 From back of car park, join bridleway heading south. Take second bridleway right and follow path straight ahead across heath. After nearly 1 mile (1.6km), where bridleway bends right at junction, bear left on waymarked footpath cutting between heather.

4 Cross over at junction of Mincing Lane and Red Lion Road and follow Footpath 95. Fork left and follow path across clear path, past buildings on left and turn left at junction with track. Keep electricity sub-station on right, pass Gorse Cottage on left and join road to B383 at Burrowhill. Turn right, pass Steep Hill and Cricketers Inn, and continue. Bear right immediately beyond The White House and follow path through trees and out across heath. Follow waymarked path to track and turn left.

2 Pass under power lines and skirt heath, keeping woodland on right. After path is lined by silver birches, join track when farm buildings are seen ahead. In a few paces fork left and cross stream, then veer right at next fork, staying close to woodland edge. Bear right at major path junction and cut between silver birches and gorse. Turn left at metalled lane leading to Albury Farm and follow it to junction. Bear left and follow road round sharp right bend. Pass bridleway on left and turn right to join path just before road curves left.

3 Go right at fork and cut along woodland edge to join track on bend. Continue through heart of wood, going straight on through gap in fence when path curves left. Approaching road, turn right over stile. With house on left, keep to left of field to track. Cross it and skirt wood, negotiating three stiles. Follow track towards houses ahead. Turn right at stile and swing left to cross stile and footbridge. Bear right to gate and follow path by stream to stile and trees. Cross into wood and follow path alongside fence. Eventually join tarmac drive straight ahead to road and turn right.

monument, Chobham Common

BROOMHALL

Ship Hill

monument

Chobham Common

WINDLESHAM

CAMBERLEY

½ mile
0
½ km

Longcross Station

VIRGINIA WATER
CHERTSEY

MOD

N

B383

B386

M3

B386

LONGCROSS

ADDLESTONE

Longcross Car Park

Albury Bottom

gorse

Valleywood

The White House

ESS

Cricketers Inn

Gorse Cottage

Four Horseshoes PH

BURROWHILL

B383

Red Lion PH

Albury Farm

Butts Hill

Butts Hill

Gracious Pond Farm

fish pool

Little Manor Farm

CHOBHAM

A319

A319

LIGHTWATER

KNAPHILL

WOKING

A3046

OTTERSHAW
ADDLESTONE

Cricketers Inn

Riverbank Tales from the Thames at Cookham

Taking in some of the finest sections of a new National Trail, this walk will delight fans of Kenneth Grahame's 'The Wind in the Willows'

Top: Ratty and Mole, illustrated by Arthur Rackham for Kenneth Grahame's *Wind in the Willows*

A stone's throw from the glorious hanging woods and elegant manicured lawns of the Cliveden estate, setting for the 1960s Profumo scandal, lies the Thamesside village of Cookham, home of the controversial artist, Stanley Spencer, until his death in 1959. The Spencer Art Gallery, formerly a Nonconformist chapel, in Cookham's main street illustrates his highly individual style. Spencer was a somewhat eccentric figure who was regularly seen pottering about the village, pushing a pram which contained his easel and paints.

A tour of Cookham's streets provides no inkling that the Thames is only a matter of yards away. The stately Thames, historically the most important river in Britain, has been used as a highway from early times. To stroll along its banks is the only way to appreciate its unique beauty and ever-changing character. This walk, which begins by following a section of the Thames Path upstream between Cookham and the dramatic chalk escarpment of Winter Hill, offers a teasing hint of the meandering river in all its glory.

Above: rowing boats on the Thames at Cookham

Officially opened by the Countryside Commission in the summer of 1996, the 180-mile (290km) Thames Path is the only national long-distance trail to follow a river for its entire length. More than 95 per cent of the trail is directly beside the Thames, which begins life as a trickling stream in a Gloucestershire field.

From Cookham the walk heads upstream to Cock Marsh, an expansive area of marshland and grass now in the care of the National Trust. The marsh has been common land since the late 13th century and is still grazed in the traditional manner. Bronze Age settlers made their home here and the site includes several prehistoric burial mounds.

Beyond Cock Marsh the walk climbs to the summit of Winter Hill, with its fine views across the Thames towards Marlow, High Wycombe and the Chilterns. Ample tree cover provides welcome shade in summer on the next stage of the walk as you pass through Quarry Wood, with Marlow's soaring church spire distantly visible.

Bisham Woods, now in the care of the Woodland Trust, were once part of a huge estate owned by nearby Bisham Abbey. Many of the trees – among them species such as beech, holly and sycamore – are 500 years old or more. The woodland once formed part of the Royal Forest of Windsor through which Queen Elizabeth I used to ride, and Quarry Wood, to the north of Bisham Woods, is thought to have provided Kenneth Grahame with the inspiration for the 'Wild Wood' in *The Wind in the Willows*. The author, who lived at nearby Cookham Dean as a child and then later with his wife and family, is known to have spent many happy hours walking among these ancient beech trees.

The final leg of the walk takes you over the high, blustery ground of the Thames Valley, dropping down gently to finish, where it started, on Cookham Moor, where stray animals were once kept. As you descend into the valley, the initial outward leg of the walk, following the Thames Path, can be identified in the distance.

Below: the Thames at Bisham

WALK 33

Riverbank Tales from the Thames at Cookham

This section of the majestic Thames inspired poets, artists and the author of 'The Wind in the Willows'

Distance: 8 miles (12.9km)
Total ascent: 316ft (96m)
Paths: mostly good; can get very wet and muddy
Terrain: riverbank, meadow, escarpment, woodland, fields
Gradients: one short steep section
Refreshments: various in Cookham; The Jolly Farmer at Cookham Dean
Park: Cookham Moor car park, west of Cookham

1 From car park walk across grass towards village. Ignore kissing gate left and follow Cookham High Street to junction with A4094. Turn left towards Wooburn and Bourne End, past Tarry Stone. Turn left through churchyard towards riverbank.

2 At Thames Path turn left, passing through two gates by sailing club. Continue upstream, crossing Marsh Meadow to kissing gate leading to Cock Marsh. Follow path by river, veering left under railway bridge.

3 With line of villas right, follow path back to riverbank. Pass through kissing gate and veer away from river at Ferry Cottage. Turn left at concrete drive and head towards Winter Hill. Follow track across field to pond. Pass through kissing gate to junction and turn right. Head diagonally up to gate and stile, then join road.

4 Turn right past Stonehouse Lane and Gibraltar Lane, following road above river. Shortly, veer half-right to path running parallel with road. Walk past several parking areas to path into woods. Turn right after several steps and follow drive to 'Rivendell' entrance. Bear immediately right of gate and follow woodland path. Veer right at fork and follow path to road. Cross and head up steep bank to seat on right. Join path just beyond seat and follow for about 100yards (91m) through Quarry Wood. Turn sharp left then immediate right fork, making for woodland corner by road.

5 Bear right into Grubwood Lane and pass houses. Turn left immediately beyond and follow path parallel to wide drive. Make for bottom of slope, then head up on path beside fence towards farm buildings. In field corner join woodland path to left. At green at Cookham Dean follow lane to war memorial. Turn right into Church Road.

6 Bear left immediately beyond church and just before Jolly Farmer Inn, then left at next footpath sign. Follow road to Huntsman's Cottage and York House as it becomes a green lane, to gate, and continue to road. Bear left to road junction. Cross to Bradcutts Lane and follow for about ½ mile (800m). Turn right at Hillgrove Farm and follow path to right, over concrete stile. Fork left to lane and cross over to footpath opposite.

7 Keep left of September Grange and follow path to field corner. Turn right past golf course sign, keeping fence and hedge on right. Cross fairways, aim left of corrugated barns and make for railway bridge ahead. Cross it and turn right to follow grassy path by fence and hedge. Join track and follow it to road. Turn left by drive to 'Fiveways' and follow path to kissing gate. Bear right and return to Cookham Moor car park, crossing footbridge over Fleet Ditch just before it.

River Thames

Bourne End railway bridge

Tarry Stone

Devil's Punch Bowl

A varied and exhilarating ramble explores some of the last remaining areas of a once large expanse of Surrey wilderness

WALK 34

Top right: bracket fungus clings to fallen wood

'The most villainous spot God ever made' is how the 19th-century diarist, William Cobbett, described Hindhead Common in 1822. He may have been referring to the bleak and desolate scenery, to its reputation as a haunt of highwaymen, or to the murder of an unknown sailor and subsequent hanging of the assailants on Gibbet Hill. Only later, with the Industrial Revolution and rail links threatening the open countryside, did this landscape become acknowledged as a precious and diminishing amenity.

This carefully managed area includes Gibbet Hill whose summit affords fine views, south across the Weald to the South Downs, and north towards the Hog's Back. Even more spectacular is the Devil's Punch Bowl, a huge natural amphitheatre sculpted by the spring water over thousands of years.

Today, despite recreational pressures and the busy A3 cutting through the Common, the open heathland and eerie, often mist-shrouded woodland still retain a wild grandeur that is hard to find elsewhere in the Southeast. Its myriad paths and tracks are best explored on weekdays and in winter.

Take time to stroll around the open common land close to the rim of the Punch Bowl and savour the dramatic views before setting out on this ramble. The early part of the route affords cameo views through the trees into the Devil's Punch Bowl and beyond, then plunges down the contours into Highcomb Bottom to a cluster of isolated houses, once home to 'broom squires', squatters who settled in the Punch Bowl and eked out a living making and selling brooms.

Below: the natural hollow of the Devil's Punch Bowl

Beyond the youth hostel you strike out on a desolate track across open heathland reminiscent of north Wales or the flanks of Dartmoor. Keep a keen eye open for a stonechat, a hobby or, in summer, a Dartford warbler, some of the 60 or so species of birds that breed on the Common's 1,400 acres (570ha).

Farmland paths, valley tracks and splendid views to the Hog's Back characterise the next stage of the walk. Despite leaving the open bracken and heather-covered hillsides and crossing the A3, the route continues to preserve that feeling of being alone in the Surrey countryside, passing only a few isolated timbered farmsteads as you head for the thickly wooded slopes of Gibbet Hill.

After a strength-sapping climb through Boundless Copse, a managed Forestry Commision area, you enter the ancient oak and beech woodland that shrouds Gibbet Hill. Pause at the summit, marvel at the views from 894 feet (272m), and seek out the inscribed stone commemorating the murder and hangings that took place here in 1786. With the incident still conjuring up wild images of a sinister past, you head ever deeper into the mysterious woodland that blankets these sandstone hills. In winter, when the wind and mist swirl through the tree canopy and the trails are blissfully quiet, let your imagination run wild – for you really could be in an uninhabited wilderness, not on the edge of Haslemere in suburban Surrey.

The Devil's Punch Bowl

A little bit of wilderness hides in the Surrey Hills

WALK 34

1 From car park follow track to left of café, heading away from A3. Keep left at path junction, walking to crossing of tracks by mast. Turn right towards height barrier and immediately bear right down steep path to Highcombe Bottom. Keep left on merging with track. Leave woodland and take next path right, downhill to cross stream.

2 Pass youth hostel and turn left beyond gate. Pass Gnome Cottage and go straight ahead at bend to gate (by cattle grid). Cross open heath, ignoring tracks left and right before taking left path at fork (animal pens in field on right). Go through gate (by cattle grid) and continue to path junction by lane.

3 Turn right up steps, pass through Upper Highfield Farm, and pass tennis court to stile by gate. Follow concrete track down to silage storage area. Cross stile on left and ascend to cross A3. Bear left down to stile and descend through trees to another stile and driveway by house. Keep left, then, at crossing of tracks, turn right, around lake, to Blackhanger Farm driveway.

4 Bear right, cross stream and stile on left. Skirt house and garden to stile in field corner and pass through copse. Follow telegraph poles across next field to gate. At waymarker post bear right and follow track to Begley Farm. Go through gate on left and keep to right-hand edge of field to lane.

8 Walk down lane (eventually metalled) and take path (Greensand Way) right, just before post box. Disregard all paths left and right, cross edge of open heath and descend, going straight ahead at crossing of paths then forking left, steeply uphill. Keep right at house, keeping to track back to A3 and start.

7 Take second path right (ahead) for ⅔ mile (1km). Descend to crossing of trails and turn right. Cross next main path and descend steeply into wooded valley. Keep ahead at crossing of bridleways, cross stream then, just past gate on left, take unmarked path left. Ascend steeply to wide trackway by house and turn left.

6 Walk south from trig point, pass car park and take path ahead. Shortly, at crossing of paths, turn left and descend to staggered crossing of paths. Take second path right and gently climb, forking left at marker post to gate. Go round gate and shortly reach junction of five ways.

5 Turn left, then just before Boundless Farm (300m), take footpath right into Boundless Copse. Keep ahead, soon forking left, steeply uphill through coniferous trees and clearing. Continue ahead as paths cross and ascend steeply to waymarker post (Greensand Way) at top and summit of Gibbet Hill.

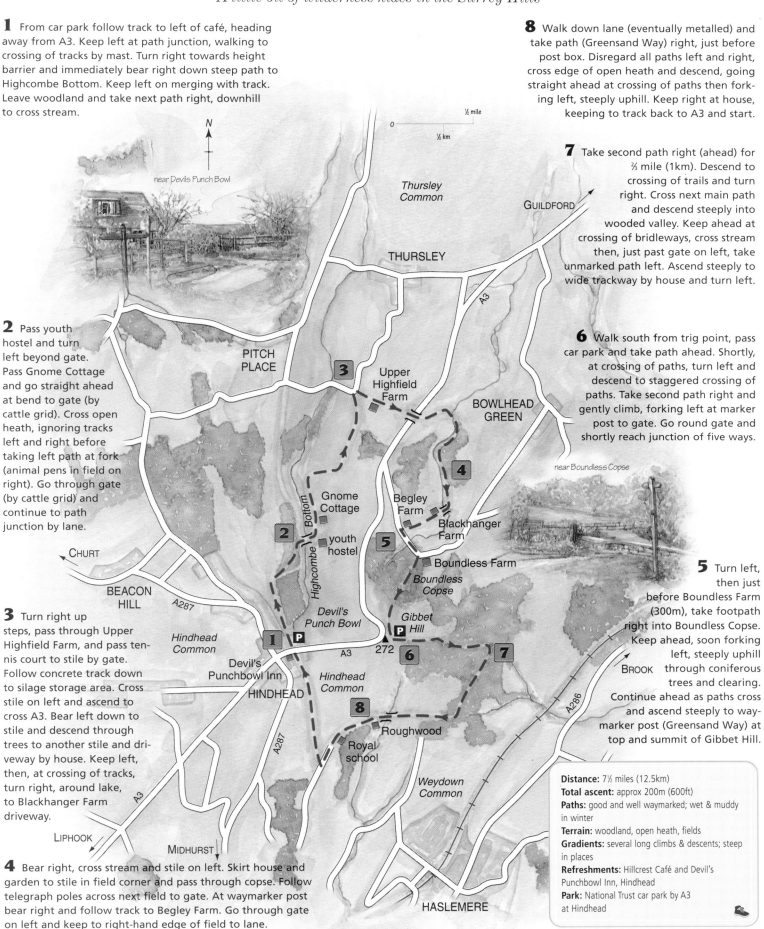

near Devils Punch Bowl

near Boundless Copse

Distance: 7½ miles (12.5km)
Total ascent: approx 200m (600ft)
Paths: good and well waymarked; wet & muddy in winter
Terrain: woodland, open heath, fields
Gradients: several long climbs & descents; steep in places
Refreshments: Hillcrest Café and Devil's Punchbowl Inn, Hindhead
Park: National Trust car park by A3 at Hindhead

Historic Routes across the Chilterns

A ridge and woodland walk reveals centuries of travelling history in the landcsape around Ivinghoe Beacon

WALK
35

Right: Aldbury village and its pond

For over 2,000 years people have crossed the Chilterns through the Tring Gap. On parts of this walk, the many centuries of transport are brought gloriously together. From the grassy knoll of Pitstone Hill the Chiltern escarpment curves away to the south and west, carrying the ancient Icknield Way towards its Thames crossing at Goring. Nestling in cuttings in the vale below, the Grand Union Canal and the London-to-Glasgow railway wend their way northwards, the silence occasionally interrupted by the rattle of a high-speed train. Immediately below you, the blue lagoons of the old Pitstone chalk quarries seem out of place. Cement from here went to many of southeast England's great transport schemes, including Waterloo Bridge and that other source of hidden background noise, the A41 Tring bypass.

But, amid all this history, it is the track beneath your feet which captures the imagination. This section of the Ridgeway National Trail follows the Upper Icknield Way, a trade route in continuous use from prehistoric times to the early 19th century. The lower route can be seen hugging the spring line at the foot of the hills, but in winter travellers were forced on to the higher ground, above the swamps and dense forest. Up here Palaeolithic civilisations buried their dead (there are dozens of tumuli on the ridge between Aldbury Nowers and Ivinghoe Beacon), and Iron Age Celtic tribes built boundary ditches between their territories (the distinctive Grims Ditch you cross as Pitstone Hill opens out).

Reluctantly leaving the splendid viewpoint of Ivinghoe Beacon, you follow the Icknield Way path as it swings east, still clinging to the hillside, towards the vast chalk lion of Whipsnade wildlife park. As woodland closes in around you, the silence must be very much as a trader would have

Above: Pitstone windmill was one of the last working mills in the southeast

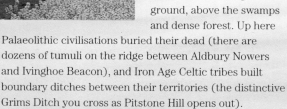

Below: a prominent landmark, the Ivinghoe Hills mark the end of The Ridgeway National Trail

experienced it, using this ancient long-distance artery between prehistoric commercial centres.

The route predates even the Roman Ermine Street, which is visible to your left as you emerge from the trees on Aldbury Nowers. This was the first route to permanently use the Tring Gap to travel through the Chilterns. Much later, in the late 18th century, the same road became a turnpike, so the northern cattle drovers who used this route to London went back to the ancient Icknield Way to avoid paying the tolls. The canal came in 1797, but its 1½-mile (2.4km) cutting is barely distinguishable amongst the fields. More noticeable are the reservoirs to the west, designed to replace the 200,000 gallons (910,000 litres) of water lost every time a boat passes through this section.

Up in the woods of the Ashridge Estate, it comes as something of a surprise to discover the 100-foot (30m) high Bridgewater Monument, built in 1832 to honour the third Duke of Bridgewater and his contribution to canal building. Its Doric splendour was almost immediately tarnished, however, by the arrival of George Stephenson's railway in 1834. This engineering triumph – its cutting visible and its trains audible across the fields beyond Pitstone village – still carries the west coast main line.

Back in Aldbury, with its pond and stocks and half-timbered cottages, you feel very removed from the centuries of transport history which surround you, but in the distance you may still hear a train rattling through the Tring Gap.

Historic Routes across the Chilterns

Along the Ridgeway to Ivinghoe Beacon, then back through beechwoods, this is a trail steeped in history

WALK 35

1 From centre of village, facing Greyhound Inn, go right, up road for 300yds (273m), past footpath and sports ground on left, to bridleway on left, by Greenings Farm. Follow this gently uphill for 500yds (455m), ignoring path off left, to footpath on right. Cross stile and take this as it dog-legs up through golf course to sign visible in front of woodland at top of course.

2 Go through fence gap, cross over track and enter woodland through kissing gate. Go through woodland, turning right to join Ridgeway National Trail, continuing down to edge of wood to view Nature Reserve interpretative panel. Retrace steps 30yds (27m) and follow Ridgeway National Trail up to left. Follow this through woods, emerging at gate in open grassland above remains of Pitstone Quarry on left.

3 Follow Ridgeway path onto ridge then straight ahead across road, aiming for right side of Steps Hill ahead. As bowl of Incombe Hole cuts in from left, traverse its edge to Steps Hill and follow track to gap in fence in far corner, ignoring gate and stile on right. Follow national trail signs through woods, then descending to road. Take care here as this was once an army range and signs warn against touching unidentified objects.

4 Cross road and take left hand track along ridge to National Trust panel on Ivinghoe Beacon. Retrace steps to road and turn left, down hill, following Icknield Way signs, over stile then along edge of field and hill. Cross stile at waymarker and enter woods after 500yds (455m). Continue through woods following Icknield Way signs.

5 After a steep ascent, turn right into farmyard. Go towards house then turn right in front of it. Follow straight farm road to minor road and turn right. After 50yds (46m) turn left, across road, to follow path into woods. Follow this path as it swings right, then left, crossing estate boundary path.

6 Cross two stiles out of woods to emerge in fields. Keep to right edge until over brow, then head straight down to metalled lane by entrance to Duncombe Farm. Cross lane and bear left through two fields to join track. Follow this left up into woods.

7 As path levels out, take right fork above cottage, then bear left into clearing by Bridgewater monument. Facing front of monument turn left and leave clearing on descending track to right of cottages. Descend quite steeply down sunken lane, staying right at any junctions, to emerge in village. Turn right on metalled road to return to village centre.

Distance: 7½ miles (12km)
Total ascent: 1,100ft (335m)
Paths: good; can be muddy
Terrain: farmland, downland and woodland
Gradients: moderate, two steeper sections
Refreshments: two pubs and a shop in Aldbury
Park: in the centre of Aldbury, by the pond

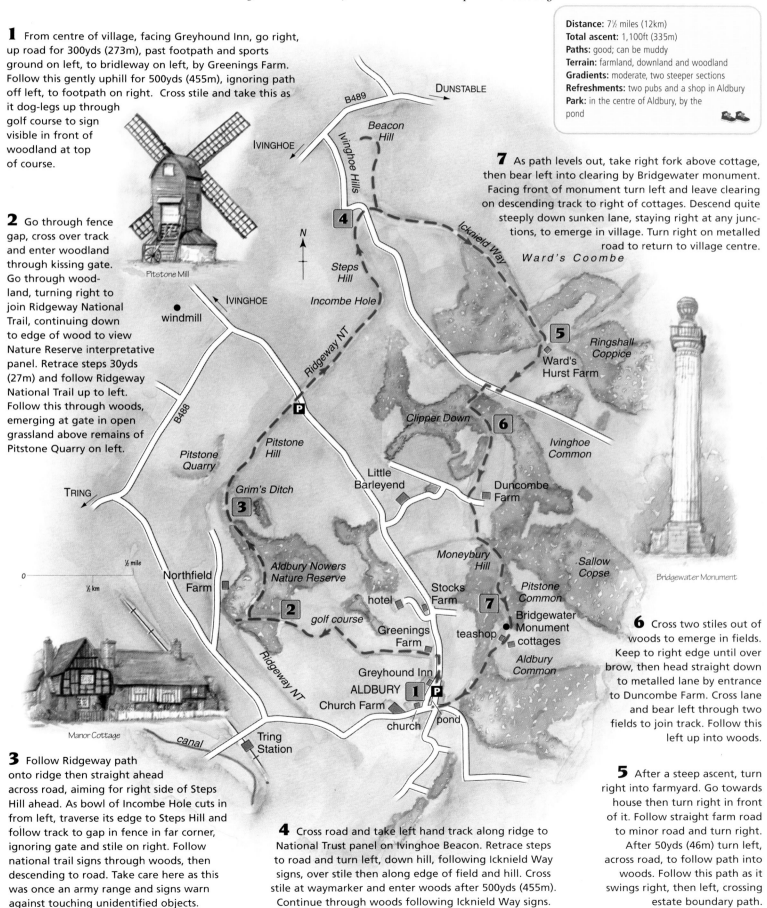

Pitstone Mill

Manor Cottage

Bridgewater Monument

In London's East End

Discover the intriguing landmarks of a thousand years of popular history in the streets between Docklands and the City

Top right: the identity of Victorian murderer 'Jack the Ripper' is still unknown

Founded by William the Conqueror, the Tower of London must be the most enduring symbol of this great city. You catch glimpses of it nestling by the river, dwarfed by Tower Bridge, as you make your way to Aldgate and the heart of the East End. All that remains of Aldgate is the name, but it is the site of one of six original gates into the Roman city of *Londinium*. The rooms above it were once leased to Geoffrey Chaucer. Emerging from an uninspiring subway, you find yourself in the bustle of Middlesex Street, better known as Petticoat Lane, the famous Sunday clothes market where poor East Enders once came to buy second-hand clothes.

Walking down Brushfield Street you have a superb view of the serene white stonework of Christ Church, acknowledged as the master-piece of Nicholas Hawksmoor, a pupil of Sir Christopher Wren. Building began in 1723, and its exuberant style was intended to impose authority and outshine the plain Noncomformist churches that were springing up all over Spitalfields at the time. Even today its impact is undiminished.

Above: the White Tower is one of London's oldest landmarks

Brick Lane, now home to a large Bangladeshi community, is where the brick-making industry once flourished. Immigrant people have settled in the East End for centuries. The attractive Georgian buildings in the little streets you pass bear testimony to the prosperity of the Huguenot merchants and silk weavers who came here as refugees. Grimmer history is recalled in Hanbury Street, the scene of one of the notorious Whitechapel Murders committed by 'Jack the Ripper' in 1888. There was much speculation as to his identity, but he was never caught.

It may feel a long trudge now up Whitechapel High Street and along the Mile End Road, but the traffic races by oblivious to the rich history that seeps from the buildings. There is the Church Bell Foundry, for instance, where Big Ben was cast; the almshouses for 'decay'd masters and commanders of ships', and the mission where the Salvation Army was born.

A hush descends when you reach Regent's Canal. As you stroll along the towpath there is only the occasional narrowboat for company until you reach Limehouse Basin, designed by Thomas Telford. Now your route takes you past converted wharves and down to the Isle of Dogs. This sweep of marshy ground used to house royal hunting dogs who, locals like to say, could be heard all the way down the Thames to Barking. Now the kennels have been replaced by the glistening glass towers of Canary Wharf, the East End's 'brave new world' of business.

Returning along the Thames Path you'll pass some of London's finest historic pubs. Most notable is the Prospect of Whitby, frequented at various times by Pepys, Dickens, Judge Jeffreys and J M W Turner. The first fuchsia plant in Britain was purchased here from a sailor for a noggin of rum. Perhaps nothing better sums up the rich history which lesser-known London hides.

Right: the graceful lines of Hawksmoor's church at Spitalfields

In London's East End

*History unfolds, street after street, in this exploration of
a lesser-known London*

1 From the Tower Thistle Hotel, by Tower Bridge, turn right and walk up St Katherine's Way. Cross the road and take the right fork which is Mansell Street. Go under the subway and take exit 14 marked Middlesex Street (Petticoat Lane).

6 Turn left and follow the signs for the Thames Path and Riverside Pubs. Follow the Thames Path signs all the way, taking the riverside links off left wherever possible. Not all are continuous and you'll need to return to the road on occasions. When you reach St Katherine's Dock, follow the signs through the dock and come out on the other side at Tower Bridge.

5 Turn right and follow pedestrian signs to Canary Wharf. At Ontario Way, on your left, is a spiral staircase at the corner of a new building. Go up the stairs and walk above the road to Westferry Circus. Walk down to Riverside Pier and Canary Wharf, then turn back, go down the steps again and back to Westferry Station.

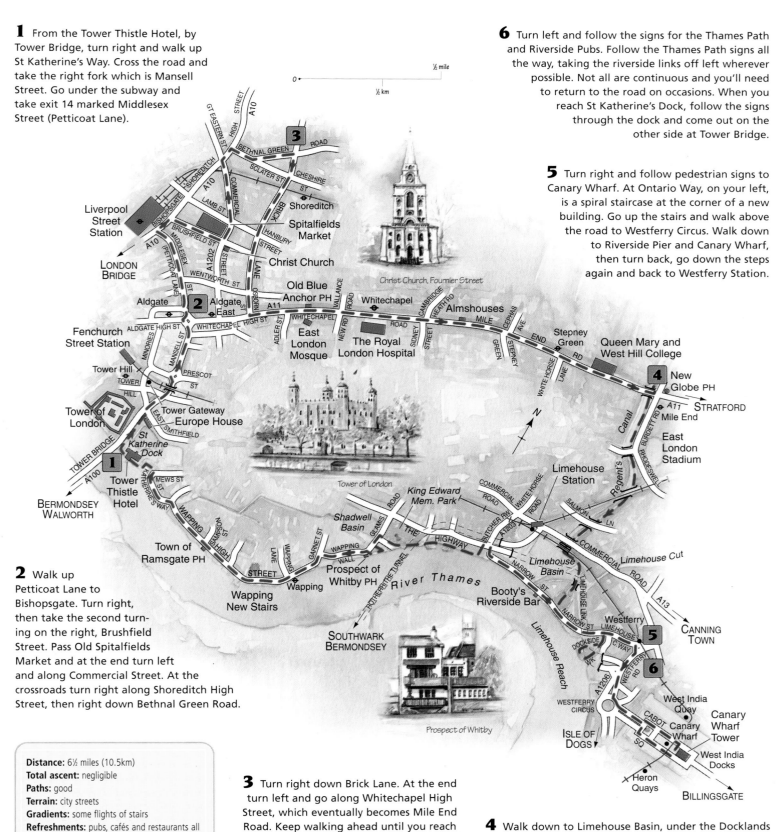

Christ Church, Fournier Street

Tower of London

Prospect of Whitby

2 Walk up Petticoat Lane to Bishopsgate. Turn right, then take the second turning on the right, Brushfield Street. Pass Old Spitalfields Market and at the end turn left and along Commercial Street. At the crossroads turn right along Shoreditch High Street, then right down Bethnal Green Road.

Distance: 6½ miles (10.5km)
Total ascent: negligible
Paths: good
Terrain: city streets
Gradients: some flights of stairs
Refreshments: pubs, cafés and restaurants all along route
Park: NCP St Katherine's Way car park, next to Tower Thistle Hotel, by Tower Bridge

3 Turn right down Brick Lane. At the end turn left and go along Whitechapel High Street, which eventually becomes Mile End Road. Keep walking ahead until you reach the bridge over the Regent's Canal. Go over the bridge and immediately turn left. Take the steps down to the canal and walk down to the left.

4 Walk down to Limehouse Basin, under the Docklands Light Railway, then turn left. Go over a bridge, through a play area then turn left at the converted wharves and walk along Barleycorn Way and Limehouse Causeway to Westferry Station.

Hethel Airfield and Norfolk's American Invasion

WALK
37

A pleasant stroll through this quiet, unassuming corner of East Anglia reveals signs of a heroic wartime past

Amidst the sleepy villages and open farmland of Norfolk lie numerous World War II airfields. Close to villages with names such as Little Snoring, Seething and Methwold, these airfields had a major impact on the countryside and the lives of the local people. This walk starts at the tiny hamlet of Hethel, home to the four squadrons of the 389th Bombardment Group, stationed here from 1943 to 1945. Their presence is commemorated in the churchyard of pretty All Saints from where the walk begins.

The airfield opened in late 1942 as Air Station No 114. In June 1943 the low-level flying training was intense and the newly arrived Americans had little time to enjoy the late English summer or sample much of the local 'warm' beer before leaving for North Africa. Today, on this walk,

you can see the end of the runway and some of the remains of the old wartime buildings – although the airfield is now a privately owned motor works, more famous as the home of Lotus Cars, and the old control tower houses the Sports and Social Club.

What was it like for the inhabitants of these Norfolk backwaters? According to one local resident, it was great fun to have the boys around. His parents' garden was used as a bicycle dump so the lads could catch the bus to Norwich for a night out. As many as 30 or 40 bicycles could be left at any one time. The walk takes you down the lane they cycled along at Bracon Ash. One Norfolk woman, who was nine when the Americans arrived, remarked that for today's youngsters it would be the equivalent to a spaceship of aliens landing. Back then, Norfolk country children were seen and not heard, yet these Americans actually talked to the children!

With 3,000 men in the region, the little villages were bursting at the seams. And these men had money. They were welcomed by the pub landlords with open arms, and often drank the pubs dry. They were less popular with the local men and soldiers on leave than with the children and the young women. In fact several US service men married local girls who joined them in the States after the war.

As you go through the wood at the beginning of the walk you can see the remains of air-raid shelters and other wartime buildings. Across the field at the end of the conservation area you can make out the former entertainment hall, which also served as a chapel. Imagine the deafening drone of the B-24s and B-17s leaving here every morning to go on bombing raids in Germany, hopefully to return later in the day. The walk takes you into open flat country which was ideal for landing and taking off. Looking left in Potash Lane you can make out the end of the runway. Pause to savour the peace and quiet, so different from the wartime bustle of the 1940s.

Top right: returning B-24s were a common sight over Norfolk

Below right: US servicemen were always popular with local children

Below: an old air-raid shelter decays in woods near Hethel

Bottom: pretty All Saints' Church in Hethel

Hethel Airfield and Norfolk's American Invasion

*On the trail of American airmen in a tiny
Norfolk village*

1 From lane by Hethel church continue to T-junction and turn right. Turn left to view air-raid shelters. Retrace steps to lane and T-junction.

2 Cross stile by gate on left and go diagonally across field towards left of White Cottage. Cross stile near pond in front of cottage, then bear left towards Hethel Thorn. Cross stile in corner then walk diagonally across field to stile in corner by trees. Walk with field left and trees right to track.

3 Turn right and follow track past farm buildings to lane. Turn right and, after 150yds (137m), take footpath left. Cross stile and continue through woods. At gate path crosses ditch to right. Cross another ditch and follow right-hand ditch past small pond to corner of wood.

Distance: 7 miles (11.2m)
Total ascent: 120ft (37m)
Paths: mostly good; can be muddy; some roads
Terrain: farmland and villages
Gradients: mainly flat; some gentle ascents
Refreshments: Bird in Hand, Wreningham
Park: on verge just past Hethel church, ¾ mile (1.2km) from B1113 at Bracon Ash

White Cottage, Hethel

Wreningham church

4 At gate turn right along edge of field, with ditch and hedge left. Turn left at road down to church on right. Cross churchyard left of church, to stile. Cross field diagonally right to stile, then over another field to telephone box.

5 Turn right on B1113. After 75yds (68m), turn right into Poorhouse Lane. At end bear left between hedges. At fields, bear left and continue left of ditch and hedge towards farm buildings. Cross lane to stile and path.

6 Continue by field edge to footbridge. Cross to next field and stile ahead. Cross to road, turn left then right, over stile to path under B1113. Continue with fence on left for 400yds (364m) to cottage. Bear right over footbridge.

7 Turn right, then immediately left with hedge and ditch left. Follow to road and cross to lane past Bird in Hand to Wreningham church. Take path opposite, along field edge to end. Turn right towards wood.

8 Don't cross stile, but turn right and after 60yds (55m) turn left over bridge. Take path to road and turn right. Where road bends right, take footpath left. After 50yds (46m) bear left over stile and bridge. Go right again, keeping ditch and hedge on right, to kissing-gate. Pass through and turn left on road.

9 Walk along road for 400yds (364m), then take footpath on right towards farm buildings. Keep left of farm and go through gap in hedge to road. Turn left and take next right into Potash Lane, signposted East Carleton. End of old runway is to left. Turn right at Brunel House.

10 Walk along track with Brunel House on left as it bears right and becomes grassy. Cross double stile into field with pond. Old Entertainment Hall is through hedge on left. Pass through gateway to track. Bear left, go through gate, turn left and walk past Church Farm. Pass through two gates and turn right to Hethel church.

The Huntingdon Home of Oliver Cromwell

The spirit of the commoner who rose to extraordinary power during the Civil War, haunts his former homeland around the Ouse Valley

WALK 38

Top right: Oliver Cromwell rose from yeoman farmer to Lord Protector

Below: the River Great Ouse at Godmanchester

Bottom: through water meadows near Huntingdon

The twin towns of Huntingdon and Godmanchester originated as Roman settlements near the junction of Ermine Street and *Via Devana*, at a fording point of the River Great Ouse, a strategic location which has ensured their continued significance. Signs of the past are still much in evidence, with a wealth of period buildings and a 14th-century bridge linking the two towns. But it is for Oliver Cromwell that Huntingdon is famous.

Born in the town in 1599, the son of a country gentleman, Cromwell became one of the most important figures in British history. As a young man he made a living as a landowner and farmer, but also became MP for Huntingdon and then Cambridge. When the Civil War broke out he joined the Parliamentary army, eventually rising to the rank of Lord General. He played a decisive role in the trial and execution of King Charles I in 1649, and from 1653 until his death in 1658 he ruled the nation as Lord Protector. Huntingdon served for a time as Cromwell's military headquarters, and several sites around the town can claim a connection. For a special insight into a rather enigmatic figure a visit to one of these – combined with this fascinating walk – could hardly be bettered. The walk guides you past the principal Cromwellian sites before heading out into the countryside of the Ouse Valley, which formed the background to his youth.

Cromwell's birthplace has been destroyed, but his coat of arms decorates the 19th-century house built on the site. This is a little further up High Street from All Saints' Church, where you can see Cromwell's baptismal record, though he was actually baptised at St John's Church, destroyed in the Civil War. The font at All Saints' is thought to have come from St John's. Close to the church stands the Falcon Tavern, used frequently by Cromwell between 1642 and 1644. Across the street is the Cromwell Museum, formerly the grammar school where Cromwell was educated before going to Cambridge University.

The rural connections are less tangible, but perhaps more evocative. Crossing Port Holme Meadow, and walking along the Cambridge road through Godmanchester and by the River Great Ouse near Houghton, you are treading footpaths and bridleways which must have been used by Cromwell himself, as a boy, as a young man and later, during the Civil War, when military preoccupations perhaps kept his mind from their beauty. The landscape has changed over the years – particularly with the building of the A14 – but lakes at Godmanchester, the legacy of gravel extraction, provide a fresh habitat for wild birds.

The Huntingdon Home of Oliver Cromwell

On the banks of the Great Ouse in search of the Lord Protector

2 Go straight on at the traffic lights. When the road bends to the right, turn left along a footpath to Mill Common. Go diagonally left to a road and turn right, past Castle Hill, under the A14 and over a brook to join the Ouse Valley Way in Port Holme Meadow.

1 From Princess Street, follow Literary Walk to High Street and turn left to All Saints' Church, the Falcon Tavern and the Cromwell Museum. Continue past the church and turn left into George Street.

Distance: 8 miles (13km)
Total ascent: negligible
Paths: good, but very muddy after rain; flooding possible in winter
Terrain: meadows, riverside, some streets
Gradients: none
Refreshments: good choice in Huntingdon and Godmanchester; pubs at Hemingford Abbots and Houghton
Park: car park in Malthouse Close off Princess Street, opposite bus station

3 Walk straight across to a footbridge at Godmanchester Lock. Having crossed, turn left to reach Chinese Bridge. Cross into Godmanchester, leaving the Ouse Valley Way. Cross the B1043 to Cambridge Street, then left into Chadley Lane to St Mary's Church.

4 Turn right through the churchyard, then right again to follow East Chadley Lane to Cambridge Road by the White Hart pub. Turn left, go under the A14, and shortly join a footpath on the left, passing a pool before turning right past a young plantation. Cross a landfill site access track and continue beside a fence.

5 Ignore access to Cow Lane and carry straight on, climbing onto an embankment to walk along the top. At the far end descend to Cow Lane. Turn left, then join the second path on the right, a bridleway running beside a dismantled railway across a common.

6 After passing a pond, the bridleway veers slightly right to join Common Lane at Hemingford Abbots. Go straight on to reach Meadow Lane and turn left. Cross Black Bridge and Hemingford Meadow to Houghton Lock. Turn left beside the River Great Ouse, rejoining the Ouse Valley Way. Just follow the frequent waymarks now as the route explores the river, a tributary and flooded gravel pits.

8 Cross a footbridge spanning the Great Ouse. Follow the road to the left, then walk through Castle Hills and along a passageway to Castle Hill. Proceed to Mill Common and turn right to Princess Street.

7 Take an underpass beneath the A14 and head towards Godmanchester. Pass a housing estate to intercept a footpath/cycleway and turn right to the B1043. Turn right towards Huntingdon, crossing at the lights.

Grimes Graves and Brooding Breckland

Set in the midst of a dark forest, a neolithic mining site is the focus for this splendid Norfolk walk

WALK 39

Top right: inside Grimes Graves

Right and below: the brooding expanse of Breckland heath and woodland

Grimes Graves was known to the Anglo-Saxons as Grim's Graves – the devil's holes of the pagan god Grim – and this area of Breckland still retains an uncanny, almost mystical feel. However, the holes you see are not graves at all but some 360 mines dug by neolithic miners 4,000 years ago. What drove these men to dig, sometimes to a depth of 40ft (12m)? Flint, the best quality of which could be found at the lowest levels, and each shaft could yield as much as eight tons. Formed by huge pressures millions of years ago, flint is found in the layers of chalk in around Breckland. The neolithic miners used reindeer antlers and stone axes to extract the flint, which was shaped into tools on site, sent away and worked at nearby settlements or transported all over the south and Midlands. The area in which you walk would have been a temporary home to these miners. One mine is accessible to the public, giving an insight to the cramped conditions the neolithic miners worked in.

Flint, however, also had ritual importance, and evidence of this has also been discovered at Grimes Graves. A small shrine was found

here, consisting of a heap of chalk surmounted by the carved figure of a pregnant woman. Other shrines were made of mounds of flint block or antler picks. The region has also thrown up evidence of other unusual non-functional activity, such as animal burials, and arrangements of mining picks and other tools, graffiti and chalk lamps. The ceremonial flint appears to have come from the deepest levels of all and was put to no other, practical use. As metal tools gradually replaced flint implements, the site adapted to the change and is known to have been used as a metal workshop in the 12th century BC. The original shafts were also used as dustbins in the Bronze Age, with bones and other rubbish thrown in.

The name Breckland, first used in the 19th century, derives from the word 'breck' – land of such poor soil it had to lay fallow between crops to recover. This soil is the product of the unusual geology and climate of the region – very cold winters, very hot summers and relatively little rainfall – factors which have combined to create a unique flora and fauna. The chalky soil yields one range of plants, while the sandy, acidic areas produce others. In midsummer the open area around Grimes Graves is ablaze with colour and abounding in insect life.

Grimes Graves and Brooding Breckland

The heathlands of central Norfolk hide a prehistoric flint mining site

1 Turn left out of the Forestry Commission office car park. Cross an iron bridge over the Little Ouse river, then up the metalled road and over the level crossing. Continue along the road for about 1½ miles (2.4km), passing a house on your right along the way.

2 Turn left along the main road, keeping to the wide verge. After about 300yds (275m), just before the 'Hidden dip' road sign, take a wide grassy track to the left. Carry straight on to the fence with a 'sheep grazing' sign. The track goes right, then immediately left by the fence, so that the grazing area is on your left.

3 Keep on the path until you reach the entrance to Grimes Graves. Turn right up the metalled road until you reach a gate by a house. Go through the gate and walk left along the wide verge.

4 Continue along the verge past a white metal gate and a public footpath sign to the left. After ¾ mile (1.2km), the road bends right and there is another white gate on your left. Take the next immediate left along a wide grassy track. Follow this straight path until another wide track crosses it. Here, turn left to follow a yellow arrow waymark.

5 Go straight on past two more yellow arrows. At the next yellow marker, turn right. After about 550yds (500m), at a clearing, five paths converge.

6 Take the path directly opposite which bears only slightly to the left, not the one by the white signpost. After 300yds (275m), the path bears diagonally right and then, very shortly, to the left. Continue, following the yellow signs.

7 After 200yds (182m) the path bears right and then after about 40yds (37m) left. Continue downhill, past two black and yellow poles until you reach the railway line.

8 Take the second left track, signposted 'conservation ride', and walk along with the railway line on your right. After 600yds (546m), go under the railway bridge and turn left. Continue to the road, then turn right over the iron bridge and return to the car park.

Distance: 6½ miles (10km)
Total Ascent: 100ft (30m)
Paths: good; grassy tracks, metalled roads
Terrain: forest and heathland
Gradients: mainly flat, some gradual ascents
Refreshments: shop in Santon Downham
Park: Forestry Commission car park in Santon Downham, off B1107 between Brandon and Thetford

Grimes Graves visitor centre

MUNDFORD

A1065

A1134

West Tofts Mere

Snake Wood

house

Grimes Graves visitor centre

West Tofts Heath

Emily's Wood

CROXTON

A1134

house

Santon Square

BRANDON

A1065

Santon Warren

N

Stone Curlew

THETFORD

SANTON DOWNHAM

level crossing

BRANDON

Thetford Forest

The Square

Little Ouse River

church

B1107

THETFORD

Warren Wood

½ mile
0
½ km

Central England

Central England

Often regarded as a vague term for an amorphous region, the Midlands have always been at the centre of the country's developing communications. The area was first criss-crossed by a series of Roman roads; indeed Watling Street and the Foss Way are still important cross-country thoroughfares.

Above: composer Edward Elgar made Malvern his home

Previous page: stepping stones span the river in Dovedale, on the border between Derbyshire and Staffordshire

Below: sunrise catches the Malvern Hills

Canals converged on the big city of Birmingham while the town of Crewe grew at a fortuitous intersection of roads and railways. In more modern times several major motorways have become interlinked in the region, home of the infamous Spaghetti Junction. Strangely enough, for all the through-traffic it sees, the Midlands are not high on the average explorer's itinerary.

There is only one national park really handy for the Midlands – the Peak District – which is very well known. Some would say it is too well known. Areas of Outstanding Natural Beauty are off-centre, over to the west, around Shropshire and the Malvern Hills. People tend to think of the Midlands in terms of simple images generated by names like the Potteries and the Black Country. Sometimes they might recall coalfields in Notting-hamshire, or open-cast mining in Northamptonshire, but there are also a few wonderful pockets of wilderness and a surprising amount of historical interest and heritage to discover in the midst of extensive agricultural acreage.

Look carefully at the landscape and you'll see that Midland folk have been sorely oppressed by their neigh-bours. Offa, King of Mercia, threw up an awesome dyke to mark his territorial limits and keep the Welsh in check. Robin Hood preferred something more akin to guerrilla warfare around Sherwood Forest. During the Wars of the Roses one of the largest armies ever assembled, drawn from all parts of the realm, descended on Bosworth Field so that rival claims to the throne could be settled. The same thing happened at Naseby Field, only this time it was full-blown civil war. In World War II the Midlands suffered mightily, and the complete levelling of Coventry in the Blitz brought a new verb into the German language, or at least into the Luftwaffe's vocabulary: *Coventrieren* – to Coventrate. This is not a full account of the 'Midland' wars, but a mere shortlist; not for nothing is this region known as the Battlefield of England. It's worth checking if there are going to be any battle re-enactments at some of the more popular sites. Depending on the era depicted, these vary from the straightforward clash of steel to spectacular cannon fire.

However you may feel about warfare, it certainly gave Stratford's most famous son something to write about. Shakespeare is one of the world's literary giants, his influence straddling the centuries, his works still the subject of hot debate. You can walk in Shakespeare's footsteps in rural Warwickshire, and, if literary themes are to your liking, D H Lawrence's old haunts can also be investigated in Nottinghamshire. A variation on the theme could take you to Malvern, where Edward Elgar found musical inspiration in the verdant landscape and the long, jagged crest of the Malvern Hills.

The Malverns offer a taste of wilderness in an essentially agricultural region, and the huddled range of the Shropshire Hills also rises abruptly from fertile plains. The real upland wilderness though, is the Dark Peak – more specifically, the grough-riven blanket bogs of the Kinder plateau. Other parts of the Peak District will at least bear old paths and packhorse tracks, but Kinder is bleak and barren bog. The eastern moorlands are lower, but still exhibit some spectacular gritstone edges. The gentler White Peak is no less spectacular, but the landforms are altogether different and much influenced by the underlying carboniferous limestone. Possibly the most popular part is around Castleton, where there are hills to climb and gorges to wander through, and even cave systems to explore. You may experience a sense of melancholy in the plague village of Eyam, or secrecy in the recessed cleft of Lud's Church – little moments where you are transported into another world, another time.

Left: a peaceful vale in the Peak District

Right: the old Monsal viaduct, Derbyshire

Below: the little town of Ironbridge, Shropshire

Central England has a reputation for being a major centre of industry, and rightly so. Ironbridge was where the Industrial Revolution started, but the place seems almost quaint these days and you explore with a sense of delving into industrial archaeology, with Abraham Darby's name to the fore. Moving eastwards across country, signs of industry diminish and there are vast, rolling fields and prosperous farmlands. If you want to find even a hint of wild country, you need to search carefully. In little upland areas such as the ancient geological inlier of Charnwood Forest and the chalky Lincolnshire Wolds you can find nature reserves where a few otherwise uncommon flowers, birds and animals take refuge. If you stretch the concept of the Midlands all the way to the coast, you can enjoy some really spectacular skyscapes around the Wash, where only the church tower of the 'Boston Stump' dares to raise a vertical line against the almost overpoweringly level horizons.

Even if your wanderings are confined to the urban sprawl around Birmingham, you can enjoy one of the finest city parks in the whole country at Sutton Park, as well as the delightful crest of the Lickey Hills and the bracken-clad open spaces of Cannock Chase. In the Midlands, more than any other part of Britain, millions of native trees are being planted in an effort to add green spaces to the grey urban environment, all part of the ongoing National Forest campaign. Give this campaign time, as you can't hurry the growth of a tree, and the countryside will look quite different within the next 50 years.

Despite the hard edges brought by canal, rail and road links, industry and urbanisation, and the feeling that the countryside exists only as thin strips alongside the Midland motorways, there is actually a lot of charming countryside to explore. Next time you pass through the area, turn onto the quiet by-roads, enquire into the heritage of the region and explore its hidden features. A little guidance is all you need in places where nature or history aren't readily apparent, and you will find it a surprising and interesting experience.

Left: the Victoria Memorial, high on Worcestershire Beacon

Best of the Rest

Dovedale Dovedale has been one of the most popular beauty spots in the Peak District for centuries – Izaak Walton came here to fish and Lord Byron compared it to Greece and Switzerland. Late spring is the best time to explore the valley of the Dove, when the wildflowers are at their best, either on a continuous walk along the river through lush meadows and woodland or on any of the circular walks starting from nearby villages such as Hartington and Biggin.

Stiperstones The last outpost of the Shropshire Hills is a mysterious spread of rocks over a pocket of sweeping moorland. So close to the Welsh border, this is a strange, unpopulated land, with peculiar Anglo-Welsh placenames and a wealth of tracks and bridleways to tempt the explorer on foot. The Stiperstones themselves can form the basis for a variety of fine circular walks from Pennerley.

Cannock Chase The Heart of England Way traverses the Country Park which protects this surprising pocket of heathland to the north of the West Midlands conurbation. Though its proximity to so many people makes the popular parts very crowded, there are still many oases of quiet to be discovered by the walker who is willing to look for them.

Monsal Trail The Peak District has an enviable network of relatively easy trails based around the former railway lines which criss-crossed its complex landscape. In Monsal Dale you can get a feel for how it must have been for passengers as the trail appears and reappears in this tight little wooded valley, much loved by photographers.

Birmingham canals It is a cliché to say that this major West Midlands city has more miles of canal than Venice, but the potential this offers the walker who wishes to explore the fascinating underbelly of a historic industrial landscape is not to be overlooked. Much of the network is waymarked and a pleasing variety of scenery can be encountered, from stately parkland to state-of-the-art new developments; still-pounding heavy industry to the haunted scars of former industrial giants.

Valley of Revolution

A world revolution began in an attractive stretch of the Severn valley

WALK

40

Top right: the belching chimneys of Coalbrookdale Ironworks, where Abraham Darby made his breakthrough

During the 18th century Britain changed from a pre-dominantly rural society to a fast-growing industrial power. The population was increasing, foreign trade was expanding, and as the century progressed new technology, new forms of transport and new towns transformed the landscape. In this deep river valley Abraham Darby helped to kick-start the Industrial Revolution that would change the world. Darby (1678–1717) had been working on an economical way of extracting iron from iron ore. The established method of heating the ore by burning charcoal was expensive and slow. In 1709 Darby discovered how to smelt the ore using coke – a coal-based product that made it a much cheaper process. The mass production of iron was underway.

Seventy years later Darby's grandson, Abraham Darby III, built the world's first cast-iron bridge. This walk begins by approaching that bridge, whose elegant, intricate design (by Thomas Pritchard) and method of construction brought admirers from all over the world. It then passes the remains of Bedlam Furnaces. With the increasing demand for iron to build ships, bridges and railways, the gorge became a little hell of furnaces, foundries and limekilns, filled with noise and noxious fumes.

At the far end of the modern suspension bridge is a fragment of the Old Free Bridge (1909), the first toll-free crossing of the gorge and an early example of reinforced-concrete architecture. From here the route continues to Jackfield, once the port that served Ironbridge and the Coalbrookdale ironworks. This role disappeared with the

introduction of the railway, but Jackfield profited from the Victorian love of decorated tiles: its tile factory flourished until the 1960s, and now contains a museum, workshops and a shop. Examples of local clay tiles can be seen at Jackfield church. Before recrossing the river, enjoy the view of the Coalport China Museum's fat, bottle-shaped kilns on the opposite bank. This was one of the country's biggest porcelain factories and has also been converted into a museum.

From the northern bank the route climbs into Ironbridge. Built above the smog and smoke of the valley floor, the town fell into decay with the 20th-century decline of the iron trade, but revived with the restoration of the gorge as a showpiece of industrial history. There are impressive views from the top of the ridge of the steep slopes and, briefly, of a contemporary industrial monument: a power station's pink cooling towers, like giant relations of the old brick kilns. The walk heads back downhill to the Museum of Iron, once Darby's powerhouse, where ironworkers laboured on 24-hour shifts to meet the industry's demands. Here, in gruelling conditions, they produced iron wheels for the first steam engine, the first iron railway tracks and, of course, the iron bridge.

Climbing beyond the museum, the route runs parallel with the old Severn Valley Railway line, almost hidden among the trees. On the final stretch the thickly wooded slopes of Benthall Edge rise ahead, a reminder of the rural tranquillity that once characterised the whole area.

Below: the ornate iron bridge across the River Severn

Valley of Revolution

*Coalbrookdale witnessed the birth of industry, but time
has healed the scars*

Distance: 5½ miles (8.8km)
Total ascent: 300ft (91m)
Paths: mostly good; riverside tracks are unsurfaced and can be muddy; steps
Terrain: roads and pavements, unsurfaced river track
Gradients: steep climb to top of ridge
Refreshments: several cafés and pubs in Ironbridge
Park: in long-stay car park beyond roundabout from visitor centre

1 From the visitor centre turn right, towards the Iron Bridge. Go under the bridge and keep ahead on the riverside path to the end, then climb the steps and turn right.

2 After about ½ mile (800m), cross the suspension bridge and turn left. From the Tile Museum, follow Church Road (left). Pass round the wooden fence to the riverside track. At the surfaced driveway take the upper path to Maws Craft Centre.

3 A little further on bear left and take the lower track to Ferry Road and on to the Boat Inn. Follow the unsurfaced track ahead for views of the Coalport China Museum.

4 Retrace your steps to the Boat Inn and cross the War Memorial Bridge. At the far side turn left. Follow the riverside track, then the pavement. After 440yds (400m) keep left with the road (don't climb to Blists Hill). In another 440yds (400m), where the road bears right, branch left over a stile and along a meandering, wooded riverside path. Eventually a waymarker points to the right. Ascend a flight of narrow steps here to emerge at a junction with Wesley Road.

7 Facing the museum gates, turn left, following the road under the railway bridge. Immediately after the bridge turn left into Coach Road. At the end (now Station Road) turn left to return to the visitor centre.

6 At the end of the road (now Hodge Bower) turn right, then after 50yds (46m) bear left past the cottages. At the White Horse pub turn left, continuing to the top of the hill before descending down Church Road. At the end of the road cross over to the Museum of Iron.

5 Follow Wesley Road (opposite) then climb the steep hill to the Golden Ball Inn. From the inn go straight ahead and, in 80yds (73m), join the pedestrian path with the railing. Cross the next road and take Belmont Road, ahead.

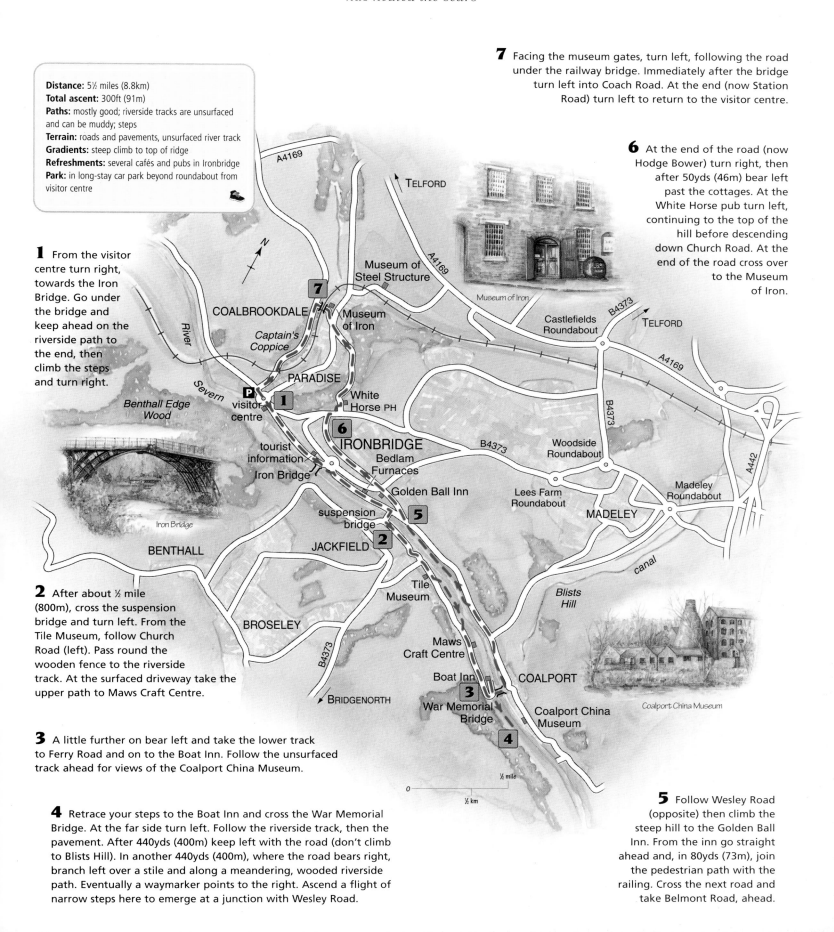

Museum of Iron

Iron Bridge

Coalport China Museum

Panorama from the Wrekin

Easy pastoral and woodland walking leads to a steep ridge, with a view of distant hills to spur you on

WALK

41

Although far from being the highest summit in Shropshire, the Wrekin is certainly the most renowned, with a special place in the affections of local people. The saying 'going all around the Wrekin' is a Shropshire way of describing a garrulous and effusive talker, while a local toast 'All friends around the Wrekin' also demonstrates why the hill, visible from much of Shropshire, is affectionately thought of as the spiritual home of all true Salopians,

Above: the Wrekin looms up out of an otherwise flat landscape

a focal point and very much the symbol of their home county.

The Wrekin, which this walk approaches by a delightful, roundabout route along an ancient green lane, through light woodland and across farm fields, stands remote from other summits, and so seems much higher than its modest height. Its distinctive shape suggests that it may be an extinct volcano. And though it is certainly volcanic in origin, it is not a volcano as such but a plug of weathered and glaciated rock, a remnant of a huge upthrust brought to the surface by subterranean volcanic activity in Precambrian times, some 600 to 800 million years ago. That places the Wrekin among the oldest rock formations in the world.

Below: looking towards Wenlock Edge and Brown Clee from the top of the Wrekin

Less prosaically, folklore captures the imagination by offering an alternative explanation for the Wrekin. In distant times, the Devil (or, in another version, a giant named Gwendol Wrekin ap Shenkin ap Mynyddmawr), decided to dam the Severn in order to flood Shrewsbury, and was on his way there with a great shovelful of soil when he met a cobbler carrying a sackful of shoes collected for repair. The Devil asked him the way to Shrewsbury, but the cobbler, guessing his purpose, complained that he had already worn out all the shoes in the bag trying to find the 'elusive' town. Frustrated, the Devil abandoned his plan and dumped his shovelful of soil where they stood, so creating the Wrekin.

The top of the Wrekin is largely bare, but the view is breathtaking and embraces not only the nearby shapely uplands of the Long Mynd, Caer Caradoc, wooded Wenlock Edge, Brown Clee and Titterstone Clee, but more distant hills – the Malverns, Bredon Hill and even, on a cold, clear day, the peaks of Snowdonia.

The summit, windswept and chilly as it must have been, was once occupied by an Iron Age hill fort, the regional 'capital' of the Cornovii, a Celtic race who came to control much of present-day Shropshire. The outline of the fort can still be traced on the hilltop, including two pronounced declivities, 'Heaven Gate' and 'Hell Gate', the main entrances through the fort's defences.

The flanks of the hill are clothed in woodland – 'forest-fleeced', as poet A E Housman describes it in *A Shropshire Lad* – and include some fine beechwoods on the western side. Much of that side is owned by Lord Barnard's Raby Estate, while the eastern slopes, bearing a fine mixed woodland of chestnut, beech, sycamore, holly, birch and larch, belong to Lord Forrester of Willey Hall near Broseley. Across the northwestern slopes there is a firing range, which has been used since World War I to provide target practice for soldiers. Warning notices are posted, and flags flown on firing days.

Panorama from the Wrekin

A walk up Shropshire's most prominent landmark reveals enormous views

Distance: 5 miles (8km)
Total ascent: 820ft (250m)
Paths: good, but muddy in places after rain
Terrain: roads, woodland, fields and steep ridge
Gradients: gentle, except for final very steep climb to the summit
Refreshments: Huntsman pub, Little Wenlock
Park: lay-by at Forest Glen, on minor road between Wellington and Little Wenlock, near a reservoir

8 Continue across the summit ridge, soon descending through Heaven Gate and Hell Gate, and following a broad track as it curves past a semi-derelict cottage. After a little more descent, another bend, and a final fling with the woodland, the track ends directly opposite the start point.

7 Here, by a prominent yew tree, turn right and climb very steeply, finally breaking free of the tree cover as you approach a conspicuous rocky outcrop. The summit of the Wrekin rises just a short distance further on, and, on a clear day, is a good place to linger. A nearby toposcope identifies distant hills and features.

1 Walk to the nearby road junction and turn right, heading for Little Wenlock. Continue (with care as there is no footway) until the road makes a pronounced bend to the right, where you leave it by branching left onto a shady green lane.

2 The green lane rises through trees to a track junction close to a group of ruined buildings. Beyond, the track – an old route to the hamlet of Huntington – descends gently, but you must leave it only a few strides after the ruined buildings by turning right onto an initially indistinct path into a narrow belt of woodland.

3 The path meanders through the woodland but eventually reaches a more direct, and slightly raised, path parallel with the woodland edge.

4 Leave the woodland at a stile and cross the field to another stile, before a short stretch of farm track leads you out to a road. Turn right and go down the road until, just before it bends sharply right, you can leave it at a stile on the left, to enter more light woodland.

5 A woodland path guides you down to a farm track. Cross this to a stile opposite, leading to open pasture. Turn left along the field edge and, after crossing an intermediate stile, continue up the field to another stile, beyond which is a broad forest track.

6 Turn left and follow the track for about ½ mile (800m) along the wooded base of the Wrekin until, just as it begins to descend, the track forks. Here, branch right into trees onto a path that also descends, as it rounds the southwestern edge of the hill. Continue with the track to an obvious path junction.

toposcope, the Wrekin

trackway, the Wrekin

SHREWSBURY
B5061
A5
Junction 7
M54
WOLVERHAMPTON
UPPINGTON
ASTON
reservoir
quarry (disused)
Wrekin Course
firing range
derelict cottage
Short Wood
Willowmoor Farm
ruined buildings
LAWLEY
Hell Gate
Heaven Gate
The Wrekin 407
Wenlock Wood
HUNTINGTON
Little Hill
Wrekin Farm
scout camp
Huntsman PH
LITTLE WENLOCK
golf course
Horsehay R/bt
A5223
GARMSTON
B4380
REWSBURY
LEIGHTON
B4380
the Wrekin
Devil's Dingle
MUCH WENLOCK
Holbrook Coppice
A4169
Jiggers R/bt
½ mile
½ km
N

Over the Long Mynd

The long, heathery crest of this rugged mountain remains markedly wilder than the surrounding cultivated lowlands

WALK

42

Top right: Church Stretton

Above: looking along the ridge of the 'Long Mountain'

Below: Carding Mill Valley

The Long Mynd towers over Church Stretton and promises an exhilarating day's walk. Rising like the armoured back of some prehistoric monster from the ordered fields of lowland Shropshire, the Long Mynd is a heather-covered mass of ancient grits and shales. Where the moorland hills fall towards Church Stretton, they are scored by numerous ravines, the lovely Carding Mill Valley being possibly the most beautiful. There is a road almost all the way to the summit, but to climb the Long Mynd on foot and trek its extensive moorlands is to appreciate the true scale and wilderness qualities of the place. Good paths and tracks can be linked to form a circular walk based at Church Stretton.

Bronze Age traders first tramped along the crest of the Long Mynd, blazing a trail now known as the Port Way. According to local legend, Caractacus, chief of the Catuvellauni, used neighbouring Caer Caradoc as a base for guerrilla action against the Roman invaders in the first century BC before he was betrayed. The Romans eventually built a road, or 'street', through the valley, from which the Strettons take their name. Saxon farmers later developed the first settlements, though the oldest datable building is the Norman church of St Laurence. Church Stretton assumed its current form in Victorian and Edwardian times, while

the railway brought tourists into the area, who were quick to discover the Carding Mill Valley.

Some say a game of golf is a good walk spoiled. When you cross the Church Stretton Golf Course, perched on a high moorland shoulder, you will have to agree that a game of golf at this height would actually make quite a challenging walk. Still, it is without regret that you leave the cultivation of the golf course behind to reach the sprawling moorland shoulders of the Long Mynd.

This walk leaves the Carding Mill Valley to the hordes, though even on the broad moorlands there can be plenty of other visitors at most times of the year. The aim is to walk along the heathery crest to the summit and enjoy the extensive views, assuming you pick a clear day. If you walk in mist, then greater care is needed at junctions of paths and tracks to complete the round in safety. There are times when habitation seems remote, even though there are several paths leading back downhill.

The National Trust holds much of the Long Mynd, and a network of paths, which has never been fully recorded on maps, offers virtual free range for walkers. Grouse are likely to break cover alarmingly underfoot, and only a few hardy trees manage to maintain a roothold on the exposed moors. There is little shelter for the walker in rain and wind, so you may need to dress for battle against the elements. That said, the place can be quite busy in good weather, with hikers and bikers – and even skiers in winter.

Over the Long Mynd

Traversing the high moorland ridge above Church Stretton

WALK 42

1 From the car park leave town by walking along the Shrewsbury Road. Turn left into a road signposted for Carding Mill Valley and golf course. Fork right up a winding road at Trevor Hill, eventually turning left to reach the golf course and clubhouse.

2 Go through the gate to the right of the clubhouse marked 'Public Footpath to the Hills'. Turn right and walk alongside beeches, then turn left and follow marker posts up a valley and across the golf course. The path runs around the head of a valley and passes a shelter, then climbs a rise before heading off to the left. Keep following the marker posts, passing a black hut, until you overlook the Carding Mill Valley.

3 Go through a gate at the top of the golf course, bear right and follow a path gently uphill, around Haddon Hill. Use the most well-trodden path. Cross two boggy patches and step over a tiny stream a little further on. The path descends slightly and crosses a wider, fast flowing stream before continuing to contour round the hillside. After stepping over another stream, turn left uphill on a faint path to intercept a wide track.

4 Turn left and rise along the broad track over extensive heather moorlands. Ignore other paths, keeping to the broad track. At one junction there is a view down Carding Mill Valley to Church Stretton. Keep straight on, rising gently to reach a complex junction. Simply step to the right to follow a narrow track uphill.

5 The track leads finally to the top of the Long Mynd (1,696ft/517m). There is a trig point (small cement pillar) and a toposcope. Snowdon is named in the view, 63 miles (101km) away. Walk straight on down to a narrow road and turn right. After passing Pole Cottage (a black hut surrounded by trees) take a grassy path on the left.

6 The path curves right and, after about 440yds (400m), joins a broad, grassy track. In bad visibility you can follow the road for another 220yds (200m) and join this track where it leaves the road. Follow the track as it cuts through heather, bilberry and bracken, rising over Round Hill then descending to a saddle. The path rises to the right, then goes round a steep slope to reach another saddle. The gentle gradient eventually gives way to a steep descent to a gate by a stream. Ford the stream and cross a footbridge to reach a lane.

7 Turn right along the lane, then left and left again in Little Stretton. Note All Saints Church at the crossroads, with the Ragleth Inn opposite. Follow the road as it passes through fields to return to Church Stretton.

Distance: 8¾ miles (14km)
Total ascent: 1,150ft (350m)
Paths: mostly clear and firm, some boggy areas and some parts muddy when wet
Terrain: extensive heather moorlands buttressed by steep hill slopes
Gradients: fairly steep early on but much gentler ascent to the top
Refreshments: various in Church Stretton; Ragleth Inn and Mynd House Hotel at Little Stretton
Park: car parks on Easthope Road in the middle of Church Stretton

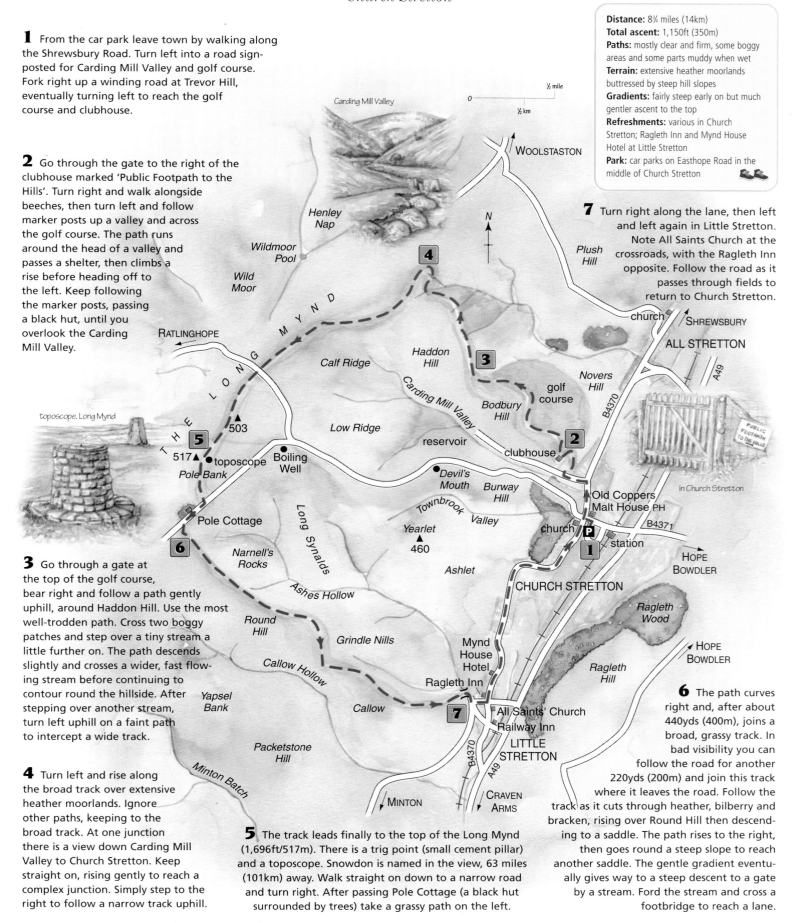

toposcope, Long Mynd

Carding Mill Valley

½ mile
0
½ km

N

WOOLSTASTON

Henley Nap

Wildmoor Pool

Wild Moor

THE LONG MYND

RATLINGHOPE

Calf Ridge

Low Ridge

503

517 toposcope
Pole Bank

Boiling Well

Pole Cottage

Narnell's Rocks

Long Synalds

Ashes Hollow

Round Hill

Grindle Nills

Callow Hollow

Yapsel Bank

Packetstone Hill

Minton Batch

Callow

MINTON

Haddon Hill

Carding Mill Valley

Bodbury Hill

reservoir

Devil's Mouth

Burway Hill

Townbrook Valley

Yearlet 460

Ashlet

Mynd House Hotel

Ragleth Inn

All Saints' Church
Railway Inn
LITTLE STRETTON

CRAVEN ARMS

golf course

Novers Hill

Plush Hill

clubhouse

Old Coppers Malt House PH

church

station

CHURCH STRETTON

Ragleth Wood

Ragleth Hill

church
ALL STRETTON

SHREWSBURY

A49

B4370

B4371

HOPE BOWDLER

HOPE BOWDLER

in Church Stretton

PUBLIC FOOTPATH TO THE HILLS

On Elgar's Malverns

Rising dramatically above the plain, the Malvern Hills are a magnet for walkers with a musical bent

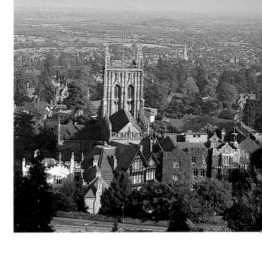

WALK 43

Top right: Great Malvern enjoyed its heyday as a spa town in Victorian times

Above: Edward Elgar, 1857–1934

Below: the Malvern Hills seen from Worcestershire Beacon

Elgar's beloved Malvern Hills, which formed a constant inspirational backdrop to his work and life, are central to this walk. He spent many hours walking and cycling in this area and some of his greatest works were composed while he was living here.

Born in Lower Broadheath, to the west of Worcester, in 1857 – his birthplace is now a museum – Elgar was the fourth child of a piano tuner and a farmer's daughter. An undistinguished scholar, he showed an impressive musical talent from an early age, playing both violin and piano. He occasionally deputised for his father, who was organist at the local Roman Catholic church, and later extended his range of instruments to include viola, cello and bassoon.

Elgar's first job was in a solicitor's office but he soon forsook the law to work in the music shop his father had opened. He also began giving music lessons, both in Worcester and Malvern. Marrying Alice Roberts, who persuaded him to concentrate on composition, in 1889, Elgar felt his future lay in London. But the move was not successful, and after a grim and frugal winter, they returned to Malvern, where Alice had lived, in 1891. The move coincided with a breakthrough in the world of composition, and his work was at last recognised by the musical establishment.

They settled in Alexandra Road, Malvern Link, an area seen from the walk, sprawling out towards Worcester, to the north of Great Malvern town. It was here Elgar composed such works as *The Black Knight*, *Scenes from the Bavarian Highlands* and the passionate *Enigma Variations*. The move also marked the critical acceptance of his work, which had eluded him up to now. In 1899 the Elgars bought a house in Malvern Wells, renaming it Craeg Lea – an anagram of E, A and C Elgar (their only child, Carice, had been born in 1891).

Great Malvern, where this walk begins, had become famous for its spring water in the 18th century and its buildings reflect the grandeur of an English spa town. From the town the walk ascends to the single north-south ridge of the Malvern Hills. From the highest point on the ridge you can experience the views that so inspired Elgar. Here is a vision of a landscape that is profoundly English, and Elgar was fervently patriotic. The surrounding countryside became very important in his work, and he drew heavily on its sounds, smell and views. Finding even Malvern a little too urban, he rented Birchwood Lodge at Great Storridge, a little further north along the ridge, in addition to the family home, and from 1898 to 1903 much of his work was done on the piano in the bedroom there.

Always searching for the ideal residence, Edward moved six more times before his death in Worcester in 1934. But his choice of final resting place – the churchyard of St Wulstan's in Little Malvern, alongside Alice, who had died in 1920 – showed his lasting love for the countryside and rising forms of the Malvern Hills.

On Elgar's Malverns

*The town and shapely string of distinctive hills inspired
one of Britain's greatest composers*

WALK
43

1 From the car park go through the red gates towards the pool's entrance, but bear right to walk beside the building. Bear left around the back of the pool, then turn right across the footbridge over the pond. Follow the path through Priory Park, bearing left in front of the theatres building to reach a prominent lamp. Here, turn right to leave the park, bearing left, then right up a lane.

2 When the lane reaches Grange Road, turn left to a T-junction with Abbey Road.

3 Turn right along Abbey Road, passing the Abbey Hotel and going through the arch of the Abbey Gatehouse. Opposite the post office, bear left up the steps and turn right along Worcester Road. Just after The Unicorn, turn left up St Ann's Road. Go up the rising road, keeping straight ahead through the trees to reach a 'Turning Place Only' sign on the right. Here turn sharply back right on a path which rises through trees and rhododendrons.

4 Ignore a crossing path, continuing to join a wider path (from left) and following it to Ivy Scar Rocks, the largest Malvern rock outcrop. Immediately beyond the outcrop, bear left up a steep, narrow path, zig-zagging through gorse, broom and bracken.

5 At a T-junction with a wider path (Lady Howard de Walden Drive), turn right, soon reaching a seat. Turn left up a steep, but obvious, grassy path. Bear right at a junction, continuing to the top of North Hill with its splendid views.

6 Go downhill towards Table Hill ahead, bearing left at the col between the peaks and following a grassy path down to rejoin de Walden Drive. Turn right and follow the track towards Worcestershire Beacon, prominent ahead. At a panorama dial, bear right off the path for a steep short-cut to the summit.

9 Just as you reach a road, bear left, uphill, along a narrow path to another road. Bear left, following the road to signs for Foley Terrace and St Ann's Road. Soon turn sharply right along the drive to *Bello Squardo*. Go down the steps to the left of the gateway to Rose Bank Gardens. Continue to a road and bear left across it to a road down to the post office. Retrace your steps from point 3 to return to the start.

8 Turn sharply left along a path between trees. Just after the reservoir railings begin, fork left along a narrow, rising, grassy path passing above a quarry to the right, then zig-zagging to the quarry base. Continue ahead, with the quarry to the right, for a few paces, then turn left down a wide path.

7 Go downhill along the ridge top to reach a wide path at the base of a hillock. Follow the path around the hillock (on left) and past a covered reservoir, to reach the Gold Mine, a cylindrical stone signpost.

Map labels:

½ mile
0
½ km

WORCESTER

BROMYARD

Malvern Hills

B4219

Cowleigh Park

N

Malvern Link Station

MALVERN LINK

A449

B4208

WEST MALVERN

5
4
North Hill
▲
400

6

St Ann's Well ●

3
1
P
2

9

Worcestershire Beacon
▲
425

Great Malvern Station

GREAT MALVERN

RHYDD

B4211

B4208

B4232

trig point

Park Wood

7

B4218

8

Railway PH

A449

UPPER WYCHE

LEDBURY

B4232

↓ LEDBURY

Abbey Gatehouse

Distance: 5½ miles (8.8km)
Total ascent: 1300 ft (396m)
Paths: excellent
Terrain: grassy ridges and woodland; town walking at start and finish
Gradients: mostly gradual, but steep on ascent of North Hill
Refreshments: lots in Great Malvern
Park: car park opposite Splash swimming pool, Priory Road, Great Malvern

Border Lines – on Offa's Dyke

Enjoy an insight into the disputed border country around Chirk and a glimpse of Wales' prettiest valley

WALK

44

Right: a primrose in flower on Offa's Dyke

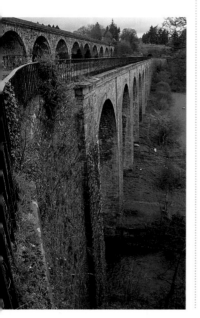

Above: the aqueduct and viaduct span the dark waters of the River Chirk

After conquering the whole of Wales in the 13th century, the powerful Norman king, Edward I, reinforced his position by building great castles in strategic places across the land. One such was built at Chirk near the start of this border walk. From its hilltop setting the huge sandstone castle oversees both the village and the Ceiriog valley, a beautiful swathe of green that scythes its way through the hills and into the heartlands of Wales.

There's an idyllic start to the walk at the secluded little village of Chirk Bank, which, unlike Chirk, lies in England. A little whitewashed post office overlooks the Shropshire Union Canal, with its hungry and ever-hopeful ducks.

After strolling along the canal towpath you're soon looking down more than 70ft (21m) over the edge of Thomas Telford's ten-arched aqueduct to the dark waters of the River Ceiriog. Next to you is Henry Robertson's even taller viaduct, built in 1840 to carry the railway.

The Ceiriog is one of Wales' finest little valleys, verdant and peaceful. But throughout the walk the castle always seems to be there, peeping through the trees. You get the feeling you're being watched, just like the Welshmen who dared to cross the dyke would have felt. Look out for the odd red hand symbol on footpath signposts. Some say that it dates back to the time when Welshmen would have had their hand cut off if they were found to be trespassing in England. There's also a tale of two youths who settled a bitter dispute by a race to the castle gates. When the leader reached the gates his hand was cut off by the sword of his enemy's aide.

For centuries fierce Welsh warlords led their armies down from the hills in attempts to force their enemies back across the Marches, and the Romans, northern Celts, Angles and Saxons forced them back. These were troubled times. In the 8th century an Anglo Saxon king, Offa, decided to settle the disputes, and he built his dyke, an earthwork border line from Prestatyn to Chepstow.

When you reach Offa's Dyke it may seem little more than an earthwork ridge, whose line is defined by hedges and overgrowths of bracken and bramble. Nowadays it is better known for the 176-mile (283km) long distance footpath running along it. On this walk, however, you will have to be content with just one of those miles, but it is a good one, climbing to a fair height. You can look back, not only to the castle, but across the wide English plains and the distant blue hills of the High Peak.

Stretches of country lane punctuate the walk back, but these attractive hedge-lined lanes are hardly used. In spring and early summer the verges are bedecked with wild flowers, and in late summer there are blackberries.

The final stretch takes you along the banks of the bustling Ceiriog back towards the viaducts. It may strike you that these feats of civil engineering are more powerful and leave a longer-lasting impression than the dyke itself, product of an era of strife.

Right: oak trees and blackthorn at Bronygarth, Offa's Dyke

Border Lines – on Offa's Dyke

A walk along England's border with Wales reveals much more than the great Saxon boundary marker

1 Across the road from the Chirk Bank post office follow the canal towpath back towards Chirk, crossing the aqueduct to a tunnel at the end of it. A footpath now climbs to the Glyn Ceiriog road.

2 Turn left down the road for 100yds (91m) to a house named Pen-y-Waen, then follow a waymarked footpath on the right, across the cutting of the old Glyn Valley Tramway. Walk through woodland, returning to the road just short of Pont-Faen (bridge).

3 Cross the bridge and turn right along the lane. After 150yds (137m), near a telephone box, go over a stile into fields. The path follows the south banks of the Ceiriog. Take the left fork on entering Woodland Trust land and climb through Pentre Wood to a country lane. turn right and follow the lane for 300yds (274m) to The Old School.

4 Go down the enclosed track to the left of The Old School. Take the second of two signposted paths, heading across the sloping fields of Bron y Garth, crossing an enclosed farm track en route. Ascend across the next field and pass through a gate. In the next field follow a fence up on the right then cross a stile. On nearing some woods on the right, the path gets rather marshy, but the difficulties are short-lived. Past the woods, aim for the whitewashed cottage directly ahead.

5 Turn left, uphill by the cottage on a path that now keeps the earthworks of Offa's Dyke to the right. Beyond a narrow tarmac road the path drops into a wooded ravine, crossing the stream via a footbridge before climbing out on some steps.

6 Shortly after the ravine, the path comes to an enclosed track. Turn left along this to meet another lane next to Mount Wood. Turn left along the lane, which descends past two farms. At a sharp right-hand bend, leave the road for a field path tracing a hedge northeastwards and pass through a gate. Continue northeast across another field to emerge at the roadside by The Pentre.

7 Cross the road to another cross-field path, heading for a gap in a hedge then veering right to the bottom right hand corner of the next field, crossing a stile into the lane. Follow the lane down to the bridge.

8 Cross the bridge and follow a path tracing the northern banks of the River Ceiriog, going beneath the arches of the aqueduct and the viaduct. On climbing to the road, turn right, then climb past the Bridge Inn back to the post office.

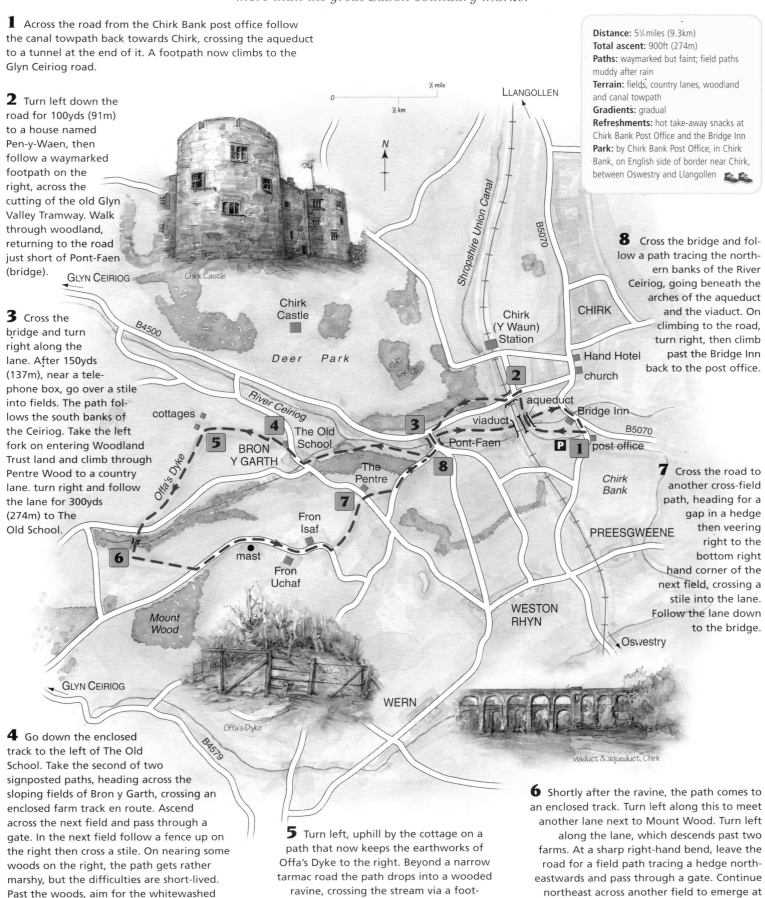

LLANGOLLEN

½ mile

0

½ km

N

Shropshire Union Canal

B5070

GLYN CEIRIOG

Chirk Castle

Chirk Castle

B4500

Chirk Castle

Deer Park

River Ceiriog

cottages

The Old School

BRON Y GARTH

Offa's Dyke

The Pentre

Fron Isaf

mast

Fron Uchaf

Mount Wood

GLYN CEIRIOG

Offa's Dyke

B4579

WERN

Chirk (Y Waun) Station

CHIRK

Hand Hotel

church

aqueduct

viaduct

Pont-Faen

Bridge Inn

B5070

post office

Chirk Bank

PREESGWEENE

WESTON RHYN

Oswestry

viaduct & aqueduct, Chirk

The Goyt Valley

This remarkable area is a microcosm of the Dark Peak, and represents a real success in the story of the National Park

WALK
45

Top right: sailing dinghies on Errwood Reservoir

Above: rushing water in the Goyt Valley

Below: the view of Shuthingsloe from the gritstone ridge of Shining Tor

The Goyt Valley on the western side of the Peak District was a place which had to be saved from its own popularity. Twenty years after it became part of Britain's first national park in the Peak District, it was in danger of being choked to death by the drivers who thronged the narrow north-south valley road, and who were ironically threatening the very tranquillity which they had come to find.

The pioneering and radical approach devised by the National Park Authority, and backed by the Countryside Commission, was a traffic management scheme which became the blueprint for many others in Britain. Large car parks were built at strategic points, a minibus service was provided, and at busy times the narrow road was closed to all traffic. The valley was thus saved from a slow, choking death, and it is a sign of the success of the park's strategy that today the scheme operates without minibuses – because most people prefer to walk.

This walk takes you from the banks of a large reservoir which, although constructed only just over 30 years ago, has been easily assimilated into the landscape, along a forestry trail through commercial woodland, through the gardens and past the ruins of a grand Victorian mansion, and finally out on to the open moorland which surrounds the valley.

In many respects, the Goyt Valley is representative of every typical habitat to be found in the Dark Peak, but it is also home to a number of rarities not found elsewhere in the millstone-grit moorlands to the north, east and west. These include the welcome recent return of breeding hen harriers to the high moors around the valley, and migrant ospreys over the reservoirs. Great crested and red-breasted mergansers can often be seen on the reservoirs, while in the woodlands, woodpeckers and nuthatches are common, as are foxes and badgers. The range of wildlife interest supported by the various habitats in the Goyt Valley has made it a Site of Special Scientific Interest and an important part of the South West Peak Environmentally Sensitive Area.

All this is set in a valley which has been significantly changed by human activity. The twin reservoirs, Fernilee and Errwood, are the most obvious artificial features. The former was constructed in 1938 to supply water for nearby Stockport. Errwood followed higher up the valley in 1967, and is now used for leisure purposes by a thriving sailing club. The construction of the Errwood Reservoir sounded the death knell for Errwood Hall, a grand Italianate mansion built a century earlier by Samuel Grimshawe, a Manchester merchant. Here the Grimshawes lived in the style of foreign princes with a large retinue of staff. They were also responsible for the acres of now neglected rhododendrons and azaleas which surround the forlorn ruins of their home.

It was at that time that the large belts of coniferous trees were planted round the reservoir, in the interests of water purity, and the modern Forestry Commission has opened up much of this forest to the public with waymarked walking trails.

The Goyt Valley

A circuit in one of the Peak District's most famously conserved valleys

WALK 45

1 Follow the nature trail signs leading up into the forest. Soon after entering the trees join a broad path and turn right, following and eventually crossing a stream. At a sharp bend and path junction, turn right to arrive at the partly reconstructed ruins of Errwood Hall.

2 Left of the Hall ruins, up way-marked steps, continue on the woodland walk as it leads off into the trees, past some gateposts and the remains of estate workers' cottages on the edge of open country.

3 Turn right by the cottages, down to some steps which lead to a footbridge and a cross-roads of paths, where you turn left, going up through the sparse trees to contour below wooded Foxlow Edge. Beyond the trees a short detour takes you to a circular shrine, erected in 1889 by the Grimshawes in memory of their childrens' governess.

4 Climb up the steps from the shrine, back on the main path which leads up to the road ahead, which is known as The Street. This was a pack-horse route from Buxton to the west. Turn uphill on the road to its summit, known as Pym's Chair, after John Pym, the 17th-century Puritan leader.

6 From the summit, which is reached by crossing a ladder stile, drop down to a stile from which a broad green track heads left above Shooter's Clough (to the left), contouring gently down. Follow a well-marked path, reaching another path. Cross this through gateposts and continue down to the Errwood car park.

5 Cross the stile on the left of the road at Pym's Chair and walk along the 2 miles (3.2km) of partly restored path, alongside a wall to the south, to Shining Tor. At 1,834ft (559m), this is the highest point on the walk.

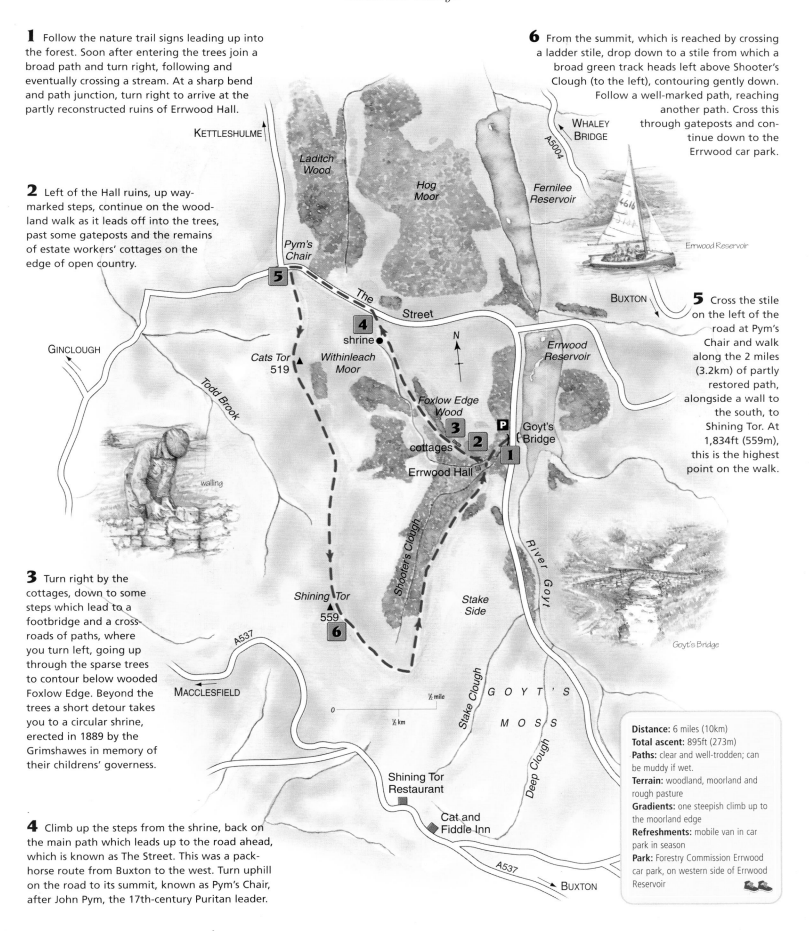

Distance: 6 miles (10km)
Total ascent: 895ft (273m)
Paths: clear and well-trodden; can be muddy if wet.
Terrain: woodland, moorland and rough pasture
Gradients: one steepish climb up to the moorland edge
Refreshments: mobile van in car park in season
Park: Forestry Commission Errwood car park, on western side of Errwood Reservoir

The Wonders of the Peak at Castleton

Where the White Peak meets the Dark, this shorter walk explores a celebrated cave and the 'shining mountain'

WALK

46

Top right: rich veins of the mineral Blue John are found at Castleton

With the interest in the picturesque and new-found mobility resulting from better communications in the 17th and 18th centuries, it became fashionable for the well-to-do to record the sights they saw on their travels.

The Seven Wonders of the ancient world were already well-established by this time, but they were out of range for most travellers. So British 'wonders' began to be dis-

Above: the mighty bulk of Mam Tor towers above Castleton

Below: Peak Cavern is one of the four 'show caves' open to the public

covered and described, and chief among these were the 'Seven Wonders of the Peak'.

They appear to have been first annotated by Michael Drayton, the Warwickshire-born poet and contemporary of Shakespeare, in his *Poly-Olbion*, first published in 1622. Describing them as 'my dreadful daughters', he records The Devil's Hole or Arse (the local name for Peak Cavern) and Sandy Hill (Mam Tor) near Castleton; Eldon Hole, near Peak Forest; Poole's Cavern and St Anne's Well at Buxton; the ebbing and flowing well at Tideswell, and the Royal Forest of the Peak.

Drayton's wonders were later recycled by the philosopher Thomas Hobbes in his Latin poem 'De Mirabilibus Pecci – Concerning the Wonders of the Peak in Darbyshire', published in 1636. But he diplomatically replaced the medieval Royal Forest of the Peak with Chatsworth House, home of the Earl of Devonshire, whose retainer he was. This fairly easy walk takes in both of Castleton's 'wonders', and includes a couple more that modern tourists might consider worthy of inclusion in the list.

The attraction of Castleton is founded on its position,

standing on the great geological divide of the Peak District, where the rolling limestone plateau of the White Peak meets the sombre moors of the Dark Peak. The town itself was founded in the 11th century when William Peveril, natural son of William the Conqueror, built his feudal stronghold on the virtually impregnable crag between the Peak Cavern gorge and Cave Dale. Peveril Castle is well worth a visit, if only to admire its fantastic position and the stupendous views across the head of the Hope Valley from its walls. The town was laid out north of the castle to a grid-iron pattern and enclosed by the still-visible Town Ditch.

But the mighty maw of Peak Cavern, said to be the largest cave entrance in Britain, was there long before the castle. Home to a community of rope-makers in 'the village which never saw the sun', the cave is one of four show caves in and around Castleton open to the public, and we pass two others on our route. They are Blue John and Treak Cliff, both famous for a wonder not on Hobbes' list – Blue John fluorspar, a sparkling blue and yellow semi-precious mineral ore that has only ever been found in the Castleton caves. All three caves are as exciting to explore now as they would have been for those earlier wonder-seekers, with their stalactites, flowstones and strange rock formations (especially in Treak Cliff Cavern).

In sharp contrast, the other wonder visited on this walk is the imposing bulk of Mam Tor – the so-called 'Shivering Mountain' – that overlooks Castleton at the head of the Hope Valley. An Iron Age hillfort encircles the 1,695ft (517m) summit, which is characterised by its sheer, crumbling east face, which gives it its alternative name. If the weather is fine, catch your breath on the summit, and take in the fabulous views over Castleton, Edale and the Hope Valley.

WALK
46

The Wonders of the Peak at Castleton

Early tourists were filled with awe at the sights around this Derbyshire village

Distance: 5 miles (8km)
Total ascent: 1,035ft (315m)
Paths: can be muddy if wet; ridge mostly paved
Terrain: rocky start then easy going on ridge and through fields
Gradients: one steep, 1,000ft (305m) ascent to the Mam Tor ridge
Refreshments: restaurants, pubs and cafes in Castleton, picnic tables at Mam Nick
Park: main car park, Castleton

7 Opposite the mine cross a fence stile and pass the lead-crushing circle associated with the mine to descend across the stream and go through a landscape of lead spoil tips to another stile. Continue through bracken, passing a farm, and return to Castleton alongside Odin Stitch via a series of stiles.

6 Take the path which contours around Treak Cliff, crossing two stiles to reach the hillside entrance to Treak Cliff Cavern, another of Castleton's show caves, with perhaps the finest underground formations. Take the steps down from the cave entrance to the road, which was abandoned in the 1970s after it collapsed beneath the shifting face of Mam Tor. It is a short distance left up the old road to the mysterious crevice of Odin Mine, on the left, one of the oldest recorded Peak District lead mines.

5 Cross the B6061 and take the slanting path which leads to a fence stile. Turn left downhill to pass the entrance to the Blue John Mine show cave. This is the source of the banded fluorspar known as Blue John.

1 From the main car park turn left up the main street, turning left again by the primary school and going straight ahead down the walled packhorse route known as Hollow Ford Road. Cross Tricket Bridge and keep left at Hollow Ford Training and Conference Centre.

2 Go through a gate and ascend the ancient packhorse route for just over a mile (1.6km), with fine views to the left of the 'shivering' east face of Mam Tor. The top of the ridge at Hollins Cross (1,260ft/384m), is marked by a viewfinder, and has wonderful views north across the vale of Edale to the plateau of Kinder Scout, the highest point of the Peak District.

3 Turn left and follow the heavily eroded ridge path along Cold Side until you reach a newly paved section, which leads up through the embankments of the hill fort which crowns Mam Tor.

4 An easy staircase of slabs leads down through the fortifications to Mam Nick (a pass). A stile gives access (left) to a path which descends through a pasture, crossing the A625 by a pair of ladder stiles. The second stile (opposite) leads down to the Windy Knoll cave, where Victorian excavators found the bones of many prehistoric animals, including rhinoceros.

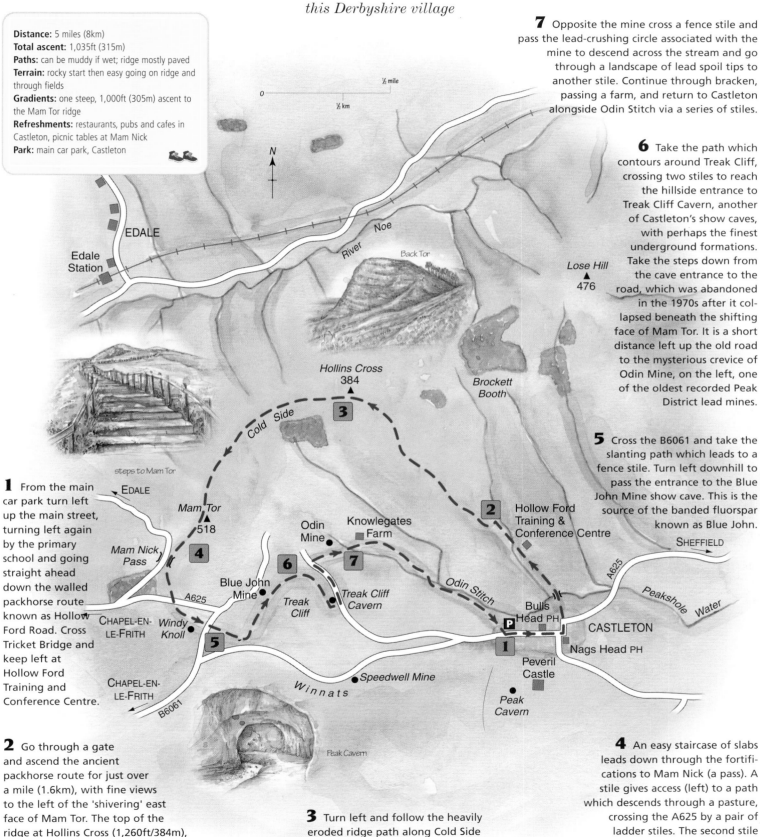

Lud's Church and the Green Knight

Legend has it that Arthurian champion Gawain faced his sternest test in this lush ravine

WALK 47

Above: the extraordinary natural chasm known as Lud's Church

Below: the ridge of the Roaches with Hen Cloud beyond

Although still marked on modern maps as a cave, Lud's Church in the Staffordshire Moorlands is really a gigantic landslip, hidden away deep among the oaks, birches and pines of Back Forest above the remote valley of the Black Brook.

It is a secret, secluded place which exudes mystery and an indefinable air of menace. To the walker who enters this strange roofless cavern, the overall impression is one of greenness – dark, dank and dripping greenness. Grass, moss and ferns hang from the 60-foot (18m) vertical sides of the deep ravine which, camouflaged by overhanging trees, is almost invisible from above. The first visit to Lud's Church is usually an eerie experience, not easily forgotten.

This is the perfect place, of course, to attract myths and legends, and Lud's Church has accrued more than its fair share. It is thought to have been named after Walter de Ludank, a Lollard follower of John Wycliffe (whose religious theories paved the way for the Reformation), who held illicit services in the remote spot, far from the prying eyes of the authorities. His daughter, Alice, is said to have been shot and killed during a raid on a service here, and her white statue (actually a ship's figurehead) stood for many years high in a cleft in the rocks. Other stories tell of headless riders being seen in the locality, and the ghost of a tall man dressed in Lincoln green.

Possibly linked with this tall apparation is the most persistent legend about Lud's Church: that it was the setting used by the unknown author of that masterpeice of medieval alliterative poetry, *Sir Gawain and the Green Knight*. This 14th-century work has been hailed as the greatest medieval poem outside the work of Chaucer.

All that can be said with certainty about the author is that language experts have concluded that the dialect used in the text places him unmistakably in the northwest Midlands, or the Staffordshire part of the Peak District. And the beheading ritual undertaken by Sir Gawain with the Green Knight, the dénouement of the vivid Arthurian tale, takes place in the Green Chapel, which has been identified with Lud's Church and the surrounding area.

This quite strenuous walk follows in the steps of Sir Gawain in the story, as he made his way 'By bluffs where boughs were bare' and 'Climbed by cliffs where the cold clung', past 'great crooked crags, cruelly jagged where the bristling barbs seemed to brush the sky.'

Most people take this to be a fair description of the area around the Roaches and Castle Cliff Rocks in Back Forest. The walk also passes Doxey Pool on the Roaches ridge, where there are legends of a mermaid and a fearsome green monster, known as Jenny Greenteeth, which lurks beneath its peaty depths.

Today the Roaches is a popular place for the climbing fraternity, and lies at the centre of an estate owned by the Peak National Park Authority. It is also the subject of a traffic management scheme, where parking restrictions and a park-and-ride service from nearby Tittesworth Reservoir operate on summer weekends.

Lud's Church and the Green Knight

Legends haunt the strange rock shapes and hollows along and beyond The Roaches

WALK 17

1 From the bus stop below The Roaches, follow the broad track up towards the gap between The Roaches and Hen Cloud. Tucked away under rocks to the left is Rock Hall, now the Don Whillans Memorial Hut.

2 Turn left just before the col and follow a wall on the right, then bear right ascending on one of several paths that climb through the woodland and later aim for a gap in the ridge to gain the top. Turn left along the partly paved ridge path for 1½ miles (2.4km). Near the highest point, pass the hollow enclosing Doxey Pool.

3 Continue on the clear, boggy path to the highest point, marked by a trig point at 1,657ft (505m) and with fine views across the Staffordshire Plain and Shutlingsloe.

4 Drop down on the path, which is later paved, through wind-eroded tors to the road at Roach End. Cross the road through a gap in the wall and immediately turn right over a stile which leads right down through heather and birch scrub to Forest Wood.

5 Enter the forest and after 200yds (182m) bear left, taking the lower path, signposted Gradbach, (ignoring the upper path signposted Lud's Church) through the woodland, with Black Brook below you to the right. Contour along the side of the valley and later descend, following way-markers, to a guide post. Bear right (signed Danebridge) to a footbridge where the Black Brook joins the River Dane.

6 Don't cross the bridge but turn left and ascend, passing a large tree, and at the second waymarker turn right, gradually ascending to Castle Cliff Rocks. This is a good place for a refreshment stop.

9 Turn right and follow the minor road, forking left for Upper Hulme after ½ mile (800m), with the outcrops of Five Clouds to the left. Return to the bus stop beneath the Roaches, and the start.

8 A sandy path leads left through birch scrub and moorland. Reaching a clearing after 300yds (273m), a sign points right to the ridge which leads back towards Roach End. The path leads to the top of the moor, where you turn left on a clear path and then follow a wall for ½ mile (800m) to return to Roach End.

7 Turn sharply left here, signposted Lud's Church, to take the upper path which leads, after 200yds (182m), to the concealed entrance to Lud's Church on your right. Take time, and care, to descend into the usually boggy depths of the chasm and emerge at the steep steps at the far end.

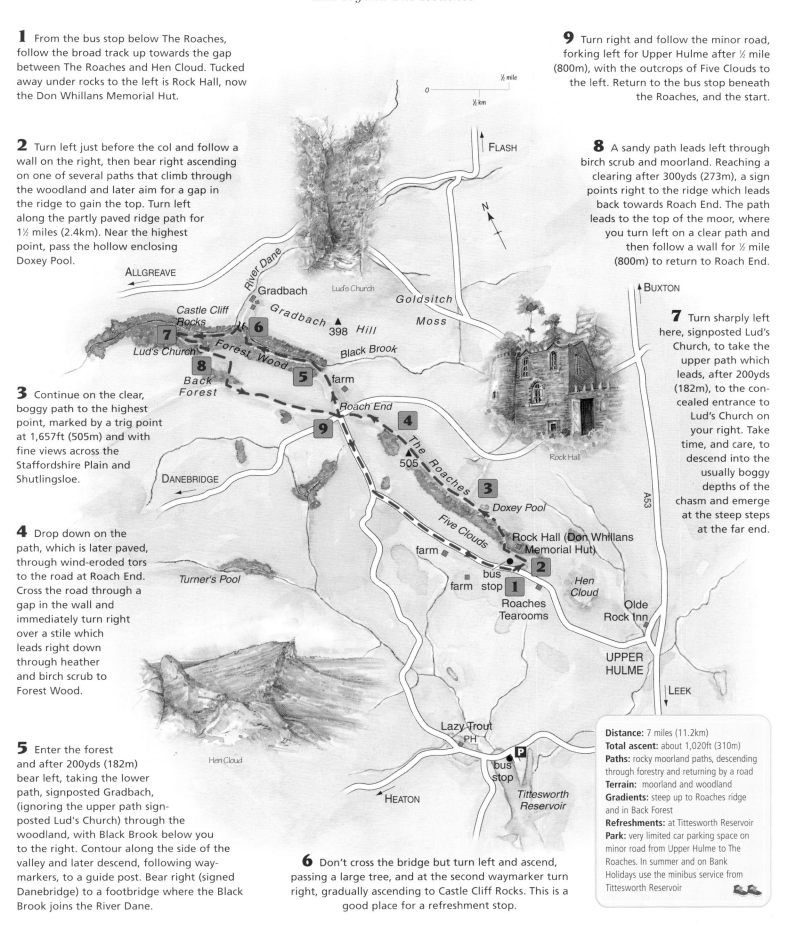

Distance: 7 miles (11.2km)
Total ascent: about 1,020ft (310m)
Paths: rocky moorland paths, descending through forestry and returning by a road
Terrain: moorland and woodland
Gradients: steep up to Roaches ridge and in Back Forest
Refreshments: at Tittesworth Reservoir
Park: very limited car parking space on minor road from Upper Hulme to The Roaches. In summer and on Bank Holidays use the minibus service from Tittesworth Reservoir

A Walk in the Dark Peak

From Edale to the dark edges of the Kinder plateau

WALK 48

Top right: the Old Nag's Head at Edale

Above: Edale marks the start of the Pennine Way

Below: sturdy sheep graze the slopes of Hope Valley

Beyond Mam Tor the Peak National Park changes from the gentle limestone hills of the White Peak to the hard gritstone Dark Peak, with its wild peat bogs, heather moors and unearthly eroded stone outcrops known as tors. Edale, where this walk begins, sits on the edge of the Dark Peak at the foot of the Kinder Scout plateau, with soft shale hills to the south and, to the north, exposed 'edges' of rock and high moorland.

People have lived in this valley, formed by the River Noe, since the Iron Age; Edale itself grew from a huddle of medieval cattle farmers' shelters, called booths or bothies. The village was originally known as Grindsbrook Booth – now the name of the approach where the Pennine Way begins. The Old Nag's Head, its official starting point, was once the village smithy. The walk sets off along the Pennine Way route, but soon swings away, following an old sled road, used by villagers in the past for bringing building stone and peat for fuel down from the edges. A sign marks the 'boundary of open country', the point of public access to private land. In the 1930s ramblers demanding the right to walk across the area's privately owned grouse moors organised a mass trespass on Kinder Scout. With the creation of the national parks in 1949, and of the Peak National Park in 1951, negotiations got underway with landowners for access to the northern moors (except on grouse-shooting days).

It's a long climb up towards the summit of Grindslow Knoll; stop occasionally to look back at the increasingly spectacular views of the wide valley below and Mam Tor beyond. The last stretch is particularly steep and rocky: take great care and don't attempt it without stout footwear and some hill-walking experience. The route skirts the summit itself along a narrow path, high above Grindsbrook Gorge. As you head towards the top of the gorge you pass the first of many tors, whose weird, crumpled forms were created when the elements wore away soft stone under harder blocks of gritstone – often leaving huge boulders balancing on slender stems.

After fording the Grindsbrook and subsidiary streams, you turn back to walk along the opposite edge. The route leads past the peat moorlands that stretch across the Kinder plateau, formed by decaying vegetation on the hard stone base. Drainage channels known as groughs cut through the peat, and heather thrives on the acidic soil. To the right, Upper Tor and Nether Tor teeter over the valley.

On the gradual descent you may hear the quacking call of the red grouse, well camouflaged in nests under the heather. The path becomes clearer on its zig-zagging course down an old sled road, and eventually emerges at Ollerbook Booth, another former 'bothy' built for livestock men, when life in the Dark Peak was a much tougher affair than it is today.

A Walk in the Dark Peak

Up to the bleak Kinder Plateau, where the Pennine hills first assert their mountain credentials

WALK 48

Distance: 6½ miles (10.5km)
Total ascent: 1,100 feet (335m)
Paths: mainly unsurfaced, some very rough; some short road sections
Terrain: fields, peat moorlands
Gradients: very steep in parts (do the walk in reverse for a more gradual ascent)
Refreshments: Ramblers Inn, Old Nag's Head, Edale
Park: Edale car park, signed off A625

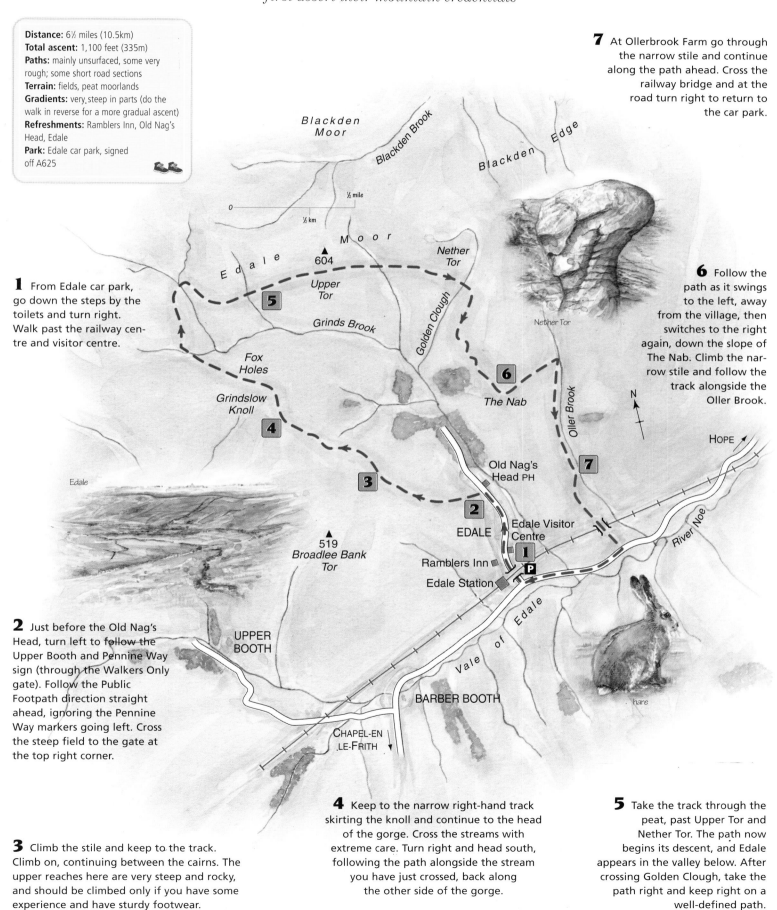

7 At Ollerbrook Farm go through the narrow stile and continue along the path ahead. Cross the railway bridge and at the road turn right to return to the car park.

1 From Edale car park, go down the steps by the toilets and turn right. Walk past the railway centre and visitor centre.

6 Follow the path as it swings to the left, away from the village, then switches to the right again, down the slope of The Nab. Climb the narrow stile and follow the track alongside the Oller Brook.

2 Just before the Old Nag's Head, turn left to follow the Upper Booth and Pennine Way sign (through the Walkers Only gate). Follow the Public Footpath direction straight ahead, ignoring the Pennine Way markers going left. Cross the steep field to the gate at the top right corner.

3 Climb the stile and keep to the track. Climb on, continuing between the cairns. The upper reaches here are very steep and rocky, and should be climbed only if you have some experience and have sturdy footwear.

4 Keep to the narrow right-hand track skirting the knoll and continue to the head of the gorge. Cross the streams with extreme care. Turn right and head south, following the path alongside the stream you have just crossed, back along the other side of the gorge.

5 Take the track through the peat, past Upper Tor and Nether Tor. The path now begins its descent, and Edale appears in the valley below. After crossing Golden Clough, take the path right and keep right on a well-defined path.

Eyam – Village of the Damned

A year of quarantine self-imposed by villagers saved the area from the ravages of bubonic plague

WALK

49

Top right: the Riley Graves

Below: a skull and crossbones marks a tomb at Eyam

Below: William Mompesson is commemorated in St Lawrence's Church, Eyam

In the summer of 1665 the Great Plague was raging through London, where it claimed over 60,000 lives. Carried by rat fleas, the disease was largely confined to the city's infested streets. But it could have swept through the entire country, had it not been for the courage of the villagers of Eyam, high in the Derbyshire peaks.

On 7 September 1665 George Viccars, a tailor, brought a box of clothing to Eyam from London. He unpacked the damp clothes to dry them and unwittingly released some plague-infected fleas. Viccars was the first to die; other villagers soon fell victim. Led by its rector, William Mompesson, the village put itself into quarantine, sealing off all direct contact with the outside world until the disease had run its course. By the end of the following year over 300 people had died – well over half Eyam's population – but the plague had been confined within the boundaries of the village.

The Eyam Museum, where this walk begins, looks at the effects of the bubonic plague itself, which brought fever, vomiting and swollen lymph glands, and almost always killed. Beyond Eyam Hall, built for Thomas Wright six years after the disease had subsided, the route first leads past a huddle of 'plague cottages' bearing plaques to commemorate those who died there; then the church, where Mompesson's wife, Catherine, is buried. She succumbed at the height of the epidemic, though Mompesson himself survived.

As you leave Eyam along Lydgate, imagine how sharp the contrast must have been between the stagnant atmosphere of the village itself and the high, open countryside beyond it. The temptation to escape must have been overwhelming but under Mompesson's guidance the villagers stayed put. The boundary stone in the field ahead marked the edge of their world. In its six holes, money was placed to pay for food left here for the residents. It's a brief walk to the next village, Stoney Middleton, and a sobering reminder of how easily the plague could have reached the villagers.

In Stoney Middleton the route passes a small restored building, the Roman Baths, which was used as a curative spring in the Middle Ages; then it climbs the steep path that leads eventually to the Riley Graves. Within a small stone enclosure, a group of simple gravestones marks the devastation of one family: here, John Hancock and his six children were buried in the space of a week in August 1666. Mrs Hancock, the only survivor, had to drag their bodies up to this field.

Back in Eyam you skirt past a patch of ground by the Miners' Arms Croft, where many villagers were buried, before climbing to Mompesson's Well, a stone wash basin where medicines and supplies were delivered, and coins brought by the villagers in payment. Vinegar was added to the water in an attempt to disinfect the money.

Mompesson carried on conducting services throughout the ordeal, moving from the church to the open air, south of the village. Services are still held here every August to commemorate the heroism and self-sacrifice of the entire community.

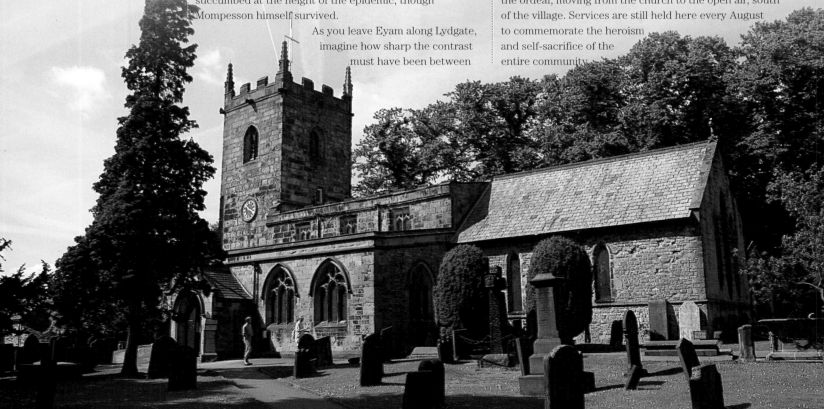

WALK
49

Eyam – Village of the Damned

A fascinating walk around the village which sacrificed
itself to save its neighbours from the plague

Distance: 5½ miles (9km)
Total ascent: 632 feet (193m)
Paths: mostly good; some parts narrow, rocky
Terrain: village roads, fields, woods, unsurfaced tracks
Gradients: very steep in parts
Refreshments: tea rooms and pubs in Eyam
Park: car park opposite Eyam Museum, Hawkshill Road, Eyam (west of Chesterfield, off A623)

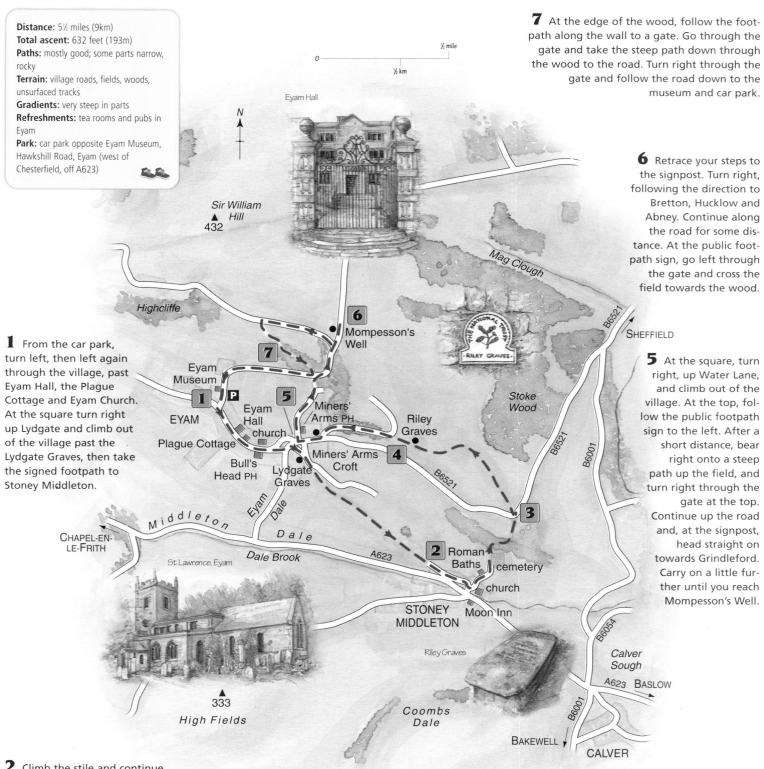

7 At the edge of the wood, follow the footpath along the wall to a gate. Go through the gate and take the steep path down through the wood to the road. Turn right through the gate and follow the road down to the museum and car park.

6 Retrace your steps to the signpost. Turn right, following the direction to Bretton, Hucklow and Abney. Continue along the road for some distance. At the public footpath sign, go left through the gate and cross the field towards the wood.

5 At the square, turn right, up Water Lane, and climb out of the village. At the top, follow the public footpath sign to the left. After a short distance, bear right onto a steep path up the field, and turn right through the gate at the top. Continue up the road and, at the signpost, head straight on towards Grindleford. Carry on a little further until you reach Mompesson's Well.

1 From the car park, turn left, then left again through the village, past Eyam Hall, the Plague Cottage and Eyam Church. At the square turn right up Lydgate and climb out of the village past the Lydgate Graves, then take the signed footpath to Stoney Middleton.

2 Climb the stile and continue along a single track road into Stoney Middleton, bearing left as you join the next road. Just before the stream, turn left towards the church. Follow the road past the Roman Baths and continue up the steep track that climbs out of the village past the cemetery.

3 At the top of the track, turn left, cross the road and pass through the narrow entrance by a gate. Follow the track alongside the stone wall. At the top corner of the field, by a trough, go through the gate ahead and continue climbing around to the right. At the top of a steep climb, turn left onto a farm track.

4 Beyond Riley Graves, continue ahead as you join the single track road that leads downhill through the trees. At the bottom, continue ahead into Eyam.

Packhorse Trails across the Peak

An easy moorland stroll crosses paths with some of the trails used by the indomitable jaggers of old

Top right: packhorses carry bread across the moors to London

When Celia Fiennes, the daughter of one of Oliver Cromwell's officers, rode side-saddle through the Peak District in 1697, she noted:

'All Derbyshire is full of steep hills, and nothing but the peakes of hills as thick one by another is seen in most of the County, which are very steepe, which makes travelling tedious and the miles long.'

Above: Longshaw Lodge, a former hunting lodge, is now a visitor centre

Following the old road from Chatsworth to Bakewell, Celia graphically described the difficulty of the route. She was an exceptionally brave and determined traveller, for at the time she passed through the Peak District, few ordinary visitors from the south would dare to venture across the moors, with or without a guide.

The exceptions were the packhorse jaggers – the men who led trains of up to 40 or 50 heavily laden animals between the major centres of production and commerce. They took their name from the sturdy Jaeger (hence jagger) – Galloway cross ponies which were their main beasts of burden. With basketwork panniers slung on either flank and jingling bells to announce their coming, the packhorse trains used well-worn and often paved routes to cross the 'howling wilderness' of the moors.

From the early Middle Ages to the 17th century, packhorses were often the only means of transporting merchandise across this difficult country. It is no exaggeration to say that they were the juggernauts of their time, and the packhorse routes the motorways.

Even up to the mid-19th century, trains of packhorses were still a common sight on the Peak District moors, and today names like Jaggers Lane and Jaggers Clough and various Hollow Ways or Hollow Gates – giving some idea of the heavy use of the routes – are still common. Modern ramblers can still follow many of these routes and find traces of the passing of the jaggers.

This easy walk on the eastern moors east of the River Derwent crosses a number of those ancient 'motorways', and passes several of the vital waymarks used by the jaggers to find their way when the mists descended on the barren moors, as they frequently do. It starts from Longshaw Lodge, a grand 19th-century shooting lodge built by the Duke of Rutland. The route passes Little John's Well, a spring named after Robin Hood's legendary colleague who is allegedly buried at nearby Hathersage; Froggatt Pole, an ancient waymark; Lady's Cross, a wayside cross which dates from the Middle Ages and is on the Hope–Chesterfield packhorse route known as Hollow Gate; and a conveniently situated wayside inn named after the ubiquitous game bird of the moors, The Grouse. If you are in this vicinity around midsummer, you can enjoy the ancient well-dressing ceremony in which the village of Hope is decked with floral tableaux.

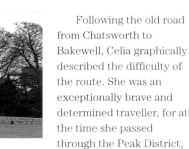

Right: sweeping views of the high open moorland from Lawrence Field on the Longshaw Estate

Packhorse Trails across the Peak

*In the footsteps of the Jaggers, whose packhorses carried
goods over the moors before the industrial revolution*

WALK 50

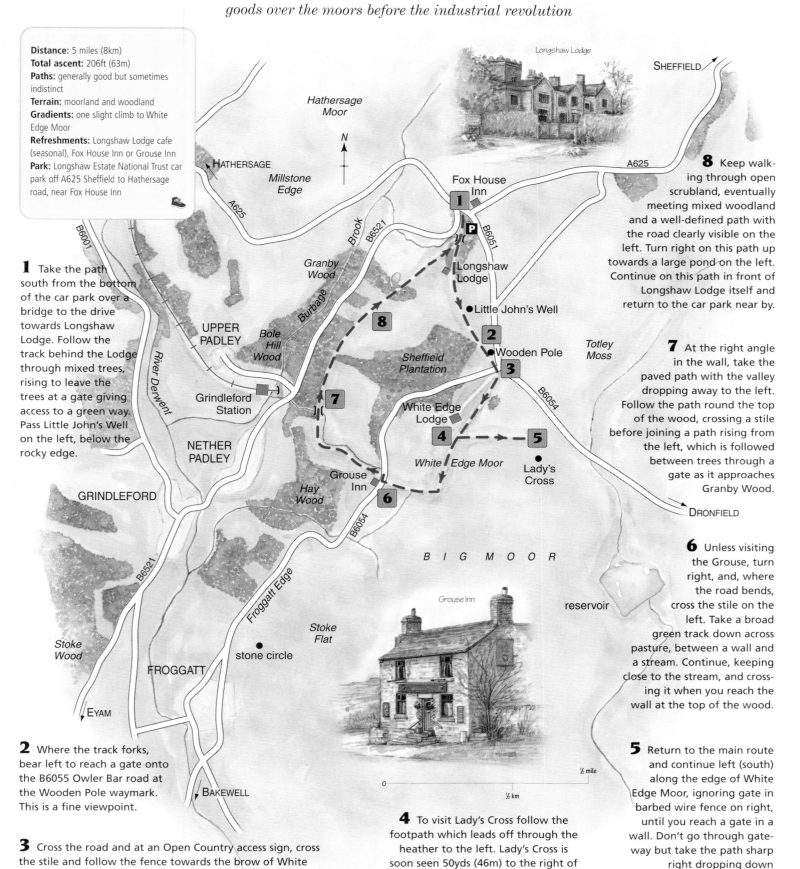

Longshaw Lodge

Distance: 5 miles (8km)
Total ascent: 206ft (63m)
Paths: generally good but sometimes indistinct
Terrain: moorland and woodland
Gradients: one slight climb to White Edge Moor
Refreshments: Longshaw Lodge cafe (seasonal), Fox House Inn or Grouse Inn
Park: Longshaw Estate National Trust car park off A625 Sheffield to Hathersage road, near Fox House Inn

1 Take the path south from the bottom of the car park over a bridge to the drive towards Longshaw Lodge. Follow the track behind the Lodge through mixed trees, rising to leave the trees at a gate giving access to a green way. Pass Little John's Well on the left, below the rocky edge.

8 Keep walking through open scrubland, eventually meeting mixed woodland and a well-defined path with the road clearly visible on the left. Turn right on this path up towards a large pond on the left. Continue on this path in front of Longshaw Lodge itself and return to the car park near by.

7 At the right angle in the wall, take the paved path with the valley dropping away to the left. Follow the path round the top of the wood, crossing a stile before joining a path rising from the left, which is followed between trees through a gate as it approaches Granby Wood.

6 Unless visiting the Grouse, turn right, and, where the road bends, cross the stile on the left. Take a broad green track down across pasture, between a wall and a stream. Continue, keeping close to the stream, and crossing it when you reach the wall at the top of the wood.

5 Return to the main route and continue left (south) along the edge of White Edge Moor, ignoring gate in barbed wire fence on right, until you reach a gate in a wall. Don't go through gateway but take the path sharp right dropping down through the heather to a bridleway, which you join and follow to reach the B6054 near the Grouse Inn.

Grouse Inn

2 Where the track forks, bear left to reach a gate onto the B6055 Owler Bar road at the Wooden Pole waymark. This is a fine viewpoint.

3 Cross the road and at an Open Country access sign, cross the stile and follow the fence towards the brow of White Edge Moor. Do not follow track on the right to White Edge Lodge. Pass above two small, windswept plantations, with White Edge Lodge beneath you to the right. The way rises to the highest point of the walk, at 1,273ft (388m).

4 To visit Lady's Cross follow the footpath which leads off through the heather to the left. Lady's Cross is soon seen 50yds (46m) to the right of the path. First mentioned in a document dated 1263, it was a guide cross on the Hope–Chesterfield and Sheffield–Tideswell routes.

Land of Legend, Lair of Outlaws

Join the hunt for Robin Hood in the ancient forest around the Saxon village of Edwinstowe

WALK 51

Top right: St Mary's Church at Edwinstowe has been woven into the legend of Robin Hood

Above: the Major Oak in Sherwood Forest Country Park

Inset below: an outdoor sculpture at the visitor centre

Below: Sherwood Forest

Robin Hood really did exist. He was a Yorkshireman who fell foul of the law in 1225 and pitted his wits against the Sheriff of Nottinghamshire, Eustace of Lowdham. Or he was Robert Fitzooth, rightful Earl of Huntingdon. Alternatively, there never was a Robin Hood at all. He's a character of the ballads and tales of the 14th and 15th centuries, drawn from a hotch-potch of folklore, religious allegory (representing the pagan Green Man) and several different lawbreakers – many of whom were given the surname Robinhood in court documents.

Whatever the truth of the matter, the legend of the outlaw and his hundred Merry Men, who lived in Sherwood Forest and robbed the rich to give to the poor, has been a favourite since it was first related in a 14th-century ballad called *A Lytell Geste of Robyn Hode*. The version that places their adventures in the 1190s, when King Richard the Lionheart was fighting at the Crusades, is the most enduring.

Sherwood Forest is today only a fraction of its size in the 12th century, when bandits could disappear into its 20-mile (32km) tangle. But the 450 acres (182ha) that now form Sherwood Forest Country Park still have an air of mystery: it's possible, especially on the first stretch of this walk, to imagine it as a vast, medieval no-go area. The path leads through beech and oak woods where, among the foliage, hollow 'stag-headed' oaks form sinister, twisted silhouettes. It soon reaches the Major Oak, now enmeshed in the Robin Hood legend as the outlaws' meeting place, though it was probably just a skinny sapling in those days. Today it is a sprawling giant of a tree, with a circumference of 33 ft (10m) and a 92-ft (28m) canopy, propped up with massive wooden beams. The name has nothing to do with its size, however: it recalls Major Hayman Rooke, who wrote a book about Nottinghamshire oaks in 1790.

As you reach the forest's western section it changes character: dark pines and holly trees line the trail, and views gradually open out across the fields to Edwinstowe. Before turning towards this village, the walk leads past an 1842 neo-Gothic folly, Archway House, built by the 4th Duke of Portland to span a turf bridleway. From the nearby road you can make out the craggy ruins of King John's hunting lodge on the horizon – all that remains of the royal palace. Sherwood Forest was the king's hunting ground: Robin's band constantly flouted the highest authorities by killing the royal deer.

As the walk turns back to the River Maun and into Edwinstowe it crosses land that was boggy before being drained in the 19th century. In the village is St Mary's, the 12th-century church where Robin is supposed to have married Maid Marian. There has been a church on the site since AD 633, when the Saxon king Edwin, after whom the village was named, was brought here to be buried.

Land of Legend, Lair of Outlaws

Robin Hood is believed to have roamed this lasting part of the great Sherwood Forest

1 From the visitor centre cafe, follow the waymarked path to Major Oak (not the path which goes through the complex and out the other side).

2 Go around the oak, following the path signed 'Visitor Centre 20 minutes', but turn almost immediately left onto the minor track.

3 After about 1 mile (1.6km), at a barrier and crossroads, turn left (before the Public Bridleway signs) on to a wide, straight route of red shingle. The path reaches the A6075 and swings right. Keep on the red path alongside the main road until it emerges on to it and you can cross safely. Take the tarmac path through the woods on the opposite side.

4 Beyond Archway House, cross the River Maun. Go under the railway bridge and turn right before the second bridge. Pass under another railway bridge (with signalbox) and follow this path to the end for a view of King John's Palace.

5 Retrace your steps to the river. Just beyond the bridge, turn right onto the waymarked track on the riverbank.

6 Continue to the Edwinstowe playing fields. Take the lower track (signed Public Bridleway) along the edge of the fields into the village.

7 Walk through the housing estate and along Sixth Avenue. Follow the road round to the left and turn right into Fourth Avenue. At the end, turn left and continue to the traffic lights; cross to St Mary's Church.

8 Leave the church by the Church Street gate (with steps, right). Continue up Church Street, out of the village. A footpath leads back to the visitor centre from the Sherwood Forest Country Park sign on the left.

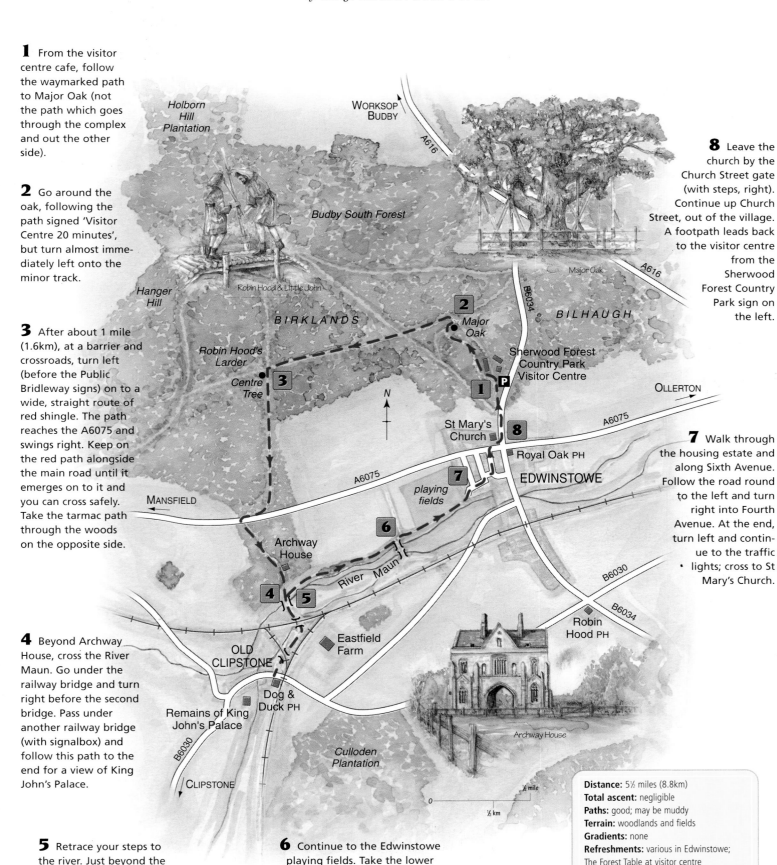

Distance: 5½ miles (8.8km)
Total ascent: negligible
Paths: good; may be muddy
Terrain: woodlands and fields
Gradients: none
Refreshments: various in Edwinstowe; The Forest Table at visitor centre
Park: Sherwood Forest Country Park visitor centre, on B6034, north of Edwinstowe

D H Lawrence's Nottinghamshire

WALK 52

A journey through the streets of Eastwood and the fields and forests beyond that inspired this controversial literary figure

Top right: home life evoked at the D H Lawrence Museum

Above: Moorgreen Reservoir features in *The White Peacock*

Below right: the streets of Eastwood were familiar territory to the young Lawrence

In the course of a relatively short and unsettled life, David Herbert Lawrence injected new vigour into English literature. Although his forthright descriptions of sex in books such as *The Rainbow* (1915) and *Lady Chatterley's Lover* (1928) caused outrage, the real impact of Lawrence's writing was in its direct and sensual accounts of working-class people and the natural world. He drew extensively on his own experiences: his early life as one of five children in a colliery town; his relationships with his father, a miner, and his schoolteacher mother; his passionate love of the surrounding countryside. This walk takes you through the landscapes of his life and imagination.

The route begins at Durban House Heritage Centre, built in 1876 as the colliery offices, where Lawrence would collect his father's wages. It's an uphill walk to Victoria Street, where Lawrence was born in 1885 at No 8a (now a museum), a terraced house with a large window where his mother, Lydia, would arrange baby clothes for sale. On Nottingham Road, the main shopping street, a plaque marks the site of the Congregational chapel where Lawrence met Jessie Chambers, the close friend who was reinvented as Miriam Leivers in *Sons and Lovers*. Walker Street leads past the Three Tuns pub (the Moon and Stars in the same novel) and swings right to present a view that to Lawrence was 'better than

any in the world'. His family moved to the row of houses on the right in 1891. It's unclear which was their home, as the numbering has changed, but the outlook is still dramatic: a wide sweep of valley towards Crich, Underwood, High Park Woods and Annesley. Turning back into town you'll reach 97 Lynncroft, a semi-detached house that marked a step up the social ladder for the Lawrences in 1905, though Lawrence described it in *Sons and Lovers* as 'old and grimy'.

As you leave Eastwood you'll pass the school where Lawrence was an unhappy pupil from 1893 to 1898, and the cottage which was the original Ram Inn and featured in his first novel, *The White Peacock* (1911). Beyond Moorgreen the route climbs towards High Park Woods (to the left, among farm buildings, are the 14th-century ruins of Beauvale Priory). From the woodlands it emerges into open, undulating countryside. In the distance ahead was Haggs Farm, the home of Jessie Chambers, where Lawrence first had the impulse to write.

Out of the woods you'll cross the old mill race to Felley Mill Farm – Stelley Mill in *The White Peacock* – and then look out over Moorgreen Reservoir, which Lawrence turned into Wiley Water. The 18th-century manor, Lamb Close House, across the lake, may have been the partial inspiration for Wragby Hall, Lady Chatterley's home.

Before his premature death of tuberculosis in 1930, Lawrence travelled all over the world, but he never forgot the Nottinghamshire countryside. This trail past the haunts of his youth makes it easy to see why.

DH Lawrence's Nottinghamshire

Tracing the characters and places of Lawrence's once controversial writing in Eastwood and its surrounding countryside

1 From Durban House turn left up Mansfield Road, then left into Princes Street. Take the first right along Victoria Street.

2 Turn left onto Nottingham Road. Opposite the war memorial turn left up Walker Street and follow it round. Take the third right onto Lynncroft. At the end turn left onto Dovecote Road and continue into Moorgreen.

3 At the Horse & Groom pub turn right, then first left up New Road.

4 Follow New Road (tarmacked) for about 1¼ miles (2km) before turning left at the public footpath sign to Hucknall, Annesley and Underwood. The track swings left, running parallel with the M1, passing a sign for the footbridge over the motorway. Eventually it leads you into the woods. At the next junction turn right to continue alongside the motorway.

near Eastwood

DH Lawrence Museum

8 At the exit, turn left (Engine Lane); this long road eventually becomes Greenhills Road and leads back to Durban House.

7 Turn left towards Moorgreen (B600). Turn right at the entrance to Collier's Wood and take the left-hand path back into Eastwood.

SHEFFIELD

FRIEZELAND

UNDERWOOD

HOBSICK

Willey Spring

Felley Mill Farm

High Park Wood

Morning Springs

Moorgreen Reservoir

Beauvale Lodge

Collier's Wood

Horse & Groom PH

Watnall Copice

Durban House

D H Lawrence Birthplace Museum

EASTWOOD

Ram Inn

Pear Tree Farm

MOORGREEN

GREASLEY

N

war memorial

NEW EASTWOOD

GILTBROOK

Nottinghamshire landscape

KIMBERLEY

HUCKNALL

NOTTINGHAM

Distance: 8¼ miles (13km)
Total ascent: 230ft (70m)
Paths: mostly good. Some shallow steps; one stile; some tracks narrow and unsurfaced, and can be muddy, especially in woods
Terrain: urban, woodland, fields
Gradients: gradual
Refreshments: Restaurant in Durban House; cafés in Eastwood; Horse & Groom pub in Moorgreen
Park: at Durban House, Mansfield Road, Eastwood

½ mile
0
½ km

NOTTINGHAM

6 Cross the stream by the little concrete bridge and enter the woods on the right. Take the track which runs parallel with the stream, leading eventually to a wider track (with a wooden fence). Moorgreen Reservoir will come into view on the right. Eventually this track leads onto a tarmac road, emerging at Beauvale Lodge.

5 At the next junction, follow the Public Footpath sign ahead to the edge of the wood, then turn left. After descending the hill, at the surfaced track, turn left to the site of Felley Mill Farm.

The Battle of Bosworth Field

A pivotal battle in the Wars of the Roses is brought to life in this peaceful, rolling landscape

Top right: a re-enactment brings the battlefield to life

Above: Richard III was cut down from his horse and killed in the battle

Below: a memorial on the battlefield

On 7 August 1485 a small army landed on the Pembrokeshire coast and began a fortnight's march through Wales. At its head was Henry Tudor, Earl of Richmond and sole surviving Lancastrian claimant to the throne. For over 80 years the houses of York and Lancaster had conducted a vicious tug-of-war over the crown. Henry's claim was through his Welsh grandfather, Owen Tudor, who had married Henry V's widow, Catherine. Now, after 14 years' exile, Henry was ready to stake that claim. It was a dangerous venture: his allies were cautious and noncommital; the reigning king, Richard III, was a clever and ruthless politician and an experienced soldier, with 12,000 troops. When Henry camped at Whitemoors on the eve of battle, he had fewer than 5,000.

The armies faced each other on 22 August. From Ambion Wood you can see Richard's standard, the white boar, fluttering over the high ground where his men were drawn up. Below was the Tudor force. The woodland was then an extensive marsh, which hemmed both armies in. The trail leads past a stone cairn, built in 1813 to mark the spring where Richard drank before fighting, and along the position occupied by his archers, infantry and mounted knights, under the Duke of Norfolk's command. To the north, towards Market Bosworth, the mighty Stanley family waited with their 5,000

troops. Henry hoped for their support but had no guarantee: Richard, fearing their treachery, had taken Thomas Lord Stanley's son hostage.

Richard's army fired a volley of cannonballs and arrows. Then Norfolk led a headlong charge downhill. The Earl of Oxford, in command of the central Tudor lines, had his standards planted in the earth and ordered his men not to budge further than 10 paces away. His soldiers held fast and Norfolk retreated to regroup. In the desperate hand-to-hand fighting that followed, Norfolk himself was cut down.

The trail now swoops downhill, giving a clear view of rolling countryside. From this vantage point, Richard watched as Henry, desperate for the Stanleys' help, galloped towards their ranks with a bodyguard of 70 men. Seeing his rival so exposed, Richard himself led a thundering cavalry charge at them, heads down and lances braced. The speed and momentum of the attack carried both parties across open ground to the place now called King Richard's Field. Now the Stanleys finally swung into action, coming to Henry's aid, and Richard, knocked from his mount, was hacked to death at the spot marked by a stone memorial.

The path loops away from the battle scene, passing Henry's camp at Whitemoors and eventually returning along the Tudor front lines. As you return towards the visitor centre, look to the right: after hearing of Richard's death, his army fled across this plain, pursued as far as Stoke Golding. There Henry VII was crowned with the retrieved royal diadem, and the first Tudor reign began.

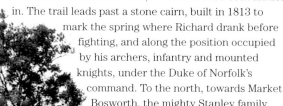

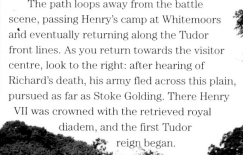

The Battle of Bosworth Field

*The dramatic scene of Richard III's death is brought
alive by this walk through the Bosworth battlefield*

1 From the car park
entrance, turn right to cross
the canal bridge; go down
the steps (right) and follow
the Ashby Canal footpath,
straight ahead.

8 Just before the visitor centre,
turn right and take the path
signed to the Marsh and Sutton
Cheney Wharf. This leads
across the field, through the
woods and along the canal
to the car park.

7 Turn into Shenton
Station, cross the railway
and turn right, following
the sign to Ambion
Wood and back to King
Richard's Well. At the
well, go through the
gate again, but now go
straight ahead.

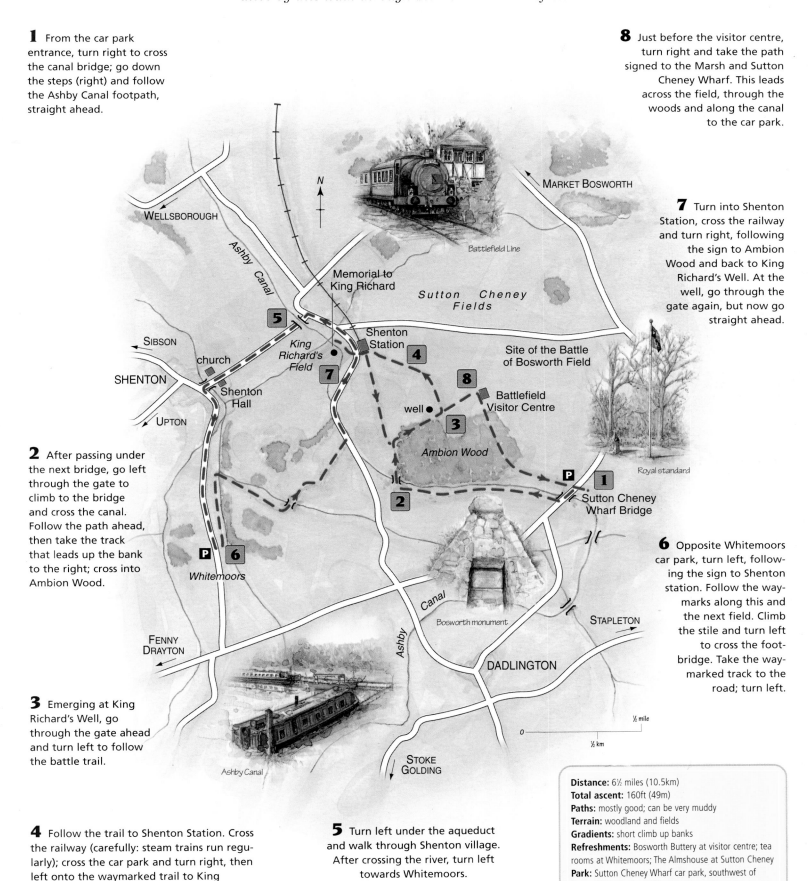

2 After passing under
the next bridge, go left
through the gate to
climb to the bridge
and cross the canal.
Follow the path ahead,
then take the track
that leads up the bank
to the right; cross into
Ambion Wood.

6 Opposite Whitemoors
car park, turn left, following the sign to Shenton
station. Follow the way-
marks along this and
the next field. Climb
the stile and turn left
to cross the foot-
bridge. Take the way-
marked track to the
road; turn left.

3 Emerging at King
Richard's Well, go
through the gate ahead
and turn left to follow
the battle trail.

4 Follow the trail to Shenton Station. Cross
the railway (carefully: steam trains run regularly); cross the car park and turn right, then
left onto the waymarked trail to King
Richard's Field. Return to the road and continue towards Shenton.

5 Turn left under the aqueduct
and walk through Shenton village.
After crossing the river, turn left
towards Whitemoors.

Distance: 6½ miles (10.5km)
Total ascent: 160ft (49m)
Paths: mostly good; can be very muddy
Terrain: woodland and fields
Gradients: short climb up banks
Refreshments: Bosworth Buttery at visitor centre; tea
rooms at Whitemoors; The Almshouse at Sutton Cheney
Park: Sutton Cheney Wharf car park, southwest of
Sutton Cheney along Wharf Lane

A Woodland Walk in Charnwood Forest

A country park and farm trail illustrate the varied countryside and farming practices of a fascinating corner of Leicestershire

WALK 54

Right: a shady path through the woods

Above: heather flourishes in the forest

Below: there are panoramic views in all directions from the viewpoint on Beacon Hill

Geologically, Charnwood Forest is one of the oldest places in Britain, an area of Precambrian rock from the earliest era of geological history – surrounded by much younger strata. This ancient rock does not support good soil, so the rugged little hills exhibit a farming pattern different from the rest of Leicestershire. Instead of arable acres, the grazing of cattle and sheep are more common. Some parts are too rugged for any type of cultivation and have been allowed to develop wild woodlands and slopes of bracken and brambles – the sorts of places children love to explore.

Bronze Age settlers cleared Beacon Hill 4,000 years ago and built ramparts of earth and stone around the summit. As the woods were cut back, a flowery heath developed. This is actively managed to keep it clear of bracken and shrubs so that heather, tormentil, sheep sorrel and other wild flowers can flourish. The trees around Beacon Hill are secondary plantings, though some invasive tree scrub has become well established. An interesting native tree collection has been planted on the lower slopes. There are 28 trees native to Britain and they are all on this walk, as well as a range of ornamental species. Informative notice boards provide interesting insights into their growth and the habitats they support.

At nearby Broombriggs, a traditional farm is equipped with a waymarked farm trail. The higher parts of the farm are used for grazing, while the lower fields are ploughed and feature continual crop rotation. While there is no access to the actual farm buildings, you can walk through almost every field and read a series of notices that explain how the farm is managed. The trail offers an insight into the methods used to farm what is really a rather difficult area to cultivate. In fact, as recently as the 1940s farms such as Broombriggs were considered suitable only for

grazing. Now the farm can produce crops of wheat, barley, oats and oilseed rape. Quite apart from the rich woodlands, fields and flowers in this part of Charnwood Forest, a variety of birds can be spotted. A hundred bird boxes have been nailed to trees and are used mostly by blue tits and great tits. Spotted flycatchers and nuthatches are also common, along with stock doves, robins, swallows, blackbirds and woodpeckers. Leicestershire is a notable fox-hunting county, so foxes learn to keep a low profile in woods close to farms.

Between Beacon Hill and Broombriggs you can enjoy a fine walk in varied countryside. While enjoying the living world all around, bear in mind that Britain's oldest fossil was found in Charnwood Forest. A schoolboy discovered the worm-like *Charnia masoni* 700 million years after it enjoyed its brief life here.

A Woodland Walk in Charnwood Forest

A Leicestershire country park preserves many fascinating pockets of a vanishing landscape

Distance: 5 miles (8km)
Total ascent: 655ft (200m)
Paths: firm paths on Beacon Hill but can be muddy around Broombriggs
Terrain: woodland, heathland, fields and farmland
Gradients: gradual
Refreshments: a variety of pubs and restaurants at Woodhouse Eaves
Park: Broombriggs car park on B591 Beacon Road above Woodhouse Eaves

6 The farm trail turns left, away from Woodhouse Eaves, passing through a couple of fields. Take the path on the right, rising towards Windmill Hill. When a path junction is reached at the top of the field, turn left. This will lead you down through fields to return to the car park.

1 From the car park, cross Beacon Road, walk uphill a few paces and turn right into Beacon Hill Country Park. A woodland path climbs up to join a broad, clear path. Turn left on this path, passing tall oak, beech and birch trees. Open heath is reached, which is being cleared of bracken and scrub.

2 Keep straight on, climbing gradually, while off to the left is a car park with toilets. To the right is the bare summit of Beacon Hill. Climb over grass and rocks to reach a trig point and an old AA toposcope.

3 Continue along the path, curving right as it descends. Banks of bilberry precede denser woods. When a gateway and car park are reached at the bottom, detour left to look at the Native Tree Collection, returning to the car park later. To continue the walk, exit from the car park near the toilets and follow a path uphill signposted for Broombriggs. Cross the road to return to the Broombriggs car park.

4 Broombriggs Farm Trail is marked with yellow rectangles, with separate paths for walkers and horseriders. Cross a stile and walk up through fields, parallel to Beacon Road, to enter Bluebell Wood. When the farm access road is reached, turn left, then turn right to pick up the next section of the trail. A broad, grassy strip has been fenced off and this climbs above the Hall Field to reach the Trust Field. This is the highest part of the farm and there are good views westwards.

5 Follow field boundaries, passing through gates and crossing several stiles. As the trail descends it turns left and runs to the right of Long Stye Wood. Notice boards along the way explain about farming at Broombriggs, with further reference to the surrounding countryside. There is an option to turn right at the bottom of the wood and detour into Woodhouse Eaves, if desired.

Map labels:
SHEPSHED
B5330
Beacon Hill
Beacon Hill
3 245 ▲●
toposcope
Native Tree Trail
Country
Beacon Plantation
Park
B591
Out Woods
Ye Olde Bulls Head
golf course
Beaumanor Hall Conference Centre
Beaumanor Park
WOODHOUSE
Quorndon
Ye Olde Bulls Head PH
old windmill
WOODHOUSE EAVES
Pear Tree PH
Curzon Arms PH
MOUNTSORREL
Broombriggs Hill
Broombriggs Farm
Bluebell Wood
Long Stye Wood
Broombriggs Farm Trail
Green Hill
on Beacon Hill
Benscliffe Wood
B5330
½ mile
½ km
N
0

stile in Charnwood Forest

The New Model Army at Naseby

In the fields of Northamptonshire a battle raged whose outcome would lay the foundations for parliamentary democracy in Britain

Top right: Charles I was defeated at Naseby by Cromwell's troops

Right: a monument marks the battle of June 1645

Of all Britain's great battlefields, Naseby must be the quietest. A slender stone monument marks the spot, otherwise you could be anywhere. It was civil war, the most shameful type of war any nation can endure, setting families, friends and neighbours against each other. Painful to remember, yet best not forgotten for the salutary lessons to be drawn from it.

Naseby is a quiet little village of some antiquity, having gained a market charter from King John as early as 1203. When King Charles I faced Parliament's New Model Army near by in 1645, no doubt normal life was suspended. An obelisk near the village on the Market Harborough road stands in memory of the Civil War, but away from where the action took place. A smaller monument stands on the actual battlefield, on the Parliamentarian side, facing 'all the King's horses and all the King's men'.

At 9am on Saturday 14th June 1645 some 9,000 men on the Royalist side were ranged against 13,500 in the New Model Army on Parliament's side. Prince Rupert, the King's nephew and a seasoned warmonger, led the first charge, uphill and against heavy fire, yet he devastated the western wing of the New Model Army. Cromwell, on the eastern side, led a similarly devastating charge against the Royalists. In the middle it was hand-to-hand fighting with the additional use of fearsome 16-foot (5m) pikes.

It could have gone either way. The Royalists had the upper hand at the beginning, but Prince Rupert made two mistakes. One was to chase fleeing soldiers off the field; and the other was to waste precious time attacking Parliament's baggage train near Naseby. By the time he was back on the main battlefield, the Royalists were almost defeated, leaving their own baggage train to be plundered. The King fled northwards, with the trained soldiers of the

New Model Army in hot pursuit, leaving a trail of bodies most of the way to Leicester. The Cromwellian victory sealed the fate of King Charles and heralded a new era of British government.

This walk takes you through the thick of the battle, from Naseby to Sibbertoft. At a strategic viewpoint you can try to re-create the scene, and wonder what chance you would have stood on the day. After leaving Sibbertoft, put yourself in the position of a villager trying to get across country without getting involved in the battle and imagine your fear as the battle suddenly shifts westwards towards Sulby.

There is an information board on the battlefield, and if further assistance is needed to appreciate the event, then visit the Naseby Battle and Farm Museum before the walk, out on the Cottesbrooke road. There you will find layouts of the battleground and various local relics. And if you are very lucky, you may be able to witness one of the battle re-enactments that periodically take place.

Below: a contemporary depiction of the battle lines

The New Model Army at Naseby

Across the battle site where Cromwell led his soldiers to change the course of British history

WALK 55

1 From the car park, walk into Naseby village to All Saints' Church and the Fitzgerald Arms. Follow the road signposted Sibbertoft, leaving the village and heading downhill. Turn right and follow a minor road, rising over a busy main road, crossing over Mill Hill and several gentle humps.

2 On the left is a stone monument, overlooking the countryside; an information board sketches out the salient points of the battle. You are now standing in Parliament's front line, facing the King's men on Dust Hill opposite.

3 Continue along the minor road, rising over Dust Hill, so that you can turn around and see things from the Royalists' point of view. When a road junction is reached, Sibbertoft is signposted to the left.

4 A bridleway is signposted at a gateway just to the left of the junction. If the fields have just been ploughed, then note that the signpost points exactly to the crucial gap in a hedge giving access to the next field. At that point, a gateway can be seen leading onto the next road. Turn left to walk into Sibbertoft.

5 To continue the walk, turn left without actually entering Sibbertoft, then left again following the signpost for Naseby. When this road suddenly bends left, walk straight on along another signposted bridleway, and turn right to follow a track past a brick building. The track runs alongside hedgerows bounding fields, so it twists left and right as it proceeds. When a junction of tracks is reached, turn right.

6 The track loses its firm surface and can be muddy. When a gate is reached on the left, go through it, then head off to the right to find a small gate leading into a woodland. There is a muddy track through the wood. When the track leaves the wood, it rises to a quiet minor road.

7. Turn left to follow the road back towards Naseby where the spire of All Saints' Church can be seen. There is a dip in the road, then later it rises over the main road and back into the village. Naseby Obelisk is in sight from the car park, and is easily visited by anyone wanting a short extension to the walk.

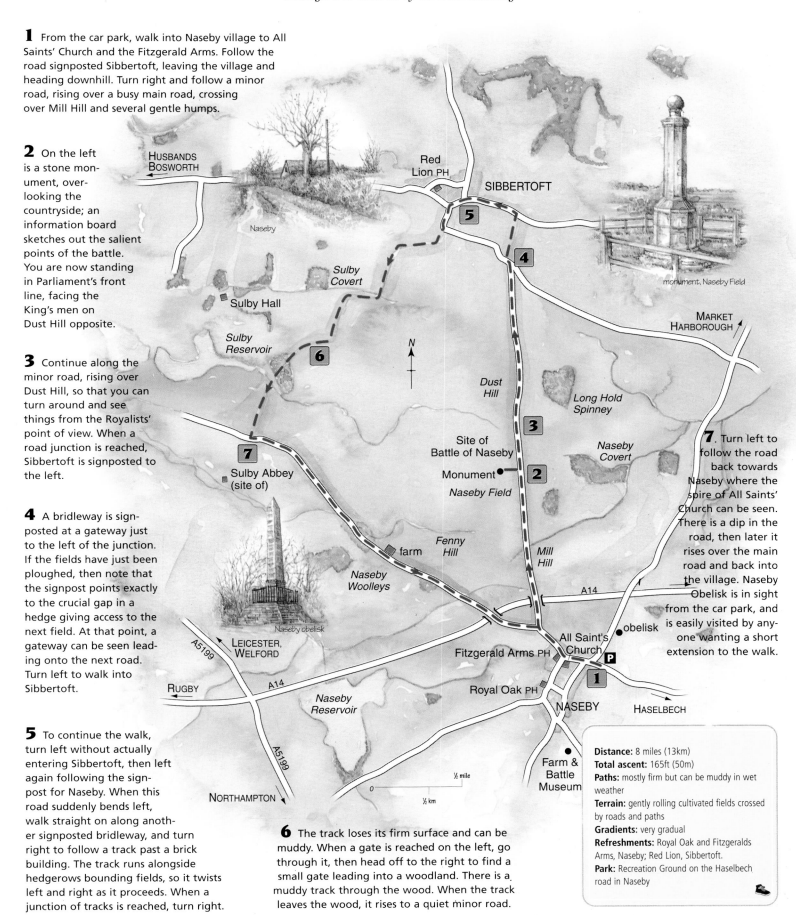

monument, Naseby Field

Naseby obelisk

Distance: 8 miles (13km)
Total ascent: 165ft (50m)
Paths: mostly firm but can be muddy in wet weather
Terrain: gently rolling cultivated fields crossed by roads and paths
Gradients: very gradual
Refreshments: Royal Oak and Fitzgeralds Arms, Naseby; Red Lion, Sibbertoft.
Park: Recreation Ground on the Haselbech road in Naseby

The Edge of the Wolds

Exploring Snipe Dales Country Park and Nature Reserve

WALK
56

Tucked in among the flatlands of the East Anglian Fens is a 40-mile (65km) patch of entirely different country. The Lincolnshire Wolds are a place of rounded hills, wooded valleys and small, scattered villages with long histories. One of these villages, Winceby, witnessed an important clash during the Civil War when Oliver Cromwell, then only an ambitious commander, defeated the Royalists at Slash Hollow. Today it is a quiet place which, along with Lusby and Hagworthingham, sits on the edge of Snipe Dales, a 220-acre (90ha) stretch of valleys, woods and streams maintained as a country park and nature reserve.

This walk begins at Lusby and plunges immediately into woodland, where broad-leaved trees – oak, lime, hornbeam and ash – are gradually replacing the pines. Climbing out of the wood, you emerge into open meadowland, with glorious views of the gentle Wolds landscape. Here the route coincides with the Bolingbroke Way, the footpath linking Winceby and Old Bolingbroke, to the south – birthplace of Henry IV and the site of a castle (now gone) held by his father, John of Gaunt. You pass briefly through Furze Hill Nature Reserve, where peacock, painted lady, holly blue and small tortoiseshell butterflies feed on the thistles and brambles; a beck twists through the reserve and the remains of an old water mill lurk in the undergrowth. The whole Snipe Dales area, with its soft Spilsby sandstone, is cut through with streams: this is one of the country's few surviving semi-natural wet valley systems. As you head towards Hagworthingham, look out for treecreepers, whitethroat, linnets and even owls.

Above: a small tortoiseshell butterfly feeding

Top right: a stream winds its way through the nature reserve

Below: the route climbs to high, rolling fields

From Hagworthingham the route climbs to a series of high, undulating fields along soft, sandy ground. To the left you can look down over the dark woods of the country park, before eventually taking the track back into them.

To your right as you return into the park is Periwinkle Wood, an area of oak, beech, ash, larch and Scots and Corsican pine, planted as recently as 1974. But here, too, the pine and larch now give way to the broad-leaved trees.

The trail leads across marshland and grassland, at one stage passing the metal cover of a water ram. This underground pump drives water to the farm on the hill ahead, using the water's energy. Its regular thump can be heard clearly from under the cover.

As you turn back towards the car park you can see areas ahead and to your right of unmanaged coarse (tall) grasses. The traditional method of cropping grass – using cows and sheep – has been reintroduced in parts of the park: the sheep nibble closely, avoiding the tough tussocks of coarse grass, which are duly tackled by the cattle.

The final stretch takes you back through the woods. Here, in the nesting season, visiting birds can include willow warblers, blackcaps, chaffinches, redpoll, blue, great and coal tits, treecreepers, goldcrests, wrens and great spotted woodpeckers. Owls, sparrowhawks and kestrels have also been seen making the most of this fascinating pocket of Lincolnshire countryside.

The Edge of the Wolds

*Rising from the flatlands, the Lincolnshire Wolds at
Snipe Dales conceal a rich variety of wildlife*

WALK 56

1 Follow Forest Trail (green fir tree symbol) and
Snipe Dales Round (red square symbol) signs to
right of main noticeboard at bottom of car park.
Route emerges from trees at flight of steps.
Continue downhill to footbridge across stream
with pond to left. Cross bridge and follow
Snipe Dales Round right along hardcore
path, now also part of Bolingbroke
Way (signposted).

Distance: 5 miles (8km)
Total Ascent: 170 feet (51m)
Paths: mostly unsurfaced; can be very
waterlogged and muddy
Terrain: woodland, grassland, fields,
village streets
Gradients: gradual
Refreshments: none
Park: Snipe Dales Country Park car park,
west of Lusby on B1195

2 After about
½ mile (800m), path
reaches another pond.
Follow Bolingbroke Way
right, skirting pond and
crossing stile. Turn immediately right up around edge
of field. At top, turn left to
follow field boundary to
end of field. Climb stile and
carry on alongside Winceby
Beck (left) to minor road.

7 After another ¼
mile (400m) reach water
ram (pump) with informa-
tion board. Continue up
path towards head of valley.
After 200yds (182m), turn sharp
left, following red squares along
oppposite bank of Winceby Beck.
Turn right up two flights of
steps to leave Nature Reserve
and re-enter woods of
Country Park. Follow
path straight ahead,
winding down to
stream. Cross by
footbridge and
ascend steeply
back to car park.

3 Cross into Furze Hill
Nature Reserve, almost
directly opposite. Once over
stile, cross footbridge, 50yds
(46m) away. Climb up field,
over three stiles to gravel
drive. Follow this left
towards Hagworthingham.
After about 80yds (75m)
drive meets road with red
brick cottages straight
ahead.

6 Head for footpath
marker, seen ahead (slightly
left) at edge of small copse. Go
through copse, over stream and
down, across field beyond to another
footbridge. On other side climb across
small field to stile. Beyond, rejoin Snipe
Dales Round. Turn right and follow red
square symbols. After 250yds (228m), go
to left of information board and follow
path downhill towards Winceby Beck. Turn
right at stream and continue up valley.
Ignore path over bridge after 400yds
(364m) and carry on along the stream side.

4 Turn left and follow road through edge of village to road
back to Lusby. Turn left and head out of village for 100yds
(91m), where stile leads to footpath to right of Crofters
Cottage. Follow narrow, green belt between two houses to
another stile, then go straight ahead across several fields.

5 Path heads down after third field turning, first sharply
right, then left, before entering an open field. Cross footbridge at far edge of field and continue straight ahead to
stile. Cross this and another stile, heading straight ahead
then bearing left to top of rise in field.

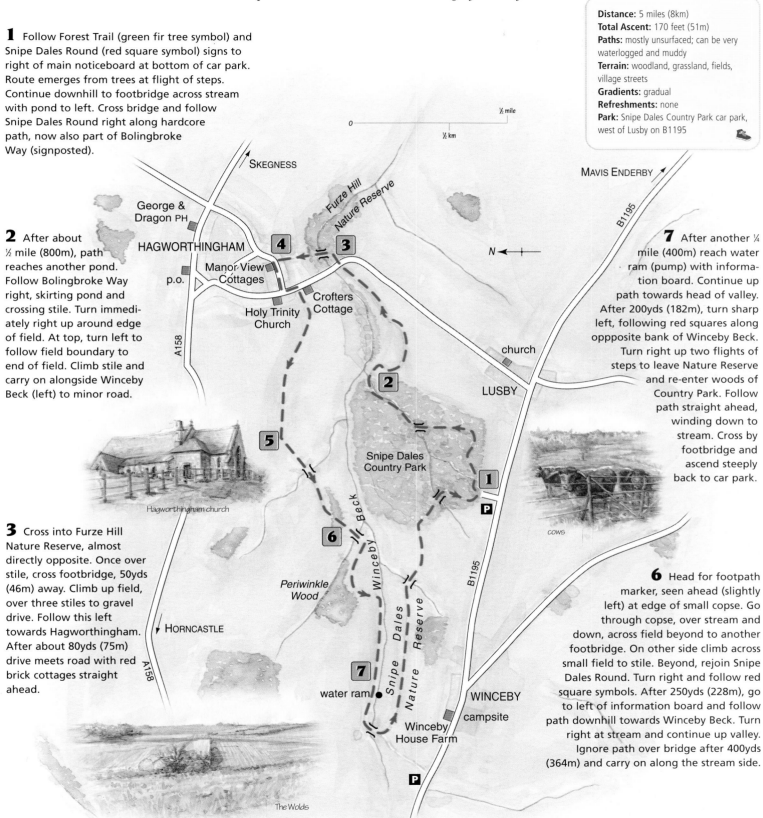

½ mile
0
½ km

SKEGNESS

George &
Dragon PH

HAGWORTHINGHAM

Manor View
Cottages

p.o.

Holy Trinity
Church

A158

Furze Hill
Nature Reserve

4

3

Crofters
Cottage

2

Snipe Dales
Country Park

Periwinkle
Wood

5

6

Beck

Winceby

7

water ram

The Wolds

HORNCASTLE

A158

Hagworthingham church

Snipe Dales Nature Reserve

Winceby
House Farm

N

MAVIS ENDERBY

B1195

church

LUSBY

1

P

B1195

cows

WINCEBY

campsite

P

Huge Skyscapes above the Wash

The salt marshes and sea-defences of this often-overlooked area offer excellent walking and bird life

WALK 57

The area east of Boston is one of the neglected corners of England. Here are no great houses, no bustling holiday resorts, no hills to climb, no tourist honeypots. The A52 on its way to Wainfleet is one of England's least straight main roads. All is quietness, with just the noise of birds on the marshes, the often scything wind and the inevitable hum of the pumping stations as they battle with the land's wish to go back to the element from which it was won.

It is this struggle to gain land from the clutches of the sea that is at the heart of this walk. You begin by following the most recent of the sea defences, a bank erected in the 1960s by the inhabitants of North Sea Camp just to the south-west of Freiston Shore, now a prison – which is why the signs at the start of the walk have been put up by the Home Office.

The land behind this bank is farmed by the prisoners, though there have been suggestions that it should be returned to the sea by flooding, so that the natural plant, insect and bird life can recolonise it. On the seaward side of the bank are miles of sea marshes and mud, channelled by inlets. This is a treacherous coastline where the tides rush in and the sands shift with surprising speed. King John found this out in 1216, when the royal treasure was lost as his entourage was caught by the tide as it crossed the Wash.

Notice that this earlier part of the bank has steep seaward slopes that have had to be reinforced. Further along, the slightly earlier bank, built by the local drainage board, has much shallower seaward slopes, better able to withstand the sea's tendency to undermine the structure.

Inland, the second bank is part of the great draining of the Fens that took place in the 17th and 18th centuries. Widely spaced, straight drainage ditches are scored across the land, and the pumping stations are the latest manifestations of various mechanical means by which the water was kept at bay. As the land was enclosed, the salt marsh changed to fresh-water marsh and eventually was drained enough to let the farmers and market gardeners move on to the fertile earth.

When you reach the innermost sea bank you will find something very different. Instead of progressing in straight lines or by gentle curves, you will find angles and sharp curves, while the bank itself here is generally not very high. Designated 'Roman Bank' on old maps, it is more likely that this has its origins with the Anglo-Saxons. Each local community would have been responsible for its own section of bank – and the lack of an overall plan accounts for the odd junctions and angles as the separate sections were joined up.

Behind this bank the drainage ditches are narrowly spaced and tangled around the villages. And dominating the vista from this stretch of the bank you will see the Stump – the 288-ft (88m) tower of Boston church – and the huge and sailing skies.

Above: the irrigation channel behind the sea wall

Below: the bank at Freiston Shore forms part of sea-defences which have been erected over the centuries

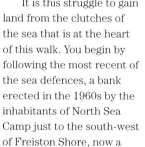

Huge Skyscapes above the Wash

*The wind and tide add drama to an otherwise
empty landscape*

1 From parking space follow path signed Freiston Shore Marsh, passing through metal gate and crossing up and over inner sea bank. Follow path to left (Prison road signed right), then curve right almost immediately to go straight on towards outer sea bank. About ½ mile (800m) further on, just before pumping station, go right through 2 metal gates and onto outer sea bank. Follow bank to left.

2 After 2 miles (3.2km) turn right by another pumping station, leaving outer sea wall, to follow path alongside drainage ditch for ¼ mile (400m) to inner sea bank. Ignore private farm road parallel to bank and climb stile onto inner sea bank, following it right for 1½ miles (2.4km), passing several pill boxes and crossing 3 stiles.

3 At another brick pumping station and red stone tablet in middle of bank, turn left down track leading away from pumping station, with wide drainage ditch on right.

7 Follow bank for 1 mile (1.6km) before route turns sharp left, then straight ahead to emerge onto another minor road. Turn right and walk towards distant houses. At T-junction turn left back towards parking area.

6 Bank emerges onto minor road opposite white house called Chimnies. Path continues to right of house, then into open ground with farmland below bank right and left. Inner bank clearly visible to left. In distance, right, the Stump of Boston's St Botolph's Church can be seen on a clear day.

5 Stick to overgrown path as it passes buildings for short distance to road by pond on right. Turn right onto road, then almost immediately left as bank continues. Walk on road, with crest of bank to right. When road swings right, bisecting bank, clamber through woodland to left. Avenue of trees along top of bank persists, with arrows carved in some trees at intervals. After ¾ mile (1.2km), path takes sharp left turn and heads almost directly back towards second pumping station. However, after 120yds (109m) turn sharply right to continue in former direction for another ¾ mile (1.2km).

4 In ½ mile (800m) continue down track 150yds (136m) beyond farm buildings on left to third, much older sea bank. As track cuts through bank, climb stile to left onto bank and go along crest. Natural avenue of trees marks route, crossing tracks as they cut through it. Eventually, after ¾ mile (1.2km), route springs out from trees into open land. Follow bank to farm visible in Benington Sea End, about ½ mile (800m) ahead.

Distance: 8 miles (12.9km)
Total ascent: negligible
Paths: generally clear; some may be overgrown and muddy
Terrain: sea banks overlooking sea marshes and farmland
Gradients: some short steps up banks
Refreshments: none
Park: by the telephone kiosk in Freiston Shore

Map labels:

SKEGNESS
SIBSEY
A52
sea bank
HURN'S END
HILL DYKE
LEVERTON
LUCASGATE
Roman Bank
Admiral Nelson PH
BENINGTON
A52
BENINGTON SEA END
BOSTON
BUTTERWICK
farm
BRAND END
Five Bells PH
Chimnies
FREISTON
TAMWORTH GREEN
SCRANE END
Freiston Low
pumping station
farm buildings
memorial stone
pumping station
THE WASH
Butterwick Low
pumping station
Roman Bank
½ mile
½ km
N

Northern England

Northern England

Bounded east and west by the North Sea and the Irish Sea respectively, and along its northern frontier by the Anglo-Scottish border, the north of England possesses landscapes that are breathtakingly beautiful, exciting, wild and desolate.

Previous page: the lush green slopes of the Newlands Valley

Bottom: the River Duddon, near Dale Head, Cumbria

Below: the remarkable Brontë sisters put Haworth on the map

Here there are rugged heights, delectable dales, invigorating coastal margins, windswept moorlands, rivers, lakes, forests, towns, villages, folklore, wildlife, history, intrigue and mystery in great abundance.

For many years the North was portrayed as a place of grime, poverty, urban deprivation, pollution, massive conurbations and coal mines. And though this imagery undoubtedly had its time and place, it only related to a small part, mostly confined to the industrial heartlands of Lancashire and Yorkshire. Beyond that lay, and still lies, a dazzling display of beautiful scenery, historically well endowed and geographically unique, that includes some of the best in Britain.

At the northern edge stands Hadrian's Wall, the greatest extant example of Roman determination in Britain, the main part of which was built between AD 122 and AD 126, *'qui barbaros Romanosque divideret'* – to separate the Romans from the barbarians. With but a brief break to try out the more northerly Antonine Wall, Hadrian's monument, now a World Heritage Site, remained occupied until AD 383, by which time the Romans were withdrawing from Britain.

Everywhere is at peace now but, long after the Romans had gone, the lands of the north were a violent and troubled place, where rustlers, outlaws and gangsters from both sides terrorised the Anglo-Scottish border of 400 years ago, and spawned the building of fortified castles and strongholds – pele towers – many of which remain to this day across virtually all of northern England. Earlier still, the north of England was the nucleus for the so-called Wars of the Roses between first the royal houses of Lancaster and York, and later those of York and Tudor, during the uncertain and turbulent world of the 15th century.

Down the centre of the region, the Pennines form the 'backbone of England', or, as the noted adventurer and author of *Robinson Crusoe* and *Moll Flanders*, Daniel Defoe, rather more dramatically put it: 'the wildest, most barren and frightful' landscape he had seen. In *Britannia* (1586), English antiquarian and historian William Camden was less daunted: the Pennines ran 'as the Apennine in

Italy, through the middest of England, with a continued ridge, rising more with continued tops and cliffs one after another even as far as Scotland'.

The Pennines were a backbone in another sense, too, providing a source of employment for many Northerners during, and for some time after, the Industrial Revolution. The highest summit, Cross Fell, was described by Defoe as 'a wall of brass'. He wasn't too wide of the mark, as the Quaker-owned London Lead Mining Company demonstrated during the many years of their operations in the Pennines.

The company also found lead to mine in the Yorkshire Dales, notably in Swaledale, where today the ancient trails of the miners enable walkers to explore vast tracts of upland. Walkers with an interest in industrial archaeology will find themselves in seventh heaven here.

The Dales, of course, are renowned for their outstanding natural beauty and dramatic scenery, as at Malham Cove, a favourite with walkers, rock climbers and botanists alike. Above the cove lies a spread of limestone pavement, one of Britain's rarest habitats. It is found only in areas of hard limestone, originally deposited in Carboniferous times, scoured by glaciers during the Ice Ages. Apart from the fascinating

Above: the blue waters of Loughrigg Tarn, Cumbria

Below: beautiful Swaledale

shapes of the rock formations, the special interest of limestone pavement lies in its plant life, which includes 18 rare or scarce species, and in its record of glacial and post-glacial history.

Rare and beautiful too, are the landscapes of Cumbria, a modern county formed in 1974 from those of Cumberland, Westmorland and Lancashire, north of Morecambe Bay. It would be a daunting, if not impossible task, to calculate how many words of praise have been heaped on Cumbria, even if only since the time of the so-called Lake Poets (notably Wordsworth and Coleridge).

It is a county of amazing and over-whelming diversity – a quality noted as far back as the 16th century when Camden wrote that it 'smileth upon the beholders and giveth contentment to as many as travaile it'. Not to be outdone, the eastern reaches flow out to the uplifting beauty of the North York Moors, the coast and the quiet folds of Northumberland and Durham. Here wartime exploits from as far back as the day the Earl of Surrey defeated the Scots and James IV at Flodden Field, are portrayed in three fascinating walks.

Elsewhere, mystery surrounds the tales of witchcraft and stone circles, while the joys of wilderness walking lead you into the rolling fells of the Forest of Bowland, the quiet reaches of Eskdale in Cumbria in the shadow of its highest peaks, and to the very summit of the Pennines.

For the simply spectacular, the walks focus on northern Lakeland, the North Yorkshire coast and the breathtaking cliffs of Malham, though there was so much to choose from.

Literary associations are woven through the fabric of northern England's society in a way that leaves them uppermost in the minds of those who enjoy the insights and pleasure they bring. Walk with the Lake Poets in Buttermere, with Lewis Carroll in Ripon, and the Brontë sisters across the rugged moors above their home in Haworth. And for good measure, tread the great upland divide between traditional Lancashire and Yorkshire, Blackstone Edge, now traversed by the greatest of all northern trails, the Pennine Way.

That this landscape is an important part of our national heritage is demonstrated by the designation here of four national parks, six Areas of Outstanding Natural Beauty, 41 national nature reserves, and innumerable Sites of Special Scientific Interest. This is a place of dramatic distinctions and captivating harmonies, of ruggedness and vigour, of pastoral landscapes and relaxation, that together produce a whole that is far greater than the sum of its numerous parts. Embracing the themes of mystery, wilderness, nature, the spectacular, the legacy of war, ancient trackways and the artistic and emotional routes of our forebears, the walks that follow take an eclectic dip into what the region has to offer.

Best of the Rest

Wharfedale Most visited of the Yorkshire Dales, Wharfedale never fails to captivate with its rich and varied scenery. Away from the honeypots of Bolton Abbey and Grassington there is a wide choice of excellent footpaths across liberating open moorlands. On the moors between Grassington and nearby Hebden extensive remains of lead-mining remind you that life was once much harder for Dales folk. There are good interpretive panels and marked trails.

North York Moors The Cleveland Way follows the escarpment of the Hambleton and Cleveland Hills before turning south again to follow the coastline to Scarborough. The best parts of the inland, moorland section can be found above Osmotherley, with enormous views across the Vale of York and north towards County Durham the reward for comparatively little effort.

Cheviots In the last hills in England deep valleys incise the huge rounded grasslands, making for excellent, remote, but quite straightforward walking. Around Ingram particularly, permissive paths have been linked up to make a series of walks which epitomise the Cheviot landscape of mountain sheepwalks and ancient settlement remains.

Howgills Like the Cheviots, the Howgills are rounded grassy mountains, cut by deep valleys leading to their remote heart.

However, they cover a much smaller area, in the 'no-man's land' between the Yorkshire Dales and the Lake District, and all their exhilarating high ridges can be traversed in a few days of good walking. A favourite is the ascent of the Calf via Winder from Sedbergh, returning by Cautley Spout's dramatic waterfall.

Keswick The rewards for escaping the seemingly endless outdoor clothing shops in the self-styled capital of the northern Lakes are many. Perhaps the best-loved getaway into this magnificent walkers' landscape is to the south of the town, up to the inspirationally-sited stone circle at Castlerigg, then on to the breathtaking viewpoint on Walla Crag. Choose an early spring morning with mist in the valley for the ultimate Lakeland view.

Garrigill The valley of the River South Tyne hides away in the North Pennines Area of Outstanding Natural Beauty. Amidst the high moorlands and below the shadow of Cross Fell, miners and farmers eked out a living from this often hostile environment. Their legacy is a fine network of footpaths and bridleways across delightful meadows and high pasture, connecting hamlets and villages like Garrigill with the upland mining areas. The Pennine Way utilises one such track as it drops down to Alston, but there are many others, little trodden by walkers, but richly rewarding when discovered by those who prefer life off the beaten track.

A Poet's View of the Buttermere Valley

This lakeside walk takes you past the tranquil waters and sullen fells that so inspired the poet and philosopher Coleridge

WALK 58

Top right: Coleridge is probably best known for *The Rime of the Ancient Mariner*

Below: autumnal colours adorn the hills around Crummock Water

Samuel Taylor Coleridge (1772–1834) came to live in the Lake District after he was introduced to the area by his friend and fellow poet, William Wordsworth. One of the places he visited on his first tour was Buttermere, a valley he said lay in a 'beautiful and stern Embracement of Rock'. They called at the Fish Inn, which you pass at the start of this walk, to see the famous 'Maid of Buttermere', otherwise known as the innkeeper's daughter, Mary Robinson – a girl so beautiful she had become something of a tourist attraction. Years later she was tricked into a scandalous marriage with conman and bigamist John Hatfield, a man Coleridge angrily dubbed the 'Keswick Imposter'.

From the Fish Inn the walk leads across boggy ground to the western side of the lake, a route Coleridge followed as part of a nine-day walk among the Western Fells which he dubbed a 'circumcursion'. The detailed notes he took as he went made this the first recorded fell walk – at least the first taken for pleasure. Coleridge was a Romantic and took to fell-walking in an attempt to discover the effect that the wild landscape and physical exertion had on his mind.

At the ruined sheepfold you can make a diversion to Scale Force, a waterfall with a 100-foot (30m) sheer drop. Coleridge knew it well and wrote that 'the chasm through which it flows is stupendous – so wildly wooded that the mosses and wet weeds … increase the Horror of the rocks'.

Continuing round the lake you feel overwhelmed by Melbreak, which rises inhospitably on your left, a mountain which Coleridge might have described as a 'Giant's Tent'. If you are lucky you might see a peregrine swoop from the bare rocks above. People once saw such mountains as dangerous, ugly places which should be avoided. Daniel Defoe described them as 'barren and wild, of no use or advantage either to man or beast'. Not until the late 18th century did it became fashionable to admire wild and picturesque scenery.

When you reach the tip of Crummock Water you get a superb sense of the grandeur of the mountains that surround it. Coleridge loved the wildness of the Lakes so much that he preferred to walk alone, and was never deterred by rain or bad weather. Unfortunately this worsened his rheumatism, a condition he tried to ease by drinking laudanum, known locally as 'Kendal Black Drop'. He was soon addicted to it.

Your route now takes you through Lanthwaite Woods and down the eastern side of the lake, where trees dip into the water like cats gently lapping at a bowl of cream. The scene can hardly have changed from Coleridge's time. An ancient bridlepath takes you away from the lake and over Rannerdale Knots, where thick carpets of bluebells wait to greet you in the spring. As you ramble back into Buttermere you begin to understand the spell cast by this hidden valley which helped to make the Lake District the Poets' Corner of England.

A Poet's View of the Buttermere Valley

The poet Coleridge stepped this way across a tranquil Lakeland scene

WALK 58

1 From the Bridge Hotel walk down to the left of the Fish Hotel, then through a gate, signposted to Scale Force and Scale Bridge. Go over a bridge, through a gate and turn right.

2 In ¼ mile (400m), after crossing a stream via a footbridge, take the path to the left which runs along the base of a rocky slope with occasional cairns. Eventually reach a gap in a wall. Descend to cross a footbridge. Scale Force waterfall is on your left.

3 Ascend for a few paces, then turn right, downhill, on a bank with a stream on your right. At the confluence with another stream, cross a footbridge then turn right. Later the path veers away from the stream towards the shore, then left alongside the lake.

4 Towards the end of the lake the track divides. Take the right-hand path through the gate and follow the water's edge. Go ahead at next gate and, just past a broken-down wall, turn left to pass a ruin, then aim for a group of pine trees by the shore. Pass through a kissing gate and then along a wall to a pumping station. Continue along the shore to cross a foot-bridge over a river. Later turn right over two bridges. Continue on shore path through Lanthwaite Woods and later past a boat house, then along by the lake. The path leads over several stiles and small bridges until it bears left at a wall.

5 Go through the gate and turn right onto the road to a parking area. Branch left across the hillside and soon cross the river and follow the bridleway. Go through a gate, to a footbridge. Cross over, then turn right to double-back and go down hill.

6 At the road walk left for a few paces then back up the bridle-way leading uphill and over a shoulder. Follow the path, keeping the lake on your right. When it comes back to the road, continue to a group of pine trees.

7 Pass through a kissing gate and follow the shore, then take a gravel path through woods. At the far end cross a footbridge, then go through a kissing gate. Turn left up field to another kissing gate, then immediately turn right around foot of crag. On reaching a foot-bridge, cross it and turn left, signed Buttermere village, and follow riverside path back to car park.

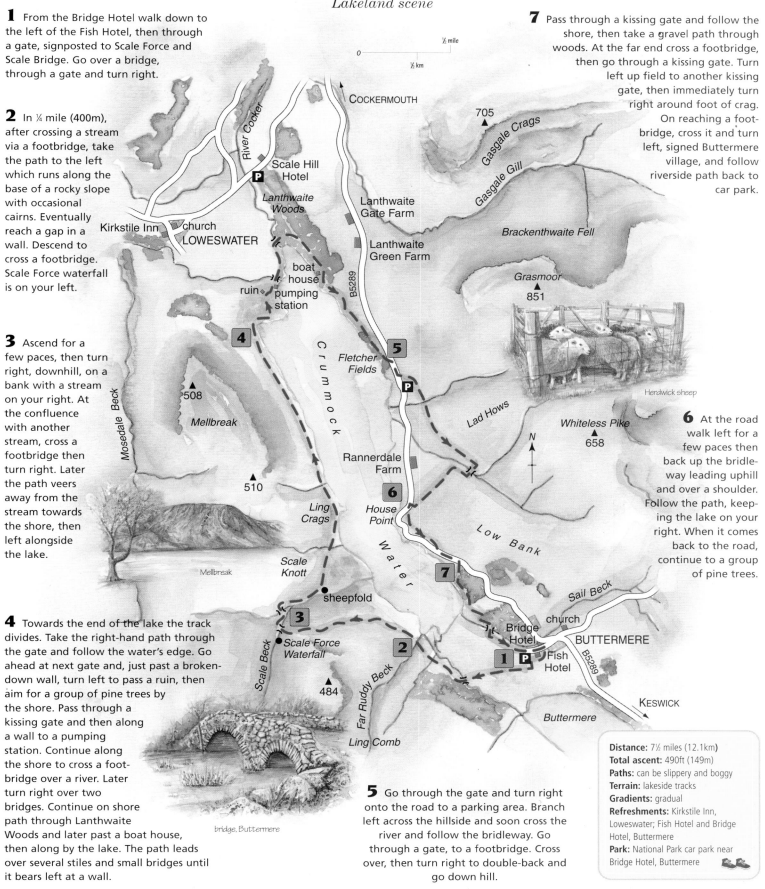

bridge, Buttermere

Herdwick sheep

Distance: 7½ miles (12.1km)
Total ascent: 490ft (149m)
Paths: can be slippery and boggy
Terrain: lakeside tracks
Gradients: gradual
Refreshments: Kirkstile Inn, Loweswater; Fish Hotel and Bridge Hotel, Buttermere
Park: National Park car park near Bridge Hotel, Buttermere

Claife Heights and the Victorian View of Windermere

A subtle balance between artifice and nature in the Lake District is revealed in this pleasant walk

WALK
59

Above: a kestrel hovers on the wind

The National Trust's estate at Claife, on the western shore of Windermere, is noted for the beauty of its setting and particularly for the rich diversity of habitats and landscapes to be found along its quiet winding paths. At the start of this walk the shoreline of the lake has the character of parkland in which nature's rougher edges have been trimmed and tamed. Beech trees overhang the water, swans bask on the close-cropped grass and even the woodland on the hills seems designed as a dramatic backdrop for gentle strolls and picnics. The grounds were laid out early in the 19th century by the Curwen family of Belle Isle, the curious circular mansion that can just be glimpsed through trees out on its private island.

The path climbs up into the hills behind Belle Grange where it runs through dense mixed woodland in which native broadleaves such as oak and ash are interspersed with larch plantations. So long as you are quiet, you may catch glimpses of red deer or notice a red squirrel darting up a tree. You may also see grey squirrels, which have advanced relatively recently into southern Lakeland and threaten to drive out the native, red species.

As you emerge from the woodland on the summit of Claife Heights the views are unexpected and superb, of open moorland backed by distant prospects of the Furness Fells and Langdale Pikes. The tarns (upland ponds) that dot the moor are havens for wildfowl in any season of the year, and overhead you are likely to spot buzzards or perhaps a kestrel hovering above the bracken. Although idyllic on a sunny day, the heights can be an eerie place on sombre autumn afternoons, when the roar of rutting stags might make you wonder if you've heard the legendary 'Claife Crier', a melancholy ghost that is said to haunt the area.

Whilst the bogs and thin soils of the moor are fit only for rough grazing, centuries of farming have transformed the sheltered valleys. As the track descends it runs between old dry-stone walls enclosing fields of lush grass that have been cleared of stones, drained and fertilised by sheep (or, more recently, by chemical means). Despite its reputation as a wilderness, the Lake District is essentially a working landscape where nature has been made to serve the needs of humans.

There could scarcely be a better symbol of society's sometimes overly romantic view of nature than the bizarre castellated ruin of Claife Station. Built in 1799, when Windermere was first becoming a fashionable resort, the tower was a 'viewing station' with its windows carefully positioned to frame prospects of the lake and hills. Visitors would pay to see real landscapes framed to resemble paintings in a gallery and on cloudy days they could, quite literally, view nature through rose-tinted glass. As you leave the ivy-shrouded ruins behind and return to the well-tended parkland on the shore, you may, like a Romantic poet, ponder on the fact that nature always, ultimately, triumphs over art.

Below: Claife Heights from Latterbarrow

Claife Heights and the Victorian View of Windermere

WALK
59

The Victorians tried to 'improve' the beauty of this lake and moorland walk with romantic architecture

1 Turn left (north) out of car park and follow the lakeside for 2 miles (3.2km). The metalled lane soon becomes an unmade track through woodland.

2 As the track approaches Belle Grange turn left just before the house up a steep and stony bridleway, signposted to Letterbarrow and Near Sawrey. Ignoring a path to the left, continue on uphill (signposted to Hawkshead) until the path levels out and reaches a broad bridleway at a complex intersection.

3 Cross the bridleway and follow path (signed to Sawrey via Tarns) that bears slightly to the left. Cross another intersection, still following the signs to Sawrey, up a steep and stony path. This soon joins a broader track that passes through a gate and stile to reach the open moorland on Claife Heights.

4 Follow faint path down towards the nearest tarn, where the route becomes much clearer. Follow trackway as it swings to left below an old stone dam, passes through a wooden gate and dips down to Moss Eccles Tarn. Continue on the track as it drops down from the moor, splashes through a little stream and runs between stone walls.

5 Where the track forks to Near and Far Sawrey bear left through a gate and follow bridleway down to join a metalled lane into Far Sawrey. Turn left along the village street to the Sawrey Hotel.

6 Just beyond the hotel car park bear left up a track signposted to ferry. The footpath skirts the gardens of a private house, then drops towards the lake beside a high stone wall. Continue on across a driveway, down a path through overhanging rhododendrons, to the road.

7 Turn left down the hill, then cross the road onto footpath separated from the traffic by a wall. Follow path downhill and across the road, through woodland to a car park.

8 At far end of this car park, take footpath into woods and up steps to Claife Station. At top of steps turn right along the terrace walk, which drops down to the road. Turn left, then bear immediately left along a narrow lane to return to car park.

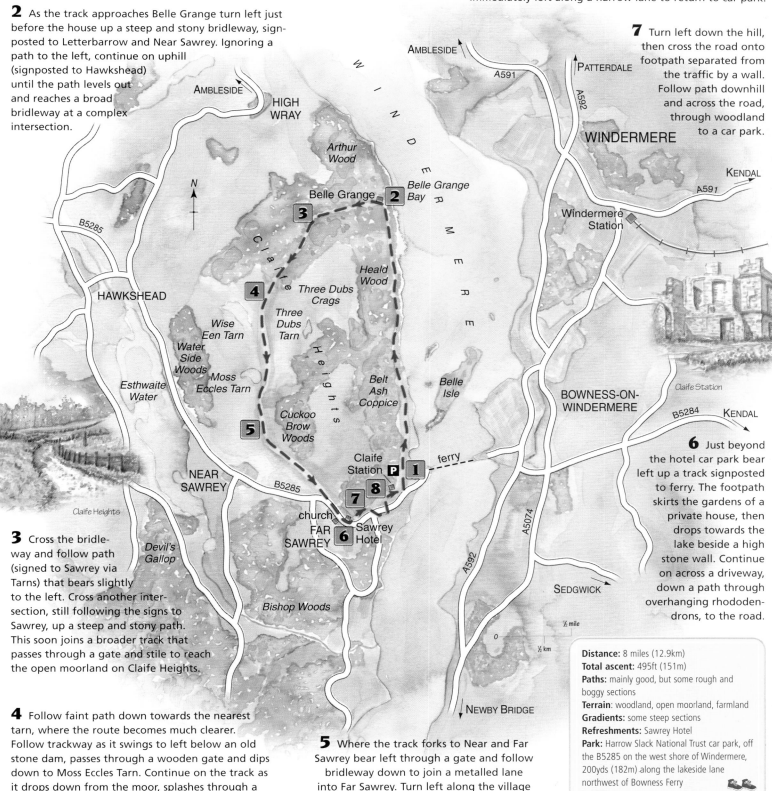

Distance: 8 miles (12.9km)
Total ascent: 495ft (151m)
Paths: mainly good, but some rough and boggy sections
Terrain: woodland, open moorland, farmland
Gradients: some steep sections
Refreshments: Sawrey Hotel
Park: Harrow Slack National Trust car park, off the B5285 on the west shore of Windermere, 200yds (182m) along the lakeside lane northwest of Bowness Ferry

The Contrasts of Upper Eskdale

One of Lakeland's finest riverside walks leads to one of its bleakest spots, returning across an eerie landscape

WALK 60

Top right: looking towards Bowfell, Upper Eskdale

Below: yellow flowers of roseroot cling to the wet crags

Bottom: a scattering of snow enhances the view to Esk Hause from Great Moss

In few places do the rivers of Lakeland truly rival those of the Scottish glens, but the River Esk, draining the vast upland sponge of Great Moss and gathering the waters of England's highest peaks, most certainly does. Between its confluences with Scale Gill and Lingcove Beck, the river puts on a fine show of white water, crashing over rock steps and diving headlong into crystal plunge pools. Above, the cliffs of Hard Knott and Heron Crags are as dark as the ravens they host, and a perfect framework for the Esk and the countless gills that feed it.

At Lingcove Bridge the setting is impressive: steep fells rise on either hand, while the way forward is split by the rocky upthrust of Throstle Garth. Here the sound of water is constant, echoing off the rock walls and adding drama to an already outstanding landscape. Mist adds a new dimension, wreathing the crags and bringing new perspectives to bear, and is a signal to the less experienced walker to proceed with caution and to retreat when route certainty ebbs towards doubt.

Beyond the bridge two distinct ascents follow, the second across the shoulder of Throstlehow Crag, which, with Green Crag opposite, compresses the river into a tight ravine. Above this constriction it is easy to become disorientated in poor visibility, though good conditions will beckon you on towards the craggy heights of Sca Fell and its neighbour, the highest summit in England.

Great Moss invokes delight or despair according to one's view of things bleak and barren. It is a vast water-gathering sponge of grass and reeds that captures rainfall from a massive ring of summits. Here the indistinct remains of a turf wall mark the boundary of a deer enclosure constructed long ago by the monks of Furness Abbey; now all this is National Trust property.

Sca Fell and Scafell Pike dominate the scene, but it is Great Moss that is the objective of this walk. Here, amid the empty vastness, the sense of isolation and loneliness is heightened by the absence of features. Bogs and deep streams await the unwary, and somehow the only certainty seems to be that you are going to get wet. So convincing is this feeling that most walkers simply choose the shallowest part of the river to cross, and surrender themselves to a foot-soaking paddle (a towel and change of socks are useful additions to the rucksack on this walk).

But the air of wilderness is powerful, the ramparts of soaring pinnacles and buttresses dramatic, and the emptiness awe-inspiring. Here is the heart of Lakeland, littered with debris from the crags above, a spectacle of nature's strength, and a humbling, magnificent place to be.

WALK
60

The Contrasts of Upper Eskdale

From a lowland vale to England's highest mountains,
following the River Esk into the remote heart of Lakeland

1 Begin from a roadside parking area at the foot of Hardknott Pass, and descend to follow the access to Brotherilkeld Farm (right, by the telephone box). As you near the farm, branch left on a path parallel with the River Esk. Ignore a footbridge and continue up-river.

2 Beyond a gate follow a broad track crossing rough pasture. This leads past a series of delightful waterfalls, and ultimately arrives at Lingcove Bridge, directly below the crags of Throstle Garth.

3 Cross the bridge and climb left, still alongside, but well above, the river. Two pronounced rises follow before the path reaches Scar Lathing, where the river makes a distinct bend westwards. Cross an inflowing stream, and bear left to pass beneath Scar Lathing, beyond which lies the bleak arena of Great Moss, spread below the soaring heights of Sca Fell and the lower cliffs of Cam Spout Crag.

4 The moss is invariably waterlogged and paths sketchy, but the objective is now to cross the river. This is usually best accomplished at or just above the confluence with How Beck, and is rarely completed dryshod. Once across, head towards the base of the waterfall from How Beck, then turn left and contour along the base of a rocky slope to reach a small knoll with massive boulders, known as Sampson's Stones.

5 A short way further on a sheepfold is reached. From it a clear path begins a gentle climb away from the river into a little-known landscape of knolls, streams, low crags and bogland.

6 The path, passing below Silverybield Crag, Round Scar and Rowantree Crags, is clear throughout, but occasionally resorts to evasion tactics before breaking free of the rocks on reaching Scale Gill. Now a clear green path zigzags down through bracken, turns right at the bottom and crosses Scale Bridge, where the gill puts on an impressive show of force.

7 A short way beyond the bridge, take the lower of two ladder stiles, and follow an improving track to Taw House Farm. Immediately turn left over a ladder stile and go down an enclosed path to the footbridge across the Esk encountered at the start of the walk, and from there retrace your steps to the valley road.

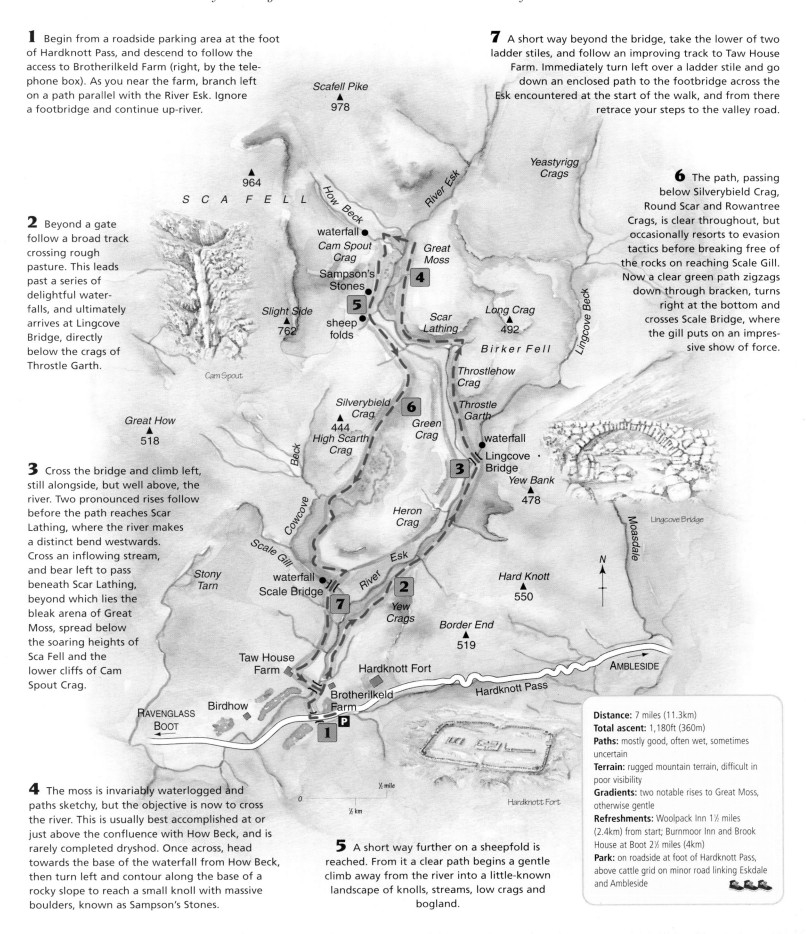

Scafell Pike
▲ 978

▲ 964

S C A F E L L

How Beck

River Esk

Yeastyrigg Crags

waterfall
Cam Spout Crag

Great Moss

4

Sampson's Stones

5

Slight Side
▲ 762

sheep folds

Scar Lathing

Long Crag
▲ 492

B i r k e r   F e l l

Cam Spout

Great How
▲ 518

Throstlehow Crag

Silverybield Crag
▲ 444
High Scarth Crag

6

Throstle Garth

Green Crag

waterfall
Lingcove Bridge ·

Yew Bank
▲ 478

Lingcove Beck

Lingcove Bridge

Cowcove Beck

Scale Gill

Heron Crag

3

Esk

River

Moasdale

Stony Tarn

waterfall
Scale Bridge

7

River

2

Yew Crags

Hard Knott
▲ 550

N

Border End
▲ 519

Taw House Farm

Hardknott Fort

AMBLESIDE

Birdhow

Brotherilkeld Farm

Hardknott Pass

RAVENGLASS
BOOT

P

1

0   ½ mile
    ½ km

Hardknott Fort

Distance: 7 miles (11.3km)
Total ascent: 1,180ft (360m)
Paths: mostly good, often wet, sometimes uncertain
Terrain: rugged mountain terrain, difficult in poor visibility
Gradients: two notable rises to Great Moss, otherwise gentle
Refreshments: Woolpack Inn 1½ miles (2.4km) from start; Burnmoor Inn and Brook House at Boot 2½ miles (4km)
Park: on roadside at foot of Hardknott Pass, above cattle grid on minor road linking Eskdale and Ambleside

Swindale and the Eastern Fells

A remote glaciated valley provides the setting for a long wild walk among the moorland fells of east Lakeland

WALK

61

Isolated Swindale – 'the valley of the swine' – offers a vivid picture of a glacier-fashioned landscape that can have changed little since the first farmers arrived some 6,000 years ago. As you cross the gorsey flanks of Dog Hill the valley eases into view below, curving progressively southward to an abrupt end, where an old road used for transporting corpses from Mardale (now under Haweswater reservoir) enters the valley en route for Shap.

Above the dale head Mosedale Beck flows through a shallow, V-shaped moorland valley before plummeting into the waterfalls of Swindale Forces. Nearby Hobgrumble Gill fills a dark gash in the cliff face with waters seeping from a high corrie on Selside Pike. When the two streams combine amid glacial moraine they produce Swindale Beck, a rare highlight in a sombre, craggy dale. Mosedale and Hobgrumble corrie are both hanging valleys, cut off by the weight of ice that ground away at the sediments and rocks of the main valley floor, lowering it appreciably.

Other than on foot, horseback or a bicycle, there is no way through Swindale, and no immediately apparent through passage for anyone. The sense of remoteness is great on the long descent into the dale. Here, after the Romans had retreated, the Vikings came. Ancient records note the name 'Thengeheved' – 'the council place at the head of the valley' – and the vision of Viking chiefs gathered in the shelter of Gouther Crag and the Knott to manage the affairs of their communities is a stirring one.

Now those same cliffs, dark and brooding, shelter peregrines, buzzards and visiting golden eagles, while the short days of winter see flocks of travel-weary fieldfares, mistle thrushes, redwings and a scattering of bramblings feeding in the fields and whirling across the cliff faces.

Above Swindale Head and the ruins of High Swindale Head Farm, Mosedale offers only the emptiness of grassy moorland across which red deer roam freely, and where, in autumn, the sound of a stag at the rut echoes sharply. Mosedale is untamed and empty, save for a collapsed wall and a small sheepfold, a flowing expanse of tough sheep's fescue and common bent. The way across it begins hesitantly and continues uncertainly, and the feeling of isolation is heightened by the barren scenery.

The distant Mosedale Cottage, surrounded by its stand of trees, lies mid-way between Swindale and Long Sleddale, and is a forlorn spot below the spoil of the disused Mosedale Quarry.

Leaving this empty quarter the walk climbs into Wet Sleddale, where countless streams feed the reservoir before flowing on to nourish the River Lowther. Here, in spring, huge flocks of black-headed gulls wheel in mutual stimulation or launch into sudden 'dreads' as they all take screaming to the air.

In the far distance, the high northern Pennines fringe the skyline, while near by the dark waters of the reservoir reflect the sky's moods in an endlessly changing display.

Above: peregrine falcons haunt the crags

Below: sheep graze the flanks of Dog Hill

Swindale and the Eastern Fells

Exploring forgotten valleys on the Lake District's eastern fringe

WALK
61

1 Leave Keld on a moorland road to Tailbert Farm. At Tailbert, abandon the road for a track across the hillside, later descending through bracken and gorse into Swindale. Cross a ford or a nearby bridge. Turn left, follow the minor road to Swindale Head Farm and go through gates onto a bridleway signed Mosedale.

2 After a final building on the left, branch left through glacial moraine, and climb through the rocky outcrops of Selside Pike. Cross open moorland to a fence at Swine Gill. Go through a gate and continue to a dilapidated building and a collapsed wall nearby.

6 When the river makes a pronounced bend to the right, move away from it to a wall. Go past Steps Hall, following a rough track towards Thornship Farm. Opposite the farm continue alongside the river to reach Keld once more.

5 Follow the road to a cattle grid. Here leave the road, turning left alongside the River Lowther. Cross a road and continue beside the river.

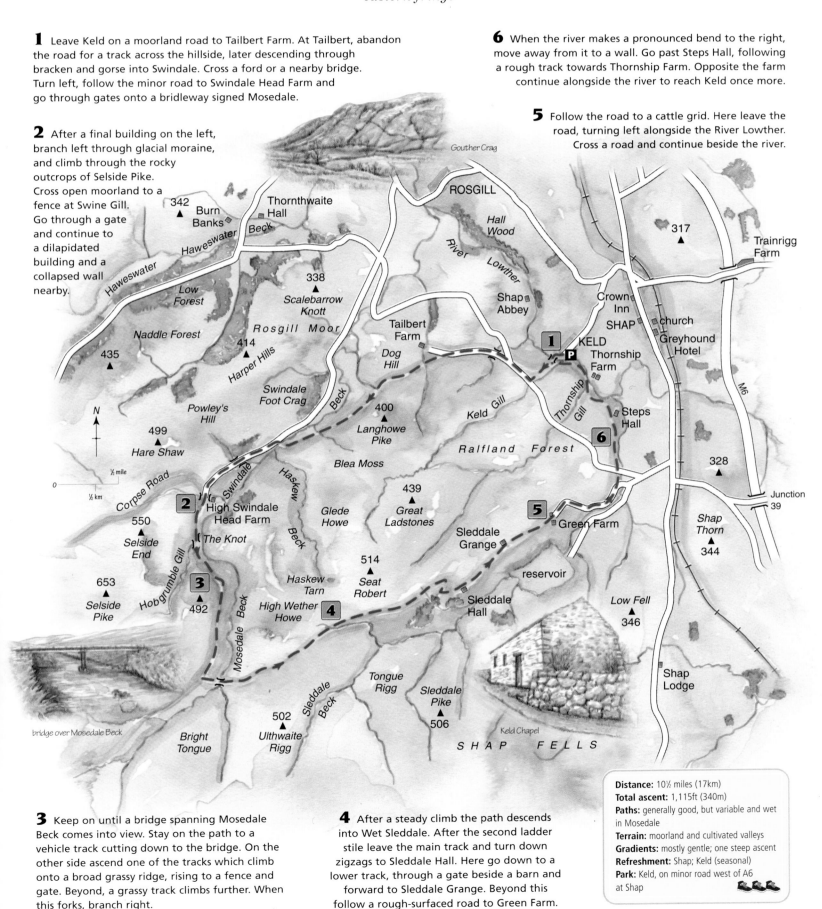

bridge over Mosedale Beck

3 Keep on until a bridge spanning Mosedale Beck comes into view. Stay on the path to a vehicle track cutting down to the bridge. On the other side ascend one of the tracks which climb onto a broad grassy ridge, rising to a fence and gate. Beyond, a grassy track climbs further. When this forks, branch right.

4 After a steady climb the path descends into Wet Sleddale. After the second ladder stile leave the main track and turn down zigzags to Sleddale Hall. Here go down to a lower track, through a gate beside a barn and forward to Sleddale Grange. Beyond this follow a rough-surfaced road to Green Farm.

Distance: 10½ miles (17km)
Total ascent: 1,115ft (340m)
Paths: generally good, but variable and wet in Mosedale
Terrain: moorland and cultivated valleys
Gradients: mostly gentle; one steep ascent
Refreshment: Shap; Keld (seasonal)
Park: Keld, on minor road west of A6 at Shap

High Pike – the Last Lakeland Hill

A steep start leads to high moorland, a prehistoric hill fort, an outstanding viewpoint – and an abundance of solitude

WALK

62

Top right: huntsman John Peel is buried at Caldbeck

Below: mining spoil on Carrock Fell

Bottom: looking back to Carrock Fell from the summit of High Pike

Behind the formidable barrier of Blencathra and Skiddaw lie the delectable Caldbeck and Uldale fells, a region of peace and isolation where rounded, grassy hills offer easy exploration, free from constraining walls and fences. Carrock Fell is the only exception, and betrays a significant change in the underlying rock strata.

This is a corner of heaven set aside for lovers of solitude, a wild and intriguing place, unique in Lakeland. Now virtually treeless and completely uncultivated, these infrequently visited northern fells were a true forest in olden times, and more recently a forest in the sense of a hunting reserve. They were also the hunting ground of John Peel, immortalised in the verses of 'D'ye ken John Peel', written by his friend John Woodcock Graves and set to music by William Metcalfe, organist at Carlisle Cathedral. Born in nearby Caldbeck in 1776, one of 13 children, Peel himself fathered 13 children. He and his bride, the daughter of a wealthy farmer from Uldale and then only 18 years old, were wed at Gretna Green after her mother had objected to the union. Begrudgingly, the family accepted that the two were indeed married, but insisted on a service of re-marriage at Caldbeck church. It was about this time that Peel started hunting with his own pack of hounds, and often followed them on foot, in the traditional Lakeland manner.

Of the two principal summits visited on this walk, Carrock Fell has the greater interest. To begin with, the Skiddaw slates that underlie the rest of the northern fells here terminate against an outcropping of igneous rocks in a way that will fascinate those with an interest in geology. The rocks have also yielded veins of copper ore and other minerals, notably at the Carrock End Mine, where the walk begins, and at Driggith Mine. Above Carrock End the crags at the eastern edge of the fell also contain outcrops of black gabbro, the rock of the Cuillins on Skye, and a rarity in Lakeland.

Carrock Fell is also unique in having an ancient hill fort, of uncertain age, on its summit. Judging by the size of the collapsed walls that ring the summit, the fort must have been a large, important stronghold and a forbidding place to live.

Once you pass beyond Carrock Fell, the influence of Skiddaw slates takes over, and the landscape becomes smooth and grassy. It is also largely featureless, and a confusing place in misty conditions. On a clear day, however, the top of High Pike – given its northerly position and the convenient memorial bench that stands there – is one of the finest vantage points imaginable. To the south, the views are confined a little by the bulk of Blencathra and Skiddaw, but northwards the eye can scan the West Cumbrian Plain, the coastal flats of the Solway, and the hills of Dumfries and Galloway.

And when Lakeland throbs beneath the weight of summer and weekend visitors, it is among the fells 'Back o' Skidda' that peace and contentment will be found.

High Pike – the Last Lakeland Hill

The Cumbrian Mountains end at a lonely viewpoint high above the Solway Plain

1 From the site of the old Carrock End Mine on Caldbeck Common head for a conspicuous grassy path slanting left and up across the lower slopes of Carrock Fell. The path climbs steeply to meet Further Gill Sike.

2 Here branch right, with the gill on your left. Higher up, the gully is dry and the path less distinct. At the top of the gully, climb straight on through heather to a less steep section, and follow a green path through heather and bracken, passing a small cairn and a ruined shelter.

3 The path rises easily to the east peak of Carrock Fell, from where a broad track strikes westwards to the main summit. On the way you pass through a ring of stones that once formed a substantial hill fort. A large cairn on a rocky plinth crowns the summit, with a shelter nearby.

4 From just north of the summit a path heads westwards across a broad ridge, passing to the north of Round Knott before reaching grassy Miton Hill. From here, walk northwest on a broad grassy track, passing Red Gate, an obvious cross-track, which offers a quick escape route northwards if necessary.

5 As you approach High Pike the path curves northwards to pass the top of Drygill Beck, a steep-sided ravine, beyond which it ascends easy grassy slopes to the summit, on the way crossing a broad stony track.

6 From the summit face the distant Pennines and descend (eastwards) across untracked ground, to intersect the broad, stony track met earlier. Turn left, and follow it until, near three large wooden posts on the right, it forks. Branch right, until you reach the top of a narrow gully. Bear right again, alongside the gully and soon cross it to pursue an old mining track above Carrock Beck.

7 Much lower down the track forks again. Branch right and go down to meet the road. Turn right to return to the start.

Distance: 6 miles (9.7km)
Total ascent: 1,560ft (476m)
Paths: mostly clear, but not advised in poor visibility; one short trackless section
Terrain: mainly high mountain moorland
Gradients: steep start but otherwise moderate
Refreshments: Mill Inn at Mungrisdale; pubs at Hesket Newmarket and Caldbeck
Park: roadside parking on Caldbeck Common, at site of Carrock End Mine, 1 mile north of Mosedale

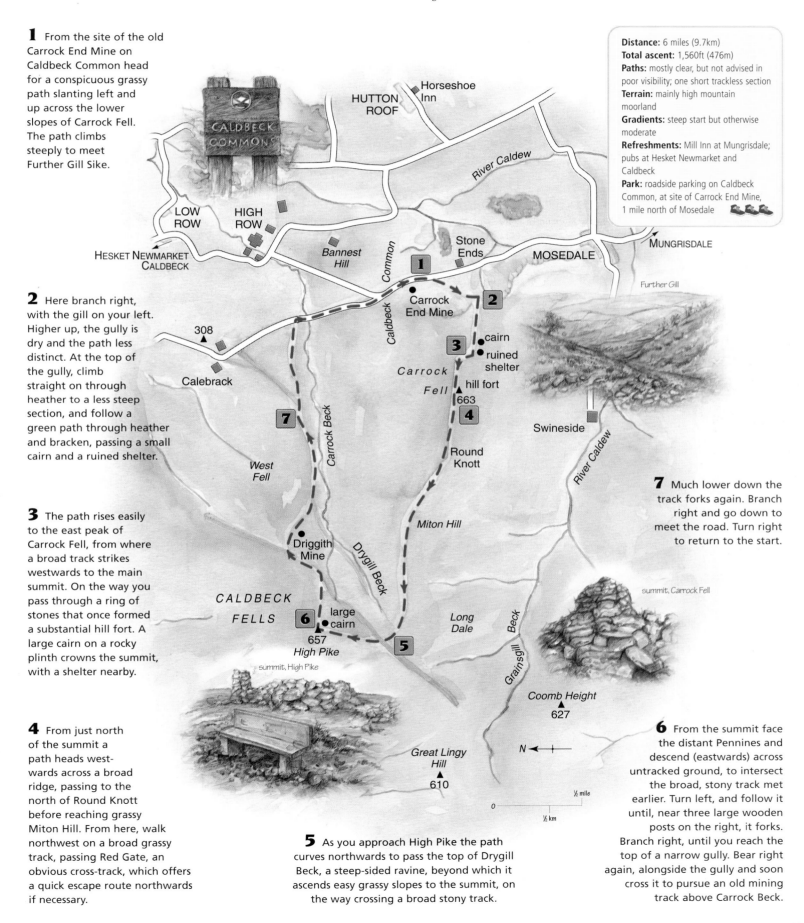

Long Meg and Lacy's Caves

An impressive catalogue of mysteries, magic and gothic romance awaits discovery in the delectable Eden Valley

Top right: no ornamental grotto was complete in its day without a live 'hermit'

Above: on the edge of the village green, Glassonby

Below: Long Meg stands apart from her 'daughters'

Names, according to some old beliefs, are imbued with magic power, embodying the spirit of the person or the place they represent. Perhaps that is why the valley of the River Eden seems such a special place, harbouring more than its fair share of secrets.

As you leave Little Salkeld at the outset of this walk, the gentle landscape of the vale appears enclosed within an amphitheatre of high hills, with the Pennines to the east, Lakeland's mountains to the west and the Howgill Fells far off to the south. In pre-historic times this fertile, sheltered valley must have seemed a paradise compared with such wild uplands: a fitting site for one of northern England's most impressive neolithic monuments, and a place to sit and ponder ancient mysteries.

We can never know who built the shrine here, or why. The tall and slender monolith, known as Long Meg, with its huge ring of recumbent boulders – her 'daughters' – dates back at least 4,000 years and bears similarities to other monuments from Orkney to Stonehenge. Long Meg herself, etched with circular and spiral patterns, was dragged for well over a mile (1.6km) to the site. Count her daughters if you dare; according to a legend, they are witches turned to stone for dancing on the Sabbath, and if you get their number right, they will come back to life.

Further on along the way, in the porch of St Michael's Church, richly carved stones commemorate another mystery, the lost village of Addingham. For centuries local tales passed down through the generations told of how a village had been washed away when the River Eden changed its course. Such stories might now be considered little more than folklore, had not a drought in 1913 revealed these stones, carved with Viking and medieval designs, embedded in the riverbed. They are presumed to have come from Addingham's drowned church.

Understandably, perhaps, the later village of Glassonby is built on higher ground and it's a long, winding road that leads down to the river. From here the walk along the Eden is sheer delight, a quiet saunter through a perfect English landscape. Then, at Lacy's Caves, you enter a world of gothic fairy tales in labyrinthine grottoes carved into the soft sandstone of the river cliff. The grottoes date back to the 18th century and were the work of Colonel Lacy of Salkeld Hall. The Colonel, clearly a Romantic, is said to have employed an ornamental hermit – effectively a living statue – to mumble in the shadows as his guests drank fine champagne.

The last stage of the walk, back into Little Salkeld, would have been a route to avoid even 30 years ago, when storage hoppers filled with gypsum towered above mine workings and rail sidings. The scene is very different today; ivy cloaks the ruined buildings of a Victorian plaster of Paris factory, trees have long reclaimed the slopes and there is a certain romance in the thought that long-neglected tunnels burrow out for miles, deep beneath the fields.

Long Meg and Lacy's Caves

A spectacular stone circle and intriguing Gothic caverns
are linked by a walk in the verdant Eden Valley

Distance: 6 miles (9.7km)
Total ascent: 230ft (70m)
Paths: mainly good, but some muddy sections
Terrain: fields, woodland and riverside
Gradients: slight; one short steep section
Refreshments: The Watermill, Little Salkeld (Mon, Tue, Wed; seasonal)
Park: beside small village green in Little Salkeld, 1½ miles (2.4km) north of Langwathby and the A686 Penrith-Alston road. Turn left off road to Glassonby at sharp right bend

7 Follow the concrete lane past Throstle Hall, a former engine house. After ½ mile (800m), as you come to a modern barn, bear left at a minor intersection to return to Little Salkeld village green.

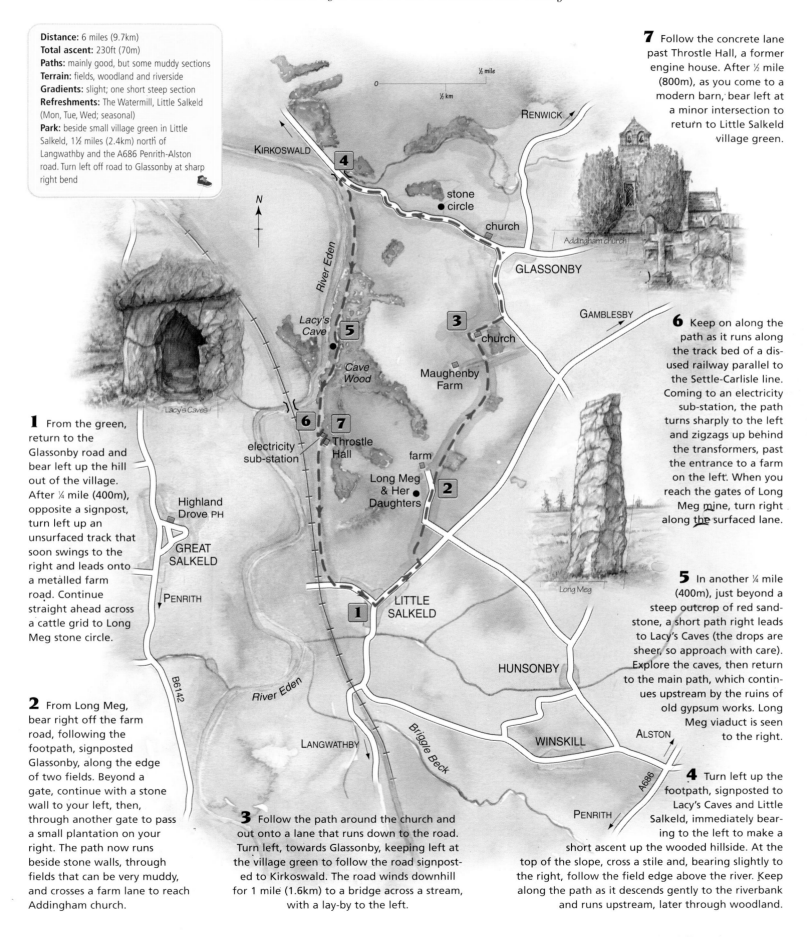

1 From the green, return to the Glassonby road and bear left up the hill out of the village. After ¼ mile (400m), opposite a signpost, turn left up an unsurfaced track that soon swings to the right and leads onto a metalled farm road. Continue straight ahead across a cattle grid to Long Meg stone circle.

2 From Long Meg, bear right off the farm road, following the footpath, signposted Glassonby, along the edge of two fields. Beyond a gate, continue with a stone wall to your left, then, through another gate to pass a small plantation on your right. The path now runs beside stone walls, through fields that can be very muddy, and crosses a farm lane to reach Addingham church.

3 Follow the path around the church and out onto a lane that runs down to the road. Turn left, towards Glassonby, keeping left at the village green to follow the road signposted to Kirkoswald. The road winds downhill for 1 mile (1.6km) to a bridge across a stream, with a lay-by to the left.

6 Keep on along the path as it runs along the track bed of a disused railway parallel to the Settle-Carlisle line. Coming to an electricity sub-station, the path turns sharply to the left and zigzags up behind the transformers, past the entrance to a farm on the left. When you reach the gates of Long Meg mine, turn right along the surfaced lane.

5 In another ¼ mile (400m), just beyond a steep outcrop of red sandstone, a short path right leads to Lacy's Caves (the drops are sheer, so approach with care). Explore the caves, then return to the main path, which continues upstream by the ruins of old gypsum works. Long Meg viaduct is seen to the right.

4 Turn left up the footpath, signposted to Lacy's Caves and Little Salkeld, immediately bearing to the left to make a short ascent up the wooded hillside. At the top of the slope, cross a stile and, bearing slightly to the right, follow the field edge above the river. Keep along the path as it descends gently to the riverbank and runs upstream, later through woodland.

Cross Fell – the Pennine Giant

At the whim of changing weather, this can be a challenging and demanding peak for walkers

WALK
64

Drawing to their greatest height where the River Tees begins its journey to the North Sea, the northern Pennines form a massive barrier between the moorlands of Cumberland and Westmorland and those of the former North Riding of Yorkshire.

In fine weather the mountain has an avuncular air and seems a calm, endearing place to visit. Alas, all is not as it appears. This is wild and inhospitable country, and Cross Fell's repertoire of dirty tricks includes subzero temperatures on at least a third of the days of the year, rain on two-thirds, and snow often well into summer. If that isn't enough, its *pièce de résistance* is a phenomenon known as the Helm Wind, a localised and ferocious gusting of the wind.

With such a pedigree it is little wonder that Cross Fell's original name was Fiends' Fell, before St Augustine, it is said, erected a cross on its summit and built an altar to celebrate the Holy Eucharist in order to scatter the resident devils. If any demons had the strength of purpose to remain in the face of such overwhelming Christianity, there is every chance they finally left when 50 brass bands gathered on the summit to celebrate the passing of the Reform Act in 1832.

In spite of its barren summit, which not even the boots of Pennine Wayfarers can scratch, and the high incidence of clouds which bedevil the mountain, Cross Fell is a magnificent viewpoint, harbouring the fells of Lakeland along the horizon beyond the Eden valley, and extending far across bright green countryside into Scotland.

The route of ascent is an old corpse road linking the church and graveyard at Kirkland with the distant community of Garrigill. In the 17th century one funeral party, caught in a blizzard high on the fellside, abandoned their burden, scurrying back to the safety of Garrigill and returning for the coffin when it was finally deemed safe to recover it, two weeks later. The mourners brought the coffin back to Garrigill where it was buried in a piece of glebe land, subsequently consecrated by the Bishop of Durham.

The top of the mountain is a vast, featureless plateau, favoured in spring by passage dotterel. But it is inordinately bleak and rendered potentially dangerous by poor visibility, as is the long descent to Wildboar Scar. At other times it is serenely peaceful and a relaxing place to be.

The long stretch of open moorland used on the descent provides an invigorating sense of freedom, with, more than likely, complete solitude. The Eden flows sedately through its valley ahead, beyond which the Lakeland fells sit like a pale blue frieze on the skyline.

At the right time of year this enchanting stretch of moorland resounds to the eerie call of the golden plover, white-rumped wheatears dart about and chatter busily, and curlew trill a constant and evocative accompaniment.

Beyond Wythwaite Farm a curious feature known as the Hanging Walls of Mark Antony adds a note of mystery. Precisely what they are, or were, is open to question, and other than a series of grassy mounds, claimed by some to be natural, there is little to see. Certainly there is no evidence that Mark Antony was ever here.

Above: Swaledale sheep, with Cross Fell behind

Below: Cross Fell and Great Dun Fell from Ranbeck

Cross Fell – the Pennine Giant

Rising up above the Vale of Eden, the Pennines' highest hill is a wild and spectacular vantage point

WALK 64

1 In Kirkland head up the road alongside Kirkland Beck. Beyond the last buildings a walled track heads out onto rough upland pastures, eventually looping north to skirt High Cap above Ardale Beck.

2 The gradient, nowhere unduly steep, is eased by a few bends. Within sight of the summit plateau, and not far from a bothy, the ascending track bears sharply left. Here leave it to strike eastwards on a cairned and grassy path, crossing the watershed and passing around the northern scree slopes of Cross Fell to locate the Pennine Way.

7 Onwards a broad green path descends easily through bracken to a sheepfold and across a tract of rough ground to Wythwaite Farm. At the farm turn right through gates, and follow a broad track back to Kirkland.

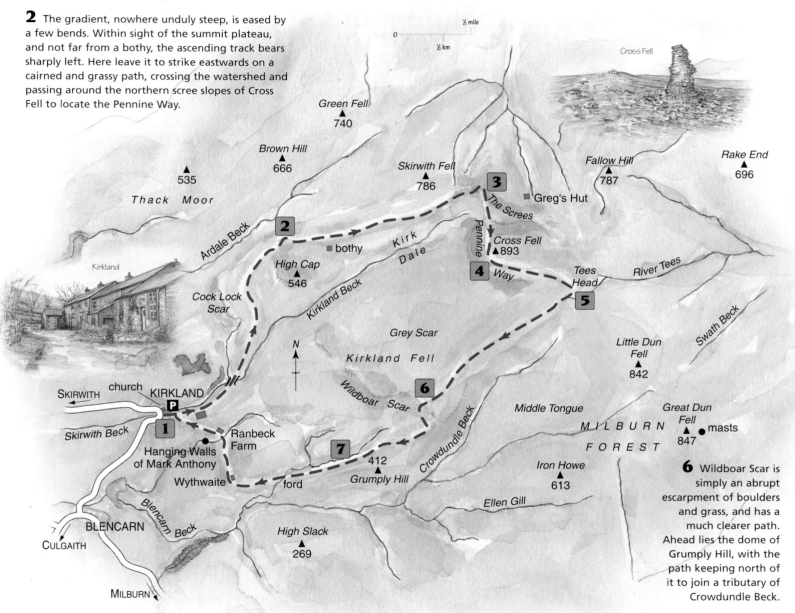

3 A waymarker indicates the line of the Pennine Way, initially wet underfoot and clear enough to follow. It soon dries out, and a few large cairns guide you to the summit shelter-cairn and trig pillar.

4 In poor visibility the surest way down is to retreat. Otherwise, press on across the summit plateau, aiming for the distant summit of Great Dun Fell and its conspicuous masts and radar station. Near the edge of the Cross Fell plateau large cairns mark the way down to Tees Head.

5 From Tees Head a cairned path, not obvious, and narrow in places, leaves the Pennine Way and heads southwest across bouldery terrain to a cairn on the edge of Wildboar Scar. If you can't locate the line of cairns leaving Tees Head, drop beneath the downfall of scree and boulders and skirt along its lower edge until cairns appear in the far distance, and head for them.

6 Wildboar Scar is simply an abrupt escarpment of boulders and grass, and has a much clearer path. Ahead lies the dome of Grumply Hill, with the path keeping north of it to join a tributary of Crowdundle Beck.

Distance: 9 miles (14.5km)
Total ascent: 2,265ft (690m)
Paths: good on ascent, thereafter sketchy
Terrain: high mountain plateau
Gradients: moderate
Refreshment: none nearby
Park: alongside river, opposite church in Kirkland, 5 miles (8km) east of A686 in Langwathby
Note: this route requires good navigational skills and should not be attempted in poor visibility

Up Gunnerside Gill with Swaledale Miners

Follow in the footsteps of the men who mined the land for lead, to explore an austerely beautiful valley

WALK 65

Top right: the village of Gunnerside

The village of Gunnerside lies in Swaledale, in the north of the Yorkshire Dales National Park, and comprises a compact huddle of stone houses lying either side of Gunnerside Beck. The village is an evocative reminder of the Norse settlers who came to the more remote dales. The name Gunnerside is a corruption of the Norse Gunnar's Saetr, and means 'Gunnar's Summer Pasture'.

Those who settled in remote Swaledale had to be both hard-working and self-reliant in order to carve a living from the land. Sheep farming has a long tradition here, but for at least three centuries lead mining dominated the local economy. Cutting across Swaledale is one of the most productive veins of lead ore in the Pennines, and nowhere in the valley was lead mined more intensively than Gunnerside Gill. The village's population figures chart the mining industry's fluctuating fortunes. When the industry was at its height, 150 years ago, the population of Gunnerside rose to around 700, about three times what it is today.

For at least a thousand years lead was won from these steep-sided valleys by a method known as 'hushing'. This meant damming upland streams and letting the water rush in a torrent down the valley side, removing rock and soil and – with luck – exposing veins of lead ore. Some of the biggest hushes in the Yorkshire Dales can be seen during this walk, some so big that they look like natural features. The mining devastation at the top of Gunnerside Gill is an awesome and unforgettable sight.

Below: the heights above Gunnerside Gill are scarred by lead mining

When hushing was no longer viable the miners created a complex system of shafts and tunnels. Apart from small explosive charges, pick and shovel were the only tools used to create them: a massive enterprise. Bringing lead ore to the surface was just the beginning; it then had to be sorted, crushed and smelted into 'pigs' of lead. Lead from Swaledale was exported all over the world – even, so it is said, to roof St Peter's in Rome.

Lead mining was always a precarious business. Long shifts underground in dark, damp, poorly ventilated conditions took their toll on the miners' health. A miner was lucky to reach the age of 50. While some mines produced rich yields for many years, financial uncertainty was the miners' lot. These Pennine hills were mined until the end of the 19th century, when cheap foreign imports of lead put the industry into a slump from which it never recovered. Miners left Swaledale in great numbers, going to the coal mines of the northeast and the textile towns of Yorkshire. Some, encouraged by reports from other settlers, decided to try their luck in America.

This is a superb walk even for those with no particular interest in industrial history. The route is easy to follow, using the tracks that the miners themselves used, and the views are breathtaking all the way. The actual mine workings are intrinsically unstable, so don't try to explore any of the mining shafts or tunnels. Wooden roof struts have seen no maintenance for a hundred years and can collapse without warning. The other mining buildings and relics should also be treated with care; a number of smelt mills have been designated as ancient monuments.

Up Gunnerside Gill with Swaledale Miners

A fine ramble up through classic Dales scenery reveals a landscape shaped by the search for lead

1 From the bridge in the centre of Gunnerside take the track on the eastern side up the beck, beginning opposite the Kings Head. After 100yds (91m), at a white gate, take stone steps to the right, then a walled path, emerging into open fields. The path descends to the beck as the valley broadens out. Cross a side beck on a tiny bridge, take two gap-stiles, close together, and follow a wall. Beyond two little gates you reach the beck again, and the first evidence of lead ore processing.

2 Pass two ore-dressing floors, one each side of the beck, and the entrance to a mining tunnel, known as a 'level'. Continue on the riverside path, following the yellow arrows, then go uphill, away from the beck. Cross a stile in the fence before going through a gap-stile in a wall. The path climbs gradually, as the valley becomes steeper-sided. Keep a wall to your left as the path levels out into the principal mining area.

3 Soon the Bunton mining complex comes into view. Pass through it and leave on a stony path uphill, with huge hushes on all sides. After 100yds (91m) uphill, fork left, downhill.

7 Keep left (the track soon becomes more distinct), heading for the roofs of Gunnerside that soon appear. The path gradually becomes clearer and leads you downhill. Go through a little wooden gate and back into the village.

6 Follow this track to the left, through a gate and past a little waterfall in Botcher Gill, before making a gentle descent. Across the valley the landscape changes back to a more familiar one of farms, walls and barns. When the track makes a long right turn, go left on a grassy path, by a small cairn.

4 Approach Blakethwaite Smelting Mill, on a cramped site where Gunnerside Beck meets Blind Beck. Take a small bridge made from a slab of stone. Behind the mill the flue (mostly collapsed) rises steeply uphill. From the mill, the return path is clear, following a well-defined path gradually climbing up the west flank of Gunnerside Gill.

5 Cross another hush on a stone parapet; soon the southern end of Gunnerside Gill comes into view. Follow the track as it becomes stonier, makes a hairpin turn to cross Botcher Gill and joins a more substantial track.

Map labels

Blakethwaite

Gunnerside Moor

Friarfold Moor
▲ 589

Blind Beck

4 limekiln
Blakethwaite Smelting Mill

ore wagon

N

Gunnerside Gill

Bunton mining complex

5

3

M E L B E C K S   M O O R

Botcher Gill

Silver Hill

6

▲ 566

Jingle Pot Edge

Winterings Edge

Gunnerside Pasture

mine buildings

2

Birkbeck Wood

Gunnerside

Elias's Stot Wood

cairn ●

7   **1**   GUNNERSIDE

IVELET

D A L E

Kings Head PH

REETH
B6270

S W A L E

River   Swale

SATRON

B6270

0   ½ mile
½ km

B6270

THWAITE

CRACKPOT

Distance: 6 miles (10km)
Total ascent: 660ft (201m)
Paths: good
Terrain: steep-sided Pennine valley
Gradients: gradual
Refreshments: Kings Head, Gunnerside
Park: opposite Kings Head, Gunnerside, on B6270 between Reeth and Kirkby Stephen

The Edge of an Empire on Hadrian's Wall

An exhilarating walk in Northumberland takes you back to paths once tramped by the legions of the mighty Roman Empire

WALK 66

Top right: the fort at Chesters

Above: the building of the wall took six long years

Below: Hadrian's great wall

The Romans invaded Britain in 55 BC and left traces of their occupation throughout the country. Yet no monument is more important, or more impressive, than the wall built by the Emperor Hadrian, which for 300 years marked the northernmost outpost of the Empire.

Starting at the little town of Halt-whistle, your route leads through a picturesque, craggy gorge known as Haltwhistle Burn. It comes as something of a surprise to find a rich industrial heritage here, crumbling quietly among the bluebells and tumbling water. The sound from the brick-glazing works, old collieries and abandoned quarries must once have echoed the length of the gorge.

Emerging from the mossy darkness of the gorge, the route now follows an old military road which once linked forts, to either side of which are dotted the sites of old Roman camps. These are sometimes visible as bumps in the fields, giving them the appearance of the burial sites of long-forgotten Roman soldiers.

Great Chesters Fort, or *Aesica* as the Romans knew it, is essentially a farm today but was once a base of 500 infantrymen, built around AD 132. A famous hoard of jewellery was discovered here which included two brooches, one shaped like a hare and another made of gold and Celtic in style. There was also a sophisticated bathhouse. The few visible remains of the fort include a stone arch which is fenced in for protection. It is the remains of an underground strong-room vault.

The walk now takes you west, following the Pennine Way, along Hadrian's Wall itself. This took six years to build and ran for 80 Roman miles (73 modern miles or 117km) across Britain. The first sections, built from Newcastle westwards, were 10 feet (3 m) thick, lessening to 6 feet (1.8m) about a third of the way along. The walkway which topped the wall was as much as 12 feet (3.5m) above ground level. As the northernmost frontier of the Roman Empire it served to 'separate the Romans from the Barbarians'. Unfortunately, many of the stones were later removed to make dry-stone walls, or even farm buildings, but it can still present a striking appearance today, snaking across the country like a slumbering moorland monster.

As you follow this walk you are rewarded with glorious views, particularly to the north where the lonely North Tyne valley stretches out to meet the Scottish border. Eventually you come to Walltown Farm, where it is possible to extend the walk to see one of the most impressive stretches of the wall. It is close to a spring known as King Arthur's Well. Tradition suggests that Roman soldiers used to plant medicinal herbs here, 'for to cure wounds'. These probably included chives, which still grow in the crevices of the crags.

Leaving the windy heights of the wall you make your way back via Lowtown, once crossed by the course of the Vallum, a huge earthwork or berm which stretched the length of the wall. It provided an extra obstacle to attackers and, as a defensive method, survives today, used famously by Iraq in the Gulf War. The Romans, you might reflect, tramping over the fields back to Haltwhistle, were remarkably sophisticated – and Hadrian's Wall must be one of their greatest achievements.

The Edge of an Empire on Hadrian's Wall

WALK 66

Walking on the wall which, for a while, marked the northern limits of the Roman Empire

Distance: 6 miles (9.6 km)
Total ascent: 560ft (171m)
Paths: mostly good but can get boggy
Terrain: fields, open country
Gradients: gradual
Refreshments: Haltwhistle town centre
Park: by Haltwhistle Railway Station

1 From the station, walk straight ahead to the main street, then right along Westgate. Follow the main road through the town, then turn left up a flight of steps, immediately before the Grey Bull Hotel. Cross the next road, to join a private road to a kissing gate and path down to Haltwhistle Burn.

2 Almost at the burn, bear left alongside a playing field to join a lane. Shortly, turn right beyond some old works, over the bridge and left through a gate. After 200yds (182m), bear left, recross the burn and turn right on a lane to Lees Hall Farm.

3 Keep to the right of the farm to a gate on the far side. Follow the track to the next gate then cross the main road, turning right, then left by a house. Keep on the tarmac road, through a gate, across the burn, then later over a cattle grid until you reach a farm – the site of Aesica, Great Chesters Fort.

4 Within the fort, turn left towards a round fenced area. Go through the gap in the wall and follow the Pennine Way markers, over ladder stiles and past Cockmount Hill Farm, keeping along the wall.

5 Turn left off the Pennine Way after a ladder stile beyond Turret 44B. Turn left again at a muddy lane, crossing a cattle grid, then after 200yds (182m), turn right on a path signed Fell End. Go through a gate to the left of a building then follow the wall around to the left. Just beyond a waymarker, go down the course of an old wall and straight on where it ends to the far side of the field. Pass through a gate then bear left to ascend to the lowest gap in the ridge ahead. Near the top, pass through a gate and cross the next field to a stile at the main road.

6 Cross the road signposted Haltwhistle and after 400yds (366m), where the road bends left, turn right on a path signposted Birchfield Gate. Head across the field to a ladder stile. Go down the centre of the next field towards a house. At the next gate, bear right, cross a burn and head for the left corner of a barn. Turn left here, recrossing the burn and ascending to the right hand corner of the field. Cross four stiles to a field on the left. Continue, to the left of Woodhead Farm, through two more gates and keep ahead, crossing a stile in the right hand corner of the field.

7 Continue to a road and after a school, turn right down an alley to a service road. Bear right on Greenholme Road, turning right at the end, then left into Greencroft Avenue. At the bottom keep forward for the railway station.

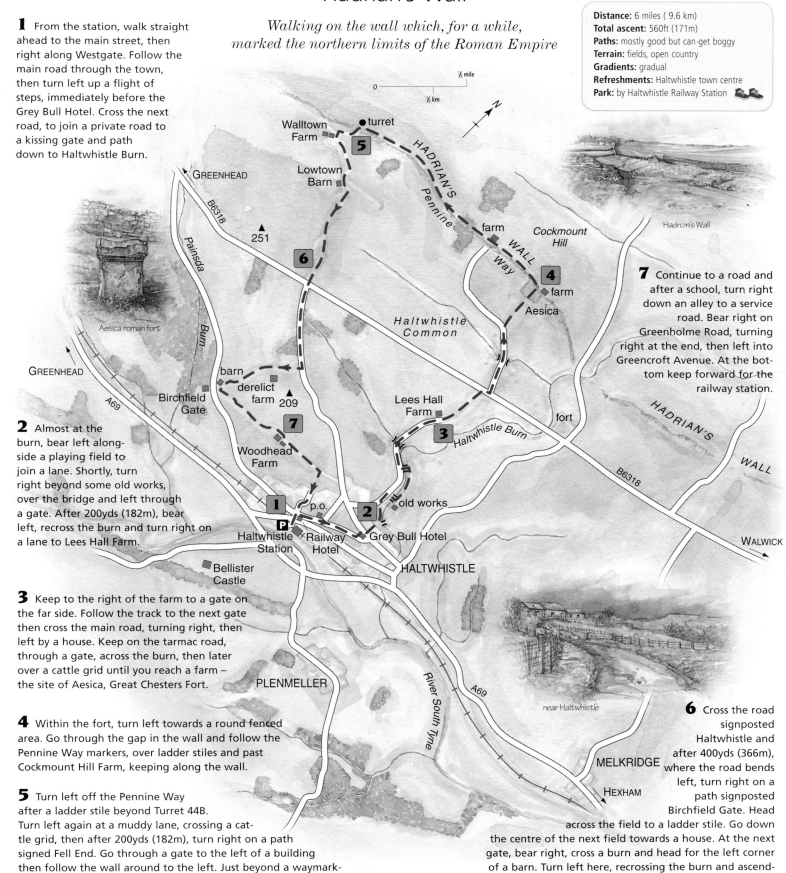

½ mile

0

½ km

N

Walltown Farm

turret

GREENHEAD

Lowtown Barn

B6318

▲ 251

Painsda   Burn

Aesica roman fort

GREENHEAD

A69

Birchfield Gate

barn

derelict farm   ▲ 209

Woodhead Farm

HADRIAN'S   Pennine   WALL   Way

farm

Cockmount Hill

Hadrian's Wall

farm

Aesica

Haltwhistle Common

Lees Hall Farm

Haltwhistle Burn

fort

HADRIAN'S WALL

B6318

WALWICK

p.o.

P

Haltwhistle Station

Railway Hotel

Grey Bull Hotel

old works

Bellister Castle

HALTWHISTLE

PLENMELLER

River South Tyne

A69

near Haltwhistle

MELKRIDGE

HEXHAM

Flodden's Bloody Field

Quiet roads and meadow paths skirt the battlefield where the flower of Scottish nobility perished in 1513

WALK

67

The countryside on both sides of the border suffered numerous raids and skirmishes over the centuries, but none so bloody as the Battle of Flodden Field, where thousands died in an afternoon. When Henry VIII attacked France in the summer of 1513 James IV of Scotland had just renewed the 'Auld Alliance' with the French. In consequence, James invaded England, and he and thousands of his men were wiped out.

The Flodden Monument, at the English battle line, has a display board which explains the positions and movements of both sides. The hill opposite is Branxton Hill, where James IV and the Scottish army lined up. Looking towards the village of Branxton you can see the tiny church of St Paul's, where many of the dead were buried in a large pit. The battered body of James IV lay overnight in this church after the battle, and it is worth exploring. Although substantially rebuilt in 1849, the original late Norman chancel arch has been incorporated as an integral part of the building, and vestiges of the older building remain in the thick stone walls. The list of former vicars and rectors starts intriguingly in 1200 with the name Merlin.

Leaving the village behind and climbing towards the Scottish position on Branxton Hill, you can see how Edward Stanley's English forces managed to surprise the Scots, advancing under cover from the lee of the hill, while the Scots were preoccupied with the enemy before them. The weather had been wet and dismal for weeks and Flodden Field was a quagmire. You can imagine the Scots rushing down the hill and becoming bogged down in the mud, their 20-foot (6m) Swiss pikes unwieldy and cumbersome, as they struggled to escape the clinging clay which would claim so many of them. The English hooked halberds were light, and lethal at close quarters. The English guns, too, were lighter and more manoeuvrable for the conditions than the heavy Scottish cannon, one of which was the mighty Mons Meg, still on display at Edinburgh Castle.

Leaving the road and heading up the rough and deeply rutted path by Flodden Hill, where the Scottish army camped prior to the battle, you can imagine the Scots toiling up the hill with their heavy cannon. The English commander, the Earl of Surrey, recognising the impossibility of assailing the Scots' position, moved north to cut off their line of retreat. Realising the danger, the Scots swiftly decamped. From the footpath you can see their entire route as they hauled guns, ammunition and supplies the two miles (3.2km) from Flodden Hill to Branxton Hill.

This peaceful landscape of gently rolling hills seems far removed from the carnage of thundering cannon and flashing halberd, and yet the shape of the landscape is unchanged by buildings or road networks.

Right: St Paul's Church, where the body of the Scottish king lay

Below: the simple memorial at Branxton

Flodden's Bloody Field

Scotland invaded England for the 'auld alliance' and the flower of its nobility was slaughtered in this Cheviot pastureland

Distance: 6 miles (9.6km)
Total ascent: 500ft (152m)
Paths: good; mostly minor roads and fields
Terrain: undulating pastureland
Gradients: gradual
Park: monument car park, Branxton

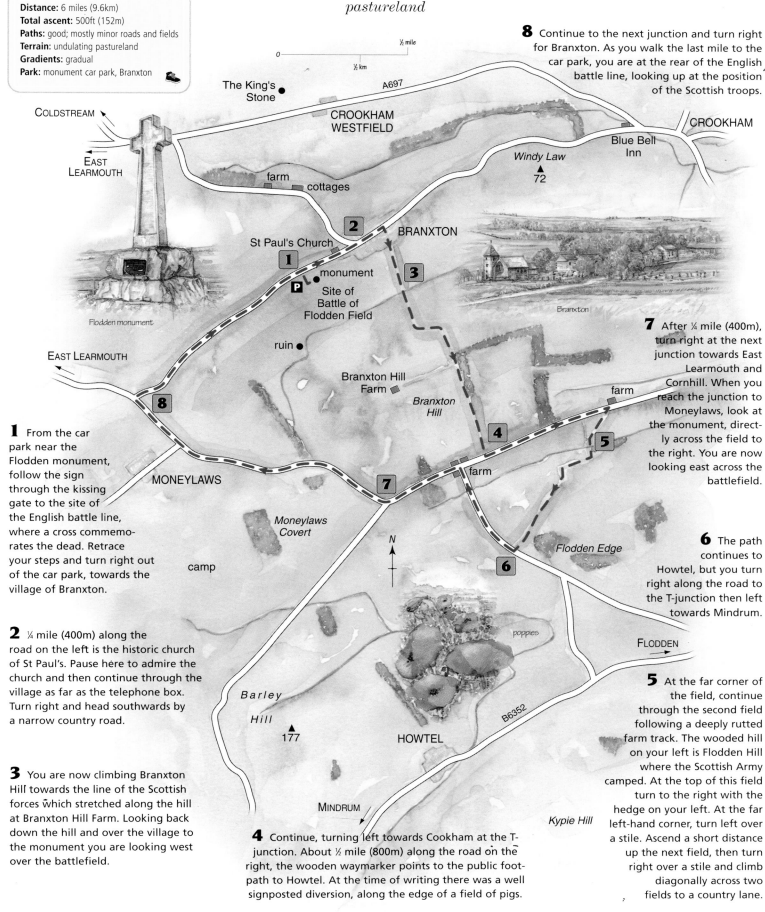

8 Continue to the next junction and turn right for Branxton. As you walk the last mile to the car park, you are at the rear of the English battle line, looking up at the position of the Scottish troops.

1 From the car park near the Flodden monument, follow the sign through the kissing gate to the site of the English battle line, where a cross commemorates the dead. Retrace your steps and turn right out of the car park, towards the village of Branxton.

2 ¼ mile (400m) along the road on the left is the historic church of St Paul's. Pause here to admire the church and then continue through the village as far as the telephone box. Turn right and head southwards by a narrow country road.

3 You are now climbing Branxton Hill towards the line of the Scottish forces which stretched along the hill at Branxton Hill Farm. Looking back down the hill and over the village to the monument you are looking west over the battlefield.

4 Continue, turning left towards Cookham at the T-junction. About ½ mile (800m) along the road on the right, the wooden waymarker points to the public footpath to Howtel. At the time of writing there was a well signposted diversion, along the edge of a field of pigs.

5 At the far corner of the field, continue through the second field following a deeply rutted farm track. The wooded hill on your left is Flodden Hill where the Scottish Army camped. At the top of this field turn to the right with the hedge on your left. At the far left-hand corner, turn left over a stile. Ascend a short distance up the next field, then turn right over a stile and climb diagonally across two fields to a country lane.

6 The path continues to Howtel, but you turn right along the road to the T-junction then left towards Mindrum.

7 After ¼ mile (400m), turn right at the next junction towards East Learmouth and Cornhill. When you reach the junction to Moneylaws, look at the monument, directly across the field to the right. You are now looking east across the battlefield.

Berwick's Bulwark against the Scots

This peaceful border town, fought over for centuries, offers a wealth of history to explore

WALK

68

Above: the huge ramparts date back to Elizabethan times

Below: the town's famous landmark, the Royal Border Bridge, was built in 1850

You could say that Berwick-upon-Tweed is the most desirable town in England. Strategically perched on the mouth of the River Tweed, it was fought over by the Scots and the English for hundreds of years. In fact, it changed hands 13 times before the English gained final control in 1482.

You leave the town over the Old Bridge. If you do this walk when the tide is out, you will be able to appreciate the river's moody mudflats. Dotted with rotting timbers that rear sullenly from the mud, they have a desolate, decaying beauty all their own. You may see birds such as ringed plovers, knots, bar-tailed godwits and oyster-catchers searching for food, or hear the mournful cry of the curlew. Looking back you get an excellent view of the town's most distinctive feature, the elegantly arched railway bridge built in 1850.

During one particularly bloody battle in 1333 the English, who occupied this side of the river, hanged the son of the warden of Berwick Castle. The spot is known as Hang-a-Dyke-Neuk. Occasionally you pass little fishing huts, or shiels – now mostly ruined reminders of the salmon-fishing industry.

The riverside is so quiet that it is something of a shock to find traffic thundering past when you reach the A1. But you are soon back by the river, heading towards the town.

There is little left of Berwick Castle as most of it was demolished to make way for the railway station. It was here that the Countess of Buchan was caged for four years and viewed by the public – her punishment for crowning Robert Bruce as king. From here you soon come to the Bell Tower, one of the few surviving parts of the medieval walls that once encircled the town.

Later you pass through the Cow Port and come up by Berwick Barracks. Designed by Nicholas Hawksmoor, these were the first purpose-built barracks in Britain. The route now takes you round the town's unique Elizabethan walls, built as a defence against the Scots. Begun in 1558, they represented the most advanced military technology of the day, with arrowhead-shaped bastions designed to withstand artillery.

On a clear day this part of the walk gives you a good view of Holy Island, Bamburgh and the Farne Islands. Down below on the rocky shore turnstones and purple sandpipers feed. Further on you can lean over the parapet and admire the famous Berwick swans, a large colony of mute swans which have made this part of the Tweed their own. Soon you reach a large black cannon, brought back from the Crimean War. Berwick-upon-Tweed was, for a long time, regarded as a foreign outpost and did not legally become part of England until 1836. Its historically unsettled status gave rise to a story claiming that Berwick was at war with Russia until 1914, as the peace treaty signed by Queen Victoria in 1856 omitted to include the town by name.

Berwick's Bulwark against the Scots

The streets, ramparts and surrounding countryside of this historic border town make for a splendid circular walk

WALK
68

1 From the Maltings car park go left, down the hill. At the bottom, cross the road, then keep ahead over Berwick Old Bridge. Once over, turn right. At corner of Blakewell Road take path to the right, beside the river.

2 Keep following this route by the river, taking care as it can be extremely muddy and wet and subject to high tides. Later go through a gate and follow the path, keeping to the line of the fence and up to the sewage works.

3 Go over the stile and follow the path, then go through the gate and turn left. At the next gate turn right onto the road. Go to the corner of the field and take the path along its right-hand edge, above the little hut.

4 Continue into the next field. At the end take the right-hand path and descend past a ruined hut and over a little bridge. Ascend and go over the stile to the picnic area with toilets.

5 Go over the next stile, by the main road, then turn right over the bridge. Take the foot-path to the right, down the steps. Go over the stile and back along the river, keeping to the line of the hedge. After ½ mile (800m), veer right to follow a series of waymarks. At the end cross the wooden bridge then a ladder stile and ascend through woodland. At the top of the wood turn right along a woodland path. (If the tide is in, stay with the hedge on your left to cross the stone bridge and turn right into the woodland.)

> **Distance:** 5 miles (8km)
> **Total ascent:** 100ft (30m)
> **Paths:** undefined in places; can be muddy
> **Terrain:** fields, town
> **Gradients:** some steps
> **Refreshments:** plenty in town
> **Park:** the Maltings car park, Berwick upon Tweed

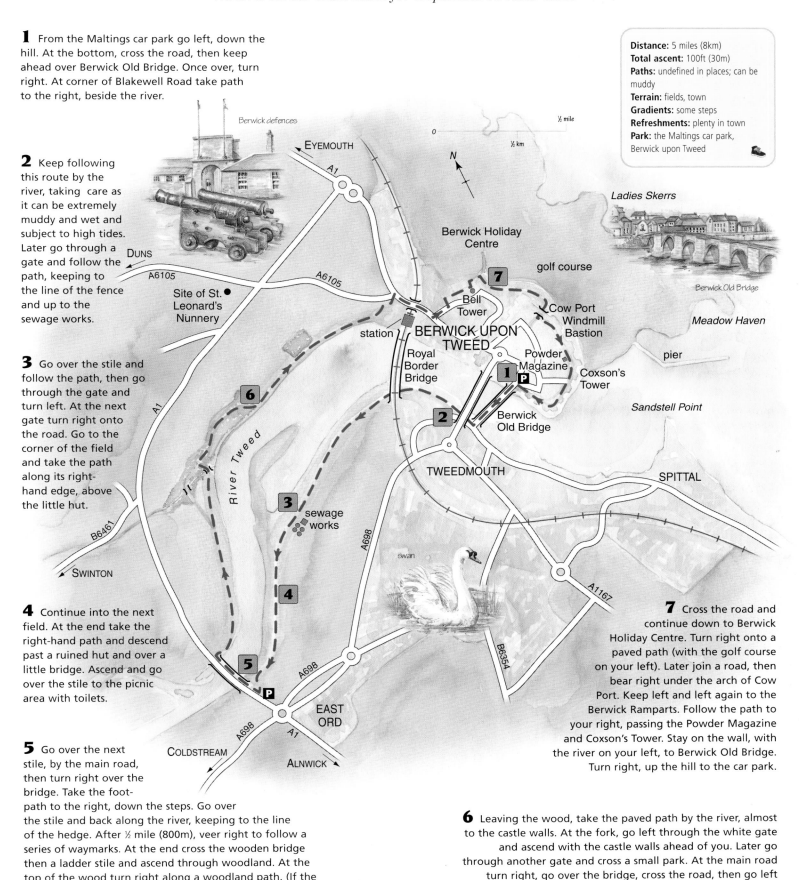

7 Cross the road and continue down to Berwick Holiday Centre. Turn right onto a paved path (with the golf course on your left). Later join a road, then bear right under the arch of Cow Port. Keep left and left again to the Berwick Ramparts. Follow the path to your right, passing the Powder Magazine and Coxson's Tower. Stay on the wall, with the river on your left, to Berwick Old Bridge. Turn right, up the hill to the car park.

6 Leaving the wood, take the paved path by the river, almost to the castle walls. At the fork, go left through the white gate and ascend with the castle walls ahead of you. Later go through another gate and cross a small park. At the main road turn right, go over the bridge, cross the road, then go left along High Greens. In 200yds (182m) turn left into Bell Tower Place then, at a school, keep right to the Bell Tower.

In the Hole of Horcum

Signs of civilisation from the Iron Age feature on this trek across fell and woodland

WALK
69

Above: look out for the tumbling flight of the lapwing

Top right: heather marks the tops of these moorland hills

Below: the sweeping hollow of the Hole of Horcum

It was Giant Wade, says legend, who created the vast, bowl-shaped depression of the Hole of Horcum by throwing a huge clod at his wife during one of their frequent arguments. He missed, the clod bounced to create the hole and came to rest in the form of the nearby hill, Blakey Topping.

Alas for romance! The geologists give us a more prosaic explanation. The many springs in the area have gradually cut their way through the heather-covered, flat-topped hills of the North York Moors to carve out one of the most spectacular sights of the area.

As you begin the walk, following the northern lip of the Hole of Horcum, look northeast to see the Fylingdales Early Warning Station, an improbably massive sandcastle-like structure that replaced the three famous giant 'golf balls' in the late 1980s. Nearer at hand, on the main road, is the Saltergate Inn, whose peat fire is reputed not to have been allowed to go out for more than 200 years.

This part of the walk has reminders, too, of earlier defences. You will go alongside an Iron Age ditch, con-structed around 4,000 years ago to protect the early settlers whose farmstead stood on a nearby ridge – a reminder that these bleak uplands were once well-populated and cultivated by our ancestors.

This is Levisham Moor, parts of it owned by the National Park Authority so that its heather moorland can be preserved. As you leave the moor and descend into Newtondale you may hear the sound of a whistle or see the smoke of a steam-drawn railway train. This is the route of the North Yorkshire Moors Railway, one of the longest and most spectacular preserved steam railways.

The walk's route takes you parallel with the line for a while, before climbing out of the dale and through woodland into the village of Levisham. A remote farming village typical of the area, it has a wide green lined with substantial stone cottages capped with red pantile roofs. To the left of the lane by which you leave the village there are the remains of pits from which iron has been dug since the Iron Age.

The path then descends into the narrowing Dundale Griff ('griff' means a hollow or pit) and reaches Levisham Beck, which flows through the heart of the Hole of Horcum, fed by the springs that gouged it out. Not for nothing does Horcum mean 'muddy hollow', and in the past it has been extensively farmed. The farmhouse of Low Horcum, beautifully set in the green bottom of the valley, is now abandoned and forlorn, with only passing walkers and hovering hang-gliders to disturb its slumbers.

In the Hole of Horcum

*Exploring this spectacular dip in the moorland plateau
of the North York Moors*

Distance: 8½ miles (13.7km)
Paths: good tracks and woodland paths; often muddy
Total ascent: 1,015ft (309m)
Terrain: moorland ridges and wooded valleys
Gradients: moderate; some steep sections
Refreshments: Levisham, or caravan in car park
Park: car park on the A169, 12 miles (19.2km) north of Pickering and 3 miles (4.8km) north of Lockton

7 At a signpost for Saltergate turn left, go over two footbridges and turn left at the waymark beyond it. The path follows the valley into the Hole of Horcum, passing a former farmhouse, then ascends to a ladder stile beside the A169. Turn right to reach the car park.

6 At the top of the green take the lane to the right of the Horseshoe Inn. At a stile beside a gate across the lane, go right and descend to follow a path along the narrowing valley, beside the stream.

5 After 500yds (457m), turn right along a bridleway, going downhill and left at a crossing track. The path winds through woodland and eventually reaches a road, where you turn left up into Levisham village.

1 From the car park cross the road and walk north, following the road's sharp left bend and then going ahead over a stile onto an uphill track as the road hairpins right. Follow this track for 2½ miles (4km), passing left of a pond, to reach signpost by a second pond.

2 Turn right (signed Station) with the pond on your right. Go ahead at a crossing track, walk beside a wall for 200yds (182m), then descend the ridge to the valley road and turn left.

4 At the second gateway take the track uphill, through a gate into woodland. Continue uphill where a track joins from the right, turning left at a crossing track, which eventually becomes metalled.

3 After 200yds (182m) take a signed track to the right. Follow bridleway signs to reach a gate by a wood. The track curves through the wood to a stile, then across fields.

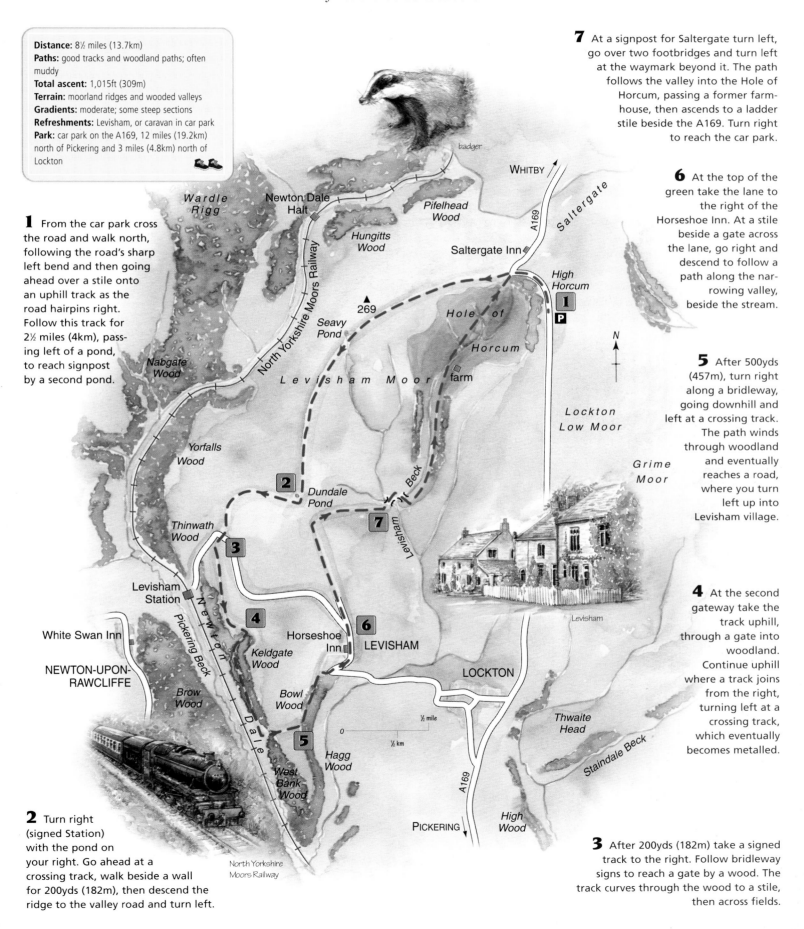

High and Deep on Yorkshire's Coast

The rugged North Yorkshire coast links Captain Cook and the mysteries of the universe near some of England's highest cliffs

WALK

70

For centuries much of the coastline of the North York Moors was only accessible from the sea, and only in a few places, like Staithes, could a small fleet of fishing boats be established. For the most part, the local communities looked resolutely inland, away from some of England's most spectacular coastline.

The walk begins in the rich, undulating farmland between moors and sea. The walk passes through fields to Roxby, now a farming community but in the Iron Age the site of an iron bloomery, turning ore into usable metal. Down the hill is the church, simple and austere from the outside but containing an unusual treasure, Lady Boynton's tomb. Erected in 1634 by her husband, it consists of a rectangular slab of jet-black stone supported on four shapely white marble urns.

From Roxby you take a circuit around Boulby Potash Mine, which processes up to 16,000 tonnes of ore a day. Potash is used in agriculture and industrial glass manufacture. Boulby is the deepest mine in Europe (3,600ft or 1,100m) and its tunnels extend 5 miles (8km) out to sea. It has been the scene of the world's deepest Morris Dance,

and, more seriously, it is used by scientists for research into Dark Matter, believed to make up as much as 99 per cent of the universe and hold the stars in place.

Soon you reach the coast and follow part of the Cleveland Way. Boulby Head is the northernmost point of the North York Moors National Park. Its cliffs rise 660ft (201m) sheer from the sea, making them the highest on Britain's east coast. They were for long mined for alum and iron ore, but the last iron ore mine closed in 1934.

As you walk along the twists and turns of the spectacular cliff-top path back towards Staithes, look out for the birds wheeling out over the sea around these mighty cliffs. Herring gulls, kittiwakes and fulmars are all regulars, while in winter you may see skuas chasing other birds to steal their food.

The tiny harbour at Staithes, formed where Roxby Beck meets the sea, is protected by the crumbling sandstone curve of Cowbar Nab and crossed by a single bridge. Here you may spot some of the older women wearing the traditional white cotton Staithes bonnet.

It was in Staithes that young James Cook – the future Captain Cook – was apprenticed to a haberdasher and grocers' merchant in the main street. This tiny, close-knit and workmanlike fishing village, its slate and pantile roofs tumbling towards the sea, inspired one of England's greatest explorers with the urge to seek adventure in the furthest corners of the globe.

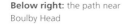

Below right: the path near Boulby Head

Below: traditional cobles in the narrow harbour at Staithes

High and Deep on Yorkshire's Coast

From the soaring cliffs above pretty Staithes to the hidden depths of Boulby Mine, this walk shows the contrasts of the North Yorkshire coast

1 From the top of the car park walk left, past garages, along a path by allotments. Turn right up the valley and follow the footpath signs through the houses to eventually meet the main road. Cross, go over a stile, through the field and cross a track by two more stiles.

8 At a crossing track (the Cleveland Way), turn right and follow it to Staithes, following signs to Cowbar. Descend to the harbour, cross the footbridge and turn right at the main village street up to the car park.

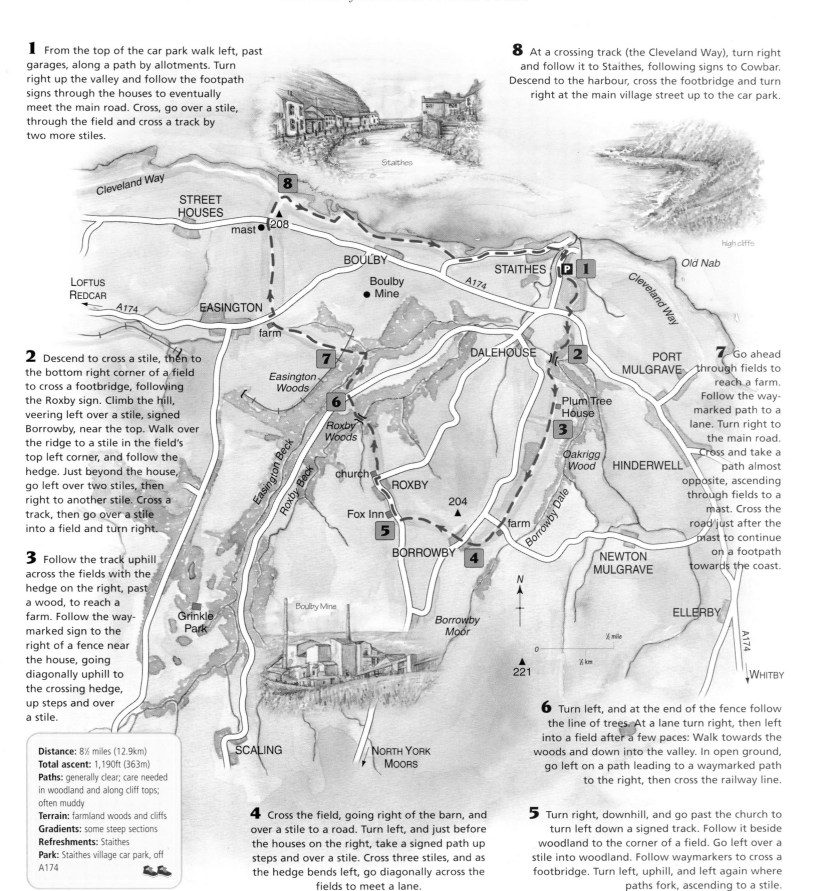

2 Descend to cross a stile, then to the bottom right corner of a field to cross a footbridge, following the Roxby sign. Climb the hill, veering left over a stile, signed Borrowby, near the top. Walk over the ridge to a stile in the field's top left corner, and follow the hedge. Just beyond the house, go left over two stiles, then right to another stile. Cross a track, then go over a stile into a field and turn right.

3 Follow the track uphill across the fields with the hedge on the right, past a wood, to reach a farm. Follow the way-marked sign to the right of a fence near the house, going diagonally uphill to the crossing hedge, up steps and over a stile.

7 Go ahead through fields to reach a farm. Follow the way-marked path to a lane. Turn right to the main road. Cross and take a path almost opposite, ascending through fields to a mast. Cross the road just after the mast to continue on a footpath towards the coast.

6 Turn left, and at the end of the fence follow the line of trees. At a lane turn right, then left into a field after a few paces: Walk towards the woods and down into the valley. In open ground, go left on a path leading to a waymarked path to the right, then cross the railway line.

Distance: 8½ miles (12.9km)
Total ascent: 1,190ft (363m)
Paths: generally clear; care needed in woodland and along cliff tops; often muddy
Terrain: farmland woods and cliffs
Gradients: some steep sections
Refreshments: Staithes
Park: Staithes village car park, off A174

4 Cross the field, going right of the barn, and over a stile to a road. Turn left, and just before the houses on the right, take a signed path up steps and over a stile. Cross three stiles, and as the hedge bends left, go diagonally across the fields to meet a lane.

5 Turn right, downhill, and go past the church to turn left down a signed track. Follow it beside woodland to the corner of a field. Go left over a stile into woodland. Follow waymarkers to cross a footbridge. Turn left, uphill, and left again where paths fork, ascending to a stile.

Down the Ripon Rabbit Hole with Lewis Carroll

A walk around the highlights of one of England's smallest cathedral cities leads out to the parkland of Studley Royal

WALK

71

Top right: Lewis Carroll

Above: Alice and the White Rabbit, by Tenniell

Below: the square towers of Ripon Cathedral

With his seven sisters and three brothers, Charles Dodgson – writer, nonsense versifier and mathematician, better known as Lewis Carroll – spent part of each year in Ripon where his father, Archdeacon Dodgson, was a canon of the cathedral. They lived first in the Old Hall south of the cathedral, where he wrote *Ye Carpette Knyghte*, then in the (now demolished) Residence, whose gateway you will see opposite the north-east corner of the cathedral. Here he wrote part of *Through the Looking-Glass* (1871).

In the cathedral you can see some of the oddities that influenced Carroll's writing. Among the carved misericords (tip-up seats) in the choir you will find a griffin, a rabbit and a turtle, all *Alice* characters, as well as 'blemya', curious creatures with their faces in their bodies, just as Alice was depicted when she had shrunk.

It may be, too, that the Saxon crypt, with its tunnels and curious niches, influenced his description of the rabbit hole Alice fell down, which 'went straight on like a tunnel for some way, and then dipped suddenly down. She looked at the sides and noticed that they were filled with cupboards.' While Charles's father was in Ripon, the crypt was proved to be Anglo-Saxon, not Roman. Hatta and Haigha, messengers with 'Anglo-Saxon attitudes', crop up in *Through the Looking-Glass*.

Other Ripon features also influenced Carroll. The Unicorn Hotel had a famous 18th-century boot boy, Tom Crudd, who could hold a coin between his protuberant nose and chin. Boots is a character in *The Hunting of the Snark*, as is the Bellman. If you are in the city at 11AM on a Thursday, you can still hear Ripon's official Bellman ringing his bell to declare the market open.

Photography, too, played a large part in Carroll's life. A keen photographer himself, he had his portrait taken twice in 1855 by Mr Booth of North Street. The process may have inspired his parody 'Hiawatha's Photographing'.

It was in another Ripon photographer's studio in 1864 that Carroll saw a photograph of Mary Badcock, a sweet little girl with long blonde hair and a ribbon round it. It is thought that he sent a copy of the picture (with her father's permission) to Sir John Tenniell, illustrator of the *Alice* books. Certainly the Alice in *Through the Looking-Glass* resembles Mary, to whom Carroll sent a copy of the book in 1871.

Mary's father, Canon Badcock, was principal of Ripon College. Carroll often visited him and his wife in the Crescent, off North Street. Local tradition says that Mrs Badcock was the model for the frequently bad-tempered Duchess in *Alice's Adventures in Wonderland* (1865).

Lewis Carroll was often invited to the Bishop's Palace northwest of the city. He wrote *The Legend of Scotland* for the bishop's children. In this work he makes oblique reference to the Valley of the Seven Bridges in Studley Park, which you will walk through. He puns on the name of the Bishop of Bec: 'A bec is no longer a bec when it is dry.' The beck that runs through the valley disappears in several places, leaving its bed empty.

Down the Ripon Rabbit Hole
with Lewis Carroll

A walk connecting Ripon with the parkland of Studley Royal – scenery which inspired Lewis Carroll

WALK
71

1 Leave Ripon market square by Kirkgate (near the Unicorn Hotel), and continue along to visit the cathedral and its Lewis Carroll links. Leave by the north door, near the Mothers' Union Chapel, and turn left, following the road as it curves left.

2 At the traffic lights turn left up Allhallowgate and, at the T-junction at the top, go right along North Street. 300yds (273m) on, turn left up Coltsgate Hill, continuing past the College and turning right in to Kirkby Road.

3 Walk up the hill, turning left into Lark Lane beyond the post box. At the bottom, turn right, then first left into Bishopton Road. Where the road bends left, go straight ahead down a track, then over a stile on the left. At a stone stile by the bridge turn right and walk beside the road.

8 Follow the path beside the river, down steps and past a footbridge, eventually to emerge into a minor road and then the main road. Turn left, over the bridge, and go straight on up the hill at the traffic lights, back to the market square.

7 Walk across the fields to a handgate into a lane, and turn left. As the houses begin, go left for 100yds (91m) along the lane to Hell Wath Cottage, turning right along a signed path where the metalled road ends.

6 Cross the footbridge, follow the path as it winds left, and turn right, uphill, at a crossing track. At the top of the hill turn sharp left, signed to Ripon, to reach a waymarked gate.

5 At the crossroads turn left towards the lake, and leave the metalled road to walk round the left end of the lake, over the dam and left, following the path over five stone bridges. Go through the gate in the wall, and walk along to a footbridge.

4 Where the road bends right by the caravan site, go through a kissing gate on the left and follow the footpath across the fields to Studley Roger. Cross the village street and go straight ahead, through two gates, to emerge into Studley Park, eventually turning right along the main drive.

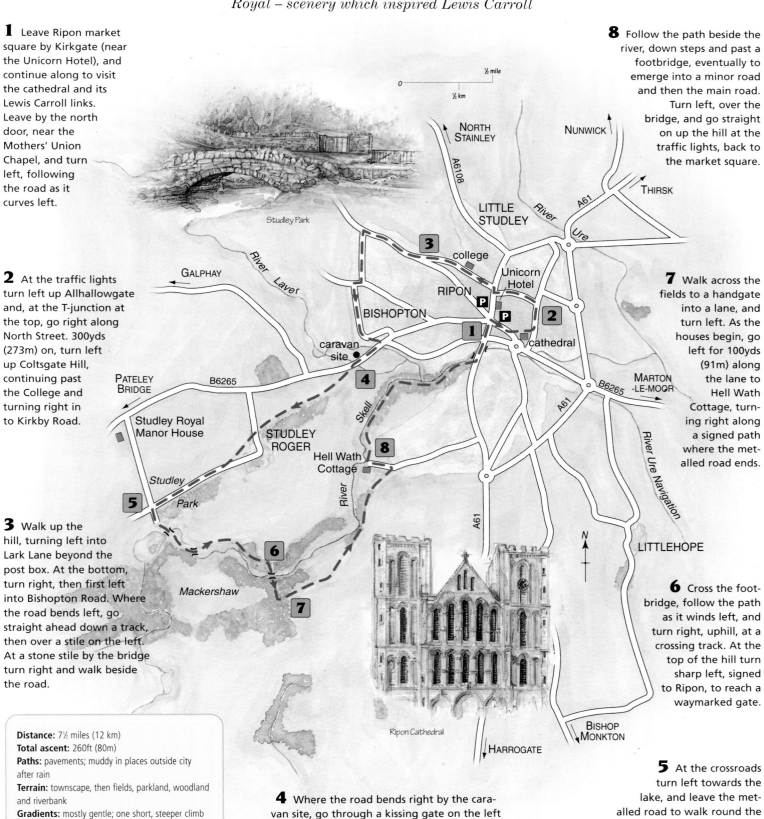

Ripon Cathedral

Distance: 7½ miles (12 km)
Total ascent: 260ft (80m)
Paths: pavements; muddy in places outside city after rain
Terrain: townscape, then fields, parkland, woodland and riverbank
Gradients: mostly gentle; one short, steeper climb
Refreshments: in Ripon or café by lake in Studley Park
Park: Ripon market square (not Thurs) or public car park near by

Wartime Remains on Spurn Point

Shifting its shoreline as the elements dictate, Spurn Point retains many reminders of its strategic and maritime importance

WALK 72

Top right: the orange berries of sea-buckthorn

Walking along Spurn, the appendix of sand dunes curving out into the mouth of the River Humber, can be an eerie experience. One of the most mobile parts of the English coast, it has been swayed back and forth, and frequently severed, by the tides over the centuries. You will see how the roadway along its spine has been diverted away from the battering waves on many occasions. Even in high summer it has an air of unreality. On gloomy days, with the foghorn booming on the point, it is easy to believe you are at the end of the earth.

It is this remoteness that gives Spurn its fascination. Bird-watchers and naturalists are frequent visitors here, and everyone should bring their binoculars with them. But as well as its native interest, Spurn holds darker, wartime memories, as it protected the vulnerable river from enemy action.

There have been lighthouses here for around 500 years; as well as the existing one, dating from 1895, you will see the remains of two others on the walk. A large circular compound once surrounded John Smeaton's 1776 light, while nearer the point itself is the stump of the Low Light of 1852.

There were fortifications here during the Napoleonic wars, but the shifting dunes and encroaching sea have removed much of the evidence. What you will notice, all along the route, are remains from the two world wars.

Weaving its way in and out of the path is the track of the former military railway line, laid in 1915 to link the large army camp at Kilnsea to the fortifications and jetty on the point. It survived until 1951. As you walk beside it, you can picture local people skimming along it on wheeled railway trucks fitted with sails to give them motive power – a type of guided sand-yachting.

Early concrete structures crop up at every step. You will see anti-tank blocks and the standing for barracks. There are former gun emplacements, still with their swivelling rails intact (there's a good example near the start of the walk, on the road near the bungalows) and, at each side of the road by Spurn Point car park, deeply slotted posts to hold an anti-tank barricade.

When you reach the point itself, you will find, beyond the modern buildings of the coastguard and lifeboat stations, a confused jumble of former army buildings, most of them dating back to World War I. Enormously thick concrete walls with narrow windows and convoluted entrances huddle down between the dunes. Gun and searchlight emplacements, some with their rusted anchorages still in place, can be identified on rooftops.

Many of these buildings are falling victim to time and nature, but you can still imagine the stresses and ennui of wartime at this remote spot.

As you leave Kilnsea on the road back to Easington, glance right to see another wartime oddity – a concrete acoustic mirror, 15 feet (4.6 m) in diameter, built around 1916 and used for detecting approaching enemy airships. Walk north along the coast from Kilnsea car park for a closer view.

Inset, below: the lighthouse on the point warns of shallow waters

Below: the shingly spit of Spurn Point

Wartime Remains on Spurn Point

Exploring the wartime remains on this remote, curling finger of land in the Mouth of the Humber

WALK 72

1 Walk to the far end of the car park and follow the Spurn Footpath sign, ascending the bank and turning right. Cross a bridge and stile and turn left then right, to follow waymarkers along the edge of the cliff. After passing two bird hides, follow the path right to descend beside bungalows towards the road.

2 Follow the yellow waymarkers to the left of the road, through the dunes and past the 'No Through Road' sign. The path will eventually join the road; continue along it until it veers right, when the signed footpath again goes to the left.

3 The path rejoins the road briefly, then turns off to the right, following the telegraph poles. Go over a ladder stile and towards the Heligoland Bird Trap. Go over another ladder stile to reach a signpost.

4 Follow the Seaside Path sign, crossing the road and ascending the dunes. The waymarked path follows the coastline and passes the lighthouse, eventually descending via a boardwalk to Spurn Point Car Park.

6 Go to the left of the information board at the north end of the car park, following the Riverside Path signs, past the former Low Light. The path joins the road briefly, but then goes left again, back to the Heligoland Trap. Go over the ladder stile and follow the outward route back to the car park.

5 Turn left and walk past the buildings and the jetty to explore the wartime buildings at the point, then return to the Spurn Point Car Park.

Distance: 8½ miles (13.5km)
Total ascent: negligible
Paths: well-signed and mostly good; muddy in places; some road walking. Obey any diversions resulting from storm damage
Terrain: sand-dunes and grassland
Gradients: none
Refreshments: seasonal at Spurn Point
Park: car park, Kilnsea (east of the village, just beyond the crossroads)

OUT NEWTON

OUT NEWTON

PATRINGTON

EASINGTON

SKEFFLING

B1445

SOUTH END

N

½ mile

0

½ km

butterfly

Skeffling Clays

Easington Clays

Riverside Hotel

Crown & Anchor Inn

KILNSEA

P 1

Kilnsea Warren

Trinity Runs

Trinity Sands

High Lighthouse

Kilnsea Clays

2

North Channel

The Old Den

3

lifeboat

Heligoland Bird Trap

Low Light

4

Spurn Point Lighthouse

war building

P

5

6

RNLI Station

Spurn Head

MOUTH OF THE HUMBER

Limestone Landscapes around Malham

Walkers are drawn from far and wide to this appealing Dales honeypot, its setting justly famous

WALK

73

Right: the fissured natural pavement above Malham Cove

The limestone landscapes of the Craven Dales have long been celebrated, and rightly so. When the exploration of Britain's wild places became fashionable during the 18th century, Malham was a habitual port of call for travellers on their way to the Scottish Highlands or the peaks of Lakeland. Those artists and writers who sought out picturesque views and 'natural curiosities' were able to find both in the environs of Malham. Today, even seasoned travellers will be impressed by the scale of Malham Cove.

A number of roads head north from the A65 between Gargrave and Hellifield, which unite into a single winding lane that leads to Malham. The village lies at the head of its own little dale: a mere 5 miles (8km) in length, but a delight from start to finish. As one of the 'honeypot' villages of the Yorkshire Dales National Park, Malham can get very crowded. On weekends and bank holidays the large car park can be filled to overflowing. The classic circular walk includes Gordale Scar, another spectacular limestone landform. This walk, however, takes you through equally interesting country, while avoiding some of the crowds. It also avoids a scramble up the rocky gorge at Gordale Scar, which can prove taxing for the less sure-footed.

Malham Cove, just a short stroll from the village, is a huge limestone cliff more than 230ft (70m) high and 885ft (270m) wide. It seems to get even bigger and more impressive as you approach. Today the Cove is a magnet for climbers, who look no bigger than ants as they traverse the overhangs and abseil down again. Centuries ago the outflow from Malham Tarn cascaded over the cliff, creating a waterfall higher than Niagara Falls. The water now makes a more circuitous journey underground before emerging downstream of Malham village as the infant River Aire.

The Yorkshire Dales National Park contains most of the limestone pavements in the country. Sadly, many have been destroyed, with the stone from too many such pavements having been looted to make garden rockeries. The pavements look much better where they are, and one of the finest examples can be found at the top of Malham Cove. It's an almost lunar landscape: a wide expanse of limestone rock created by glaciers during the last Ice Age with deep fissures, subsequently widened by the action of water. The flat areas of limestone are known as clints, while the deep clefts are grikes. Be careful as you walk across the pavement; it's very easy to twist an ankle. In icy conditions the pavement is best avoided altogether.

The windswept limestone pavements of the Dales are not as devoid of life as they initially appear. The grikes offer shelter for a remarkable variety of plant life, including the hart's tongue fern. The view from the top of Malham Cove is spectacular; look out for the strips that signify ancient field systems, and the satisfying pattern of dry-stone walls and field barns that is so typical of Pennine Yorkshire.

Above: Malham Tarn

Below: the celebrated Dales beauty spot of Malham Cove

Limestone Landscapes around Malham

Above the spectacular face of Malham Cove lies a less-visited world of classic limestone scenery

WALK 73

> **Distance:** 5 miles (8km)
> **Total ascent:** 985ft (300m)
> **Paths:** good; some steep, stepped sections
> **Terrain:** limestone landscape and upland pasture
> **Gradients:** mostly easy, apart from steps up side of cove
> **Refreshments:** pubs and cafés, Malham
> **Park:** car park by visitor centre, Malham

6 At this corner, take a gate on the right onto a field track (signed Malham 1 mile), soon enclosed between limestone walls. Follow this green lane past the water treatment works to join another, stonier track to a T-junction of tracks. Go right to return to Malham car park.

1 From the car park walk into the village. Where the road forks at the little bridge over Malham Beck, keep left, signed to Settle. About 200yds (182m) past the last building, go through a pair of gates on the right, to follow the well-trodden path towards Malham Cove. Descend to accompany Malham Beck, passing a little clapper-bridge on the way.

5 Go through the gate (signed to Cove Road), and follow a path downhill. Pass a way-marker sign (Malham 2 miles) and head towards Malham Cove in the distance. Descend gradually, going through a gate near where dry-stone walls meet and continuing down the broad track to a minor road. Walk right, down the road, for 200yds (182m), to a sharp hairpin bend to the left.

2 Just 300yds (274m) from the base of the cliff, take steps on the left climbing steeply to the extensive limestone pavement on top of the cove. Cross the pavement (with care) to a wall, and follow it to the left, along the dry valley of Watlowes. Beyond a wall-stile the valley narrows into a rocky gorge, that you leave by steps at the far end.

3 Take a step-stile at the top. Ignore a track to the right (signed Malham Tarn) to continue straight ahead alongside the wall. After just 30yds (27m), take a ladder stile on the left, over the wall. Follow the wall on your right; a finger post indicates Langscar Gate. Walk up to a road, cross it, and continue in the same direction, now on a rutted track. Follow the track uphill to a meeting of walls.

4 Take the gap in the walls and bear half-left to join a grassy track, uphill, to a gate in a wall. Continue in the same direction, through two more gates, after which you bear half-left towards Nappa Cross, a stone pillar on top of a wall (a medieval guide-stone). Follow the wall uphill to a gate and a three-way fingerpost. This, at 1,640ft (500m), is the highest point of the walk.

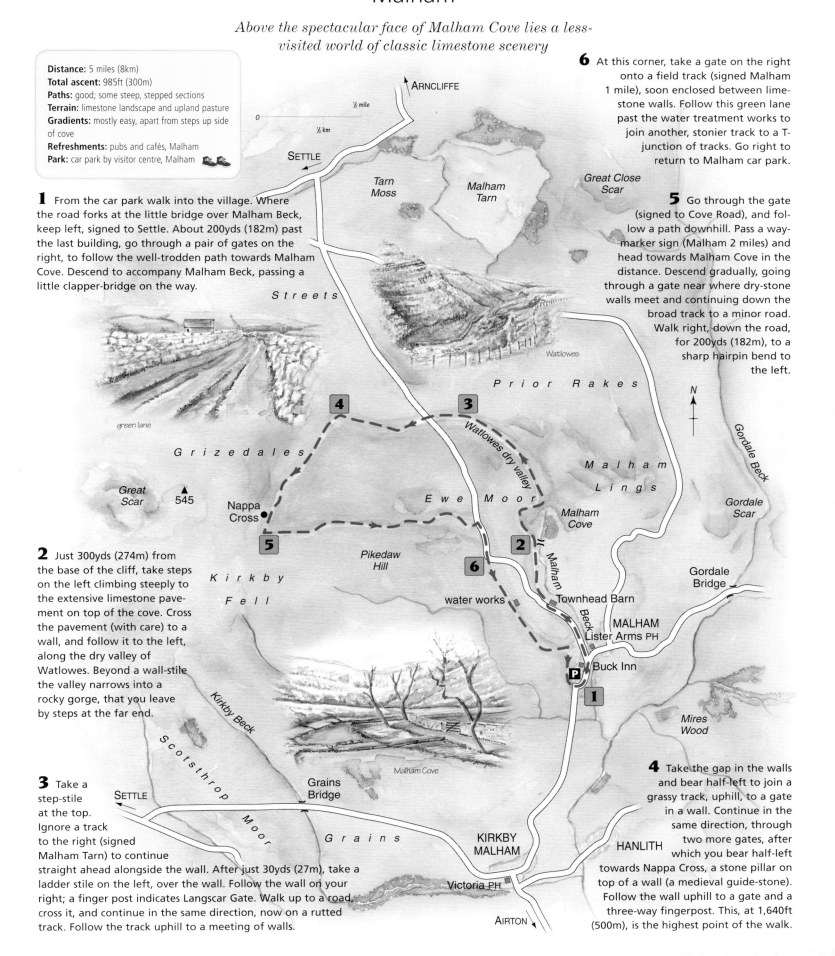

Malham Cove

Haworth and the Brontë Moors

Cross the wild Yorkshire moors to a romantic ruin, following in the footsteps of three precociously talented sisters

WALK
74

Above: the Brontë Parsonage, now a museum

Top right: Anne, Emily and Charlotte Brontë in a portrait by their brother, Branwell

Below: the ruined farmhouse of Top Withins, open to the elements

Who could have imagined, when the Reverend Patrick Brontë became curate of the Church of St Michael and All Angels in 1820, that the little gritstone town of Haworth would become a literary Mecca to rival Grasmere and Stratford-on-Avon? But it has, and visitors from all over the world flock here in great numbers, some to gain insight into the books of Charlotte, Emily and Anne, others just to enjoy a day out.

The shy sisters would recognise the steep main street, still cobbled, though they would no doubt be amazed to see the tourist industry that has built up around their names and literary reputations. They would recognise the Georgian parsonage too. Now a museum, it has been painstakingly restored to reflect the lives of the Brontës, with rooms filled with their personal treasures. That three such prodigious talents should be found within a single family is remarkable enough. To have created such towering works as *Jane Eyre* and *Wuthering Heights* while living in what was a bleakly inhospitable place is almost beyond belief. The Victorian public were unprepared for this trio of lady novelists, which is why the books published in their short lifetimes bore the androgynous pen names of Acton, Currer and Ellis Bell.

From the day that Patrick Brontë came to Haworth with his wife and six children, tragedy was never far away. His wife died the following year and two daughters did not survive to adulthood. His only son Branwell succumbed to drink and drugs; Anne and Emily died aged 29 and 30 respectively. Charlotte, alone, lived long enough to marry. But after just one year of marriage – to her father's curate – she too fell ill and died, at the age of just 38. Reverend Brontë survived them all, living to the ripe old age of 84.

Tourism is no recent development in Haworth: by the middle of the 19th century the pilgrimages were underway. No matter how crowded this little town becomes (and those who value their solitude should avoid visiting on a sunny summer weekend), it is always possible to escape to the moors that surround Haworth. You can follow, literally, in the footsteps of the three sisters as they sought freedom and inspiration away from the stifling confines of the parsonage and the adjacent graveyard.

It's startling to think that from start to finish this walk never leaves the borough of Bradford. The lonely outpost of Top Withins, the ruined farm which is believed to have inspired the setting of Emily's great novel *Wuthering Heights*, seems very remote from that cosmopolitan city.

This is not as undemanding a ramble as some guidebooks might suggest, so wear sturdy boots and carry weatherproof clothing to cope with the fickle Pennine weather. Once you leave Haworth behind, you'll leave most of the crowds too. By the time you take a well-earned rest on the conveniently-sited bench at Top Withins, you'll probably only have grouse for company, and perhaps some hardy Pennine Wayfarers.

Haworth and the Brontë Moors

The moors above the Brontë's West Yorkshire home were a source of both inspiration and solace in their briefly flourishing lives

1 From the car park, go through gate posts opposite the museum and turn right. The lane soon becomes a paved field path that leads to the Haworth-Stanbury road. Walk left along the road and, after about 80yds (75m), take a left fork, signed to Penistone Hill. Continue along this quiet road to a T-junction.

2 Take the track straight ahead, soon signed Brontë Way and Top Withins, gradually descending to South Dean Beck where, within a few paces of the stone bridge, you'll find the Brontë Waterfall and Brontë Seat (a stone that resembles a chair). Cross the bridge and climb steeply uphill to a 3-way sign.

3 Keep left, uphill, on a paved path signed to Top Withins. The path soon levels out to accompany a dry-stone wall. Cross a stile and then keep left. Cross a tiny beck on stepping stones; a steep uphill climb brings you to a waymarker by a ruined building. A short detour of 200yds (182m), left, uphill, is needed if you want to investigate the lonely ruins of Top Withins.

7 From here you retrace your outward route: walk left along the road, soon taking a stile on the right, to follow the paved field path back into Haworth.

6 Bear right along the road through Stanbury, then take the first road on the right, signed to Oxenhope, and cross the dam of Lower Laithe Reservoir. Immediately beyond the dam, bear left on a road that soon reduces to a track, uphill, to meet a road by Haworth Cemetery.

5 Pass a white farmhouse – Upper Heights Cottage – then bear immediately left at a fork of tracks (still signed as Pennine Way). Walk past another building, Lower Heights Farm. After 550yds (500m), where the Pennine Way veers left, continue on the track straight ahead, signed to Stanbury and Haworth. Follow the track to meet a road near the village of Stanbury.

4 Turn right at the waymarker, on a paved path, downhill, signed to Stanbury and Haworth; you are now joining the Pennine Way. You have a broad, easily-followed track across the wide expanse of moorland.

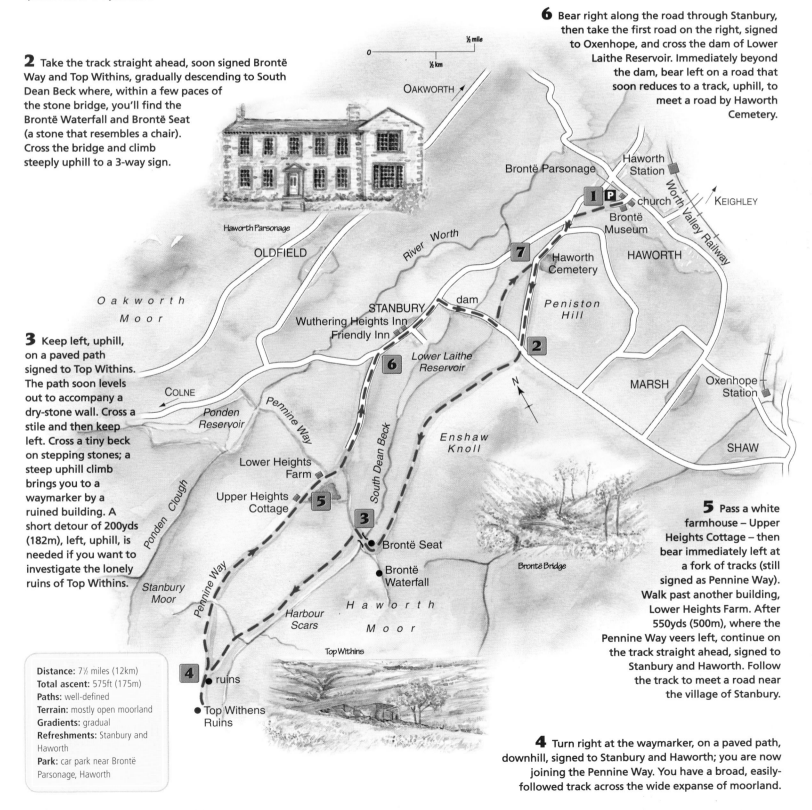

Distance: 7½ miles (12km)
Total ascent: 575ft (175m)
Paths: well-defined
Terrain: mostly open moorland
Gradients: gradual
Refreshments: Stanbury and Haworth
Park: car park near Brontë Parsonage, Haworth

Slaidburn and the Forest of Bowland

Explore the high, open fells of the Forest of Bowland on this wilderness ramble up hill and down dale

WALK 75

The Forest of Bowland, as this big chunk of northern Lancashire is officially known, has long since been stripped of the trees among which the de Lacy lords of Bowland hunted deer in Norman times. These days the area offers one of the largest stretches of open moorland walking in the North of England – high, lonely and unfrequented.

The Hark-to-Bounty Inn in the remote village of Slaidburn got its unusual name courtesy of jolly Parson Wigglesworth back in Victorian days. The sporting parson – who was also the squire of Slaidburn – was fortifying himself in the inn for a day's hunting out in the wastes of the Forest of Bowland, when he heard his dog Bounty outbarking the rest of the pack. 'Oh, hark to Bounty!' exclaimed the delighted owner, flushed with pride and ale.

Slaidburn itself is a snug little moorland village full of old stone houses, many with external flights of steps. It lies tucked down in the valley of the River Hodder, with the Bowland fells rising to the north. A century ago this was still a very isolated place, its sole lifeline to the outside world being a carrier's wagon which trundled over the fells twice a week to Clitheroe, 10 miles (16km) to the south.

The Slaidburn bell ringers were famous for their skill, and also for exercising their prerogative to repair to the

Hark-to-Bounty as soon as they had finished ringing, without attending the church service.

At first you walk along the flowery banks of the Croasdale Brook and through lowland pastures, but once you're up above the valley bottom the harsh loneliness of Bowland begins to assert itself. Small, thick-walled stone barns stand along the roadsides and out in the fields, left behind as you climb the broad shoulder of Dunsop Fell. The long dark back of Burn Fell humps into prominence on your left, its flanks striped with dry-stone walls. This is a moody, atmospheric stretch of moorland tramping, before the ground steepens and plunges dramatically away into the crumpled green depths of Whitendale and the rushing River Dunsop.

Down at Dunsop Bridge, the meeting place of sister rivers Dunsop and Hodder, a cluster of houses huddles around the bridge. Wagtails and chaffinches are usually to be seen here, bobbing and fluttering over the stony shallows.

Long before the Normans came to lord it over Bowland, Norse invaders had arrived here. There was ground for the taking for anyone prepared to clear a patch in the forest, and plenty of good hunting. The farms they founded on the fell slopes between Dunsop Bridge and Slaidburn are still there, and on the homeward journey you may spot some of the old Norse names, adapted over the centuries, such as Beatrix (Bothvar's 'ergh' or farm) and Gamble Hole (Gamel's Hall).

Above: the Forest of Bowland remains unpoilt by mass tourism

Below: sheep graze the lower pastures of the Hodder valley

Slaidburn and the Forest of Bowland

Exploring the great tract of moorland which opens out between the Yorkshire Dales and the Lancashire Plain

WALK 75

Distance: 11 miles (17.7km)
Total ascent: 985ft (300m)
Paths: good meadow paths, moorland roads and tracks.
Terrain: wild, open moors and hillsides, with steep stream valleys
Gradients: several longish gradual climbs, and one or two short sharp ones
Refreshments: Hark to Bounty Inn, Slaidburn; village shop, Dunsop Bridge
Park: public car park on edge of Slaidburn, 9 miles (15km) north of Clitheroe on the B6478
Note: not recommended in poor visibility

1 Walk into the village to the Hark to Bounty Inn. From the inn turn right. Past the health centre, turn right ('Wood House' sign) on a path by Croasdale Brook, then through meadows. At a T-junction, go right down the grassy path to Myttons Farm.

8 Follow the farm track to the road, where you turn right for 600yds (548m), to reach the Hark to Bounty Inn at Slaidburn.

7 Go straight across a field, crossing first a wall stile, then a fence stile, then another wall stile. Aim diagonally right here across a field, bearing away from a fence. Keep left of a farm on your right, heading northeast until a gate and stile in a wall. Cross stile and follow the track to Pain Hill Farm. Go through farmyard, past buildings and out through a gate onto a track with several cattle grids.

2 Turn left to the road, then right for 1½ miles (2.4km) to go through a gate marked 'No vehicle access'. Turn immediately left up a bridleway, where a wall on the left soon swings away; follow the track uphill for 1 mile (1.6km) to a gate.

3 From this gate at the top of Dunsop Fell, bear diagonally right on a path, following yellow-topped marker posts for 1¼ miles (2km) down into Whitendale. Turn left on the road here beside the River Dunsop, for 3½ miles (5.6km), to Dunsop Bridge.

4 Turn left to cross the bridge then immediately left again up a marked bridleway. At Holme Head Cottages go through a gate (blue and yellow arrows) .In 20yds (18m), turn right to climb steps up a steep bank. Cross a wall stile and follow telegraph poles to Beatrix.

5 At Beatrix turn left along the road. Pass houses, and take the track to Back of Hill Barn. Follow arrow waymarks down to the valley bottom, cross the stream and climb the track to Rough Syke Barn.

6 Continue uphill, keeping on the right-hand track, eastward, to go through a gate. In 150yds (137m), turn left into a walled lane, for 600yds (548m) to a road. Turn right here, and in 250 yds (229m) go left over a stile with a footpath sign.

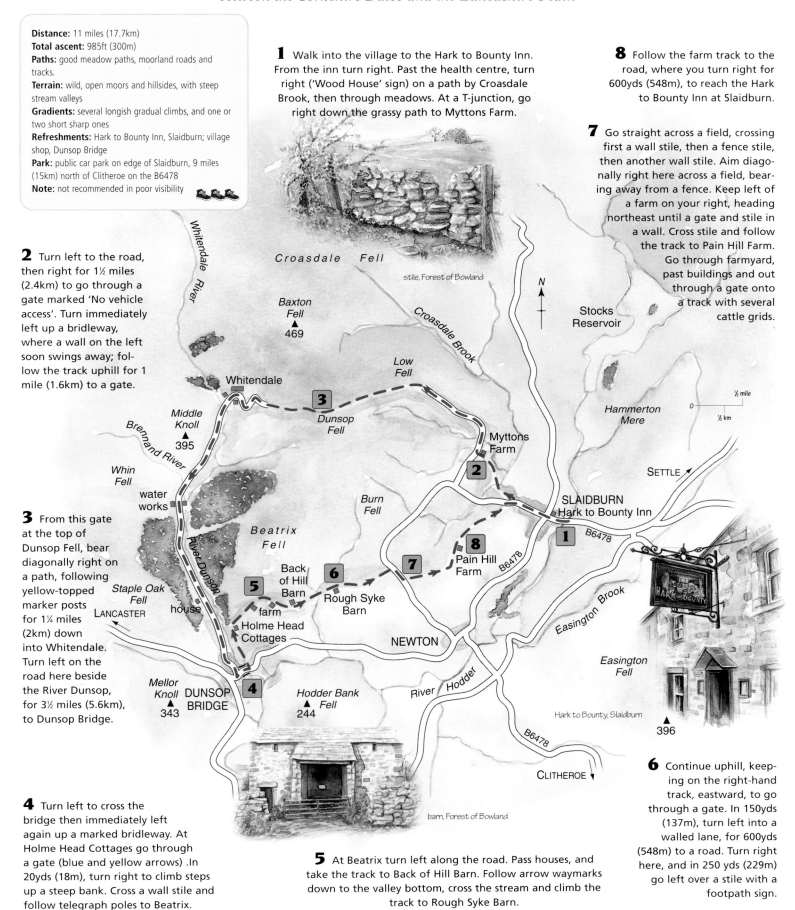

stile, Forest of Bowland

Croasdale Fell

Whitendale River

Baxton Fell ▲ 469

Croasdale Brook

Low Fell

Stocks Reservoir

N

Whitendale

Middle Knoll ▲ 395

Brennand River

Dunsop Fell

Hammerton Mere

½ mile

½ km

Whin Fell

water works

Myttons Farm

SETTLE ↗

Burn Fell

SLAIDBURN
Hark to Bounty Inn

River Dunsop

Beatrix Fell

2

1

B6478

Staple Oak Fell

LANCASTER ↙

house

Back of Hill Barn

6

7

8
Pain Hill Farm

B6478

Easington Brook

5
farm

Rough Syke Barn

Holme Head Cottages

NEWTON

Easington Fell

Mellor Knoll ▲ 343

DUNSOP BRIDGE

4

Hodder Bank Fell ▲ 244

River Hodder

B6478

CLITHEROE ↓

Hark to Bounty, Slaidburn

▲ 396

barn, Forest of Bowland

Cloth and Canal-folk in Calderdale

Old packhorse routes from Hebden Bridge lead you on the trail of the Yorkshire weavers

WALK
76

Hebden Bridge, just 4 miles (6.5km) from the Lancashire border, has been a popular place to visit ever since the railway was extended across the Pennines by way of the Calder Valley. The beautiful wooded valley of Hardcastle Crags, now looked after by the National Trust, is a justifiably famous beauty spot.

This walk links the little town of Hebden Bridge with the old hand-weaving village of Heptonstall, using sections of two waymarked walks: the Calderdale Way and the Pennine Way. The hill village of Heptonstall is the older settlement and was, in its time, an important centre of the textile trade. A cursory look at a map shows Heptonstall to be at the hub of a complex network of old trackways, mostly used by packhorse trains carrying wool and cotton. And Heptonstall's Cloth Hall – where pieces of cloth were bought and sold – dates back to the 16th century, when Hebden Bridge was little more than a river crossing on the old packhorse causeway between Heptonstall and Halifax.

Heptonstall's importance came at the time when textiles were a cottage industry, with spinning and weaving being undertaken in isolated farmhouses. When the processes began to be mechanised, during the Industrial Revolution, Heptonstall – with no running water to power the water wheels – was literally left high and dry.

Allow time to explore the village and soak up its unique atmosphere. In the old part of Heptonstall (now a conservation area) there is much to see. The country's oldest Methodist chapel in continuous use dates back to 1764. The churchyard is shared, unusually, by two churches: a capacious Victorian edifice and the evocative ruins of the old medieval church. The gritstone houses huddle closely together, as though sheltering from the prevailing wind.

As soon as spinning and weaving developed on a truly industrial scale, communities sprang up wherever there was a ready supply of running water. So Hebden Bridge was established in the valley, where two rivers meet. The handsome 16th-century packhorse bridge that gives the town its name still spans Hebden Water. At one time there were more than 30 mills here, specialising in cotton, fustian and corduroy. Hemmed in by hills, and with the mills occupying much of the valley bottom the workers' houses had to be built up the slopes, and an ingenious solution was to build 'top and bottom' houses, one on top of the other. They can be clearly seen on the last leg of the walk, which offers a bird's-eye view over the town.

Few looms clatter today, but Hebden Bridge has reinvented itself as the 'capital' of Upper Calderdale. It's known today for its excellent walking, bohemian population, trips along the Rochdale Canal by horse-drawn narrowboats and its midsummer arts festival.

Above: travelling on the Rochdale Canal

Below: tall houses defy the steep hills around Hebden Bridge

Cloth and Canal-folk in Calderdale

Explore Calderdale's charming tangle of lanes and bridleways between working villages

1 From the crossroads in the centre of Hebden Bridge go down Holme Street to the Rochdale Canal and walk right, along the towpath. After about 1 mile (1.6km) you come to a broadening of the canal, next to a mill and lock; immediately before the next bridge over the canal, go right to meet the A646.

2 Cross the road and walk right for 110yds (100m) to take a track left (signed Pennine Way), through a tunnel beneath the railway. Go steeply uphill on an unevenly paved, walled path, past old houses. At a high retaining wall and small graveyard turn sharp right, through a gate (signed as Pennine Way: official route).

3 Follow a grassy track then take stone steps past a waterfall issuing from a small stone building. Go left at the houses, on a more substantial track. Keep left at a house called Long Hey Top, then go immediately right along a waymarked field path, which leads to a road.

4 Cross the road and continue on the field path, then between walls, to meet an unmade track. (The New Delight Inn is left along this track.)

5 Walk steeply down to the beck – Colden Water – and cross it on a stone clapper-bridge. Climb steeply up the other side, to join a paved causeway at the top of the woodland. Follow the causeway over a stile to the left and over a field; at the second wall-stile bear slightly left to keep following the causeway, with a wall initially to your right and then your left. With Heptonstall church tower coming into view, turn right along a gravel path by a farm outbuilding. Keep left of a house, soon to go over a stile and onto a paved path.

7 Bear left at a wall-end on a walled path leading into Heptonstall. Explore this fascinating village, then follow the cobbled main street downhill. Take a paved set of steps on the left after a set of houses on the right, accessed via a gap-stile. Go right, at a road, past houses, for 200yds (182m) following the brown sign off to the left, to take the steep, cobbled packhorse road – known as The Buttress – which takes you back into Hebden Bridge.

6 After a gap in a wall, at a meeting of tracks, keep straight ahead, slightly downhill. Continue along the level track to join a metalled road. Go uphill for 220yds (200m), then take a gap in the wall to the right. The path meanders through woodland and care is needed in places. Turn uphill slightly at an old waymarker to follow the top path, emerging near the vantage point of Hell Hole Rocks.

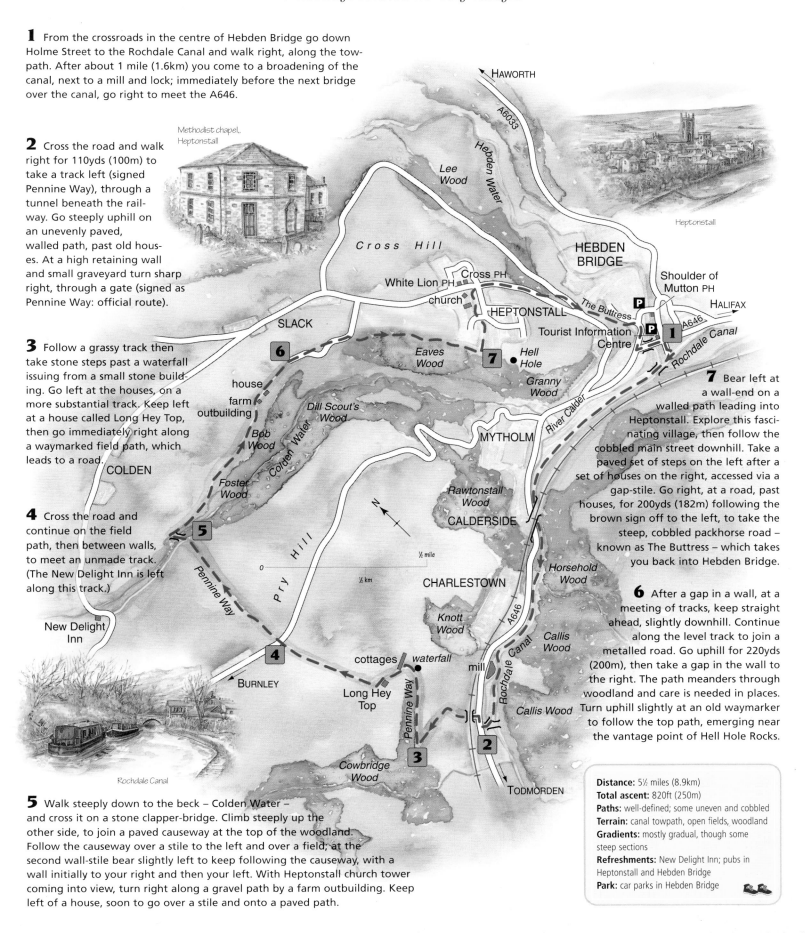

Methodist chapel, Heptonstall

Heptonstall

Rochdale Canal

Distance: 5½ miles (8.9km)
Total ascent: 820ft (250m)
Paths: well-defined; some uneven and cobbled
Terrain: canal towpath, open fields, woodland
Gradients: mostly gradual, though some steep sections
Refreshments: New Delight Inn; pubs in Heptonstall and Hebden Bridge
Park: car parks in Hebden Bridge

The Witches of Pendle Hill

Once believed the highest mountain in England and now notorious for tales of witchcraft, Pendle looms dramatically

WALK 77

Top right: Pendle proved itself a hotbed of witchcraft

Inset below: a peaceful scene at Barley

Bottom: the distinctive profile of Pendle Hill

Witches and Quakers are improbable bedfellows, but both are linked with Pendle Hill, which dominates the attractive village of Barley. The region forms part of the former Royal Forest of Pendle, once remote from outside influence, and where all newcomers were regarded with suspicion. Such insularity also fostered a strong belief in superstitions and the retention of old customs, and proved a potent breeding ground for ideas which were only a step away from black magic and witchcraft. From this volatile mix some folk joined in what they called covens, indulged in strange rites and worshipped the devil. It was a practice that proved profitable, as many discovered, for their neighbours were intimidated and easily blackmailed.

Out of this developed the tales of the Pendle witches. They were real people, living during the reign of James I – a king who believed strongly in the power of witchcraft.

Foremost among the 'witches' was Elizabeth Southernes, who sold her soul to the devil, and was feared as Old Mother Demdike, living in nearby Malkin Tower. She lived as a witch, and brought up her children and grandchildren as witches also. She made the grave mistake, however, of recruiting into the devil's service one Anne Whittle (later known as Old Chattox) – the two families were soon at loggerheads and became bitter rivals. Nevertheless, between them they effectively terrorised the Pendle area.

Sadly, suspicion of witchcraft sometimes fell on innocent people, the most renowned of whom was Alice Nutter of Rough Lee Hall. When the Demdikes were condemned they brought down Alice Nutter too. In 1612, 19 witches from Pendle were tried at Lancaster, and many were hanged. Old Mother Demdike herself, however, escaped the gallows by dying in her cell.

Until quite recently it was the custom never to mow a particular field in Barley at hay-gathering because witches are said to have fouled it. And there are accounts of two old ladies who visited the churchyard at Newchurch each year to place a wreath on a witch's grave, reputedly that of Alice Nutter. Many of the witches and wizards lived around Newchurch, a village you cannot leave without climbing up and going down. Don't be surprised to find witches gathered outside one of its shops, even today.

But not everything around Pendle is about witchcraft. Shortly after the witchcraft trials, George Fox, a young man from Leicestershire, climbed Pendle Hill and had a vision in which 'the Lord let [him] see in what places he had a great people to be gathered'. From this grew the Society of Friends, better known as Quakers.

Barley, once a meeting place for witches, is today the main starting point for walkers to Pendle Hill. For the superstitious, tradition decrees that to avoid being cursed, those who venture up it must carry a stone to the top and place it with the hundreds already there. The hill – a vast and hauntingly beautiful upland moor, site of a Bronze Age burial mound and a beacon to warn of enemy invasions – is irresistible.

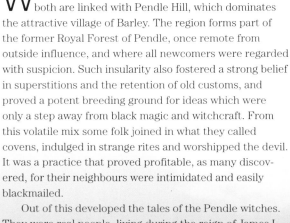

The Witches of Pendle Hill

A walk up this prominent Lancashire hill reveals a landscape where witches were once thought a problem

WALK
77

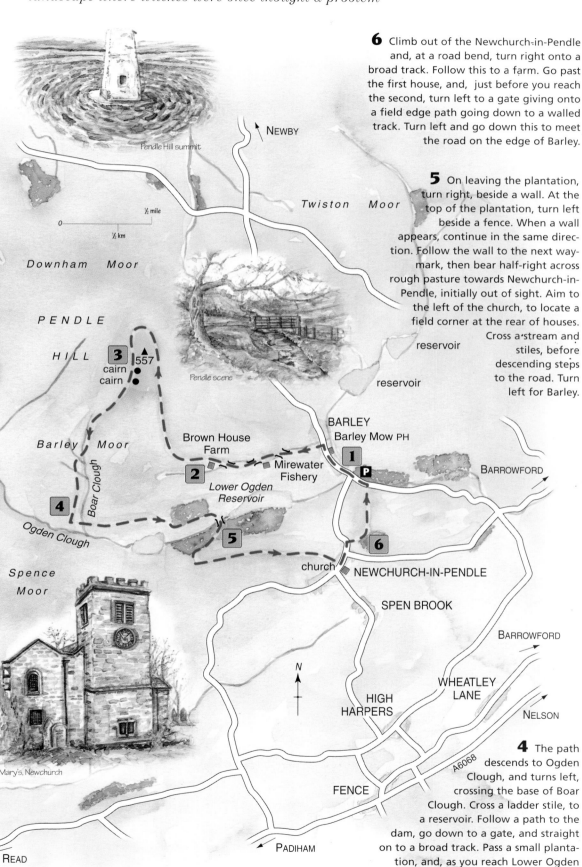

Distance: 5½ miles (9km)
Total ascent: 1,310 feet (400m)
Paths: clear, but not obvious in poor visibility; muddy in places
Terrain: mountain and upland pasture
Gradients: one steep ascent and a lesser climb through a plantation
Refreshments: pubs, restaurant and refreshments in Barley
Park: car park in Barley, north of Burnley, off A6068

1 From the car park, take the path towards the village. Walk past the Barley Mow restaurant, and at Meadow Bank Farm turn left beside a stream. At a foot-bridge, turn left onto a lane and, just before Mirewater Fishery, go through a kissing gate on the right onto a foot-path that leads to Brown House Farm. Continue up a grassy bank opposite the farm, to a stile.

2 Over the stile, cross a gully and bear right in the next pas-ture, below power lines, to another kissing gate. Ascend the right-hand edge of the next field. At the top, go through a gate and across a sloping field to more gates, where the steep path onto Pendle Hill begins. At the top, turn left beside a wall, ignoring a ladder stile, and following path towards the summit trig point.

3 Cross the summit, and descend to the second of two large cairns. Bear half-right, following the path across moorland. Near a small cairn, branch right to a waymarker pole, continuing into Boar Clough.

6 Climb out of the Newchurch-in-Pendle and, at a road bend, turn right onto a broad track. Follow this to a farm. Go past the first house, and, just before you reach the second, turn left to a gate giving onto a field edge path going down to a walled track. Turn left and go down this to meet the road on the edge of Barley.

5 On leaving the plantation, turn right, beside a wall. At the top of the plantation, turn left beside a fence. When a wall appears, continue in the same direc-tion. Follow the wall to the next way-mark, then bear half-right across rough pasture towards Newchurch-in-Pendle, initially out of sight. Aim to the left of the church, to locate a field corner at the rear of houses. Cross a stream and stiles, before descending steps to the road. Turn left for Barley.

4 The path descends to Ogden Clough, and turns left, crossing the base of Boar Clough. Cross a ladder stile, to a reservoir. Follow a path to the dam, go down to a gate, and straight on to a broad track. Pass a small planta-tion, and, as you reach Lower Ogden Reservoir, leave the track, turning right onto a path, soon descending left down steps to a footbridge. Beyond, you climb into a plantation.

Pendle Hill summit

NEWBY

Twiston Moor

Downham Moor

CLITHEROE

PENDLE

HILL

3
▲ 557
cairn
cairn

Pendle scene

reservoir

reservoir

Mearley Moor

Barley Moor

Brown House Farm

BARLEY
Barley Mow PH

1
P

BARROWFORD

2
Mirewater Fishery

Lower Ogden Reservoir

4

Ogden Clough

Boar Clough

5

6

Spence Moor

church NEWCHURCH-IN-PENDLE

SPEN BROOK

St. Mary's, Newchurch

reservoir

BARROWFORD

WHEATLEY LANE

NELSON

N

HIGH HARPERS

FENCE

A6068

READ

PADIHAM

½ mile
0
½ km

Saltaire's Model Streets and the Five Rise

Follow the Leeds & Liverpool Canal to Bingley, skirting the moors to return along the valley heights

Right: Bingley's staircase lock, the Five Rise

Saltaire is an early example of a planned industrial village, founded by shrewd businessman Sir Titus Salt. He made his money by cornering the market in alpaca wool, which he wove into high-quality cloth in the huge mill which dominates the start of this walk. The canal towpath passes beside his domed church, where he is buried.

Industry falls away almost at once, and the canal passes through peaceful woodland, crossing the River Aire on an aqueduct. The towpath switches to the other side of the canal as it approaches Bingley. Near the town centre you will see to the left the modern headquarters of the Bradford and Bingley Building Society. The towpath ascends beside three locks, and then reaches the spectacular Five Rise locks.

One of the major engineering structures on the 127-mile (204km) Leeds & Liverpool Canal, the Five Rise Locks were designed by John Longbotham, the canal's engineer, and opened in 1770. The flight had a sensational opening ceremony, complete with bands, bunting, cannon fire and the ringing of church bells. Each of the five staircase locks – with the top gate of each lock acting as the bottom gate of the next – is 66ft (20m) long and 14ft 4in (4.4m) wide, and holds 90,000 gallons (409,140 litres) of water. It alters the level of the canal by 60ft (18.3m), and it takes at least 30 minutes for each boat to pass through.

Leaving the canal above the locks, the route makes its way uphill, away from the valley of the River Aire. These are the lower slopes of the famous Ilkley Moor. The path continues through farmland, and eventually joins a paved, switch-backing track, part of a former packhorse route that crossed the moors to link up the Aire and Wharfe valleys. Soon after passing the 17th-century Eldwick Hall the path reaches the Dales Way Link which joins Shipley with the start of the 80-mile (129km) Dales Way long distance path.

Your route takes you on to Baildon Moor and along the hillside road with its fine views over the Aire Valley. Below is the rocky valley of Shipley Glen; call in at Brackenhall Countryside Centre as you pass to learn more about the wildlife and geology of the area.

If you time your walk to reach the Shipley Glen Tramway on an afternoon between May and September, you may well be able to make the last part of your journey in the way local people have done since 1895. The cable-hauled tram, with open carriages, travels for nearly ¼ mile (400m), with a maximum gradient of 1 in 7 (14 per cent). Opened on 18 May 1895, it has in turn been powered by a suction gas engine, oil and, since 1928, electricity.

Right: Salt's Mill is now a local arts centre and world-class art gallery

Saltaire's Model Streets and the Five Rise

Titus Salt built his vision of an industrial village beside the engineering triumph of the Leeds-Liverpool Canal

WALK 78

1 Cross the canal by the swing bridge, turn left onto the canal towpath and follow the canal for 2 miles (3.2km) to Five Rise Locks.

Distance: 8½ miles (13.7km)
Total ascent: 430ft (131m)
Paths: generally clear and well-signed; boggy in places
Terrain: canal bank, woodland and open moorland
Gradients: some steep sections
Refreshments: Saltaire, Bingley, Shipley Glen
Park: at Hirst Wood, 1 mile (1.6km) along Hirst Lane from A650 Saltaire roundabout

2 At the locks' summit turn right over the metal bridge and walk up the road, bending right alongside the stone wall. Just before a road joins from the right, turn left up a narrow metalled lane between two walls.

3 Follow this path, with a stream on your right, uphill, crossing two roads and passing through a small housing estate, to reach the hilltop on Lady Lane, where you turn right.

9 Cross the river by a footbridge, then go straight on to the canal towpath, turning right to reach Hirst Wood after 1 mile (1.6km).

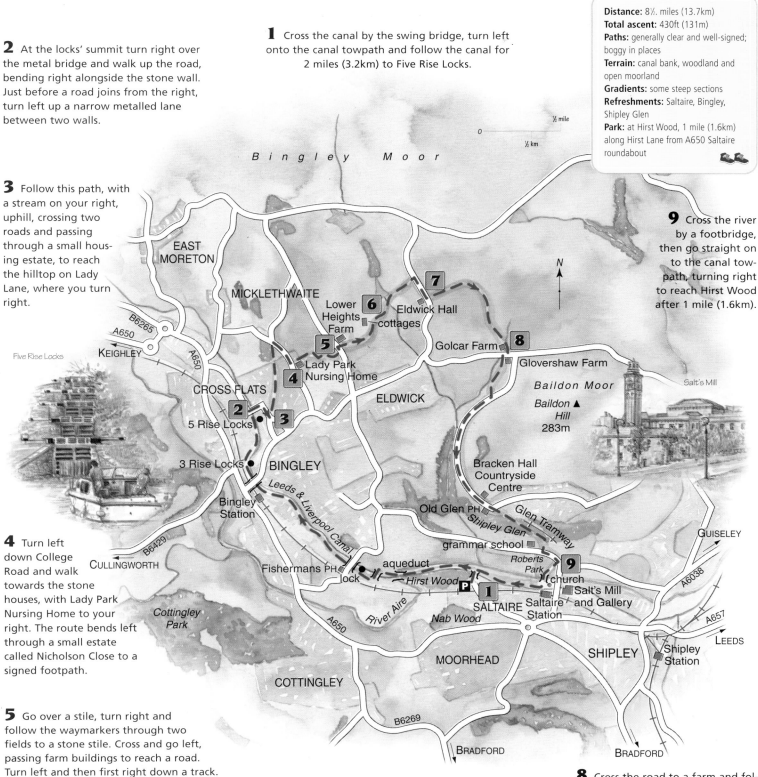

4 Turn left down College Road and walk towards the stone houses, with Lady Park Nursing Home to your right. The route bends left through a small estate called Nicholson Close to a signed footpath.

5 Go over a stile, turn right and follow the waymarkers through two fields to a stone stile. Cross and go left, passing farm buildings to reach a road. Turn left and then first right down a track.

6 After a right-angled bend beyond the cottages turn left, downhill on the packhorse track between walls. Pass the reservoir to reach a road, then turn right to reach Eldwick Hall on your right.

7 Turn left opposite the hall and follow the path through fields to reach a signpost. Turn right, along the Dales Way Link. On reaching a farm, go left over a stile and follow the farm drive to the road.

8 Cross the road to a farm and follow a path next to a beck until you reach a road, which you follow to the Glen Tramway entrance. Take the tramway down the hill, or the path beside it. At the foot of the hill go straight ahead through Roberts Park.

High Pennine Byways over Blackstone Edge

Discover the paved routes of early commercial travellers in this wild hike

WALK
79

Right: before the mechanisation of the Industrial Revolution, spinning and weaving were cottage industries

Below: the steep road is believed to date back to Roman times

Bottom: the crags of Blackstone Edge

The South Pennine moors have traditionally offered the chance for millworkers and other wage slaves to be, in the words of the song, 'a free man on Sunday'. Though they are easily accessible from the industrial towns of east Lancashire and west Yorkshire, a tramp across the tops makes you feel a long way from civilisation. The moors provide excellent walking, panoramic views and fresh air aplenty.

Note that this walk takes you out into the wilds and should not be attempted in bad weather or poor visibility. Wear sturdy footgear, take waterproofs and pack some sandwiches: you won't find a welcoming pub until the walk is nearly over. Despite these provisos, the route-finding is easy, and the steepest gradient is up the old Roman road.

These high, lonely moors are criss-crossed by old tracks. Before the Industrial Revolution the textile trades of Yorkshire and Lancashire were cottage industries, carried out in isolated farmsteads and communities. Raw

materials were delivered to the spinners and weavers; finished cloth 'pieces' had to be taken away to cloth halls and merchant clothiers.

With the valley bottoms being largely undrained, transport was by packhorse over the higher ground. The routes were typically marked on the ground by closely fitting stone flags, creating what are known as 'causeways' or 'causeys'. Other tracks are known as 'hollow-ways', centuries of traffic having worn them into steep-sided thoroughfares. This walk includes sections of both causeways and hollow-ways. You may not see another soul for miles, but a few generations ago these tracks must have been very busy, the motorways of their day.

Blackstone Edge holds few terrors for the travellers of today, now that modern roads have tamed the steepest gradients. The M62 motorway slices through the landscape, allowing motorists to traverse the Pennine watershed in a matter of minutes. But for centuries Blackstone Edge was a notorious barrier for travellers between Lancashire and Yorkshire. Celia Feinnes, coming this way in 1698, described Blackstone Edge as a dismal high precipice, steep in ascent. Even that doughty traveller, Daniel Defoe, had cause to declare that the depth of the precipice and narrowness of the way looked horrid.

This walk includes that steep ascent, up a fascinating paved causeway that continues to puzzle historians. Is it Roman, as some suggest, or a pre-turnpike packhorse road? If it is Roman, then it is the best-preserved example in the country. One thing is certain: the Aiggin Stone, at the top, is a guide stone and dates from medieval times.

High Pennine Byways over Blackstone Edge

A beautifully preserved section of ancient road leads over the moors between Yorkshire and Lancashire

1 From station take underpass beneath railway. Walk left, along tow-path, crossing canal at first set of locks, to follow path that emerges onto Ealees Road. Continue straight ahead on metalled track, passing a mill and Old Mill Cottage. As track curves right, take steps on your left and follow path uphill. Bear left, immediately before farm at top, to walk up a wooded valley. Cross footbridge; when path levels out, you see a canal drain. Don't cross it, but follow it to the left, to Owlet Hall.

6 Keep to lakeside road before going right, past visitor centre. At far end of car park join metalled path. Cross footbridge and follow stream to bigger track. Go left here and retrace your earlier steps, keeping straight ahead on path to canal, and back along towpath into Littleborough.

Roman Road

R i s h w o r t h   M o o r

reservoir

Aiggin Stone

Robin Hood's Bed

RIPPONDEN

Aiggin Stone

RIPPONDEN

3

HUDDERSFIELD

Rishworth Drain

472

Broad Head Drain

Blackstone Edge

Roman Road

A58

LYDGATE

reservoir

High Peak Cottages

TODMORDEN

M o s s   M o o r

Junction 22

LITTLEBOROUGH

Owlet Hall

2

golf course

A6033

Old Mill Cottage

C l e g g   M o o r

Low House Moor

4

mast

A672

N

Windy Hill

mill

Littleborough Station

1

Cleggswood Hill

½ mile

½ km

0

Bleakedgate Moor

M62

ROCHDALE

River Roch

canal

P

visitor centre

Fishermans Inn

Hollingworth Lake

6

RAKEWOOD

5

5 At a T-junction take right fork to follow a deep hollow way and keep right, following brown arrow way-markers. The surface improves beneath pylons, then comes to a crossroads with a wooden gate. Don't go through it, but turn right, through a metal gate. Walk down track for about 100yds (91m), before bearing left over stile onto track, descending towards Rakewood Viaduct. Take right fork beyond viaduct to cross rugby field to a road. Turn left, passing mill, to Hollingworth Lake.

hare

Rakewood Viaduct

reservoirs

ROCHDALE

4 Follow path uphill, to mast. Bear right onto a track, then, at far end of the mast's perimeter fence, bear half-left on rutted track, downhill. Go through a wall-gap, then by a wall over Windy Hill. Eventually it becomes a walled track or hollow way.

2 Go through wooden gates and around front of house to join a field path, and follow a wall on your left with a golf course right. Go left along a stony track, keeping left past a farm, then turning left on bridleway to Blackstone Edge Road by High Peak Cottages. Turn right on path directly in front of cottages, continuing on a field path with a wall on right. At farm track go right for a few paces, then head left, up the hill on obvious path. Soon you are on the famous 'Roman Road' to the Aiggin Stone, a medieval waymarker.

3 Go right from the stone, through a gate, to join the Pennine Way. Small cairns mark the path along Blackstone Edge. Past a trig point (the highest point of the walk), follow a sandy track (aim for mast in the middle distance), bearing left to cross the M62 on a footbridge.

Distance: 9 miles (14.5km)
Total ascent: 1,148ft (350m)
Paths: mostly well-defined; may be boggy after rain
Terrain: mostly open moorland; best not attempted in bad weather or poor visibility
Gradients: mostly gradual
Refreshments: Littleborough
Park: Littleborough railway station

Wales

Wales

Cymru, the land of compatriots, our land; a land that is distinct and unique in so many ways; a land intrinsically rugged and wild, with a character all its own, and a fascinating history and culture.

Previous page: moody skies over Llyn y Dywarchen, near Rhyd-Ddu, Snowdonia

Below: dramatic Cwm Idwal, Snowdonia

Here in Wales are craggy heights, rock-strewn, heather-clad hillsides, barren moors, bright green valleys, silver rivers, mountain lakes, rocky, storm-tossed coastlines and sublime golden beaches. And over it all lies a mantle of history and mystery as complex as any.

This is a most beautiful and varied country, one where there is still resistance to cultural change and a strong desire to retain an identity quite uninfluenced by external forces whether invading, subsuming or economic. In his publication *Visions of Snowdonia* (1997) Jim Perrin explains: '…whatever else Wales is, it is not England, it is other.'

Ever since Mercian King Offa ordered the building of his now renowned dyke in AD 779 – for reasons that have never been totally clear, but probably have more to do with defining a national boundary than with a need for defence – the people of this wild country have been known as *wealas*, the Anglo-Saxon word for 'foreigners': and from this came the word Wales. Today, Wales seems to be a confusing muddle of counties and unitary authorities

salvaged from a modest spread of counties manipulated, in 1974, out of a slightly more complex but more memorable group of counties and a few large borough councils – almost back to square one. For walkers, thankfully, Wales has traditionally been a country of three parts – North, South and Mid-Wales – and each has its own distinctive flavour and characteristics.

In the late 12th century a native of South Wales set out on a journey to North Wales in company with fellow churchmen. His name was Giraldus, and his mission was to do with both church politics and drumming up support for the Third Crusade. The journey, undoubtedly arduous, was almost certainly fascinating and full of intrigue. In the Wales of those times all the roads would have been green roads, and the only alternative was to follow the coastline – and that usually meant no roads at all.

To follow that route today would prove no less fascinating, and take you through the three regions of Wales in a way that would almost certainly leave you captivated by the variety, enthralled by the sheer beauty of the landscapes and excited by the discovery of a land of richness. Indeed, the walks that follow pursue ancient footsteps and trackways from those of prehistoric man and the Romans, to those of Bible-seeking Mary Jones, whose memorable walk to Bala was one of great devotion and faith.

Much of walkers' North Wales is contained within the Snowdonia National Park, from time immemorial known to its inhabitants as Eryri, the 'Place of Eagles'. Eagles did once haunt the cliffs and cwms of North Wales, and kings too, for here the Welsh King Gwrtheyrn, better known as Vortigern, sought safe retreat from the attacks of the English in the land called Gwynedd.

The popularity of Snowdon (Yr Wyddfa), the Carneddau, the Glyderau, the Rhinogs and the other mountains of Eryri has scarcely abated since the first recorded ascent of Snowdon in 1639 by botanist Thomas Johnson. And though all the early ascents were by scientists, by the time the English traveller George Borrow (author of *Wild Wales*) appeared on the scene in the 1850s to quote Welsh poetry from Snowdon's summit, the ascent was already a popular excursion.

Below: the rugged Llanberis Pass, Snowdonia

Above: the mighty towers of Harlech Castle

Below: Threecliff Bay and Great Tor, on the Gower Peninsula

But it was not Snowdon alone that drew the visitors. Black's *Picturesque Guide to North Wales*, published in 1857, comments that 'in savage grandeur the Glyder is not surpassed by any scene in Wales'. A question of preferences, undoubtedly, but already Wales was beginning to draw comparisons and tease out its devotees. And though the Glyderau are virtually all rocks, the adjacent Carneddau (in spite of some notable cliffs) are essentially rounded, grassy hills, a perfect contrast to much of the rest of North Wales.

Nor is the whole of North Wales Snowdonia. The eastern moorlands of Denbighshire are a kind of sleeping policeman, and flow westwards to the great natural barrier that is the River Conwy below the eastern fringes of the Carneddau. North and west, the isle of Anglesey, the 'Mother of Wales', and the delectable Lleyn Peninsula boast renowned landscapes that make your heart ache and your spirit rejoice.

Further south, the Rhinogs are as rugged and rough as anything to be found in Britain, and certain to exact perspiration by the bucketful, as they no doubt did when traders first constructed their route through Cwm Bychan. Yet for the appellation of 'most dangerous mountain in Wales', we must look to Powys and the vast sprawl of Plynlimon, high above the Hafren Forest. It is the 'frequency of bogs, concealed under a smooth and apparently firm turf' that deterred the author of the *Picturesque Guide*, for this is the cradle of rivers: the Severn and the Wye rise within a short distance of one another, and the Ystwyth begins close by.

A hundred years after the Domesday Book, Archbishop Baldwin of Canterbury began his mission to preach the Crusades in Wales in the quiet heartlands of Mid-Wales, at New Radnor, part of the great hunting Forest of Radnor. But, for the next two and a half centuries, it was an unhappy, oppressed place, where the Lords Marchers held power of life and death over the inhabitants, ruling them by the sword under the Jura Regalia, a severe form of martial law.

And in the south, the borderland Black Mountains (Mynyddoedd Duon) are a paradise for walkers who revel in long, lofty ridges separated by valleys of quiet calm. Further west rise the distinctive, flat-topped summits of the Brecon Beacons, another Black Mountain (Mynydd Du) and the Fforest Fawr, names that speak of wilderness and desolation, and all contained within the Brecon Beacons National Park. The further west you go, the greater the feeling of isolation, but never in an overpowering way, for here the seclusion works as a panacea for workaday ills, and the wild, ponied expanses are the most refreshing of ingredients in the panoply of Wales.

Best of the Rest

The Monmouthshire and Brecon Canal The only canal through a national park, the Monmouthshire and Brecon Canal offers easy walking amidst spectacular scenery. The ridges of the Brecon Beacons loom above, but the way along the towpath remains completely level, all the way into the centre of Brecon itself.

The Valleys The harsh edges of South Wales' industrial heartlands were always softened by the proximity of steeply wooded hillsides and liberating open moorlands. Now the industry has departed and the walker can return to the valleys, making good use of disused railway lines and the network of paths and tracks that kept workers and materials moving throughout the Industrial Revolution. The head of the Rhondda valley is particularly worth exploring.

Mid-Wales To the south of Strata Florida Abbey the wilds of Mid-Wales are often overlooked by walkers aiming for the mountains of Snowdonia or the high hills of the Brecon Beacons. And yet here is a landscape of intricate upland valleys, not at all spoiled by its forestation or reservoir developments. In fact it is these corporate utility invaders which have opened up the place for walkers, with car parks and nature trails. The serene upper reaches of the Afon Tywi, in particular, support a fine network of paths and trails for the walker in search of solitude.

Gower The beautiful sweeps of sand which characterise the handful of beaches on the Gower Peninsula attract thousands of holidaymakers in the summer months. Less well known is the fine stretch of cliff path which connects them – as dramatic as anything in Cornwall or Pembrokeshire. If you have a few days, the coast can be walked as a continuous path, otherwise extensive inland links allow each section to be done as a circular walk.

Betws-y-coed In the shadow of the great mountain mass of the Carneddau in Snowdonia a series of pretty valleys spreads like fingers to that of the much larger Afon Conwy. The environment here, though remote and sometimes inhospitable, has been much utilised, by early farmers, miners, reservoir-builders and foresters. The resulting landscape, around Llyn Crafnant and Llyn Geirionydd is a delightful tangle of lanes and paths amid small lakes, intriguingly overgrown old workings and ancient hill farms.

Left: reflections in Llynnau Mymbyr, Snowdonia

Breidden Hills – the Gateway to Wales

A walk with fine views on the first mountains in Wales

WALK
80

Top right: Rodney's Pillar towers above the border country

If you've motored down the A458 from Shrewsbury into Wales, you've no doubt noticed the place where the first big hills rise from the fields of Shropshire. Usually, they signal that you're well on your way to the more celebrated Cambrian Mountains. They might hold your interest for a mile or two, but soon pass as you speed on into Snowdonia. Well, those big hills are the Breiddens. Formed by a volcanic upheaval, these hard dolerite outcrops have withstood the eroding elements of time better than the softer rocks of the surrounding countryside. Complex geology hereabouts has allowed both acid- and lime-loving plants to flourish. Edward Lhuyd made the first recorded British sighting of spiked speedwell here, in the 17th century.

More than 200 years ago Sir George Brydges Rodney regularly climbed to the top of Breidden Hill, where he said he could spy ships sailing in and out of the Severn Estuary. The locals of Montgomery honoured him in 1792 by erecting an obelisk atop the summit rocks. They were proud of this man who had joined the navy at 13, and who had risen to the ranks of admiral, inflicting many famous victories over the fleets of the French, Spanish and Dutch.

Today when you stand beneath Rodney's Pillar you can see much the same view as did the Admiral. The River Severn slithers like a serpent past the buildings of Welshpool, and through mile upon mile of lowland plain

Below: Breidden's views have been famous for centuries

etched with a web of hedgerow and forest, framed by the rolling Welsh foothills.

There are three ancient settlements in these hills: one on Middletown Hill, one on Breidden Hill and one in the forests of New Pieces, between the two hills. They were probably occupied until the Roman invasion in AD 57.

The first fort is reached after a steep but exhilarating climb from Middletown. Middletown Hill is the least wooded of the hills, and as such has uninterrupted views on the climb. One by one the towns and villages of Shropshire are laid out beneath your feet like blue-grey patches on a huge real-life map. The fields are punctuated by the odd church spire or tower, and a faint plume of smoke from a Chirk factory, with hills in the distance.

The land in between Middleton Hill and Breidden Hill consists of a narrow band of farm pasture and large tracts of conifer forest. Easy, well-marked paths thread through the forest to Rodney's Pillar, but it's the nearby crag-topped wooded hill, Moel y Golfa, that takes the eye. Paths to it are steep, though, and some may prefer the walk through the oak woods that cloak its lower slopes. The summit has rocks on the top to scramble over and another monument to look at. This one, a more modest pillar than Admiral Rodney's, is dedicated to Romany leader Ernest Burton, who died in 1960, and carries another plaque to his son, Uriah, who died in 1986.

Breidden Hills –
the Gateway to Wales

*Long famed for their extensive views, the Breidden Hills
hint at the great mountains beyond*

1 From car park, walk up lane directly opposite Breidden Hotel. Ignore footpath left and follow lane towards Middleton Quarry. Fork right at junction, soon turning left on path uphill through gorse and bracken. Keep climbing through all path junctions to ridge at the top. Turn right on wide track to Middletown Hill.

2 Walk along ridge to summit then down to saddle. Descend left to lane and turn right. Pass Belleisle Farm and carry on to track on left, taking you past another farm, into pastureland. Maintain direction through first field, then follow left-hand hedge to woods. Cross stream and follow waymarked bridleway rising through woods. It crosses a flinty forestry road then continues to climb up to Rodneys Pillar, taking two left forks along the way. Beyond stile in fence, path traverses open hillside to another stile preceding steep climb to Rodney's Pillar.

7 At signpost by fence corner, near lower edge of wood, turn right. Two routes meet up by stile at edge of wood. Turn sharp left if you have just descended from higher route. Another stile leads to field. Turn left along its edge, past pig enclosure to farm track. Turn right to road, a little way out of Middletown, and follow it left, back into village.

3 From the summit, head along ridge (southwest) to edge of wood, then turn sharp left to double-back down hillside and through sparse woodland to open area.

Ernest Burton's monument, Moel y Golfa

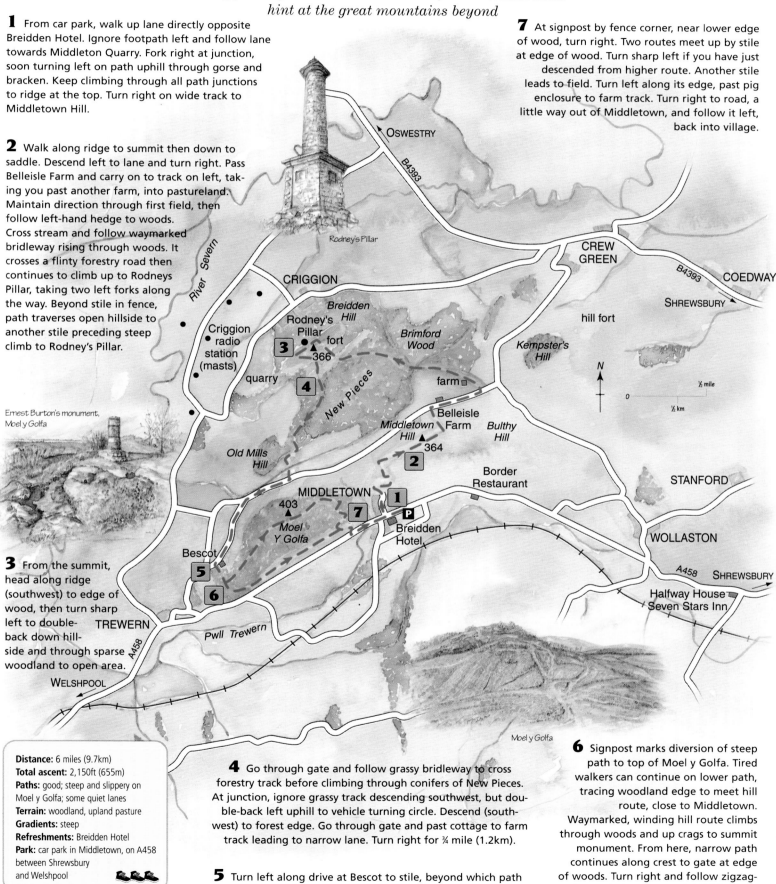

4 Go through gate and follow grassy bridleway to cross forestry track before climbing through conifers of New Pieces. At junction, ignore grassy track descending southwest, but double-back left uphill to vehicle turning circle. Descend (southwest) to forest edge. Go through gate and past cottage to farm track leading to narrow lane. Turn right for ¾ mile (1.2km).

5 Turn left along drive at Bescot to stile, beyond which path traverses afforested western slopes of Moel y Golfa.

6 Signpost marks diversion of steep path to top of Moel y Golfa. Tired walkers can continue on lower path, tracing woodland edge to meet hill route, close to Middletown. Waymarked, winding hill route climbs through woods and up crags to summit monument. From here, narrow path continues along crest to gate at edge of woods. Turn right and follow zigzagging path down towards Middletown.

Distance: 6 miles (9.7km)
Total ascent: 2,150ft (655m)
Paths: good; steep and slippery on Moel y Golfa; some quiet lanes
Terrain: woodland, upland pasture
Gradients: steep
Refreshments: Breidden Hotel
Park: car park in Middletown, on A458 between Shrewsbury and Welshpool

Monmouthshire's White Castle

*A grim castle guarded the border in medieval times and served
a curious purpose in World War II*

WALK
81

The shadows of two men of war pervade this stroll through the gentle green countryside of Monmouthshire. One was a famous man of honour, whom Shakespeare acknowledged. The other was a pathetic, hollowed-out shell of a man, a tragic and futile figure of modern times.

We meet the first at the village of Llantilio Crossenny, in the valley country of tumbling streams west of Monmouth. A square, grassy platform surrounded by a moat, hard by the B4233 road, shows the site of Hen Cwrt, or Old Court, once a palace used by the medieval Bishops of Llandaff when visiting their estates at Llantilio Crossenny. In the 15th century it became the dwelling of the celebrated Welsh warrior Dafydd ap Llewelyn, Shakespeare's 'Fluellen valiant, and touch'd with choler, hot as gunpowder', who in *Henry V* force-feeds a leek to the mocking Pistol. Dafydd ap Llewelyn was not only valiant on the battlefield: he was said to have begotten so many children that they could form an unbroken chain between Hen Cwrt and the church 400 yards (365m) away. He had one blemished or gammy eye – hence his nickname of 'Sir David Gam'. He was knighted on the field of Agincourt in 1415, and died there immediately afterwards.

Sir David's coat of arms hangs outside the Hostry Inn, the ancient hostelry where your walk begins. The church

Above: White Castle dominates the surrounding countryside

of St Teilo is well worth a look (collect the key from the nearby vicarage). It was built to serve the visiting Bishops of Llandaff and their big retinues, and retains its tall nave and lovely 14th-century chancel windows.

The outward route from Llantilio Crossenny lies along Offa's Dyke long-distance footpath, a very well-marked route. This brings you in 2 miles (3km) to White Castle, one of the grimmest and grandest of the great early medieval castles built along the Welsh border when the English and Welsh were at each other's throats. The inner ward, or walled enclosure, is flanked by a hornwork (an unusual crescent-shaped defensive earthwork in the moat) and a semicircular outer ward. Drum towers with gatehouses rise from the curtain walls that surround the fortress. It all looks dourly impregnable.

White Castle dominated its surrounding countryside. Men felt safe enough under its protection to build a market town outside its walls. Today, however, there is not a trace of that once thriving borough.

The lonely castle holds the memory of our second man of war, Adolf Hitler's deputy, Rudolf Hess, who arrived by aeroplane in Britain in 1941 under mysterious circumstances, armed with proposals for a deal to end the war. Between 1942 and 1945 Hess was kept secretly in a military hospital just outside Abergavenny, a few miles away, and was brought to White Castle for recreation from time to time. His unnerving stare from under bushy eyebrows led one of his guards to describe him as 'a wild man with the look of the animals in Bristol Zoo.' On his White Castle outings Hess would stand for hours, glaring into the moat and dropping breadcrumbs to the giant carp.

Below: Hen Cwrt was once a palace of the Bishops of Llandaff

Monmouthshire's White Castle

*The gentle Monmouthshire countryside hides a grim
castle with a dark past*

1 From the Hostry Inn turn right down the lane. In 300yds (275m), on a left bend, keep ahead to St Teilo's Church.

2 Walk down the stone steps from the west end of the graveyard and take the signed footpath between a wire fence and the churchyard wall. Go through a kissing gate and over a field to the B4233. Across the road is the moated site of Hen Cwrt, the Old Court.

3 Turn left along the B4233. In 90yds (82m) turn right over a stile, and follow Offa's Dyke Path signs across five fields to a farm track at Great Treadam. Turn left to the road, and right for 150yds (137m), to turn right into a lane.

4 Follow the lane northwards for ¾ mile (1.2km) to a road by a large white house. Keep forward for 250yds (229m) to White Castle.

8 Don't cross this stile, but follow the fence uphill to the lane. Turn right and walk for 1 mile (1.6km) to the B4233. Turn right and, in 350yds (320m), follow a footpath sign on the left across the fields to Llantilio Crossenny church. Return from here to the Hostry Inn.

7 From the saddle of ground at the top of the slope aim ahead across a field to a stile in a post-and-wire fence. Follow yellow arrows and Three Castles Walk signs across the next field, then over a stile and round to the right, to reach a stile in the corner of a fence.

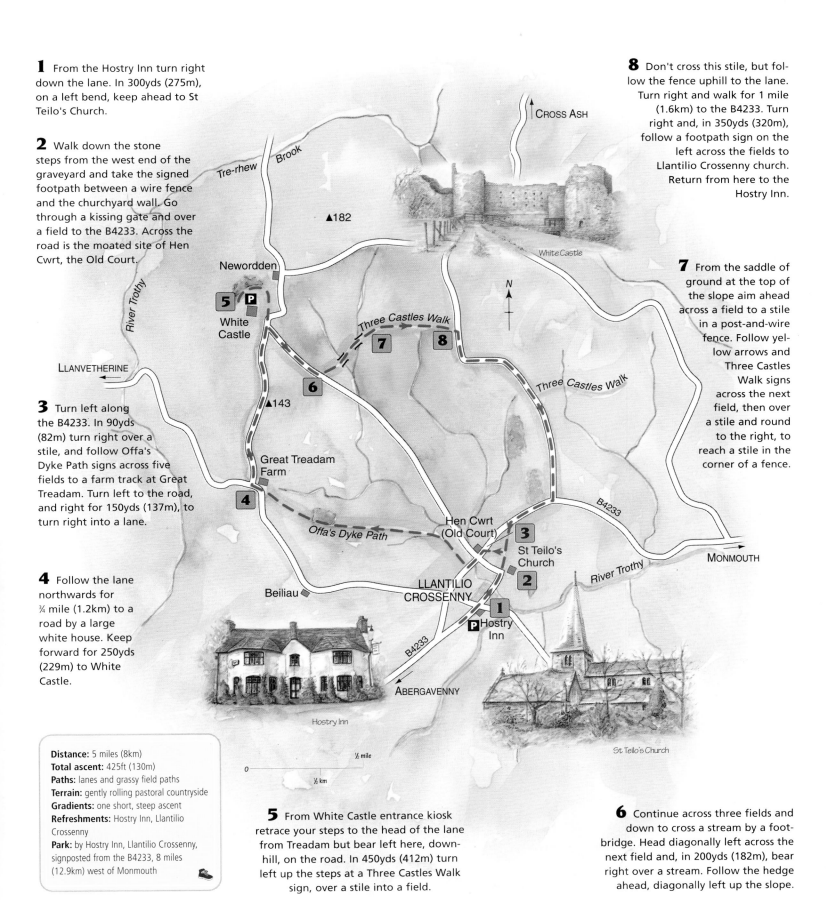

Distance: 5 miles (8km)
Total ascent: 425ft (130m)
Paths: lanes and grassy field paths
Terrain: gently rolling pastoral countryside
Gradients: one short, steep ascent
Refreshments: Hostry Inn, Llantilio Crossenny
Park: by Hostry Inn, Llantilio Crossenny, signposted from the B4233, 8 miles (12.9km) west of Monmouth

5 From White Castle entrance kiosk retrace your steps to the head of the lane from Treadam but bear left here, downhill, on the road. In 450yds (412m) turn left up the steps at a Three Castles Walk sign, over a stile into a field.

6 Continue across three fields and down to cross a stream by a footbridge. Head diagonally left across the next field and, in 200yds (182m), bear right over a stream. Follow the hedge ahead, diagonally left up the slope.

Eric Gill in the Black Mountains

For a few short years an eccentric English artist found inspiration – and free materials – in a remote Welsh village

Top right: Eric Gill's Prospero and Ariel for Broadcasting House in London reflected his diverse influences

Below: the little chapel at Capel-y-ffin, as remote a place as Gill could find to work

Bottom: the Black Mountains rise to emphatic crests

In August 1924 the artist and craftsman Eric Gill arrived in a lorry at Capel-y-ffin – 'The Chapel at the End' – with four other adults, seven children, many cats, chickens, ducks and geese, two magpies, a pony and a rank-smelling goat. The lorry was large, the lanes were small, and the journey was difficult. The impact of the eccentric, enthusiastic, religious and hedonistic Gill on this tiny and remote village must have been electric.

The scatter of cottages and larger houses in and around this junction of two valleys has a feeling of finality. The lane you will walk along used to end here, though now it eventually climbs over the Gospel Pass to plunge down into Hay-on-Wye.

For Gill this remoteness was a release from the difficulties he had found in both his work and his private life at his previous home at Ditchling in East Sussex. He delighted in Capel's local walks, especially the track along the side of Darren Lwyd, the tongue of mountain that divides the valleys. He also, according to his autobiography, joined his family and companions in naked bathing in the Nant Bwch, the stream that tumbles down the valley to join the Afon Honddu below the village.

As you round the bluff of the Darren Lwyd the steep crags of Tarren yr Esgob – 'The Bishop's Rock' – tower before you. Below it to the left are two white houses. The left-hand building is The Monastery, Gill's home. When his family and friends moved in it was dilapidated and depressing. It was formerly home to another eccentric, Father Ignatius of Llanthony. A Church of England deacon, he founded a religious order here in 1870, which folded on his death in 1907. By Gill's time the house was owned by the Benedictine monks from Caldey Island, off the Pembroke coast.

Gill abandoned Ignatius's unfinished church (you can see its gaunt ruins beside The Monastery) and had a chapel constructed within the house, served by a resident monk.

Living in various places over his relatively short life, Gill still maintained a steady artistic output, including the sculptures at Broadcasting House and Westminster Cathedral's 'Stations of the Cross'. But he did some of his best work at Capel. Sculpture was at first carried out in the coal cellar, a setting that appealed to his love of the dramatic. A special advantage of his residence here was the fact that there was abundant local stone, which he could collect from the mountains for nothing.

In this household of freedom and experimentation, he drew and engraved his often erotic illustrations. Here, too, he designed some of his most famous works, the typefaces Gill Sans and Perpetua. Many clients found their way up the winding roads from Abergavenny, and his commissions came thick and fast. Other artists too, visited him and stayed in The Monastery, especially his friend David Jones, the English poet and artist, who was also inspired by the local landscape.

Suddenly, in 1928, the caravan was on the move again. In another, typical, swing of lifestyle, Gill moved from his mountain fastness to High Wycombe, within easy reach of London. He left behind two carved stones at the church, local tales of odd 'goings-on' on the hillside, and some of the best graphic and sculptural works of the 20th century.

Eric Gill in the Black Mountains

In this high valley in the Black Mountains, the artist and sculptor Eric Gill settled into an eccentric lifestyle with his extended family

1 Take the lane between the chapel and the telephone box, climbing the hill. After 800 yards (730m), by a sign to the youth hostel, go right through a gate, down the track, over the river and up to a second gate.

6 When the path reaches the lane, turn left down the hill, go over a ford and pass The Monastery back to the village.

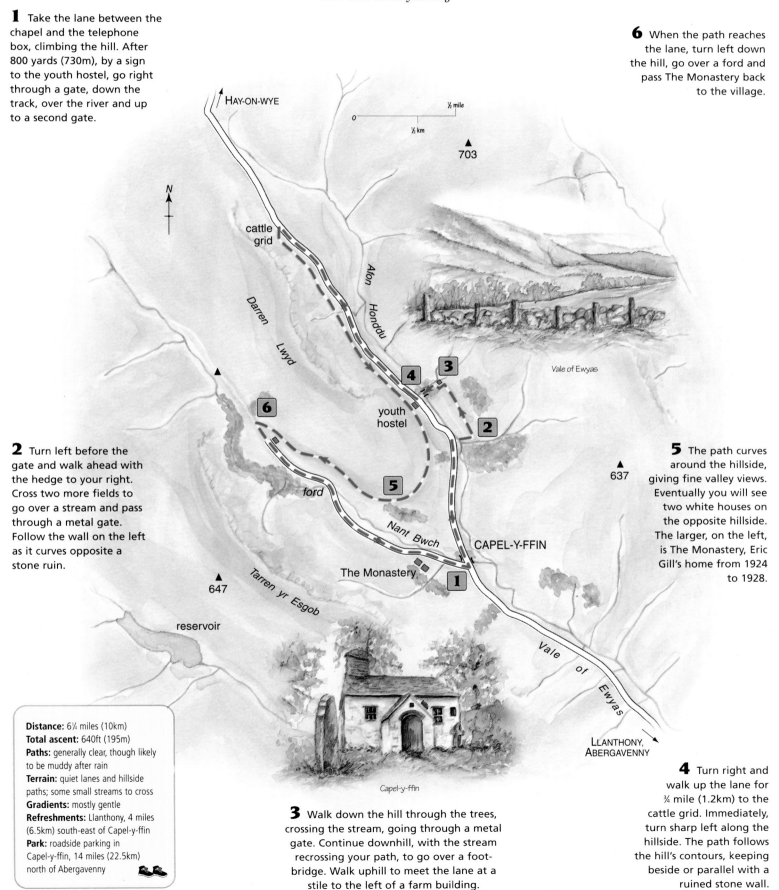

2 Turn left before the gate and walk ahead with the hedge to your right. Cross two more fields to go over a stream and pass through a metal gate. Follow the wall on the left as it curves opposite a stone ruin.

5 The path curves around the hillside, giving fine valley views. Eventually you will see two white houses on the opposite hillside. The larger, on the left, is The Monastery, Eric Gill's home from 1924 to 1928.

Capel-y-ffin

Distance: 6¼ miles (10km)
Total ascent: 640ft (195m)
Paths: generally clear, though likely to be muddy after rain
Terrain: quiet lanes and hillside paths; some small streams to cross
Gradients: mostly gentle
Refreshments: Llanthony, 4 miles (6.5km) south-east of Capel-y-ffin
Park: roadside parking in Capel-y-ffin, 14 miles (22.5km) north of Abergavenny

3 Walk down the hill through the trees, crossing the stream, going through a metal gate. Continue downhill, with the stream recrossing your path, to go over a foot-bridge. Walk uphill to meet the lane at a stile to the left of a farm building.

4 Turn right and walk up the lane for ¾ mile (1.2km) to the cattle grid. Immediately, turn sharp left along the hillside. The path follows the hill's contours, keeping beside or parallel with a ruined stone wall.

Raglan's Civil War Fortress

The walk circles a fine castle, built by Marcher lords and famously besieged in 1646

WALK 83

Above: Charles I twice retreated behind Raglan's sturdy walls

Below and top right: Raglan's defences were finally undermined by tunnelling

It is not known with certainty when the first castle was built at Raglan, but it is likely to date from soon after the Norman Conquest, when a string of castles was built in southern Wales – Chepstow, Monmouth, Caerleon, Abergavenny and, probably, Raglan. The castles were erected by the Marcher lords, those who held estates on the 'march', or border, between Norman England and the Welsh. The eastern boundaries of the Marcher lords' estates were well-defined, but to the west they were allowed to own anything they could take from, and hold against, the Welsh. The resentment this caused simmered for centuries and resulted in numerous conflicts.

But the conflict now most associated with Raglan is the English Civil War. On 14 June 1645 the Royalists were defeated at Naseby and Charles I rode west to stay at Raglan, home of the aged but loyal Lord Worcester. The following year, on 3 June, a Parliamentarian army arrived at Raglan and called on Lord Worcester to surrender. Worcester was by now 85 years old, but he remained steadfastly loyal to his king. His response to the surrender call was: 'I make choice, if it so please God, to die nobly than to live in infamy.'

The Parliamentarian army, reinforced after the fall of Oxford, circled the castle and settled down for a long siege. Then in early August Sir Thomas Fairfax arrived. Fairfax had no interest in a protracted campaign and set his men to tunnelling under the walls of the castle. By 17 August it was clear to Lord Worcester that the castle walls had been almost completely undermined and that his castle would be destroyed

unless he negotiated a surrender. After two days of talks he surrendered Raglan and was taken to the Tower. There his age and demeanour aroused compassion in Parliament and it was decided to move him to Windsor Castle. On being told, Worcester is said to have cried 'God bless my soul, they will give me a grander castle than they took away.' But it was not to be. The old man died in the Tower before being moved.

At Raglan the fearful Parliamentarians decided to ensure that never again would the castle threaten them. Bombardment with cannon failed to make any impression, so the tunnelling beneath the walls was resumed. Wooden props were placed beneath the walls and set ablaze. Their collapse brought down the outer walls, creating the imposing ruins we see today.

Our walk heads south from Raglan Church crossing Leaguer Fields, where the main Parliamentarian army camped. It continues to the castle which, despite its ruinous state, is still impressive and must have struck fear into the hearts of the advancing Parliamentarians. Having rounded the castle's east and north sides, walking through the fertile land that the Marcher lords coveted, we pass along the western approaches. Over to the right is Gwarlod-y-Beddau, the Meadow of Graves, where the (relatively few) men killed in the action lie buried, but the eye is drawn towards the brooding castle walls. It was built to defy the Welsh and it is easy to judge the air of menace it must have given its Norman lord.

Raglan's Civil War Fortress

During the Civil War Charles I retreated to this imposing castle in the beautiful Welsh Marches

Distance: 5 miles (8km)
Total ascent: 250ft (76m)
Paths: good; can be muddy after rain
Terrain: fields, enclosed bridleway
Gradients: few ascents and very gradual
Refreshments: various in Raglan
Park: Castle Street, Raglan or by Raglan Castle

11 Go through and turn right, crossing bridge into Castle Street.

10 Then, cross and turn left along a verge about 330yds (300m), to reach gap in stone wall on the right.

9 Go through gap and bear away from left field edge to reach hedge elbow across field. Bear left to walk with hedge to stile on to A40.

1 From Castle Street, take Chepstow Road, past St Cadoc's Church, towards Chepstow. Ignore the footpath on the left after the school and health centre.

2 Ahead, stay on left-hand side of road and, opposite Brooklands Farm B&B sign, enter gate with path leading towards sewage works to right. Before sewage works continue over concrete bridge, go straight across field and cross next field diagonally to far left corner. Cross stile and sleeper bridge and bear slightly left, following edge of sports field to gate onto lane.

8 When road turns sharp right, cross stile on left into field and walk to right, round edge of field to stile in wire fence. Cross field, bearing left but aiming well to right of castle and church tower. Cross stile in far hedge and bear left, aiming for large hedge gap.

7 Turn left along enclosed bridleway. Follow this downhill, then uphill, to reach road opposite Lower House. Turn left.

3 Cross lane, go through gate and bear left, uphill, towards stile behind railway wagon shed. Cross to lane and go over stile opposite into cattle field. Follow hedge to right and cross stile into another field. Keep to right of field to reach stile onto road. Turn right and walk towards A40.

6 At bottom of field cross stile and turn right, leaving hedge to go through left-hand gate ahead. Follow hedge on right, maintaining direction when it bears away. Cross ditch and continue to stile. Follow hedge on right, crossing stile over it and turn left uphill. Where field widens, turn left to cross stile.

4 Turn left and cross to far side of A40. Walk along verge to steps down to signed footpath and stile into field. Cross field uphill to reach gate onto lane leading to Raglan Castle car park.

5 Turn right towards Castle Farm. Where lane bears left cross stile on right and with field edge on your left walk to another stile. Cross and follow left edge, crossing stile in it and bearing right to stile. Cross and turn left through gate. Cross track, go over stile and turn half-right across field beyond, passing small hillock.

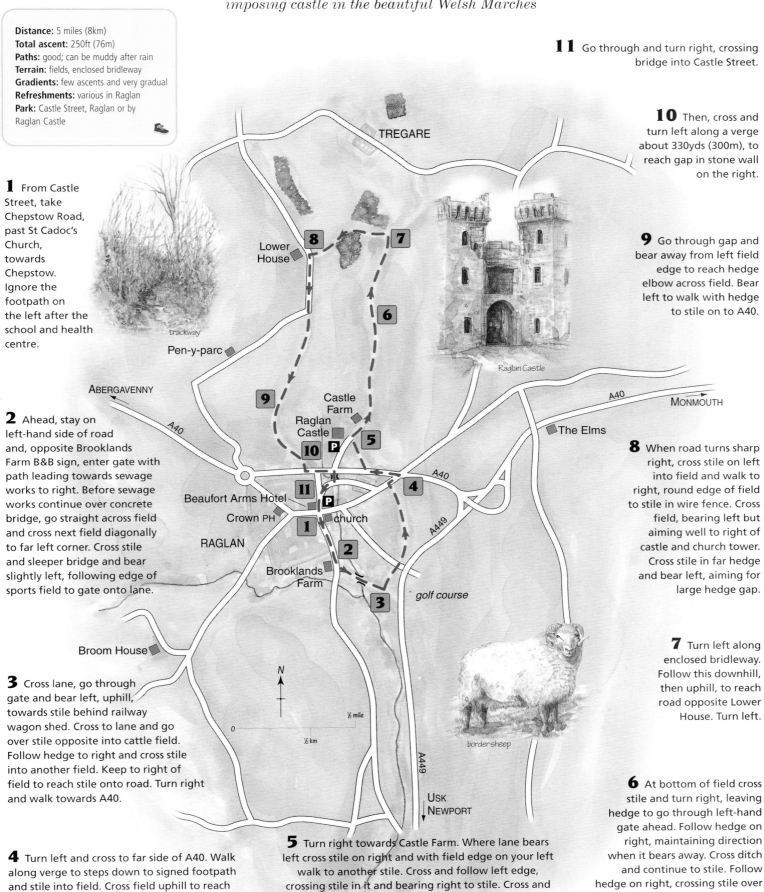

TREGARE

Lower House

Pen-y-parc

trackway

ABERGAVENNY

A40

Beaufort Arms Hotel

Crown PH

RAGLAN

Brooklands Farm

Broom House

Raglan Castle

Castle Farm

Raglan Castle

church

golf course

The Elms

A40

MONMOUTH

A449

A449

USK
NEWPORT

border sheep

N

½ mile

0

½ km

A Fairy Lake and the Black Mountain

Discover a watery tale of mystery in this beautiful and isolated wilderness

WALK
84

Top right: the Beacons were the red kite's last outpost until recent reintroductions

Above: path erosion threatens a fragile landscape

Below: Llyn y Fan Fach below towering Bannau Sir Gaer

The Black Mountain, or Mynydd Du as it is known in Welsh, lies at the unfashionable end of the Brecon Beacons National Park. Surrounded by a wide expanse of moorland with few roads, it's not quite as easy to get to as the Beacons themselves. But this is a mysterious wilderness with secretive corners that draw you in, and there's a strange tale to be told.

The tiny village of Llanddeusant lies at the end of a long, winding lane threading through the Sawdde valley. Its pub has been turned into a youth hostel and there are few spaces to leave a car, so you motor on, down a little hedge-lined lane signposted to Llyn y Fan. On the hillside to your right, there's the farmhouse of Blaen Sawdde, part of that mysterious tale – but that's for later. The road degenerates into a stony track that descends to a car park by a little bridge. From here your journey must be on foot.

After climbing south along the stony track you're soon staring down at Llyn y Fan Fach. Towering above the black waters, the cliffs of Bannau Sir Gaer are layered with dark, crusty gritstone and tawny red sandstone. Little has changed in this magical place since medieval times, when young Rhiwallon first saw a golden-haired maiden sitting on the lakeshore. This farmer's son from Blaen Sawdde was instantly smitten by her beauty and vowed to marry her. Eventually she agreed, but told him that she was no ordinary mortal and that she would return to her kind if he struck her three times.

It is said that the third time he struck her was after she had giggled at a funeral. Although it was a mere tap, the lady disappeared from his life, returning to the waters as mysteriously as she had first appeared. Rhiwallon died of a broken heart, but his three sons were able to see their mother on frequent trips to the lake. She taught them the secrets of medicine, showing them herbs from the mountain and where they grew. The boys were to become the first in a long line of Myddfai physicians, the last being Dr John Williams, physician to Queen Victoria.

The next bit of the route is even more spectacular, tracing the top of the cliffs, first to Picws Du, the highest of the Carmarthenshire peaks or fans (Bannau Sir Gaer), then to Fan Brycheiniog, the Brecon peak, the highest of the group. Several deep and exciting gullies split the tiered cliffs, giving bird's eye views of the lake.

On reaching Fan Brycheiniog another lake, Llyn y Fan Fawr, appears beneath the steep cliffs. This one has a more open aspect, and its cold waters are often whipped up by the wind into white horses. At Fan Foel a little path scuttles down to the lower moors. Tracks dive for the cover of the moor grass in places, but it is good to roam free on these fenceless hillsides. Maybe the late sun will be colouring the red sandstone cliffs even redder. In this soft evening light and flickering shadows it would be easy to conjure up images of the Lady of the Lake picking wildflowers on the mountainsides.

A Fairy Lake and the Black Mountain

A fine mountain walk in the backwaters of the Brecon Beacons National Park

1 From the car park at Blaenau, follow the stony reservoir supply track by the Sawdde stream up to the shores of Llyn y Fan Fach, taking the right fork just before the reservoir.

6 Turn left on a path descending above the north banks of the stream. The path comes down the sides of Bryn Mawr, towards a bridge conveying the outward track across the stream. It then swings right to avoid some squat cliffs. Look out for a little path on the left which makes the final descent to the car park at Blaenau.

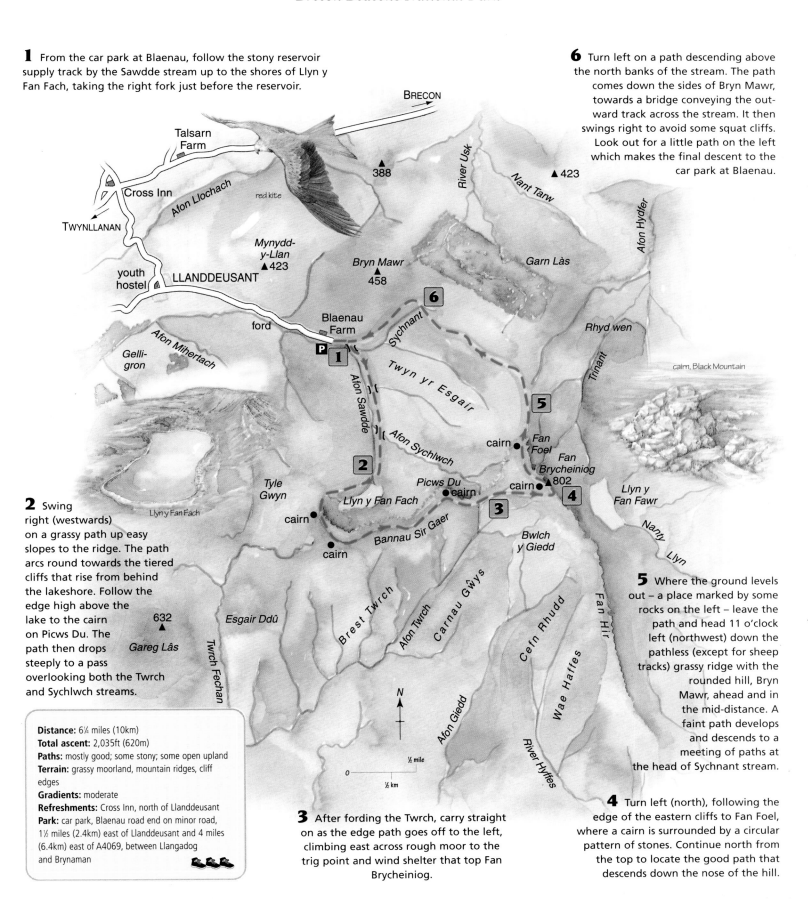

2 Swing right (westwards) on a grassy path up easy slopes to the ridge. The path arcs round towards the tiered cliffs that rise from behind the lakeshore. Follow the edge high above the lake to the cairn on Picws Du. The path then drops steeply to a pass overlooking both the Twrch and Sychlwch streams.

Distance: 6¼ miles (10km)
Total ascent: 2,035ft (620m)
Paths: mostly good; some stony; some open upland
Terrain: grassy moorland, mountain ridges, cliff edges
Gradients: moderate
Refreshments: Cross Inn, north of Llanddeusant
Park: car park, Blaenau road end on minor road, 1½ miles (2.4km) east of Llanddeusant and 4 miles (6.4km) east of A4069, between Llangadog and Brynaman

5 Where the ground levels out – a place marked by some rocks on the left – leave the path and head 11 o'clock left (northwest) down the pathless (except for sheep tracks) grassy ridge with the rounded hill, Bryn Mawr, ahead and in the mid-distance. A faint path develops and descends to a meeting of paths at the head of Sychnant stream.

4 Turn left (north), following the edge of the eastern cliffs to Fan Foel, where a cairn is surrounded by a circular pattern of stones. Continue north from the top to locate the good path that descends down the nose of the hill.

3 After fording the Twrch, carry straight on as the edge path goes off to the left, climbing east across rough moor to the trig point and wind shelter that top Fan Brycheiniog.

Dale – a Pembroke Peninsula

A dramatic coastal walk with spectacular scenery and a magnificent natural harbour

WALK
85

Top right: the Skomer ferry

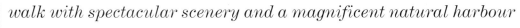

Above: the village and harbour of Dale

Below: the rugged shoreline of Mill Bay

This walk follows part of the Pembrokeshire Coast Path, a 168-mile (269km) public right of way opened on 3 July 1953, a year after the Pembrokeshire coast was designated Britain's only coastal national park. It is easy to see why, for the scenery, with its rich variety of plant and bird life and fascinating geology, is a visual feast with spectacular panoramic views, rugged cliffs and lovely sandy coves and beaches.

The twin islands of Skomer and Skokholm beckon offshore at the beginning of the walk. These are both nature reserves where a variety of sea birds and seals can be seen. Their names – like many in this area – are of Norse origin, recalling the Viking invasions across the Irish Sea in the 8th, 9th and 10th centuries. Dale itself also bears a Norse name, marking this as being south of the Landsker, Pembrokeshire's linguistic divide. The north of the county has a substantial Welsh-speaking population, whilst this, the southern half, is largely anglicised, having long been known as 'little England'. The peninsula is also south of a geological fault line – the old red sandstone is a reminder of the Gower Peninsula, and this part was an island before the Ice Age.

The rocks at the foot of St Ann's Head overlooking Milford Haven were considered so treacherous that two lighthouses were deemed necessary. These were originally built in 1714, in alignment to aid navigation. The higher one closed in 1910 and is now a coastguard and cliff rescue station, while the current lower lighthouse, still in use, replaced a coal-fired beacon in 1841. There are wide-ranging views from here down the expanse of Milford Haven. This is a ria, the former valley of the River Cleddau, which was flooded at the end of the last Ice Age by meltwater. The wide, deep waters of the Haven form a magnificent natural harbour, used by pleasure craft and commercial shipping alike. Brightly coloured yachts from the local sailing clubs ply the in-shore waters, while the deeper channels are used by the ferries from Pembroke Dock to Rosslare in Ireland and the giant oil tankers making their way to the refineries, glimpses of which can be seen along the shores. The most notorious of these tankers was *The Sea Empress*, which was wrecked off shore here on 15 February 1996. Although the full lasting effects are still unknown, there is no obvious sign of the spilt oil to spoil the area's lovely beaches now.

Just around St Ann's Head is Mill Bay, which took its place in British history when the Tudor dynasty launched its claim to the throne. Henry Tudor, the future King Henry VII, landed here on 7 August 1485 before going on to victory over Richard III at the Battle of Bosworth Field. A little further on, the fort at West Blockhouse Point was built in 1857 in response to unrealised fears of French invasion, and the strategic nature of this headland is underlined once again as you pass the fortified manor house of Dale Castle. Such turbulent times are hard to imagine now. The peaceful cliffs and coves of this wonderful coastline are just waiting to be explored, to the accompaniment of little more than crashing waves and seagulls' cries.

Dale – a Pembroke Peninsula

At the entrance to Milford Haven, the Dale Peninsula has always played a strategic role in maritime history

1 From the National Trust car park return to the road and go left where the road bends right towards Dale. Turn left to follow a concrete track which bears left to a stile beside a gate. Cross this, turn right and take another stile to reach the coast path.

7 Turn left with the signposted coast path to walk with the sea on your right. After crossing a series of stiles, take a kissing gate and look out for the stile beside a gate on your left, which you used on your outward journey. Turn left, inland, to cross this and retrace your steps to the car park.

2 Go left to walk with the sea on your right (leaving the islands of Skokholm and Skomer behind you). Follow the coast path to the road as it approaches St Ann's Head.

3 Go right along the road to pass the old High Lighthouse on your right, then turn left through a gate and turn right immediately to take a signposted path towards the Low Lighthouse. Turn sharply left, as signposted, to follow the coast path towards Mill Bay, still walking with the sea on your right.

4 Descend steps to cross a footbridge and climb up the other side. Continue with the sea on your right around West Blockhouse Point (with it's three transit marks – navigational aids). Follow the coast path around Watwick Point (where there is a single transit mark), cross a footbridge above Castle Beach and climb to join a road on Dale Point.

6 Go left along the road to pass St James' Church on your left. When the road turns left, leave it by going straight ahead on a track which passes Dale Castle on your right. When this track bends left, take the signposted footpath ahead to Westdale Bay.

5 Turn left to follow the road downhill into Dale. Ignore a turning on your left and reach the Griffin Inn. Take a footpath on your left immediately after the pub and just before a boathouse. This leads to a road. Cross this and go ahead over a stile beside a gate and turn right to cross a stone stile and reach another road.

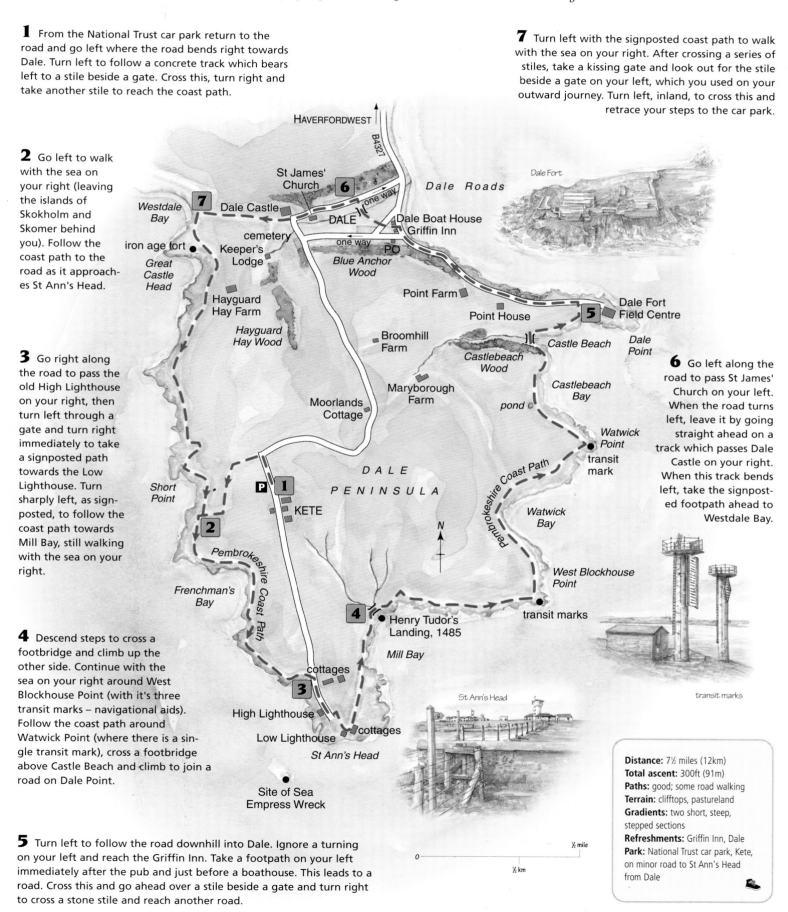

Distance: 7½ miles (12km)
Total ascent: 300ft (91m)
Paths: good; some road walking
Terrain: clifftops, pastureland
Gradients: two short, steep, stepped sections
Refreshments: Griffin Inn, Dale
Park: National Trust car park, Kete, on minor road to St Ann's Head from Dale

Strumble Head and the French Invasion

The Pembrokeshire coast witnessed the last hostile invasion of British soil, in 1797

Top right: the lighthouse on Strumble Head

Above: a tapestry celebrates the unlikely events of 1797

Below: the monument on Carregwastad Point

The glorious stretch of coastline near Strumble Head is so well endowed with intoxicating scenery and the promise of marine mammals such as seals and dolphins that the drama of its history seems superfluous. Yet this is the place where Britain confronted her last invaders. Ending in near-farcical defeat, the French Invasion of 1797 can at least boast its own tapestry, housed at nearby Fishguard – about the only thing it has in common with a rather more successful venture at Hastings in 1066.

The 18th-century invaders had been led to believe that the oppressed Welsh peasants were like dry heather just waiting to blaze up in revolt against the tyranny of the English Crown. So, in order to light the spark, a company of around 1,400 French troops set sail from Brest, landing in Pembrokeshire on 22 February 1797. The confidence of the French in their venture evidently did not extend to risking their crack troops, as their legion was largely made up of convicts under the leadership of the Irish-American Colonel Tate. Each man was issued with 100 rounds of ammunition and four days' rations of food and double brandy.

One of the invaders was James Bowen, who had been transported from this part of Pembrokeshire for horse-stealing. Whether he was homesick, or bent on revenge, the original plan of landing at Bristol was conveniently changed to capturing Fishguard. When the alarm was raised quickly there, James Bowen knew just the spot at Carregwastad Point – his old haunt – to disembark on a calm, moonlit night.

The invaders made their headquarters at the nearby farm of Tre-Howel and set about drinking Portuguese wine salvaged from a shipwreck the previous month. By the afternoon of 24 February most of them were helplessly drunk. By this time, too, Lord Cawdor had assembled 575 local men to save the kingdom, but tradition has it that it was the timely appearance of the doughty Jemima Nicholas and her cloaked and bonneted companions that persuaded Colonel Tate to sign the document of surrender. These ladies circled the hill where the French soldiers were based, and it is said that, mistaking their red flannel costumes for the uniforms of defenders' forces (no doubt while still under the influence of their Portuguese booty), the invaders soon lost heart and surrendered. They had lost 12 dead in some early skirmishes, and 8 were drowned when coming ashore. The only Welsh casualty was a woman killed accidentally in a pub whilst a pistol was being loaded. The centenary of the invasion was marked by the erection of a monument on Carregwastad Point in 1897.

A few years later, in 1908, Strumble Head lighthouse was built on Ynys Meicel (accessible by bridge), to guard against perils of a different kind.

Strumble Head and the French Invasion

A memorial stone on this spectacular coastal walk marks the point where a Napoleonic army invaded Britain

6 Bear right at a fork to follow the road down towards the lighthouse on Strumble Head. Ignore a drive for Llanwnwr Farm on your left. Return to the car park on your left.

5 Take Tre-Howel's access drive through the yard and then turn left up to a quiet road and turn right, with sweeping views over the sea on your right.

4 Go ahead over a stile beside a gate to follow a green lane. This bends left. Continue inland, ignoring another green lane on your right. Pass through a gate, ignoring another track signposted on your left, shortly before bearing right to Tre-Howel farm.

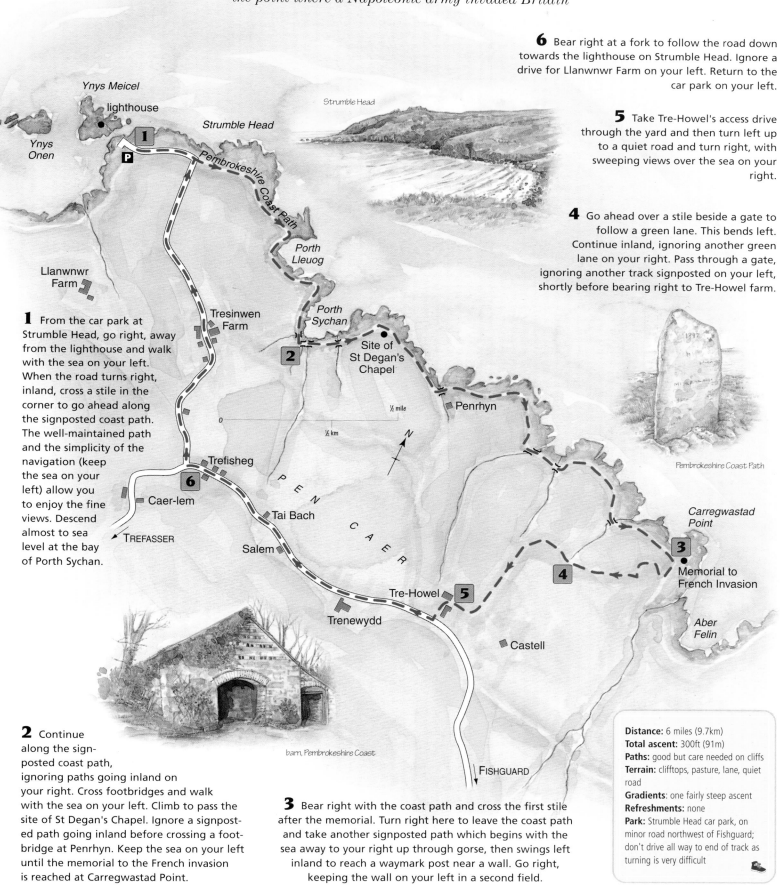

1 From the car park at Strumble Head, go right, away from the lighthouse and walk with the sea on your left. When the road turns right, inland, cross a stile in the corner to go ahead along the signposted coast path. The well-maintained path and the simplicity of the navigation (keep the sea on your left) allow you to enjoy the fine views. Descend almost to sea level at the bay of Porth Sychan.

2 Continue along the signposted coast path, ignoring paths going inland on your right. Cross footbridges and walk with the sea on your left. Climb to pass the site of St Degan's Chapel. Ignore a signposted path going inland before crossing a footbridge at Penrhyn. Keep the sea on your left until the memorial to the French invasion is reached at Carregwastad Point.

barn, Pembrokeshire Coast

Strumble Head

Pembrokeshire Coast Path

3 Bear right with the coast path and cross the first stile after the memorial. Turn right here to leave the coast path and take another signposted path which begins with the sea away to your right up through gorse, then swings left inland to reach a waymark post near a wall. Go right, keeping the wall on your left in a second field.

Distance: 6 miles (9.7km)
Total ascent: 300ft (91m)
Paths: good but care needed on cliffs
Terrain: clifftops, pasture, lane, quiet road
Gradients: one fairly steep ascent
Refreshments: none
Park: Strumble Head car park, on minor road northwest of Fishguard; don't drive all way to end of track as turning is very difficult

Abbey in the Wilderness

Explore the ruins of Strata Florida, a once rich and powerful abbey set in a remote valley in mid-Wales

Top right: terraced cottages at Pontrhydfendigaid

Above: a griffon clearly appears on an abbey tile

Below: the memorial to Dafydd ap Gwilym in the abbey ruins

Strata Florida was once a rich and influential abbey, a focus for literary, religious and political activity in Wales. Little of its structure now remains, but the site still has special significance in Welsh culture as the burial place of Dafydd ap Gwilym, the nation's most celebrated medieval poet.

This walk focuses on an exploration of the abbey ruins, set in the wild and remote Cambrian uplands. Cistercian monks first established an abbey hereabouts in 1164, but most of the remains you see today, including the striking arched doorway at the west end of the church nave, date from 1184, when Rhys ap Gruffudd, ruler of the Deheubarth (southern princedom) refounded the community. The Cistercian order appealed to many Welsh leaders as an austere and self-supporting rule, and the movement flourished throughout the country.

Strata Florida (the Latin name for Ystrad Fflur, or 'Flowering Vale') was an ideally isolated setting for the monks, set between the River Teifi and its tributary, the Glasffrwd, among the high moors of central Wales. The abbey grew steadily in wealth and importance. In 1238 the Welsh princes gathered here to give their allegiance to Llywelyn the Great and his descendants. Buildings were added and improved: in the 14th and 15th centuries three chapels were tucked into the south transept of the church,

and their floors decorated with patterned tiles, some of which survive.

Today many visitors come here to pay their respects to Dafydd ap Gwilym (1320–80), a poet of noble descent who produced robust and elegant verses about love, lust and nature. A slate memorial plaque, erected in 1951, notes (in Welsh and Latin) that the bard lies 'under the yew against the wall'. A simple stone memorial has been placed in the hollow of a large yew tree in the adjacent churchyard.

Before reaching the abbey itself, the route crosses peaceful hillsides where the monks once farmed their sheep. The abbey did well from the sale of wool, and at its peak had flocks grazing as far as Rhayader, 15 miles (24 km) to the east. After passing the edge of the wild and lonely moors of the Cambrian mountains, you enter a section of dark, evergreen forestry. Its eerie silence provides a stark contrast with the variety of bird and plant life which flourishes in the welcoming mixed deciduous woodland as you head down towards the river.

Past the abbey the route leads cross-country to the village of Pontrhydfendigaid, passing an abandoned lead mine – one of many workings that once operated in the mid-Wales mountains. Beyond the village are sweeping views of the surrounding countryside, including Tregaron Bog, a series of raised peat bogs straddling the Teifi and now a nature reserve.

Abbey in the Wilderness

In the heart of Wales, Strata Florida Abbey was an important oasis amidst wild but beautiful uplands

1 From lay-by at south end of village, continue south along road towards Tregaron, going gently uphill to stile and ancient wooden footpath sign on left.

2 Cross stile and follow track beyond towards caravans. Go on to caravan site road and bear left, between vans. As road bears right, bear left past last caravan to stile in corner.

10 At farm lane bear left to road. Turn left, crossing hump-backed bridge and passing road, on left, for Strata Florida, to return to start.

9 As road turns sharp left, go right past telephone box and, soon, cross waymarked stile on left. Cross footbridge and bear left towards waymarked stile by gate. The path now follows Afon Teifi (left) all the way to Pontrhydfendigaid, with occasional waymarkers, stiles and gates.

Distance: 5½ miles (9km)
Total ascent: 500 ft (152m)
Paths: mainly obvious paths and lanes
Terrain: fields, country lanes and forestry
Gradients: gradual
Refreshments: Red Lion and Black Lion, Pontrhydfendigaid
Park: along main street or in lay-by at southern entrance to village, Pontrhydfendigaid

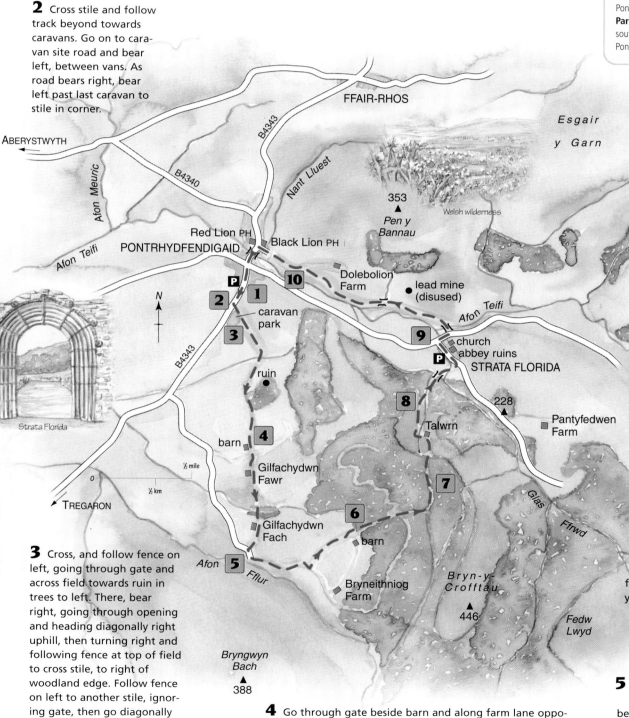

Strata Florida

tile, Strata Florida

8 An occasionally indistinct path follows stream down, crossing it once, to footbridge. Cross and follow stream bank to gate. Keep ahead along road beyond. Strata Florida car park is to left, ruins and church to right.

7 Follow track to gate and continue along lane beyond to ruin (Talwrn). Go left along ruin's top, near wall, to follow another lane to end. Go through gate and turn right, following stream. Soon bear left to gate, bearing right beyond to regain stream.

6 Follow bridleway through forest to forestry road. After 50 yds (46m), as it goes sharp right between trees, bear left along another bridleway. Follow to path coming down from right. Bear left with waymarker.

5 Turn left. When road ends, go through gate and follow lane beyond. As farm comes into view about ¼ mile (400m) ahead, take lane coming in from left, following it uphill. Approaching barn, go through gate on left and turn right along fence to gate into forest.

3 Cross, and follow fence on left, going through gate and across field towards ruin in trees to left. There, bear right, going through opening and heading diagonally right uphill, then turning right and following fence at top of field to cross stile, to right of woodland edge. Follow fence on left to another stile, ignoring gate, then go diagonally right across field to reach gate in top right corner. Go through and turn left immediately through another gate. Go diagonally right towards barn.

4 Go through gate beside barn and along farm lane opposite. Beyond first farm, lane degenerates to track, but remains obvious. Beyond farmyard keep to left of hut and take lower, right-hand track into trees. Ford stream, go through gate and follow track uphill to second farm. Go through gate and ahead along farm lane to road.

Sarn Helen – the Roman Highway through Wales

A walk along an ancient road leads to a prehistoric burial mound associated with an enigmatic medieval bard

Top right: Bronze Age remains at Bedd Taliesin

Above: Gwar-cwm-uchaf, on the highway of Sarn Helen

Below: the Dyfi Estuary stretches out beyond Bedd Taliesin

The Roman highway of Sarn Helen bears an intriguing name. Whilst it could merely be a corruption of the Welsh name 'Sarn y Lleng', meaning causeway of the legion, it could equally refer to the wife of Macsen Wledig (Magnus Maximus), the warrior who drained Britain of troops in AD 383 in his abortive bid to become Emperor of Rome. There is also an earlier Helen, or Helena, the mother of Constantine the Great, who may have been British. Maybe these spirited women oversaw maintenance of the road, but this route of some 150 miles (240km) between Carmarthen in the south and Caerhun (now Conwy) in the north, was defended by a chain of Roman forts long before either woman was born.

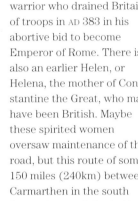

Another theory has it that 'Helen' is a corruption of 'halen' (salt). Salt was a valuable commodity in Roman times, and often formed the main constituent of legionaries' pay. Traders in this and other merchandise probably passed this way long before Roman times, in the Bronze Age, for the burial chamber known as Bedd Taliesin (the grave of Taliesin) is dated to the second millenium BC. The Celts have always been fond of associating geographical features or ancient remains with their own historical or mythical figures, which explains why this Bronze Age burial mound is reputed to be the last resting-place of a 6th-century bard.

Little is known of the historical Taliesin apart from the poetical works ascribed to him. The majority of these have come down to us in the 13th-century *Book of Taliesin*, although the bard himself lived and wrote in the 6th century in the service of Urien, King of Rheged, a British kingdom which covered modern-day Cumbria and parts of the borders and southwest Scotland, and shows just how far Welsh culture once extended. Oral tradition was responsible for keeping alive the works of Taliesin from when they were composed until they were finally set down in writing some seven centuries later. This, and the early Welsh bards' love of embellishment and exaggeration, led to the growth of numerous fantastical legends surrounding him and attributing to him the qualities of magician, sorcerer and prophet. It is little wonder, then, that the prehistoric burial mound with its obscure origins has come to be associated with a colourful figure, part historical and part legendary, from the equally obscure but revered medieval past.

Returning to the present, the views from this section of Sarn Helen, in the vicinity of Bedd Taliesin, extend across the flat plain that borders the estuary of the Afon Dyfi. This landscape, all the more surprising in contrast to the ubiquitous mountains further inland, encompasses a raised bog, Cors Fochno, bordered by the sand dunes that line the southern Dyfi estuary. The area is a nature reserve, notable for its wading and sea birds and colourful butterflies. As if by poetic contrast, the far-reaching views also take in the colourful seaside resort of Aberdyfi, a popular tourist destination in summer.

Sarn Helen – the Roman Highway through Wales

A stretch of Roman Road leads to the legendary burial place of a great Welsh bard

1 Start at the Wildfowler Inn in Tre'r-ddôl. On the village street, face the pub, go right, past the garage, shop and café, to join the A487. Turn right towards Machynlleth, and, after passing the last house, turn right through a wooden gate into a forestry plantation. Climb with an attractive, narrow, path.

2 Bear left when the path forks. Ignore paths descending from your right. Go ahead across clear-felled hillside. The path becomes a firm track before reaching a lane. Go right uphill, passing a number of houses and, eventually, farm buildings at Cefngweiriog.

3 Reach the junction with Sarn Helen, coming as a track through a gate on your left. Turn right to walk along this quiet lane. Follow this section of Sarn Helen for over 1 mile (1.6km), ignoring a lane descending on your right. Cross a bridge over the Afon Clettwr and climb towards Gwar-cwm-uchaf farm. Turn left before you reach it, onto a rising track and ignore all branching paths.

7 Take a gate ahead to descend on a tree-lined hollow way towards Tre'r-ddôl. Emerge on the road, with a chapel on your left, and turn right across a bridge over the Afon Clettwr to return to the start.

6 Enter woodland at a bridleway waymark post and soon turn sharp right to descend a rough path which zigzags steeply down between oak trees. Go ahead through a gate into a plantation of conifers.

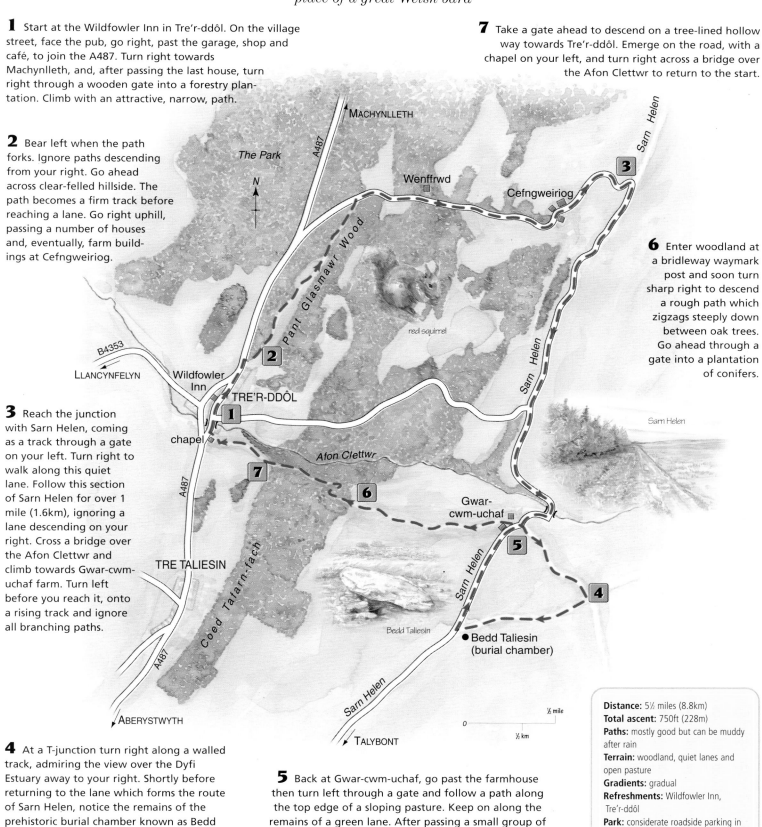

4 At a T-junction turn right along a walled track, admiring the view over the Dyfi Estuary away to your right. Shortly before returning to the lane which forms the route of Sarn Helen, notice the remains of the prehistoric burial chamber known as Bedd Taliesin on your left. Go through a gate to turn right along Sarn Helen, with fine views towards Aberdyfi over the stone wall on your left.

5 Back at Gwar-cwm-uchaf, go past the farmhouse then turn left through a gate and follow a path along the top edge of a sloping pasture. Keep on along the remains of a green lane. After passing a small group of trees, go forward to pass through a gate then proceed first by a stream and then beside a line of tree stumps. Keep on in the same direction along a hedged section and then along a rutted path.

Distance: 5½ miles (8.8km)
Total ascent: 750ft (228m)
Paths: mostly good but can be muddy after rain
Terrain: woodland, quiet lanes and open pasture
Gradients: gradual
Refreshments: Wildfowler Inn, Tre'r-ddôl
Park: considerate roadside parking in Tre'r-ddôl, just off the A487 between Aberystwyth and Machynlleth, 2 miles (3.2km) north of Tal-y-bont

Cadair Idris – the Mountain Nature Reserve

Visit one of the most popular summits in Snowdonia, via a remote mountainside where Ice Age plants still flourish

Cadair Idris stands at the southern extremity of the Snowdonia National Park, and forms a compact, imposing mountain range which towers above the beautiful Mawddach Estuary to the north, with the classic fault trough filled by tranquil Tal-y-llyn lake lying to the south.

The name means the Chair of Idris, and this is usually identified as Cwm Gadair on the north-facing slopes of the mountain. The Idris in question may have been either a local giant or Idris ap Gwyddno, a Celtic prince who died in battle against the Saxons or Irish in the early 7th century. Yet another story, in this land rich in myths and legends, claims that the mountain was named after Idris Garw, a local poet who walked on the mountain at night, seeking inspiration from the stars. It was this Idris who may have given rise to the often-quoted saying that anyone who spends a night on Cadair Idris will awake either a madman or a poet – but this is a common story on many Welsh hills.

Myths and legends will not be your only companions on this high-level walk to Cadair's summit. You will see the menacing shape of the raven – a sacred bird to the Celts – and hear its harsh croak echoing off the imposing cliffs of Craig Cau, once described by mountain photographer W A Poucher as one of the wildest places in Wales. You may also be lucky enough to spot the elegant, fork-tailed shape of the chestnut-backed red kite spiralling in the thermals high above the cliffs – this species has been successfully encouraged to return to these parts after years of patient work by the RSPB. If you are on your way to Llyn Cau in summer you may also hear the loud, fluty song of the white-chested ring ouzel or mountain blackbird, drifting up from the Afon Cau. And don't be surprised if you trip over a molehill on your way to the top. Moles have been recorded just 141ft (43m) below the 2,930ft (893m) summit of Cadair Idris.

The cliffs of Craig Cau are a mixture of hard, acidic rocks and calcareous ashes and lavas. Their fertility and inaccessibility, added to their north-facing aspect, provide a rare habitat for arctic and alpine plants that survived the Ice Age. These include the delicate pink flowers of moss campion, which appear in mossy cushions from June to July, and mini-forests of arctic dwarf willow. Both purple and mossy saxifrage flower in the damp recesses of the lime-rich cliffs, which are brightened in summer by the yellow flashes of globe flower and the ubiquitous Welsh poppy. The walk starts from the Idris Gates at Minffordd, constructed by Ivor Idris of the famous soft drinks firm, who was responsible for planting the many exotic trees, including North American sequoias, on his estate.

Higher up, the path is engineered into steps as it passes above a series of waterfalls through the ancient oakwoods on Ystrad Gwyn. These gnarled woods, now protected from the sheep by fences, are also thought to date from the end of the last Ice Age.

Top right: purple saxifrage flourishes in the mountain environment

Above: Llyn Cau is a perfect corrie lake

Below: dramatic cliffs front the Cadair ridge

Cadair Idris –
the Mountain Nature Reserve

A challenging mountain walk around the bowl of
Cwm Cau in the Cadair Idris National Nature Reserve

Distance: 5½ miles (8.8km)
Total Ascent: 2,950ft (899m)
Paths: good; some rough; stream crossing difficult after heavy rain
Terrain: rocky, mountainous
Gradients: steep; occasionally very steep
Refreshments: none
Park: Minffordd car park at junction of A487 and B4405

1 Walk to the back of the car park, where a well-signed path leaves through a gate. Follow a raised causeway to a kissing gate and visitor centre. Follow the path over a bridge to a gate into the nature reserve.

2 Follow the steep, mostly stepped path up through the woods, with the stream to your right.

3 Go through a gate to reach more open country, continuing to climb to a point where the plantation on your right swings away and the path runs very close to the stream. Note the path down to the water here. Take it to study the stream crossing. The stream must be crossed on the return route. In dry weather it can be crossed easily. **If not, you should reverse the route from Pen-y-gadair, rather than complete the circuit.**

4 Return to, and continue along, the path. High up to the right a ladder stile over a fence can be seen, the diagonal path descending to the stream is the return route. The outward path now takes you into Cwm Cau.

8 Descend on the path to Nant Cadair and carefully cross the stream to reach the outward path. Turn left downhill, and follow the outward route back to the start.

7 Continue downhill, close to the fence, to cross the ladder stile seen from the path to Cwm Cau. Look for the conifers below you to the right of the fence. If you reach these you have gone too far. You must cross the ladder stile to a clear path, descending initially diagonally, to the conifers at the stream.

6 From the summit, continue along a broad ridge (ENE). After about 15 minutes, at the low point of the ridge, before it rises to Mynydd Moel, a minor path forks right, terracing above Cwm Cau, then descending gently and later undulating past a number of springs to a fence and following it down to cross a ladder stile. If you miss this path, don't panic: the fence ahead rises almost to the top of Mynydd Moel so, wherever you meet it, cross it and follow it right downhill.

5 Just before a huge whale-back rock, bear left, climbing steeply to the top of the ridge. Turn right and continue along the ridge, always tending a little to the right, to the summit of Craig Cau, marked by a ladder stile and small cairn. Continue on the ridge, descending (NNE then N) past the top of a stone shoot, then swinging right uphill on rougher ground to the summit of Pen-y-gadair, marked by a trig point and a substantial stone shelter.

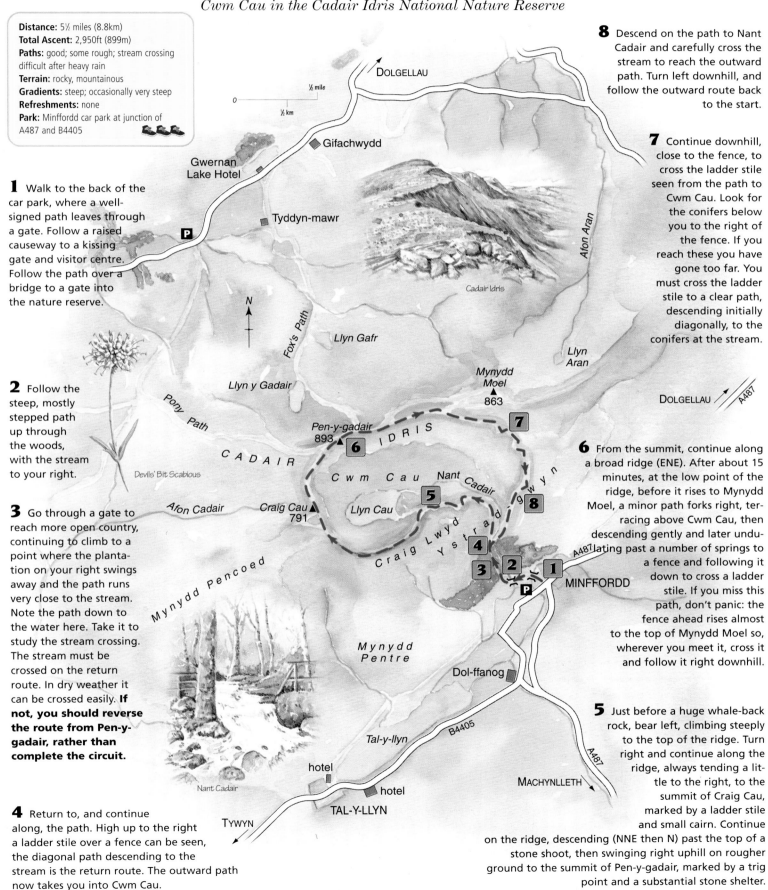

On the Roman Steps through the Rhinogs

For centuries these rugged hills, criss-crossed by ancient tracks, presented a formidable barrier to travellers

WALK 90

Top right: a merlin surveys the mountain scene

Below: the Roman Steps probably never carried Romans

Inset: Gloyw Llyn, surrounded by mountain bog

The rocks of the Rhinogs are among the oldest in Britain. They are Precambrian – older than the oldest that can be realistically dated. This rock is very hard, weathering slowly and so forming a poor soil. As a result the Rhinogs are a range of sharp edges, whose angled rock beds frequently make walking difficult and slow, though, by compensation, the landscape is wonderfully wild.

For centuries the range formed a barrier to those wanting to reach Ardudwy, the fertile coastal plain to the west, an isolation which allowed a band of outlaws to set up a hiding place on Ardudwy, using a pass which only they knew to raid the lands to the east. On one raid they kidnapped the womenfolk of a Clwyd village. Outraged, the village men pursued them back towards the coast, found the secret pass, and hastened to rescue their women. But the women, having fallen for the outlaws, no longer wanted to be rescued. Rather than return to their old lives in Clwyd, the women threw themselves into a mountain lake and drowned. The lake is still called Llyn Morwynion, the Lake of Maidens.

The outlaws' pass across Bwlch Tyddiad – the way you are about to go – is only one of several routes through the hills. To the north, between Harlech and Trawsfynydd, is the most ancient route, probably walked since Bronze Age times and which can still be followed today, while south of the Bwlch Tyddiad route is Bwlch Drws Ardudwy, the most obvious pass when the Rhinogs are viewed from the east. It is also the one which names the range: the pass is flanked by Rhinog Fawr and Rhinog Fach (the big and small doorposts). South again the range declines towards the River Mawddach and

here there is a final ancient track, and one of the strangest. Those walking in the wilderness of the south Rhinogs for the first time will be amazed to discover a humpback bridge in the middle of nowhere – Pont Scethin – which lies on the old coach road from Harlech.

Our route through the range is an enigmatic one, well-engineered, with slabs of local stone laid along much of its length. But these slabs are called the Roman Steps. Why? It is very likely that there was an ancient way – one that existed before the Ardudwy outlaws followed the route – over Bwlch Tyddiad, one that may even have been taken by the Romans, who had a large fort at Trawsfynydd. But there is no evidence for a Roman construction, or even any certainty of where the name came from. Most experts now agree that the slabs were laid for a medieval packhorse trail, the spacing occasionally looking more suited to a packhorse than a man (though often the reverse is true). We follow the Steps, then a rugged path to a high mountain lake. This is magnificent but uncompromising country, the climb to the lake steep and poorly trodden, the only company the wind and the croaking of ravens. To return we descend equally steeply to a larger lake, also set in a beautiful, but harsh, landscape. From it, an anglers' path descends, reaching the Steps again.

On the Roman Steps
through the Rhinogs

This ancient pathway through the heart of the Rhinog
hills was one of many trade routes across the mountains

1 Leave the car park through the gate at its top end and turn right. Cross the causeway over the stream, then a ladder stile, following the path rising through a wood.

Distance: 4½ miles (7.2km)
Total ascent: 1,150 ft (350m)
Paths: excellent as far as the path to Llyn Du, rugged or poor thereafter
Terrain: heather clad and rocky mountains
Gradients: gradual, then steep and difficult
Refreshments: none
Park: car park at Llyn Cwm Bychan at end of minor road, 5 miles east of A496 in Harlech

2 At the end of the woodland, cross another ladder stile and continue along the path to reach a little humped bridge. Beyond, the slabs of the Roman Steps appear.

3 300yds (274m) beyond the humped bridge, where a slab bridge crosses the stream, note a path forking right: this is the return route. For now, continue along the steps, following the stream and sometimes crossing it. Occasionally the steps disappear, but the way is always obvious, heading up towards a narrow, rocky cleft.

4 Go between round, wooden gateposts in a wall and continue along the steps. As the pass narrows, cross through another low wall. Some 600yds (546m) on, another wall crosses the route.

5 Go right immediately after this wall on a path climbing steeply beside the wall. Follow it, staying close to the wall to the crest of a ridge. Now descend, still following the wall, then climb again.

6 On the final climb the path bears left, away from the wall, to a viewpoint above Llyn Du. Bear right from here to return to the wall and cross it by the stone stile. Follow the path beyond to pass through a wall gap. In a few minutes there is a view of Gloyw Llyn.

7 Be cautious now. Below you is a large boulder ruckle. Trace the line of a path which turns left under a cliff and skirts across the top of the rockfall, then makes its way down the left (as viewed) side. At the base of the ruckle, as you enter a small gully, break out, bearing right across boggy ground on a terrace above the lake. Pass through alternate boggy patches and areas of heather, and tend right towards the finger-like end of the lake.

8 Don't go down to the lake, but stay on the terrace, ignoring paths to the far end of the lake. Bear right, away from the lake and from the network of paths select one which heads towards Clip. If you head directly for Llyn Cwm Bychan, you are too far left.

9 Follow the path downhill, briefly indistinct in boggy ground, but soon re-appearing. Pass a ruined sheepfold, then go through a gap in a wall. The path descends soon to the steps at the point noted on the outward route. Turn left to the little humped bridge and return to the start.

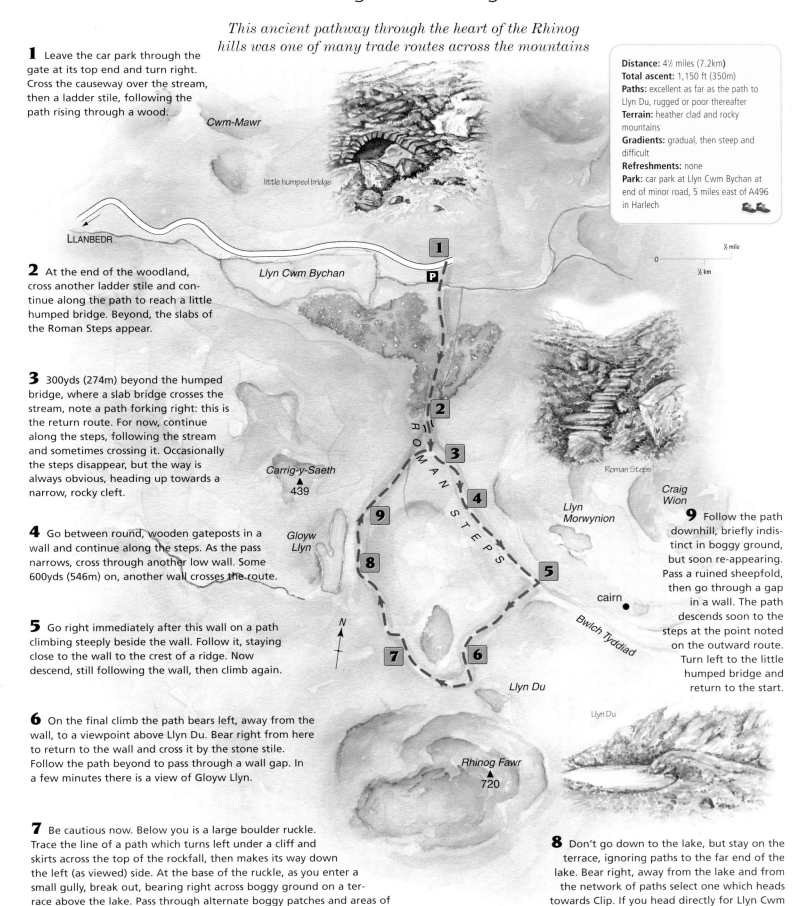

Cwm-Mawr

little humped bridge

LLANBEDR

Llyn Cwm Bychan

Carrig-y-Saeth
▲
439

Gloyw
Llyn

ROMAN STEPS

Llyn
Morwynion

Roman Steps

Craig
Wion

cairn •

Bwlch Tyddiad

Llyn Du

Rhinog Fawr
▲
720

Llyn Du

N

½ mile
0
½ km

Mary Jones in the Dysynni Valley

Wander through a valley beneath Cadair Idris, home to the girl who inspired a remarkable world movement

WALK
91

The Dysynni Valley forms a wide, flat tongue of land leading into the heart of Snowdonia, and to the feet of the impressive mountain, Cadair Idris. From the hamlet of Llanfihangel-y-Pennant you start by taking a hillside

Above: Craig yr Aderyn (Bird's Rock) looms over the Dysynni Valley

Top right: the Victorian monument to Mary Jones

Below: Castell-y-Bere is unusual for its indigenous Welsh origins

circuit, with fine views up and down the valley, that will soon bring you down to the Afon Cadair and Tyn-y-ddol.

It was from this remote place, the story says, that 15-year-old Mary Jones set off in 1800 to walk barefoot for 30 miles (48km) through the mountains to Bala to purchase a copy of the Bible in Welsh from the minister there, the Reverend Thomas Charles. By the time she arrived they were all sold, and no more would come from the printers.

She was deeply disappointed – so Thomas Charles gave her his own copy. And he was so impressed by her desire for the scriptures in her own tongue that he was inspired to found the British and Foreign Bible Society, which continues to provide copies of the Bible throughout the world. The Bible he gave Mary is now in Cambridge University Library.

Mary's story first appeared in print in 1867, the year after her death, and it is not clear whether Thomas Charles was really inspired by her visit or just encouraged in his aims by such determination. Certainly the Victorians loved the romance of Mary's walk, and put up the granite memorial to her in her roofless cottage, still standing at Tyn-y-ddol. Alas for romance: she was described at the age of 80 as being 'small and thin with a melancholy, ungrateful expression.'

As the walk continues along the side of the valley the improbable bulk of the 760ft-high (233m) Craig yr Aderyn – Birds' Rock – gradually dominates the landscape. The Dysynni Valley has silted up over the centuries, and the rock, once a sea cliff, is now 4 miles (6.4km) from the coast. The cormorants who continue to nest here have not noticed this, and it is their only inland nesting site in Europe. There are the remains of an Iron Age fort at the Rock's summit, and it is also the home to a rarely-seen herd of wild goats.

The walk crosses the valley floor and turns northeast, the views now terminated by the majestic heights of Cadair Idris. Below it, on a rocky outcrop in the valley bottom, are the remains of Castell-y-Bere, once the largest and most ornate castle in Wales. Always open for visits, it was built by the Welsh (unlike many Welsh castles, which the English kings built to subdue the natives). Llywelyn ap Iorwerth – Llywelyn the Great – is said to have been born here, and his brother Dafydd twice defended it against English sieges. It was eventually taken in 1294 and mostly destroyed, leaving the few remains – the remnants of three towers, a rectangular keep and triangular bastion – you can see today. Dafydd escaped to maintain a guerrilla campaign against the invaders from the almost impenetrable mountains.

Mary Jones in the Dysynni Valley

*In the footsteps of a remarkable woman, whose exploits
were commemorated by Victorian missionaries*

1 Walk north up the lane between the church and the cottage. As it bends left on the approach to a farm, go right, over a ladder stile or through the gate and along a track. Having passed through a gate behind the farm, fork right, climbing steadily on a stony track, and continue past an old quarry and a small larch plantation. Soon after a stream crosses the track, climb a stile on the left.

2 Descend to cross a footbridge over the Afon Cadair, then climb diagonally left to a stile onto a bridleway. Turn left and follow the track to reach Tyn-y-ddôl, where Mary Jones lived.

3 Just beyond the remains of her cottage go straight ahead at a footpath sign. The path runs beside the river, passing two farms, until it meets a stone wall. Keep on in the same direction, but just to the right of the wall. A series of stiles leads you on to pass a third farm, after which you turn left by a stream to a stile beside a chapel.

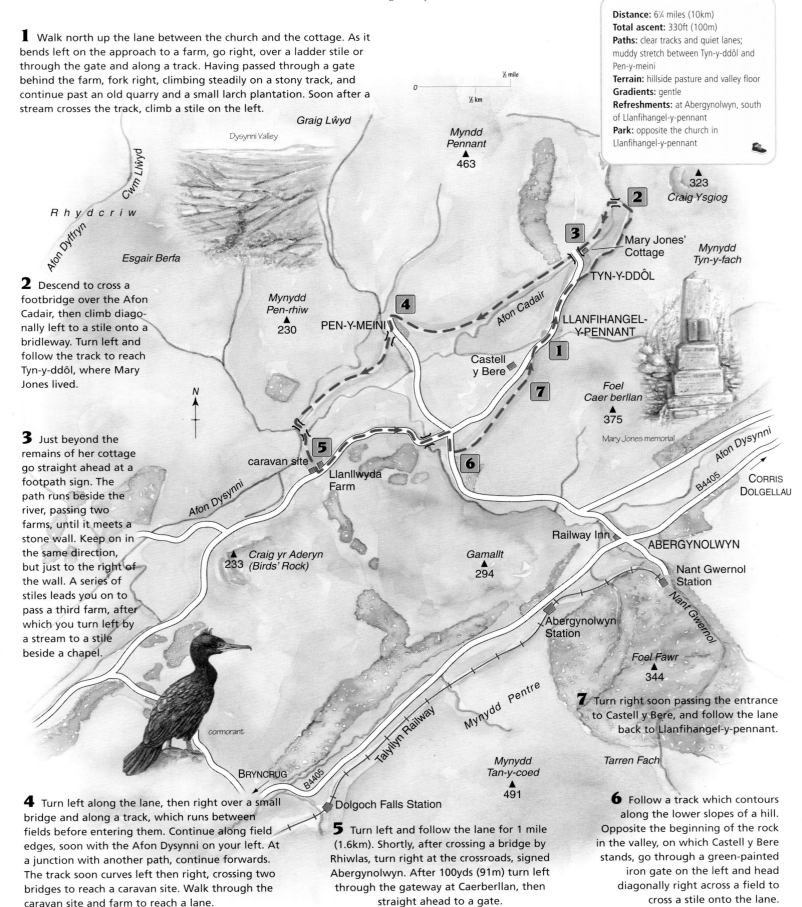

Distance: 6¼ miles (10km)
Total ascent: 330ft (100m)
Paths: clear tracks and quiet lanes; muddy stretch between Tyn-y-ddôl and Pen-y-meini
Terrain: hillside pasture and valley floor
Gradients: gentle
Refreshments: at Abergynolwyn, south of Llanfihangel-y-pennant
Park: opposite the church in Llanfihangel-y-pennant

4 Turn left along the lane, then right over a small bridge and along a track, which runs between fields before entering them. Continue along field edges, soon with the Afon Dysynni on your left. At a junction with another path, continue forwards. The track soon curves left then right, crossing two bridges to reach a caravan site. Walk through the caravan site and farm to reach a lane.

5 Turn left and follow the lane for 1 mile (1.6km). Shortly, after crossing a bridge by Rhiwlas, turn right at the crossroads, signed Abergynolwyn. After 100yds (91m) turn left through the gateway at Caerberllan, then straight ahead to a gate.

6 Follow a track which contours along the lower slopes of a hill. Opposite the beginning of the rock in the valley, on which Castell y Bere stands, go through a green-painted iron gate on the left and head diagonally right across a field to cross a stile onto the lane.

7 Turn right soon passing the entrance to Castell y Bere, and follow the lane back to Llanfihangel-y-pennant.

Rhaeadr Ddu – the Black Waterfall

A peaceful woodland walk taking you from crystal-clear waters, the inspiration for artists, to memories of glittering gold once sought by prospectors

WALK
92

Top right: rocks split the falls

Above: ferns flourish in the damp conditions

Below: waters spout into the gully

The Coed-y-Brenin, or king's forest, which provides the setting for this walk, is a wonderful haven of beauty and tranquillity. Most of the woodland you pass through is made up of native deciduous trees which support a rich variety of wildlife. The canopy formed by the oak trees (mainly the sessile oak, the ancient species native to this area) supports an abundance of mosses, liverworts and rare ferns. This is a fine place to watch birds too, with fly-catchers, wood warblers, jays, siskins and, above the trees, birds of prey such as buzzards and sparrowhawks, all to be seen. You might even catch a glimpse of deer, descendants of a herd introduced before the estate was bought by the Forestry Commission after World War I.

Another natural wonder gives the walk its focal point, the beautiful Rhaeadr Ddu, or black waterfall. This earns its name from the hard rocks which make up the bed of the Afon Gamlan and provide a dark backdrop to the white spray of the falls. This is one walk where wet weather can even prove an advantage, as the rains swell the torrents. Landscape artists such as Richard Wilson, Gainsborough and Turner and poets such as Shelley and Thomas Love Peacock have been drawn here since at least the 18th century. A lasting memorial to the muse which inspired them has been carved into a rock overlooking the waterfall, in the form of lines from an ode by Thomas Gray. The National Trust has erected a slate tablet with the verse carved on it.

A sense of a quite different past is felt at the site of the former Cefn Coch gold mine. Opened in 1862 and closed in 1914, this was once the third richest of the Meirionydd gold belt. Mining for minerals, notably copper and lead, has been carried out for centuries in the Mawddach Valley, but it was not until the middle of the 19th century that Dolgellau became the centre of a mini-gold rush. Welsh gold is considered particularly fine, and to this day is used for jewellery for the royal family. This particular mine, however, ceased to be viable decades ago, and the adits – horizontal tunnels bored into the hillside marked by spoil heaps at their mouths – can be very dangerous. So however tempting it may be, do not enter them or let children play there. Instead, pause a while to enjoy the ghosts of history evoked by the ruins; imagine the hive of activity when the mine was at its prime and the site was covered by heavy machinery, and consider the lives of those who came to work underground in this and many other remote sites throughout the Welsh countryside, many moving around from place to place as old mineral veins dried up and new ones yielded their wealth.

Rhaedr Ddu – the Black Waterfall

Deep forests cloak a lovely waterfall, where poets and writers found inspiration

1 From car park, follow main road left (south) for a few paces to black corrugated village hall and turn right between hall and river on gated lane. Climb gradually upstream with river away to left. Ignore drive to Ty-cerig on right.

2 About 200yds (182m) beyond drive, where lane bends right, look for waymark post in woodland ahead. Go to it and bear left along waymarked path towards footbridge over river. Just before footbridge, keep to path which leads directly to viewpoint of waterfall upstream from bridge. See lines of poetry carved on rock then retrace route a few paces and cross footbridge.

7 As track swings left, go ahead through small gate and descend with walled path. Pass buildings of Tyddyn-y-bwlch and through gate into woodland and, in 20yds (18m), after second gate, bear right at fork. Drop down to lane, go right (downhill) and follow it back to village and car park in Ganllwyd.

6 At track junction, turn right to follow track across river. Take track on right and, ignoring tracks through forest on left, bear right at two forks, keeping alongside river. At mountain bike waymark, take lesser track right, dropping downhill.

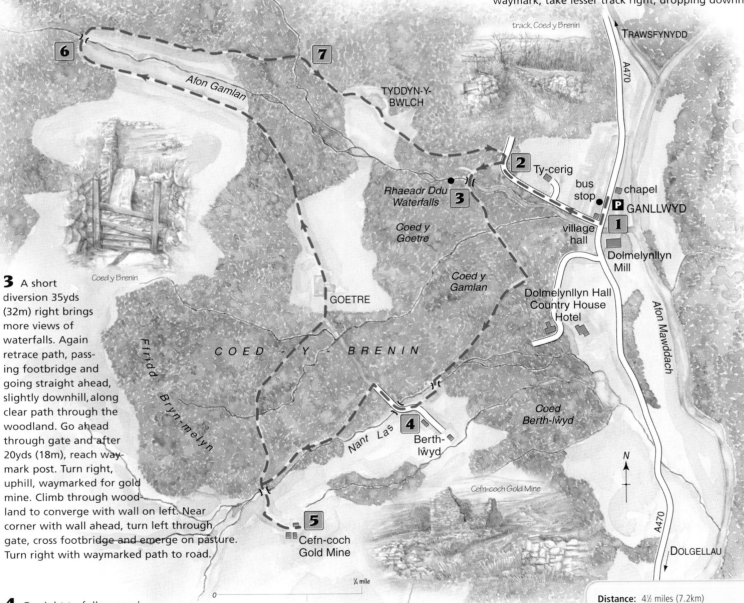

3 A short diversion 35yds (32m) right brings more views of waterfalls. Again retrace path, passing footbridge and going straight ahead, slightly downhill, along clear path through the woodland. Go ahead through gate and after 20yds (18m), reach waymark post. Turn right, uphill, waymarked for gold mine. Climb through woodland to converge with wall on left. Near corner with wall ahead, turn left through gate, cross footbridge and emerge on pasture. Turn right with waymarked path to road.

4 Go right to follow road across bridge and gate to re-enter woodland. After 80yds (73m), turn left along track between trees. Again converge with stream on left and ignore tracks on right. Turn left through narrow gap in wall, over collapsible stile and footbridge. Climb with paved way to ruins of Cefn-coch Gold Mine.

5 Retrace steps and cross footbridge and collapsible stile again. Go 35yds (32m) downhill on outward approach route to track junction and take track going ahead (ignoring track bearing left uphill and track used to reach here on right). Follow downhill to major track and go left through gate to pass buildings of Goetre. Continue along firm track through open space and back into forest. Then, back into open country, track rises to converge with river (Afon Gamlan) on right.

Distance: 4½ miles (7.2km)
Total ascent: 600ft (189m)
Paths: good
Terrain: oak woodland, conifer forest, pasture, quiet road
Gradients: some gradual climbs
Refreshments: none
Park: National Trust car park on eastern side of A470 in Ganllwyd, 5 miles (8km) north of Dolgellau

Pilgrims and Mysteries on Lleyn's Peninsula

The monastry on Bardsey Island was the ultimate goal for devout early Christians

WALK 93

Top right: a finger-post on the route

Below: Bardsey lurks, whale-like, off the Lleyn

Inset: a landing craft serves as a ferry for modern pilgrims to Bardsey

For modern ramblers the windswept Penrhyn Llyn (Lleyn Peninsula) provides a sense of adventure in a remote spot. For walkers of bygone centuries, however, the wild surroundings brought the sort of hardships normally to be avoided – yet people came here in great numbers. Assembling at Aberdaron, they gathered in Y Gegin Fawr (the Great Kitchen), a 14th-century stone building whose fare still draws and sustains visitors today, and prayed in a magnificent church on the sands dedicated to the 6th-century St Hywyn, before setting out on the hazardous crossing to the monastery on Ynys Enlli (Bardsey Island).

Their purpose was not leisure but spiritual renewal, for the pedestrian 'tourists' of the Middle Ages were pilgrims. Their final destination was the mystic isle of Bardsey and the large and famous monastery founded in AD 615 by St Cadfan, its first abbot and a cousin of St Hywyn (himself a later abbot of Bardsey). These early Christian visitors believed they were following in the footsteps of 20,000 saints, although this number is more likely to reflect the vast number of pilgrims who came to find sanctuary and end their days here. So highly was this journey to the edge of Wales rated in the Middle Ages, that three pilgrimages to Bardsey were deemed equal to one to Rome. Today all that survives of the religious community is the 13th-century bell tower, a poignant reminder of the once thriving spiritual centre which was the Augustinian abbey of St Mary.

This route passes the cove of Porth Meudwy, from which the pilgrims' boats set sail. The climax of the walk is the view of Bardsey Island and the companionship of its whale-like bulk as you go round the tip of Lleyn. Looking at this sight, standing where so many pilgrims stood and saw it, is a moving experience.

Even before Christianity, Lleyn was clearly a place of spiritual importance. Significant representation is found here of the network of ley-lines, pathways of mystic energy marked by standing stones and other ancient monuments erected by our prehistoric ancestors and believed to criss-cross the landscape. When these paths were mapped on the peninsula two leys were found to converge on Bardsey from the mainland, one through Mynydd Anelog and the other through Capel Fair. This alignment would seem to focus the spiritual energies through Lleyn to the holy isle, bringing them together in harmonious fusion. The early Celtic church, with its roots in contemplation of the beauties and mysteries of the natural world, was sensitive to the significance of such ancient sacred sites, and it is no coincidence that a hermitage and later a community was founded on this remote yet inspirational island.

If all this makes you want to brave the crossing to the island as a modern-day pilgrim, note that the weekly boat usually sails on Saturdays; note, too, that people are often stranded for long periods on the island by bad weather. Take your own provisions and step back in time to a world without electricity. (For details on visiting Bardsey, telephone 01758 730740, 01766 522239 or 01626 773908.)

Pilgrims and Mysteries on Lleyn's Peninsula

A coastal walk through a landscape dominated by rituals

1 From car park, return to road junction and turn left, without crossing either bridge. Bear left uphill, ignoring turnings to right. When level with entrance to Dwyros camping site on right, turn left down signposted path. Pass houses and cross footbridge over Afon Saint to enter National Trust land.

6 On right is gate, stile and National Trust pillar, with track dropping down to Porth Meudwy valley. This is short cut described earlier. Continue past Cwrt (left) and go right at successive road junctions to retrace steps into Aberdaron, passing Dwyros on left.

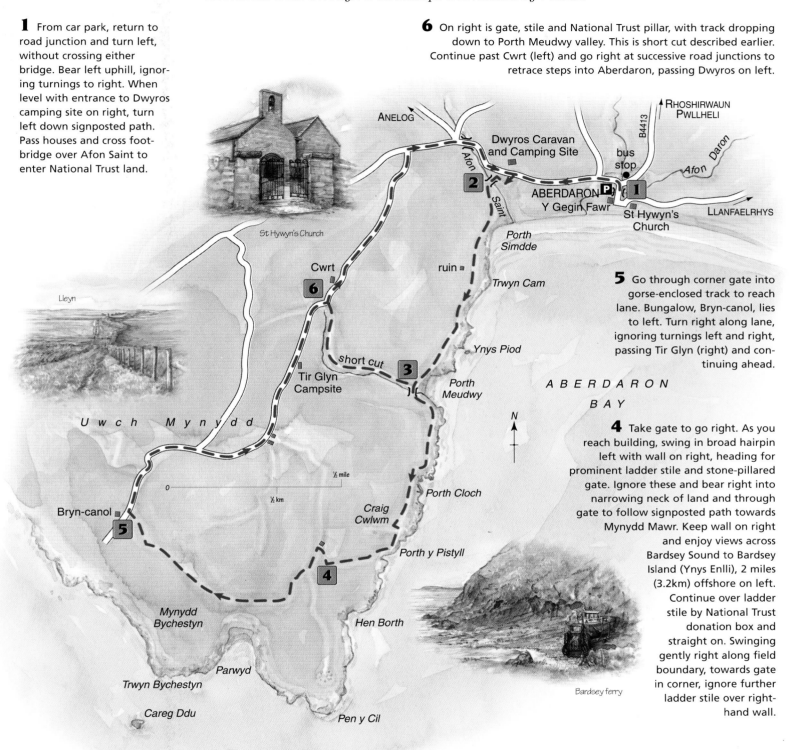

Bardsey ferry

5 Go through corner gate into gorse-enclosed track to reach lane. Bungalow, Bryn-canol, lies to left. Turn right along lane, ignoring turnings left and right, passing Tir Glyn (right) and continuing ahead.

4 Take gate to go right. As you reach building, swing in broad hairpin left with wall on right, heading for prominent ladder stile and stone-pillared gate. Ignore these and bear right into narrowing neck of land and through gate to follow signposted path towards Mynydd Mawr. Keep wall on right and enjoy views across Bardsey Sound to Bardsey Island (Ynys Enlli), 2 miles (3.2km) offshore on left. Continue over ladder stile by National Trust donation box and straight on. Swinging gently right along field boundary, towards gate in corner, ignore further ladder stile over right-hand wall.

2 Follow coast path, keeping sea on left and ignoring path descending to beach at Porth Simdde. Continue past ruin (right) and through kissing-gate to log seat, then another kissing-gate before descending steps to inlet of Porth Meudwy. Track right offers short cut from here to stage 6 (near Cwrt). If you use this, keep to main track in valley bottom, ignoring side tracks.

3 Going ahead with signposted coast path, cross footbridge and climb steps up to stile. Ignore further stile, immediately on right skyline. Resume clifftop walk, keeping sea on left, passing Porth Cloch, then rising to pass Craig Cwlwm with its summit pond. Descend awkward outcrop to disused quarry. Ignore path and stile leading inland and continue on coast path, descending initially for 15 minutes to Porth y Pistyll. At its inland point, fork right, keeping to right-hand edge of field as you climb to gate in top right-hand corner.

Distance: 5½ miles (8.8km)
Total ascent: 350ft (107m)
Paths: good; some roads
Terrain: clifftop, pastureland
Gradients: some steep, stepped sections
Refreshments: many places in Aberdaron
Park: car park in Aberdaron, on B4413 16 miles (25.6km) west of Pwllheli

Quarrymen's Trails around
Blaenau Ffestiniog *Drama and history are*

embedded deep in the grim but beautiful slate workings of the Moelwyns

WALK
94

Tanygrisiau's terraced houses lie beneath the slate-grey Moelwyn Mountains. Piles of slate are heaped up to the sky like pyramids, looking black in contrast to the foaming waterfalls that tumble down to the reservoir. Occasionally, little narrow-gauge steam engines chug by, their smoke billowing through the falling rain and up into the clouds. It's a sombre scene, but typical of a Ffestiniog day, and one that has its share of drama and history. That history is one of hardship and austerity, for the Ffestiniog quarrymen and miners lived by this slate, breathed the dust of this slate, and often died getting this slate from the mountain.

Tanygrisiau means 'Place under the Stairs'. As you leave the last of its little houses behind, you climb into the grey-blue world of Cwmorthin, a dramatic crag-bound valley, biting deep into the Moelwyn mountainsides. Gaunt skeletons of the Cwmorthin Barracks and its crumbling chimneys loom before you. Slate even forms the fence that guides the track by the black waters of Cwmorthin's lake. Hiding behind some pines are yet more relics – a chapel where a few remaining slates cling to the rafters, waiting for the next wind to blow them back on to the hillside from where they came.

The old track climbs out of the cwm to the Rhosydd Mine, which, at 1,600 feet (500m), was one of the highest workings in Snowdonia. At one time the whole place would have reverberated to the sound of

gunpowder explosions, the noise of a couple of hundred men, and the creaking wheels of quarry wagons taking the slate down the hill. It is said that the quarrymen had a good choir, and that on a summer night the hills would also echo to the sound of hymns and anthems.

The steep tramways take you from Rhosydd up on to the slopes of Moelwyn Mawr. The original Rhosydd workings, West Twll and East Twll, are gigantic open pits that are unstable and liable to frequent collapse, as are the long shafts that tunnel through the mountainsides back to the lower mines and the barracks.

Crossing the depression between Moel yr Hydd and Moelwyn Mawr, the change is one from moorland to mountain, as a miners' track takes you along a ledge on steep, stony slopes, high above the Vale of Ffestiniog. Ahead, Moelwyn Bach boasts rocky buttresses and screes. One of its crags resembles the head of a lion. Beneath it a wild mountain tarn, Llyn Stwlan, has been tamed by a concrete dam. It's part of the Tanygrisiau Pump Storage Scheme, where off-peak electricity is used to pump water from the larger Tanygrisiau Reservoir 1,000 feet (305m) below to Llyn Stwlan. At peak times the intake gates are opened, and Stwlan is emptied of its contents, allowing the head of water to power the turbines.

You will see the power station on the final promenade by the shores of Tanygrisiau Reservoir, but first the descent must be made down the rocky, bracken-cloaked hillsides, with a derelict wall and the lively Nant Ddu stream as company.

Above: mountains of slate loom over Blaenau Ffestiniog

Below: Cnicht and the Moelwyns rise above the upper Rhosydd mines

Quarrymen's Trails around Blaenau Ffestiniog

A fascinating mountain walk amidst the ruins of a once-thriving slate industry

Distance: 6 miles (9.7km)
Total ascent: 1,275ft (389m)
Paths: rough
Terrain: old quarry workings, rough moorland and bouldery mountainside
Gradients: fairly steep in places
Refreshments: café at power station visitor centre
Park: car park on minor road to power station visitor centre, Tanygrisiau, north of A496 between Blaenau Ffestiniog and Maentwrog

7 Immediately before power station go left on waymarked path behind buildings and recross railway before climbing to metalled lane. Follow to junction just above visitor centre, then turn left on lane climbing back to car park.

6 Follow tramway for 100yds (91m). Remains of wall lead off at right angle right. Follow this down to north banks of Nant Ddu. Keep to faint path down left bank of stream, around isolated building and back towards stream, down to footbridge. Don't cross, but turn left through short tunnel to follow path swinging left, above shores of reservoir, before crossing Ffestiniog Railway to shoreline track towards power station.

1 From car park entrance turn right and, in a few paces, cross river bridge to top houses of Tanygrisiau. Turn left on slaty track, parallel to stream, to shores of Llyn Cwmorthin.

2 Cross slate footbridge beneath ruins of quarry barracks, then follow track round shore past derelict chapel. Continue on main track to right of more quarry buildings, and upward, climbing past further quarry buildings to Rhosydd Mines plateau.

3 From rear of rows of buildings (workers' barracks) and left og giant spoil heap, climb the slate incline to the top pulley house. Go straight ahead for 100yds (91m), but just before more derelict buildings, fork left on grassy track, passing right of spoil heap and buildings, then swinging half right to fence and ladder stile. Don't cross stile but follow fence and diversion markers skirting pit, eventually swinging back to re-join original path at metal gate. Follow grassy path to pass between Moel-yr-Hydd and Moelwyn Mawr.

5 On nearing high col beneath rockfaces of Moelwyn mawr, the track deteriorates as it crosses boulderfields. On reaching col, double back left for 50yds (46m), then descend on a faint path past Llyn Stwlan's southern shores. Path squeezes between the wall end of dam and a rocky bluff. Go down concrete steps and sharp left to main section of dam. Round end of low wall and return to butress of dam. Keeping very close to butresses, descend steeply on path to outlet stream at base. Don't cross fence, but go downhill with fence on left, aiming for top of tramway.

4 Go through gate, turn right for a few paces, then left to large cairn where quarry track traverses bouldery slopes beneath cliffs of Cragysgafn and high above Llyn Stwlan.

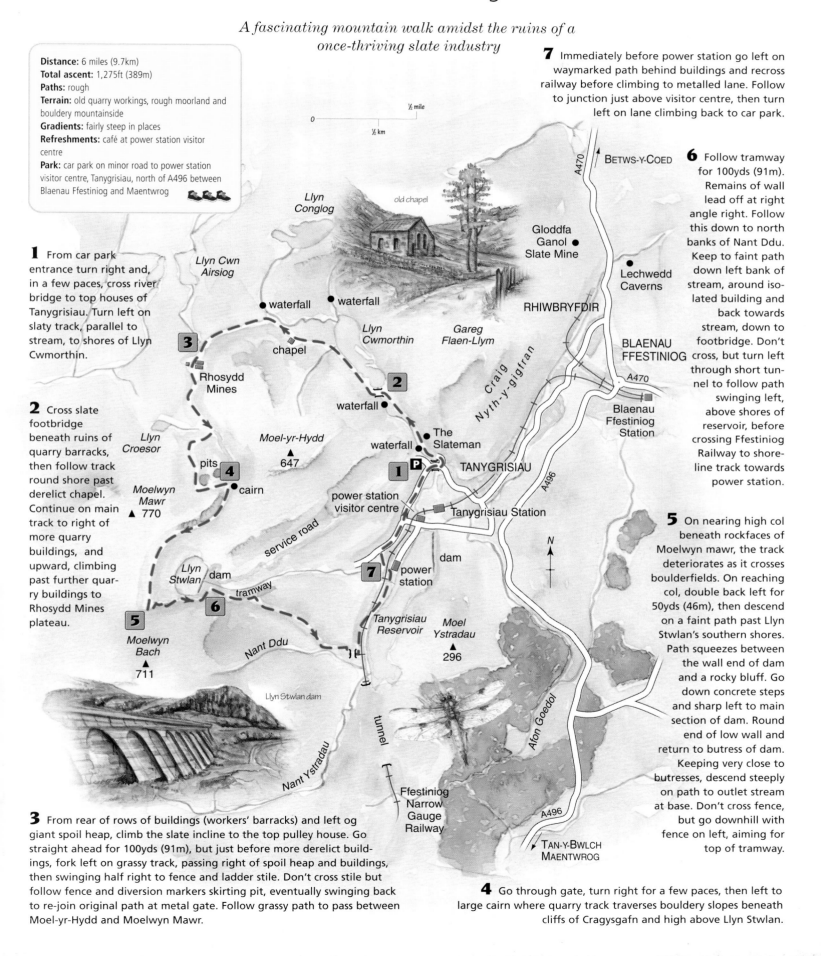

Llyn Conglog · old chapel · Llyn Cwn Airsiog · waterfall · waterfall · Gloddfa Ganol Slate Mine · Lechwedd Caverns · RHIWBRYFDIR · BETWS-Y-COED · A470 · **3** · Rhosydd Mines · chapel · Llyn Cwmorthin · Gareg Flaen-Llym · Craig Nyth-y-gigfran · BLAENAU FFESTINIOG · A470 · Blaenau Ffestiniog Station · **2** · waterfall · Llyn Croesor · pits · **4** · cairn · Moel-yr-Hydd ▲ 647 · waterfall · The Slateman · Moelwyn Mawr ▲ 770 · power station visitor centre · **1** P · TANYGRISIAU · A496 · Tanygrisiau Station · service road · Llyn Stwlan · dam · **6** · tramway · **7** · power station · dam · N · Moelwyn Bach ▲ 711 · Nant Ddu · Tanygrisiau Reservoir · Moel Ystradau ▲ 296 · Afon Goedol · Llyn Stwlan dam · tunnel · Nant Ystradau · Ffestiniog Narrow Gauge Railway · A496 · TAN-Y-BWLCH MAENTWROG

Groves and Graves in Anglesey

A Stone Age burial mound vies with a Druidic stronghold on this winding route which links the island's sacred sites

WALK

95

Below: a lichen-covered standing stone along the route

Below right: inside the ancient burial chamber of Bryncelli-ddu

Bottom: Moel-y-don, where the Druids fought their last stand

Moel-y-don, where the walk begins, is a bulge of flat, windswept land that juts out into the Menai Strait, the channel of water that divides the rugged fastnesses of Snowdonia from the gentler farmlands of Anglesey. In Welsh *moel* can imply a bare and empty place, so it must long have been treeless and subject to the elements. It would have been a great contrast to the rest of the heavily wooded island in the time of the Celts, ancestors of the Welsh people. Arriving here in the Iron Age, they displaced or intermarried with the Bronze Age Britons.

With them came their priests, the Druids. Brynsiencyn, 2 miles (3.2km) west of Moel-y-don, was a main centre for the Celts, and when the Druids were outlawed in AD 54, ostensibly because of the human sacrifices they practised, they retreated here to Anglesey where they would make their last stand against the advancing Romans. The Roman historian Tacitus described the scene, with the soldiers on the mainland side of the Menai Strait and the Druids on Moel-y-don: 'By the shore the opposing battle line was formed, thick with men and weapons; between the ranks dashed women dressed in funeral black like the Furies, with flowing hair and carrying torches. The Druids stood among them, issuing frightful curses, with their hands raised high to the heavens. Our soldiers were so frightened by this unfamiliar sight that their limbs were paralysed, and they stood motionless, vulnerable to wounding.'

Alas for the Druids, the impact did not last. The Romans crossed the strait and, in a bloody struggle, extinguished the last defiance of the Druids. Moving forward into the interior of the island, the invaders ruthlessly cut down the sacred groves of

oak trees and harried the natives.

The walk takes a winding route through this once-ritual landscape, now overlain with farmland and smallholdings. The thick oak woodland has given way to fields, crossed by ancient tracks. Your route follows one of these, just before you reach the village of Llanddaniel Fab. The path is deeply scarred into the landscape and lined with mossy walls.

Although the Celtic Druids played a major role in Anglesey's history, they were preceded by a still more ancient religious tradition. In the latter stretch of the walk you will pass Bryncelli-ddu, a burial chamber dating from between 2000 and 1500 BC. Built in the late Stone Age, it replaced an earlier circle of standing stones. Passages lead inside to a central chamber with a large, free-standing stone pillar at its centre. There is also a replica of a stone incised with maze-like spirals (the original is held in the National Museum, Cardiff).

Groves and Graves in Anglesey

Peaceful lowland Anglesey is home to a wealth of prehistoric landmarks

Distance: 8¼ miles (13.3km)
Total ascent: 280ft (85m)
Paths: mostly clear tracks and field paths; often muddy
Terrain: undulating farmland, with some woodland
Gradients: slight
Refreshments: Plas Coch or Brynsiencyn
Park: at the end of the Moel-y-don peninsula, south of the A4080

8 At the gate, go across the field to a waymarker, then turn right towards the cottage and chapel. Immediately before the cottage, go left through its grounds to the road. Turn left, cross the main road and follow the road signed Moel-y-don for a mile (1.6km) back to the car.

7 50yds (46m) beyond the gate turn right along a track. After the second stile, go right of a brick building, then diagonally left towards a rhododendron thicket, going right of it to a stile into woodland. Follow the track through the wood, keeping the wall to your left.

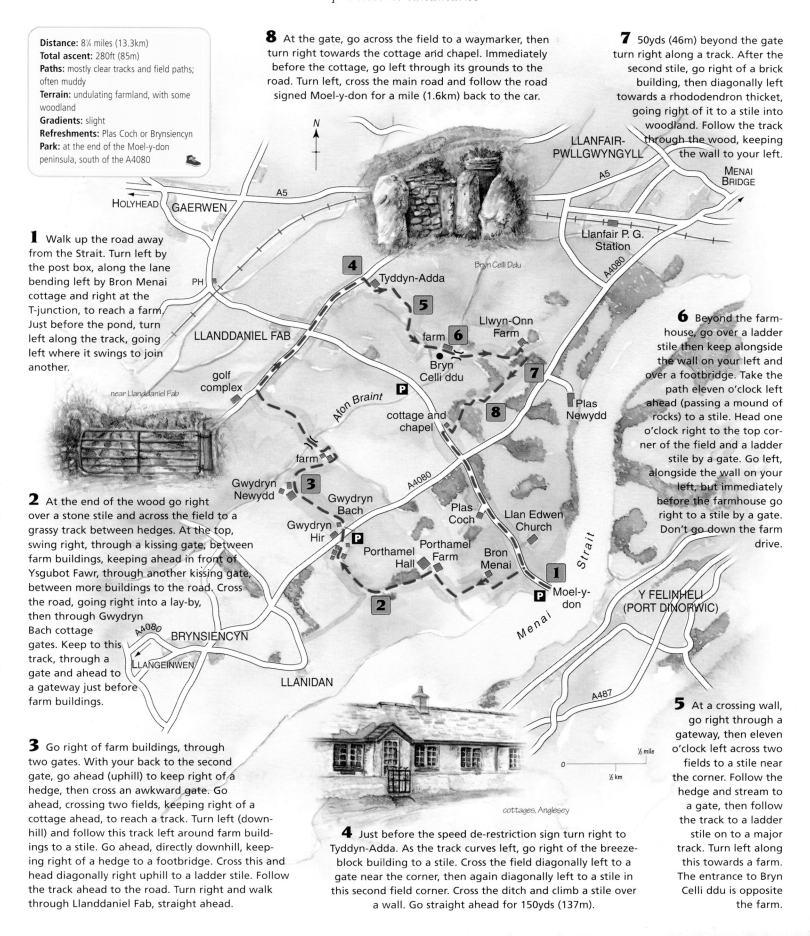

1 Walk up the road away from the Strait. Turn left by the post box, along the lane bending left by Bron Menai cottage and right at the T-junction, to reach a farm. Just before the pond, turn left along the track, going left where it swings to join another.

near Llanddaniel Fab

6 Beyond the farmhouse, go over a ladder stile then keep alongside the wall on your left and over a footbridge. Take the path eleven o'clock left ahead (passing a mound of rocks) to a stile. Head one o'clock right to the top corner of the field and a ladder stile by a gate. Go left, alongside the wall on your left, but immediately before the farmhouse go right to a stile by a gate. Don't go down the farm drive.

2 At the end of the wood go right over a stone stile and across the field to a grassy track between hedges. At the top, swing right, through a kissing gate, between farm buildings, keeping ahead in front of Ysgubot Fawr, through another kissing gate, between more buildings to the road. Cross the road, going right into a lay-by, then through Gwydryn Bach cottage gates. Keep to this track, through a gate and ahead to a gateway just before farm buildings.

3 Go right of farm buildings, through two gates. With your back to the second gate, go ahead (uphill) to keep right of a hedge, then cross an awkward gate. Go ahead, crossing two fields, keeping right of a cottage ahead, to reach a track. Turn left (downhill) and follow this track left around farm buildings to a stile. Go ahead, directly downhill, keeping right of a hedge to a footbridge. Cross this and head diagonally right uphill to a ladder stile. Follow the track ahead to the road. Turn right and walk through Llanddaniel Fab, straight ahead.

Bryn Celli Ddu

cottages, Anglesey

4 Just before the speed de-restriction sign turn right to Tyddyn-Adda. As the track curves left, go right of the breeze-block building to a stile. Cross the field diagonally left to a gate near the corner, then again diagonally left to a stile in this second field corner. Cross the ditch and climb a stile over a wall. Go straight ahead for 150yds (137m).

5 At a crossing wall, go right through a gateway, then eleven o'clock left across two fields to a stile near the corner. Follow the hedge and stream to a gate, then follow the track to a ladder stile on to a major track. Turn left along this towards a farm. The entrance to Bryn Celli ddu is opposite the farm.

0   ½ mile
0   ½ km

Watkin Path and the Heart of Snowdonia

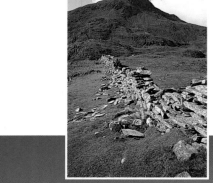

WALK 96

A trail through breathtaking scenery was familar to quarry workers, a legendary king and a prime minister alike

Top right: pretty waterfalls below Cwm Llan

Inset below: Yr Aran towers over Bwlch Cwm Llan

Bottom: everything here is made of slate

The road from Pen-y-Gwryd to Beddgelert runs past Llyn Gwynant, nestling below the huge flank of Y Lliwedd to reach Nantgwynant and the 'secret' side of Snowdon. The walk from here is the longest climb to the highest summit, but a climb through some of the most varied and spectacular scenery in the National Park. From the start Snowdon appears as a high, flat ridge set far above rugged Craig-ddu, dauntingly far off, but the interest never flags and keeps tiredness at bay.

The delights begin with the oak woodland of Parc Hafod-y-Llan, a superb section of ancient oak wood, the best in Snowdonia. The wood once stretched far up Cwm Llan, but was cleared for mining and sheep rearing. When the path emerges above the wood, Cwm Llan opens up, a magnificent jumble of rocks and waterfalls. After heavy rain the falls are among the best in the National Park.

A gate gives access to the Snowdon National Nature Reserve. Sheep have reduced the plant life of the floor of the valley to grasses, but heather flourishes on the rock ledges, with parsley fern and maidenhair spleenwort on the damper and steeper rock faces. Pied flycatchers flit through the oak woodlands and ring ouzels – looking like blackbirds wearing parsons' collars – are seen on the more open ground. There are also likely to be feral goats.

But the wildlife is the icing on the scenic cake. Towering ahead now is Snowdon's southern face, forming the back of this superb mountain cwm. Y Lliwedd, to the right, and Yr Aran, to the left, form the vast sidewalls of the cwm. The Watkin Path – named after Sir Edward Watkin, a Victorian railway magnate and Liberal MP who gave it to the nation after his retirement – climbs to Bwlch y Saethau, the Pass of the Arrows, legendary site of King Arthur's last battle against Mordred. Our walk does not follow the path all the way, bearing left for the less arduous climb of Yr Aran, but does reach Gladstone Rock, which commemorates the path's opening by W E Gladstone, then in his fourth term as Prime Minister, on 13 September 1892. Gladstone was 84 but, in pouring rain, walked up to the rock. There he asked for an encore from the choir Watkin had organised and gave a lengthy speech on 'The Land Question in Wales'. The crowd then retreated down the path, about which not one word had been said – which was rather sad, considering that the whole show had been arranged in its honour. The next day several members of the official party did come back, including Gladstone's wife, and some even followed the path to Snowdon's summit.

Watkin Path and the Heart of Snowdonia

Gentle walking in the heart of the Snowdon range, with a challenging option for greater views

1 From car park follow road towards Beddgelert for 50yds (46m), then cross to reach signed path. Cross cattle grid and follow tarmac lane away from main road, with river on right and woodland on left.

2 Leave tarmac lane at footpath sign, bearing left through gate on rough track, with wall on left and rhododendrons on right. Go ahead through gate and follow track curving right to reach kissing-gate, shortly after obvious incline up and down hillside.

8 To descend, retrace path to ladder stile, cross it and follow to left of wall. Descent flattens, before low point of ridge. Carefully turn left and descend steeply heading cross-country, northeast. Aim just a little right of prominent waterfall in valley below, so as to avoid cliffs of Clogwyn Brith. When tramway is reached, a short detour right visits ruins of drumhouse at top of incline. Don't be tempted to climb down incline. Instead, return along tramway and descend to regain Watkin Path. Turn right and reverse route back to start.

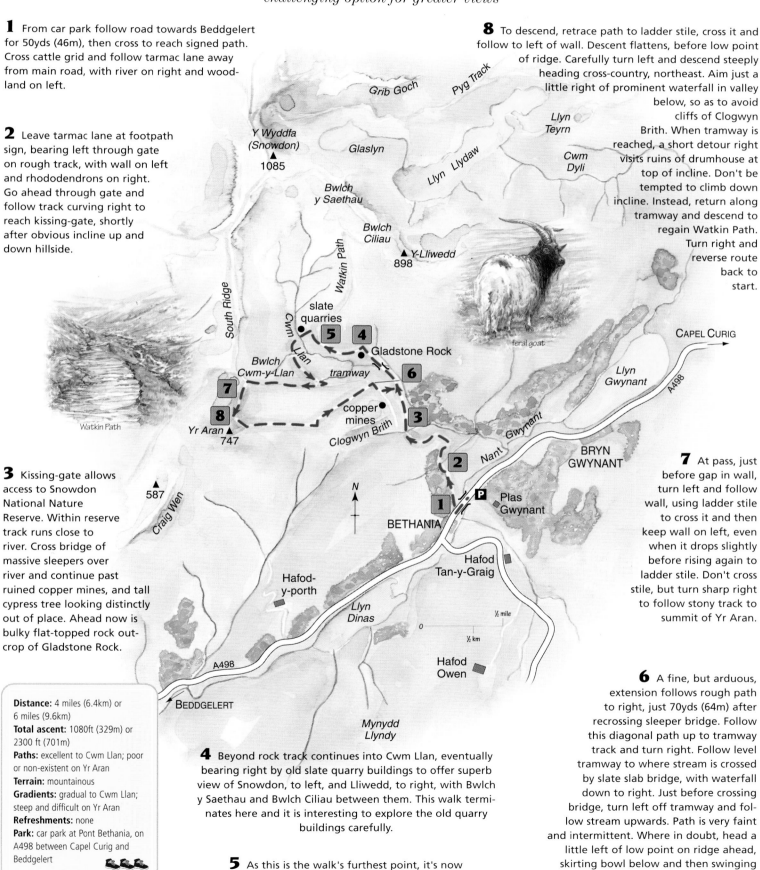

Watkin Path

feral goat

3 Kissing-gate allows access to Snowdon National Nature Reserve. Within reserve track runs close to river. Cross bridge of massive sleepers over river and continue past ruined copper mines, and tall cypress tree looking distinctly out of place. Ahead now is bulky flat-topped rock outcrop of Gladstone Rock.

7 At pass, just before gap in wall, turn left and follow wall, using ladder stile to cross it and then keep wall on left, even when it drops slightly before rising again to ladder stile. Don't cross stile, but turn sharp right to follow stony track to summit of Yr Aran.

Distance: 4 miles (6.4km) or 6 miles (9.6km)
Total ascent: 1080ft (329m) or 2300 ft (701m)
Paths: excellent to Cwm Llan; poor or non-existent on Yr Aran
Terrain: mountainous
Gradients: gradual to Cwm Llan; steep and difficult on Yr Aran
Refreshments: none
Park: car park at Pont Bethania, on A498 between Capel Curig and Beddgelert

4 Beyond rock track continues into Cwm Llan, eventually bearing right by old slate quarry buildings to offer superb view of Snowdon, to left, and Lliwedd, to right, with Bwlch y Saethau and Bwlch Ciliau between them. This walk terminates here and it is interesting to explore the old quarry buildings carefully.

5 As this is the walk's furthest point, it's now simple to reverse route back to start.

6 A fine, but arduous, extension follows rough path to right, just 70yds (64m) after recrossing sleeper bridge. Follow this diagonal path up to tramway track and turn right. Follow level tramway to where stream is crossed by slate slab bridge, with waterfall down to right. Just before crossing bridge, turn left off tramway and follow stream upwards. Path is very faint and intermittent. Where in doubt, head a little left of low point on ridge ahead, skirting bowl below and then swinging right, directly to pass of Bwlch-Cwm-Llan.

Lost Civilisations on Tal y Fan

History and prehistory cross paths in the rugged hills above the North Wales coast

WALK
97

Top right: Maen y Bardd cromlech on Tal y Fan

The whole of the Carneddau, the coastal mountains of North Wales, were peopled from the earliest times, and the legacy of their presence remains for today's visitors to see and wonder over. Tal y Fan, the most northerly of the range, gazes down on the historically important town of Conwy and boasts more than its fair share of prehistoric and Roman interest.

The 2,000-foot (610m) summit is a fine vantage point, a ragged upthrust of crags and rocky knolls that punctuate

edly erected by man for a purpose. On the eastern slopes of Cefn Llechen a small group of stones forms an indistinct circle, while on the northern slopes of Tal y Fan, just below the quarries, a huge monolith is neither erratic nor accidental. Someone placed it here, aeons ago, but their reasons are lost in the mists of time.

Across the southern slopes runs the course of a Roman road, passing to the southwest of Tal y Fan's neighbour, Foel Lwyd, at the Bwlch y Ddeufaen, the Pass of the Two Stones. But these stones were old when the Romans came, in the 1st century AD, and stand on a Bronze Age track, usurped by the invading forces, between the Conwy Valley and the coast at Aber.

Above: the rugged hills around Tal y Fan tower over Penmaenmawr and the coast

Below: a stone circle perches on the slopes of Cefn Llechan

After visiting the summit of Tal y Fan, this walk eases down to the ancient road and, for a few minutes, allows you to walk in the footsteps of Roman soldiers and prehistoric man.

More prehistoric interest awaits along the way, but first there is an optional diversion. For here, just beyond Cae Coch Farm, stands Maen y Bardd, the Bard's Stone, a splendid cromlech, or burial chamber, built by an ancient megalithic population. The additional effort of the ascent is well worthwhile.

rough upland pastures dotted with low gorse bushes and spread with bracken and heather. The view embraces the whole of Anglesey in one direction, and the hazy sprawl of the Denbigh moors in the opposite. Southwest rise the bald, tumescent domes of the high Carneddau, while northeast you gaze out over Conwy, Llandudno and Liverpool Bay.

Huge standing stones dot this landscape, each with some past significance lost from certainty, but undoubt-

But on this walk, of all the ancient monuments, it is the hill fort of Caer Bach that especially pleases, a raised circular mound with obvious earth ramparts and an inner circle of stones. It commands a wonderful view of the Conwy Valley, and is an excellent spot from which to enjoy the sound of silence and, perhaps, to imagine what life would have been like in these windswept hills thousands of years ago.

Lost Civilisations on Tal y Fan

The hinterland of the North Wales coast is dotted with mysterious stones and circles

Distance: 9½ miles (15.3km)
Total ascent: 1,725ft (526m)
Paths: mainly grassy and clear, but confusing in poor visibility
Terrain: mountain upland, hill pastures and rocky outcrops
Gradients: moderate
Refreshments: nothing near by; many places in Conwy.
Park: on roadside at the top of Sychnant Pass, the old hill road between Conwy and Penmaenmawr

9 Retrace your outward journey for ½ mile (800m), then continue ahead on a good track descending to turn left onto a gravel track. Follow this to a car park and turn left again onto the road back to the start.

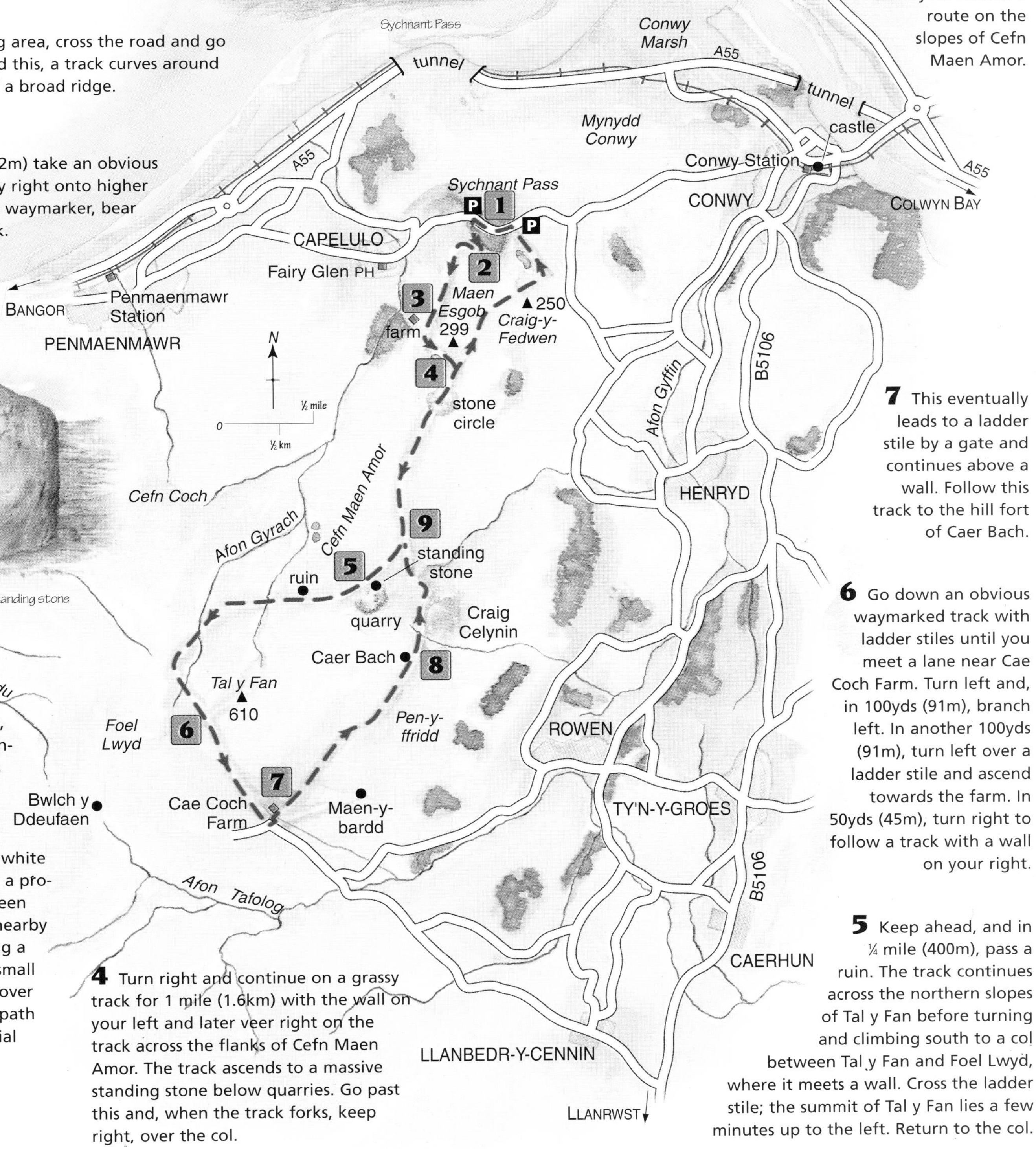

8 Pass around the hill fort and bear left to walk beside a collapsed wall, heading for Craig Celynin. A terraced track passes round the western side of Craig Celynin. From its northwestern edge, cut across hill pasture to a wall gap in a corner. Through this, turn right, beside a wall, and follow it until you meet your outward route on the slopes of Cefn Maen Amor.

1 From the parking area, cross the road and go up to a gate. Beyond this, a track curves around the northern end of a broad ridge.

2 After 200yds (182m) take an obvious track turning sharply right onto higher ground and, at next waymarker, bear left on a green track. In 300yds (273m), at power lines, branch right and head across heather moorland to a wall and ladder stile.

3 Beyond the stile, descend a little (signposted North Wales Path) across the western slopes of Maen Esgob, and turn left above the white farmhouse through a pronounced pass between low hills (ignore a nearby waymark). Following a stony track, pass a small lake, and continue over the col on a grassy path to reach a substantial wall on your left.

4 Turn right and continue on a grassy track for 1 mile (1.6km) with the wall on your left and later veer right on the track across the flanks of Cefn Maen Amor. The track ascends to a massive standing stone below quarries. Go past this and, when the track forks, keep right, over the col.

7 This eventually leads to a ladder stile by a gate and continues above a wall. Follow this track to the hill fort of Caer Bach.

6 Go down an obvious waymarked track with ladder stiles until you meet a lane near Cae Coch Farm. Turn left and, in 100yds (91m), branch left. In another 100yds (91m), turn left over a ladder stile and ascend towards the farm. In 50yds (45m), turn right to follow a track with a wall on your right.

5 Keep ahead, and in ¼ mile (400m), pass a ruin. The track continues across the northern slopes of Tal y Fan before turning and climbing south to a col between Tal y Fan and Foel Lwyd, where it meets a wall. Cross the ladder stile; the summit of Tal y Fan lies a few minutes up to the left. Return to the col.

Map labels: Conwy, Sands, Conwy Marsh, Sychnant Pass, tunnel, A55, Mynydd Conwy, tunnel, castle, Conwy Station, A55, COLWYN BAY, CONWY, Sychnant Pass, **P 1**, **P**, CAPELULO, Fairy Glen PH, **2**, **3**, farm, Maen Esgob 299, ▲250 Craig-y-Fedwen, **4**, stone circle, Penmaenmawr Station, BANGOR, PENMAENMAWR, N, ½ mile, 0, ½ km, Cefn Coch, Afon Gyrach, Cefn Maen Amor, **9**, standing stone, **5**, ruin, standing stone, quarry, Craig Celynin, Caer Bach **8**, Afon Ddu, Tal y Fan ▲ 610, Foel Lwyd, **6**, Pen-y-ffridd, Bwlch y Ddeufaen, **7**, Cae Coch Farm, Maen-y-bardd, Afon Tafolog, LLANBEDR-Y-CENNIN, LLANRWST, Afon Gyffin, B5106, HENRYD, ROWEN, TY'N-Y-GROES, B5106, CAERHUN

Eastern Moorlands *Offa's Dyke*

and the curiously pitted, rolling landscape of Ruabon
Mountain have been left oddly shaped by history

WALK
98

To experience the stark contrast between the brouhaha of urban life – not far distant from this walk across Ruabon Mountain – and the soft undulations of windswept open heather moorland that this mountain and its neighbours provides, is to go some way towards balancing the scales of life. On the one hand, clutter and noise; on the other, peace and a gently flowing uniformity that is both

Offa's Dyke Path, one of the finest long-distance walks in Britain. The construction of the dyke itself was ordered in AD 779 by Offa, King of Mercia from AD 757 to 796. Today it represents something of a puzzle. Nobody really understands why Offa might have wanted it; perhaps it was the first serious attempt to establish a fortified boundary with Wales. Most experts consider that it was originally intended merely to define the boundary, but that it may also have served as a sort of customs barrier where tolls were imposed on cross-border trade.

Within minutes of the start you are romping across invigorating, open moorlands from the cover of which red grouse chuckle at you and tell you to 'go-bak, go-bak'. Superficially uniform and with few prominent features, these yawning expanses played a vastly important role during World War II. For years during the war, local people built fires across the moors to decoy Luftwaffe pilots into believing they were gazing down on the ruins of burning Liverpool. As a result, the moors are liberally dotted with the bomb craters – proof, if proof were needed, that the ploy worked. But there are other, smaller 'bomb' sites. These are, in fact, bell pits that once formed the focus of a viable lead-mining industry in the region, and two of these are passed during this walk.

High on the moors, and close by the path, stands an unfinished viewfinder, started by a local school, while near by is a massive cross, constructed on the ground from small boulders. It marks the crash site of a Bristol Beaufighter aircraft that came down here during the war with the loss of its crew.

The attractions of moorland wandering may be less instantly obvious than those of the high mountains, but they are present nonetheless, and give every bit as much satisfaction and enjoyment.

Above: a bell pit or bomb crater on Ruabon Mountain

Top right: the red grouse is a familiar sight

Below: Cyrn-y-Brain from Ruabon Mountain

cathartic and relaxing. For regular walkers, there is a point to introducing balance into one's walking repertoire. The rugged, rocky crests of Snowdonia may excite and galvanise, but the heather-purple acres of vibrant moorland provide less demanding fare and do much to uplift the soul, in a tranquil and soothing way. Without doubt, you feel good after a day on the moors.

At the very start of the walk you cross the course of

Eastern Moorlands

*The exhilarating open moorlands of Ruabon Mountain
protect North Wales from the hubbub of English industry*

1 Leave the car park at its top corner by crossing a stile and turning left along the road. Cross the road and in a few strides turn right onto a signposted track, which curves right and rises onto heather moorland.

2 A number of tracks soon branch from the main track. Keep to the highest, and after ¼ mile (400m) go on past an isolated tree. A second isolated tree stands near a path junction, where the most prominent track turns right and descends. Ignore this, and go forward on a narrow and boggy path through heather.

3 At a waymark post, keep forward into a rising gully, beyond which you emerge onto the open top of Ruabon Mountain. Go forward, descending easily in a south-easterly direction towards a clump of trees at Mountain Lodge, about ¾ mile (1.2km) away.

Distance: 6 miles (9.7km)
Total ascent: 1,100ft (335m)
Paths: boggy but clear; potentially confusing in mist
Terrain: heather moorland and plantation
Gradients: two steady ascents
Refreshments: pubs in Minera
Park: car park on forest fringe, just north of World's End, on hill road between Minera and A542, north of Llangollen

4 The path later veers north of Mountain Lodge, and finally eases down via a kissing-gate to a road. Turn right and follow the road across a stream and, later, the inflow to a small reservoir.

8 Take an obvious path through a dip, and continue on the other side to join a good path parallel with a plantation boundary. Later, join the outward route just a few minutes from the start.

7 Beyond the plantation boundary, there is a steady haul on a narrow path across the heather moor, crossing the high point, veering right and descending to a waymark post at a path junction. Bear left and descend to another track. Turn right for 50yds (46m) passing a small pond, and then go left on a faint green path to pass around a circular bell pit after 100yds (91m).

6 Enter the plantation and follow the path with a stream on your right, to reach a clearing after ½ mile (800m). Cross the clearing to take the path on the right (now with a stream on your left). Shortly, at a fork, veer right uphill on a rocky path to the top of the plantation, ignoring the path from the left crossing the stream.

5 A few minutes further on leave the road for a bridleway on the right, going forward through a metal gate and along a delightful green track that soon rises to the left above a stream. As you near Newtown Mountain Plantation, watch for a path branching right, down to the stream, and taking you into the plantation.

Map labels

rabbit

MINERA

memorial cross

Aber Sychnant

562 ▲ Cyrn-y-Brain

MOUNTAIN

▲ 460

490 ▲

492 ▲

315 ▲

1 P

2

3

8

4

World's End • cross

pond

Craig Arthur

EGLWYSEG

RUABON MOUNTAIN

Mountain Lodge

5

6

511 ▲

502 ▲

7

Newtown Mountain Plantation

Bryn Adda Flat

364 ▲

red grouse

PENYCAE

Creigiau Eglwyseg

LLANGOLLEN

N

Trevor Rocks

½ mile

0

½ km

Shropshire Union Canal

LLANGOLLEN

GARTH

A539

TREVOR

A539

RUABON

aqueduct

A5

CHIRK

A5

River Dee

Scotland

Scotland

A tour of Scotland offers the chance to see Britain's landscape on a grand scale. All the island's highest mountains lie north of the border, along with an incredibly rugged coastline and vast tracts of wilderness.

Above: Robert Louis Stevenson's tales of adventure romped across the countryside

Previous pages: the mountainous pass of Glen Coe

Below: Loch Tummel, in central Scotland, from the Queen's View

Not only that, but there is a greater degree of freedom to roam than elsewhere in Britain, as well as a distinct culture and tradition evident wherever you travel. Scotland displays many faces, even on first acquaintance: the rolling hills of the Southern Uplands, the industrial urban belt between the Clyde and the Forth, then the Highlands in all their splendour, breaking up west and north into a succession of headlands and sea lochs, islands and stacks. There is a huge amount to see and a lifetime simply isn't long enough to explore the country properly.

In your wanderings, remember that Scotland has a history, law and culture all of its own; but also bear in mind that its affairs have been inextricably linked with Ireland and England, to say nothing of a profound Nordic influence over the centuries. Waves of invaders from Europe were always slow to penetrate into the last rugged recesses of Scotland, but once in place they would turn and defend their hills and glens with great ferocity. The Picts, we know for certain, had a well-established social structure and a capital at Kilmartin, but they were under pressure from the Roman advance northwards through Britain. What we don't know is where the Picts came from, or where they went – but then, Scotland is a land of mist and mystery.

Two men, both from Donegal in Ireland, helped to define and shape much of Scotland's early culture: St Columba, who settled on Iona and sent his followers to preach Christianity on the mainland, and Somerled, who was the progenitor of the great clan MacDonald. Many other people made their mark, including St Ninian, for

Left: Caerlaverock Castle, Dumfries and Galloway

Below: the view over Edinburgh
from Arthur's Seat

example, who brought Christianity into Scotland by way of Whithorn – and successive English kings who raged almost continual warfare against the Scots. Wherever you look, you can find evidence of strife: Largs, Bannockburn, Stirling and Culloden all saw great and decisive battles, while the 'Debatable Land' was for centuries a no-man's land between Scotland and England. In fact, Scotland's relationship with England was always dominated by the need to establish some kind of border. While countless lives were lost in that struggle, an amazing Gaelic civilisation remained largely intact and isolated from the rest of the world in the rugged Highlands and Islands. Then there are shameful episodes: the Massacre of Glen Coe, paifully seared into the folk memory of Scotland, and the brutal Clearances of the 19th century, in which thousands were evicted from the land and forced into migration to the industrial south or further afield to North America.

One thing you see aplenty while travelling around this land is monuments. There are monuments to the great battles and to all kinds of people, from nobles killed in battle to the postman who died of exposure while carrying the mail over the hills. The weather, it has to be said, can be extreme on the high ground, so approach with due caution. You can walk up towards the jagged Cuillins from Sligachan on the Isle of Skye without too much difficulty, but to grapple with the high ridges requires rock-climbing skills. You can wander in the wilds of Moidart or onto the bleak bogs of the Flow Country, but you need to know when it's time to turn back. If the really high mountains look daunting, there are plenty of smaller hills you can scramble up. You can climb Criffel, one of the first Scottish hills seen on the approach from England, or Hart Fell, one of a range of more challenging summits separating the border region from the central belt of Scottish population in Glasgow and Edinburgh.

There are many old tracks you can follow in other places. The first rough highways were trodden by drovers through the glens and high passes. The first concerted attempt to establish a real road network came under the auspices of General Wade after the 1745 Jacobite Rebellion. Amazingly, for a country that was just ending

centuries of strife and war, tourism was very quick to catch on, no doubt spurred by the enthusiastic writings of native Scotsmen and visitors alike. You could walk around Alloway with Robert Burns as your companion, investigate tales of the notorious Rob Roy MacGregor around Balquhidder, or stroll through the city of Edinburgh in search of several notable worthies in one short walk. Others may look above the chimney tops of 'Auld Reekie' at the Pentland Hills and wonder what the walking is like in that direction. It's interesting – and if you're searching for the Holy Grail, you might just find a mention of it at Rosslyn Chapel.

It may sound strange, in a country with so much wilderness and so many natural wonders, to actually go in search of these themes. There are parts of Scotland where unusual species cling to a precarious existence in safe havens. The ancient Caledonian pine forest at Roth-iemurchus is a mere remnant of a much more widespread wildwood. Then of course, in a country with so many mountain and hill ranges, coastal wetlands are at a premium, which is why bird reserves such as the one at Caerlaverock are so important for overwintering geese and other species. Ptarmigan seem to thrive even on the most barren rocky peaks. It's worth asking the question 'What is wilderness anyway?' because even in the apparent wilds of Scotland most of the landscape is man-managed. Sheep are grazed in many places, continually nipping back any tree seedlings that take root, leaving the hills looking quite bare. Deer roam huge upland estates and are subject to annual shoots and culls. Even extensive heather moorlands may be strictly managed for grouse shooting, with 'vermin' being controlled and strip-burning taking place in rotation to create an environment to favour the needs of the birds.

Scotland is a land of conflicts and contrasts, of lovely scenery and loveless battlefields. Romantic-looking castles sit uneasily with their history of appalling bloodshed. Craggy peaks can look welcoming one moment, then threatening the next, as the weather clouds over. This endless variation is an essential part of Scotland's fascination and explains why few people ever tire of exploring it.

Below left: the Jacobite Monument at Glenfinnan, on the West Highland coast

Best of the Rest

Trotternish There is something surreal about the pillars and spikes of Quiraing, the intriguing end to the Trotternish uplands of northern Skye. Walkers who approach from the road crossing the centre of the island are rewarded by an unfolding view of towers and pinnacles, which swirl in and out of the mist like the landscape in a Chinese painting. Although the pillars present problems to even the most experienced scrambler, there are good paths around the strange arenas created by this unique rock formation, making them accessible to most fit walkers.

Trossachs The Victorians were first drawn by the scenic splendours of the Trossachs, another point of entry from the lowland world to the upland wilds of the Highlands, and the area became a fashionable stopping place for tourists. As the road from Callander winds its way through forests and past lakes, the placenames turn from Anglicised lowland Scots to bewildering Highland Gaelic. The difference should not be lost on walkers who will find much to delight and challenge them in this introduction to the Highland landscape.

Glen Clova Glen Clova strikes out into the rising eastern Highlands, offering many Lowlanders the first glimpses of the great mountain ranges beyond the Highland line. Jock's Road is an ancient highway linking Kirriemuir with the splendour of Royal Deeside and can be used to access the Caenlochan National Nature Reserve, high in the Grampians above the head of the glen.

Hoy The Old Man of Hoy is a landmark to any visitor arriving in the Orkney Islands by sea. The hinterland to this famous sea cliff pillar is a rich landscape of moorland and pasture, little changed since Viking settlers named its natural features. A ferry links the island with the main Orkney port at Stromness, and walks radiate from Hoy village and nearby Rackwick to the surrounding coast.

Sandwood Bay Few places epitomise the essence of remote northwest Scotland than this spectacular sweep of sand on Sutherland's wild Atlantic coast. Accessible only on foot from a road end three miles (4.8km) away, walkers who make it this far (the drive out to the roadend is as challenging as the walking) are rewarded by solitude and a perfect beach. Backpackers might be tempted to continue up the wild coastline to Cape Wrath, but most will be happy to walk back the way they came, having caught a glimpse of a world little changed since the first prehistoric settlers.

Merrick The feral goats which loiter on the wild hillsides of the Southern Uplands are often the only company walkers have as they make their way up southern Scotland's highest peak, the Merrick. From the campsites and facilities in Glen Trool there is a good track, though very steep in places, to the upper parts of this lonely mountain, and the views in clear weather are unsurpassed.

Arran Often fêted as Scotland in miniature, there is a wealth of good walking at all levels on this Clyde island. For an introduction to Scottish mountain walking, the ascent of Goat Fell, the island's highest peak, from Brodick Castle by Glen Rosa and the Saddle, is hard to beat.

Edinburgh's Literary Past

A walk through the medieval closes and elegant Georgian terraces of Scotland's capital reveals a world-class literary heritage

WALK
99

Top right: author of *Kidnapped* and other great tales, Robert Louis Stevenson

Below: looking up to Edinburgh Castle from Calton Hill

Edinburgh has been both home and inspiration to writers and poets for hundreds of years. Even the station is named after the 'Waverley' novels of Sir Walter Scott, who is himself commemorated in the grand Gothic spire of the Scott Monument, at 200 feet (61m) the largest monument to an author in the world.

From bustling Princes Street you come to the quieter streets of the New Town, the Georgian area laid out in the 18th century for wealthy residents who wished to escape the squalor of the Old Town, the area by the Castle. Its associations with the literary glitterati are numerous. Castle Street, for instance, claims two honours: No 30, the birthplace of Kenneth Grahame, author of *The Wind in the Willows*, and No 39, the home of Sir Walter Scott. Then you walk along quiet, airy terraces to 17 Heriot Row, the elegant childhood home of Robert Louis Stevenson.

Emerging into the hustle and bustle of Picardy Place, you see a statue of Sherlock Holmes peering suspiciously at the traffic. It commemorates his creator, Sir Arthur Conan Doyle, who was born close by. The climb up Calton Hill is rewarded by a superb view, particularly of Arthur's Seat, one of Robert Louis Stevenson's favourite spots.

Now you descend to the medieval closes and tottering tenements of the Old Town. Here is Canongate Kirk, where Robert Burns' love, 'Clarinda', is buried, and a spot outside St Giles Cathedral marking the site of the prison which gave its name to Scott's novel, *The Heart of Midlothian*.

At the corner of Candlemaker Row you pass the statue to Greyfriars Bobby, the Skye terrier who kept a 14-year vigil at his master's graveside, inspiring many books and a Disney film. Then down a dark street to the Grassmarket, where Burke and Hare, the body-snatchers, lured their victims. Making your way back down the Royal Mile from the Castle you can almost hear the whispers of the literary figures who haunt these dark closes. There is James' Court, where Dr Johnson stayed with James Boswell on their return from their tour of Scotland. The great lexicographer was 'assaulted by the evening effluvia of Edinburgh' – a comment on the filth and stench that were once the signature of the Old Town. Next you pass Lady Stair's Close, where Robert Burns stayed when he was launched into high society, and Brodie's Close, named after Deacon Brodie who inspired Stevenson's *The Strange Case of Dr Jekyll and Mr Hyde*. Respectable by day, he became a robber at night.

As you leave the Royal Mile behind, you become aware that, like Jekyll and Hyde, Edinburgh has two faces. No wonder that this city, with its elegant New Town and murky Old Town, has inspired so many writers over the centuries.

Edinburgh's Literary Past

*A walk around the elegant streets of the Scottish capital,
with a proud tradition of literature*

Start: Edinburgh Waverley railway station
Distance: 5 miles (8km)
Paths: pavements throughout
Terrain: city streets
Gradients: a few short, steep sections
Refreshments: plenty in city centre
Park: Waverley Station

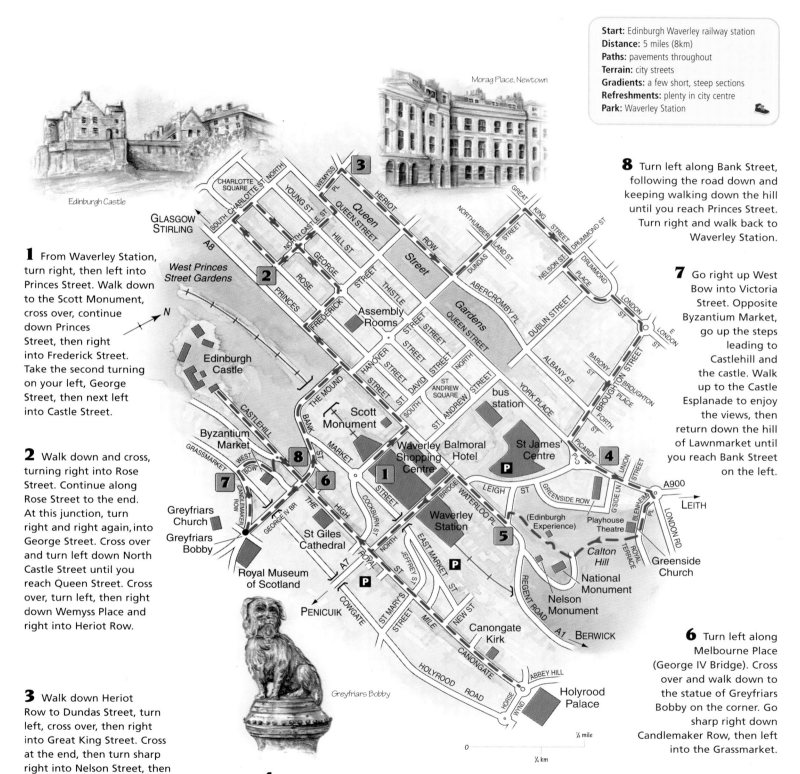

Morag Place, Newtown

Edinburgh Castle

Greyfriars Bobby

1 From Waverley Station, turn right, then left into Princes Street. Walk down to the Scott Monument, cross over, continue down Princes Street, then right into Frederick Street. Take the second turning on your left, George Street, then next left into Castle Street.

2 Walk down and cross, turning right into Rose Street. Continue along Rose Street to the end. At this junction, turn right and right again, into George Street. Cross over and turn left down North Castle Street until you reach Queen Street. Cross over, turn left, then right down Wemyss Place and right into Heriot Row.

3 Walk down Heriot Row to Dundas Street, turn left, cross over, then right into Great King Street. Cross at the end, then turn sharp right into Nelson Street, then left into Drummond Place. Follow Drummond Place into London Street, then turn right, up Broughton Street. Keep going to the main road junction at the top of the hill, then turn left into Picardy Place.

4 Cross the road opposite the Playhouse, turn left, then right at the roundabout with the clock and immediately right up Blenheim Place. Take the path on the right by Greenside Church, climbing up to Calton Hill. Taking the the left hand path, walk across towards the Edinburgh Experience and descend by the path leading to Waterloo Place.

5 Turn right, cross over then turn left at the Balmoral Hotel and up North Bridge. Turn left down the High Street (Royal Mile) and walk down to Holyrood Palace. Walk back up the other side of the road.

6 Turn left along Melbourne Place (George IV Bridge). Cross over and walk down to the statue of Greyfriars Bobby on the corner. Go sharp right down Candlemaker Row, then left into the Grassmarket.

7 Go right up West Bow into Victoria Street. Opposite Byzantium Market, go up the steps leading to Castlehill and the castle. Walk up to the Castle Esplanade to enjoy the views, then return down the hill of Lawnmarket until you reach Bank Street on the left.

8 Turn left along Bank Street, following the road down and keeping walking down the hill until you reach Princes Street. Turn right and walk back to Waverley Station.

The Mysteries of Rosslyn

As development sprawls south from Edinburgh, this legendary glen is an unexpected oasis

Top right: the towering walls of Rosslyn Castle

Below: intricate carving on the beautiful Apprentice Pillar

Below: the significance of Rosslyn Chapel far outweighs its diminutive size

Half ruined, Rosslyn Castle stands on the edge of Rosslyn Glen as if still protecting Scotland from invasion, as it did in centuries past. Near the other end of the glen is the cairn marking the site of the Battle of Roslin where in 1303, during the Scottish Wars of Independence, a small force of Scottish soldiers repelled a much larger invading army in three separate conflicts within 24 hours. But Rosslyn Chapel, built at the order of Sir William St Clair in 1450, is the gem in this walk.

This exquisitely carved masterpiece of the mason's art is a medieval cathedral in miniature. Nowhere in Europe will you find stone carvings so full of mystic significance, so intricate and so delicate as at Rosslyn Chapel. You can see green men, a complete Danse Macabre, Masonic symbols and, if you know where to look, a carving of Robert the Bruce, copied from his death mask. The St Clairs were closely associated with the Knights Templar, a mysterious order of wealthy warrior monks. They were reputed to have found the Holy Grail and the treasures of Solomon's Temple, including ancient scrolls with rituals dating back to ancient Egypt which they adopted.

Within the chapel are two great pillars, one plain and the other ornate and elaborately carved. When the first, plainer pillar was complete, Sir William instructed the master mason on the design of the second, which was extremely complex, and required extraordinary skill. Daunted, the master mason went to Rome for further study before embarking on the task. In his absence a young apprentice, who claimed to have seen the pillar in a dream, was instructed to make it. The Apprentice Pillar is an ethereal, interwoven composition of spirals more reminiscent of icing than solid stone. When the master mason returned and saw the pillar, he was so enraged that he killed the boy with a blow from his mallet. He was subsequently hanged for the crime. His head and those of the apprentice and his widowed mother are graven in stone near the ceiling of the chapel.

With all these medieval faces looking down on you, it is an atmospheric place. At the side of the chapel, steep, time-worn steps lead down to the crypt. This is empty save for a few relics and a Templar stone, yet as you cross the threshold you may feel a cold shiver. A former curator reports having seen the ghostly figure of a monk praying at the altar, while four spectral knights, clad in monks' habits stood guard around him. Twenty of them, in full battle armour, lie beneath the chapel in a huge vault. They are the Guardians of the Templars' treasures and of the Holy Grail which, according to legend, is concealed within that beautiful, fateful Apprentice Pillar.

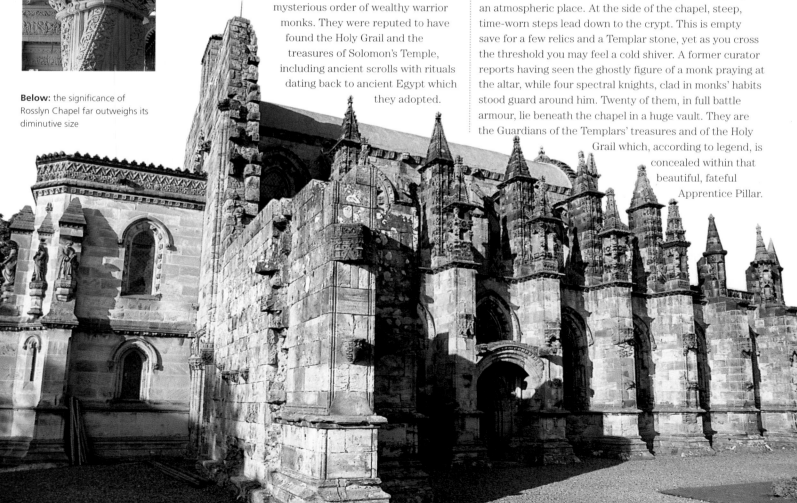

The Mysteries of Rosslyn

*On the trail of the Holy Grail in a wooded glen near
Edinburgh's suburbs*

1 From the car park, take the path leading towards the river and cross the metal foot-bridge. Follow the path uphill and pass under the arch of the castle bridge. At the T-junction, turn left along Gardener's Brae.

2 Follow the path along the side of the river. This will take you uphill to a wall on the left. Keep the wall on your left as you follow the path back down towards the river, then continue over three stiles.

3 When the river splits in two and loops back on itself, follow the path across another stile and continue, going up the banking to the top of a narrow ridge.

5 From the cairn, continue along the road into Roslin itself. At the end of the road, follow the signs to the left, to Rosslyn Chapel. From the chapel, retrace your steps, then turn left towards the cemeteries and left again between the cemeteries, towards the castle. Return from the castle to the steps on the left, which will return you to the car park.

4 Follow the path to a stile beside a large gate. Turn left along the road, eventually passing through the remains of an old railway bridge. Continue, past the animal research centre, until you reach a cairn on the right.

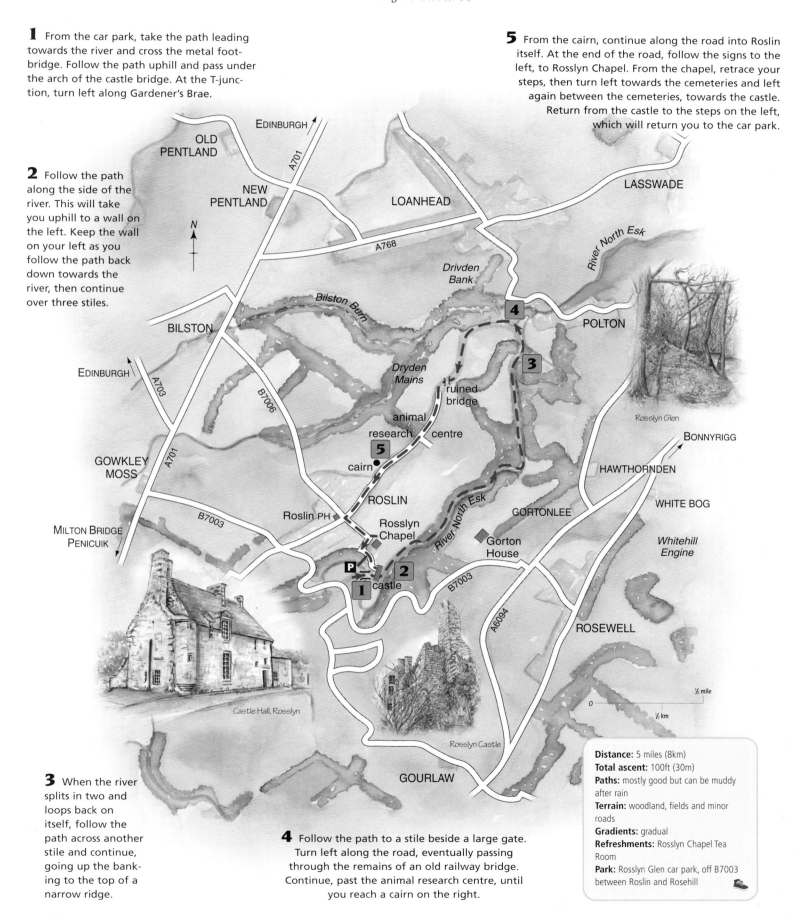

Rosslyn Glen

Castle Hall, Rosslyn

Rosslyn Castle

Distance: 5 miles (8km)
Total ascent: 100ft (30m)
Paths: mostly good but can be muddy after rain
Terrain: woodland, fields and minor roads
Gradients: gradual
Refreshments: Rosslyn Chapel Tea Room
Park: Rosslyn Glen car park, off B7003 between Roslin and Rosehill

Through the Wild Pentlands

The steep moors and rolling tops of the Pentland Hills offer a quick escape from the city of Edinburgh

**WALK
101**

Top right: a snipe hides out in the rough grazing

The Edinburgh suburb of Balerno, with its trim estates of modern houses, might seem an unlikely gateway to wild country. The Pentland Hills are not, however, just a cosy green belt for the capital of Scotland, but a range of steep, uncompromising peaks rising 1500 feet (457m) above sea level, where even in the valleys the walker can experience a sense of utter isolation.

Above: the avenue at Bavelaw

The first part of this walk skirts the nature reserves of Red Moss and Bavelaw Marsh. Set out early in the morning as the mist is rising from the water and a cacophony of wildfowl fills the air, and you might well believe that you are passing a primeval swamp rather than a reservoir. The drive, along an avenue of stately beeches, leads to Bavelaw Castle, a 16th-century laird's house (not open to the public) with walled grounds that back directly on to open moorland. This land has never been improved or cultivated. It remains just as it was when the castle was first built – rough grazing for livestock and a source of wild game.

The path climbs steadily into the hills, winding through a narrow pass beneath slopes of scree and heather. The hardy black-faced sheep that overwinter on these barren hillsides are still shepherded in 'hefts' – flocks with an inbred loyalty to their ancestral territories that ensures they do not stray or intermingle. As you pause below a little waterfall that tumbles from a rocky gorge, you feel you are in some Highland glen rather than within a few miles of the crowds on Princes Street.

The heart of the Pentlands is a long, deep valley hidden by high ridges from the outside world. Two large reservoirs, dating from the 1850s, still provide Edinburgh with water, although they now appear as natural as mountain lochs. If water levels are exceptionally low you may see the ruins of St Catherine's Chapel, dating from the reign of Robert the Bruce (1274-1329), which lies beneath the surface of Glencorse. You may also hear the sound of gunfire, either from the army range on Castlelaw or from grouse butts on the heather moors.

The path back over to Balerno from Glencorse is along a very ancient way known as Maiden's Cleuch. There's an intriguing old stone stile near the summit of the pass, from where there are tremendous views across the Moorfoot Hills towards the English border. Then, as you breast the pass, a still more splendid panorama opens up before you along the Firth of Forth and deep into the Trossachs to the summit of Ben Ledi 50 miles (80km) away.

Walking back towards the car park along the banks of Threipmuir Reservoir, you can appreciate the Pentlands' stubborn character. Above a lonely farm on the far shore of the lake, old cultivation furrows can be seen etched into the moorland of Black Hill. Man has made his mark here, scratching at the barren soil for a living before abandoning the fields to heather. Although within sight of a busy city, these hills cannot be tamed.

Below: snow picks out the rolling shapes of the Pentland Hills

Through the Wild Pentland Hills

A pleasingly gentle tour through the heart of this surprisingly severe little range of hills

1 From the car park, pass an information board on your left, turn left up the track, then immediately right along a footpath (Nine Mile Burn and Glencorse). After ¼ mile (400m), cross a stile and turn left into Bavelaw. Cross over a bridge and pass through the white gate to go uphill through an avenue of trees. Turn left at the junction, then follow drive to right. As the drive turns into private grounds of Bavelaw Castle, go straight ahead to a gate out onto moorland.

7 Beyond the cottage, follow the path to the right at the head of Harlaw Reservoir and, after crossing a dam, follow the track around to the left and along the shore. After ½ mile (800m), turn right along the side of a concrete spillway and follow the path as it swings left by Threipmuir Reservoir. Veering from the bank, the path turns right just before a hut. Pass through a gate and continue along a cinder track, which, after passing through another gate, continues to the car park.

6 Cross the stile and continue downhill across moorland. Further down the slopes, ignore a path to Currie and go straight ahead, crossing a stile and then along field paths to a T-junction. Turn right towards a belt of trees, then turn left, just before a gate, to a road. Follow the track to Warlaw House Rangers Centre (displays on local wildlife), passing through a gate to the cottage and ignoring sign to Balerno.

5 Turn left through a gate, following a footpath signed to Balerno by Harlaw. After 300yds (275m) continue ahead, ignoring path to right. Continue up the valley, known as Maiden's Cleuch, to a stone stile near the summit of the pass.

4 Crossing a wooden bridge in front of the house, turn right down the lane, following the shore of Loganlea Reservoir and then Logan Burn down to Glencorse Reservoir. Continue along the lakeside for ½ mile (800m) until the shore is lined by pine trees.

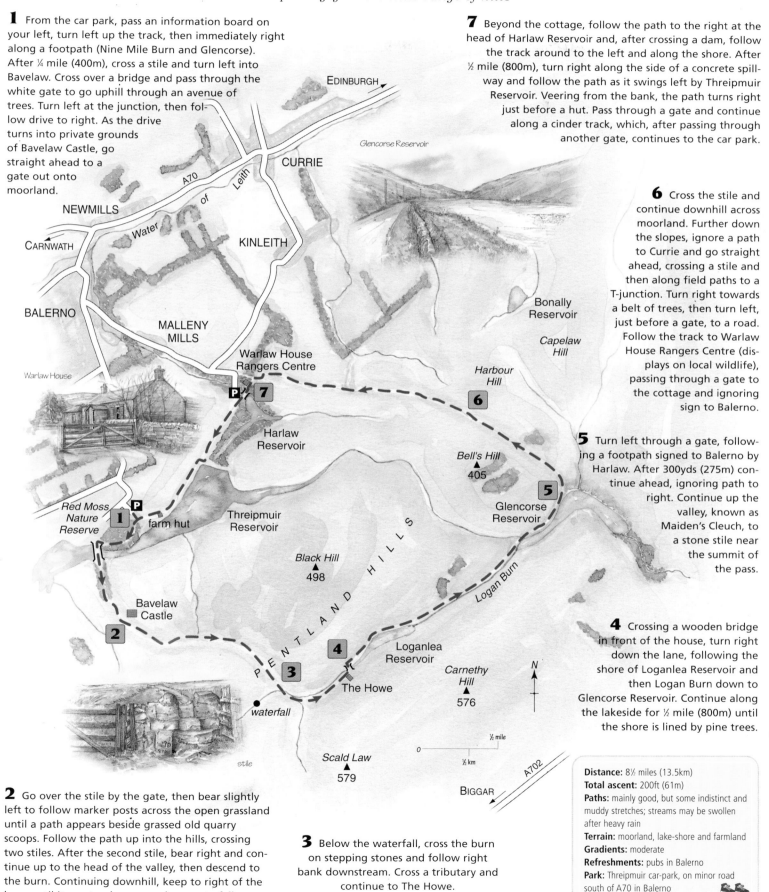

2 Go over the stile by the gate, then bear slightly left to follow marker posts across the open grassland until a path appears beside grassed old quarry scoops. Follow the path up into the hills, crossing two stiles. After the second stile, bear right and continue up to the head of the valley, then descend to the burn. Continuing downhill, keep to right of the burn until it meets a larger one by a waterfall.

3 Below the waterfall, cross the burn on stepping stones and follow right bank downstream. Cross a tributary and continue to The Howe.

Distance: 8½ miles (13.5km)
Total ascent: 200ft (61m)
Paths: mainly good, but some indistinct and muddy stretches; streams may be swollen after heavy rain
Terrain: moorland, lake-shore and farmland
Gradients: moderate
Refreshments: pubs in Balerno
Park: Threipmuir car-park, on minor road south of A70 in Balerno

Magic Waters from Hart Fell

Drink from a healing spring rising in the hill where Merlin lived – according to Nicolai Tolstoy

Today, as you walk up the Auchencat burn, it is difficult to imagine living in such a desolate spot. But when the great Caledonian Forest covered most of the countryside, the dense trees would have provided shelter, building materials, clothing, and even nuts, berries and roots for food. Now the only shelter is an overhang of rock as the ravine narrows just before the spa.

Here it seems the past is separated from the present by a very thin veil, and you can imagine a ragged hermit crouching in the small narrow cave under the rocks, casting his baleful eye upon you. Merlin, like his monarch, King Arthur, is one of those shadowy characters of prehistory and legend of whom tales are told in many places. He was the archetype of the shaman or wise man – perhaps the Druid priest at nearby Lochmaben, where the god Mapponus was worshipped at a site still marked by the mighty Clochmab-bonstane.

The hill running up from the spa is called Arthur's Seat, possibly because of the Merlin connection or possibly because hills with springs were regarded as part of the underworld and, according to legend, Arthur and his knights were sleeping in a hollow hill, awaiting the time to re-emerge. Whatever the reason, it is worth the steep climb to the summit of this hill and

Above: Hart Fell's rounded slopes are cleaved by steep ravines

Top right: the magician Merlin is associated with several springs

Below: the rolling flanks of Hart Fell, from the southwest

then on to Hart Fell for the majestic views over the Devil's Beeftub and the Lowther Hills.

Hart Fell was identified as Merlin's home by Russian author and historian, Nicolai Tolstoy, in his book *The Quest for Merlin*. Researching ancient Welsh annals and epic poems of Arthurian legend, he concluded that Merlin fled into the Forest of Caledon after the Battle of Arderydd in Cumbria. Driven insane by the carnage, particularly the killing of his niece and nephew, he took refuge at Hart Fell, where, according to Tolstoy, 'There was a spring on the very top of a certain mountain surrounded on all sides by hazel and dense thorns.'

In ancient times, water which flowed from a hillside like this was considered to be sacred and to have magical healing properties. This drew holy men or healers to live near by. In Victorian times people also believed the water to have natural curative properties, and the spring became an important part of the local economy. Moffat was a famous spa and people came in droves to take the waters, rich in iron and calcium. Sad to say, the Victorian visitors' health probably benefited more from the walk to the spa than from the water, which tastes rather metallic.

To sample the water, crouch down and creep through the small doorway in the dome which houses the spa. Look on your left for the small stone bowl where the natural spring water bubbles up from the ground. The domed stone construction dates from the midddle of the 18th century.

Magic Waters from Hart Fell

*In the Southern Uplands with the magic of Merlin and
the healing waters of the Hartfell Spa*

WALK 102

1 From Annan Water Hall, follow the signpost to Hartfell Spa. Follow the path along the Auchencat Burn, then through a gate in a dry stone wall. The track heads up away from the burn. Beyond the next wall, the first waymarker can be seen.

2 The path continues along the edge of the hill. Go through the gate in the wall and keep the fence on your right. Cross the stile at the next waymarker.

3 Descend to the burn and cross two bridges made from telegraph poles. Ignore the third bridge. A small sign points the way to the spa. The glen starts to widen at the next waymarker.

4 Head towards the narrow ravine for ½ mile (800m), past some sheep pens on the right and across another path. As you ascend, the ravine narrows just before a rocky outcrop on the left. The spa is on the right. Retrace your steps to the sheep pens.

5 Turn left up the main valley to a wire fence after ½ mile (800m). Head left along it and ascend to an opening. Turn right then ascend northeastwards across featureless terrain for ¾ mile (1.2km) to a small cairn on Arthur's Seat. Beyond it, continue north-easterly to pick up a track to Hart Fell summit.

Distance: 7 miles (11.2km)
Total ascent: 2,400ft (732m)
Paths: generally good but indistinct in places
Terrain: fields, riverbank and grassy mountain
Gradients: slight to moderate; one very steep section
Refreshments: Star Hotel, Moffat
Park: Annan Water Hall, near head of minor road north of A701 in Moffat

9 Keep ahead, passing farm sheds on your left. Cross two cattle grids to reach the lane. Turn left along the lane to return to Annan Water Hall.

8 Bear right on a track for 100yds (91m), then bear left to a gate. Beyond, cross a plank bridge and continue across a field to the left hand corner of a wooded ravine. Keep ahead, with the wood on your right to reach a gate to the right of a grey-roofed shed. Continue down the track to the next gate by a bridge.

7 Towards the end of the ridge, bear right to a sheep pen then descend on a faint track ahead, in the direction of Annan Water Hall, to a gate.

6 Return by way of Arthur's Seat to the gap in the wire fence. Take the path directly ahead and in 100yds (91m), take the right fork.

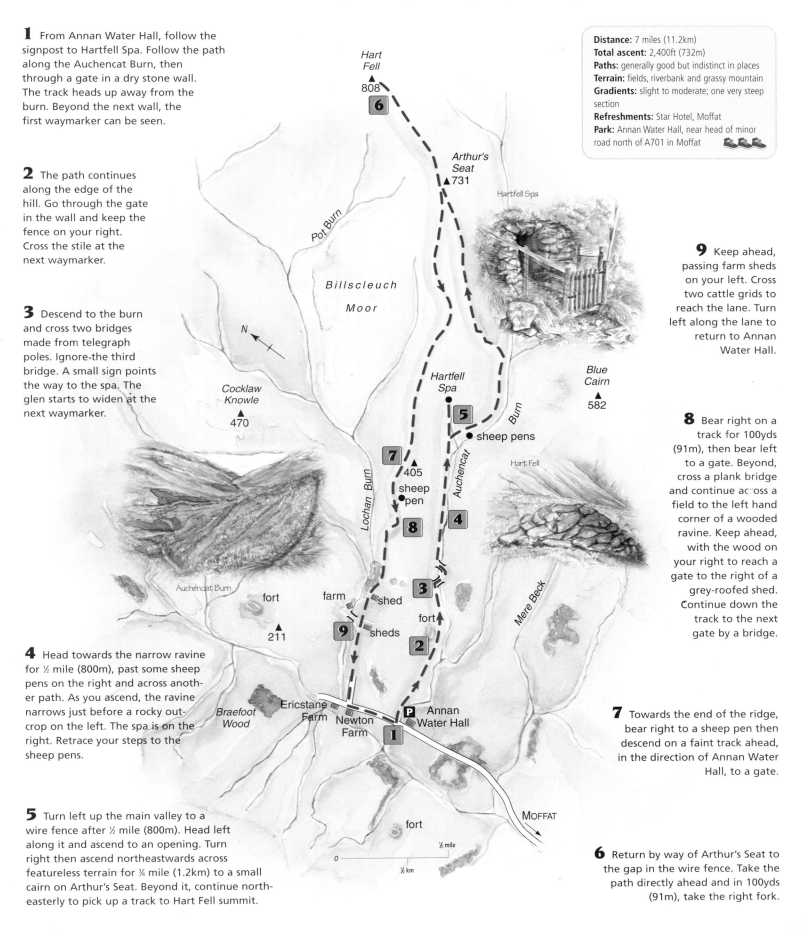

Caerlaverock and the Rich Solway Marshes

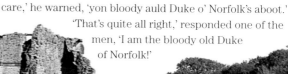

Explore the marshes of the Solway Firth

in the company – for half the year at least – of 20,000 Norwegian visitors

WALK
103

Top right: thousands of barnacle geese congregate on the marshes of the Solway Firth

The lush green wetlands of the Solway Firth (don't forget your wellingtons) are lovely at any time of year, and notably rich in bird life. But to see the wildfowl at their most spectacular you need to come to Caerlaverock between October and March, when the barnacle geese are here. The journey that these 20,000 hardy little dark-backed and pale-breasted birds make from their native Norwegian island of Spitsbergen is an astonishing one.

Escaping the rigours of the far northern winter, they leave the Arctic Circle and fly south almost 2,000 miles (3,000km), arriving with pinpoint accuracy on the Solway as they have done for thousands of years. When the nesting and mating urge comes over them at the advent of the following spring, they make their way back to Spitsbergen to breed.

Photographs of their Arctic breeding ground – the bare islets just offshore where they hatch, the flat grassy sward of the Spitsbergen coast where they feed under an immense

curtain of wrinkled cliffs – are on display at the Wildfowl and Wetlands Trust's centre at East Park, where the walk starts. East Park forms part of a national nature reserve established about 40 years ago on 20,000 acres (8,100 hectares) of mudflats, foreshore and merse (salt marsh) on the Duke of Norfolk's estates at Caerlaverock. The reserve was created just in time for the barnacle geese, whose numbers – thanks to indiscriminate shooting – had fallen to less than 500 just after World War II.

Out in the marshy grounds of East Park, a couple of drove roads lined with sheltering hedges and craftily concealed bird hides lead to the tall observation towers from which – through binoculars – you can watch the barnacle geese as they feed, quarrel, flirt, land and take off in big, loudly gabbling packs. Flighting time at dawn and dusk is best, when all 20,000 move at the same time between their night-time roosting place out on the mud and marshlands, and their daytime feeding grounds inland – one of nature's really awe-inspiring spectacles.

East of the WWT centre stands Caerlaverock Castle, a three-sided romantic ruin of jagged red sandstone walls and drum towers rising from a moat. It was built in about 1270, and enjoyed its full share of sieges, burnings, hangings and slaughter. In 1300, the English king Edward I brought 87 knights and 3,000 men to attack the castle. Giant siege engines lobbed great stone balls over the walls (several are on display) until the 60-man garrison surrendered. Many paid for their defiance with their lives, hanged from the castle walls – a terrible public death.

Down on the merse shore, don't be surprised if you hear the pop of a shotgun. The barnacle geese are protected, but about 200 birds of other species are shot each year. One story tells of the local man who met a party armed with shotguns and took them for poachers. 'Tak' care,' he warned, 'yon bloody auld Duke o' Norfolk's aboot.' 'That's quite all right,' responded one of the men, 'I am the bloody old Duke of Norfolk!'

Above: a hide at East Park

Below: the moated ruin of Caerlaverock Castle

Caerlaverock and the Rich Solway Marshes

*In the shadow of this unusual castle a nature reserve
protects a rich marshland habitat*

1 From the car park, turn back along the approach road for ½ mile (800m) then turn left, passing Scottish National Heritage's information point on your left.

2 In 300yds (275m), bear left by a house, along a hedged track to the edge of the Merse (saltmarsh). Turn right before the next fence and keep left for 150yds (136m) then turn right along a low bank for 1 mile (1.6km). Near the end, veer left to cross two wooden bridges and then a stile.

Distance: 6 miles (9.5km)
Total ascent: 310ft (95m)
Path: country roads, lanes and foreshore tracks; very muddy after rain
Terrain: flat estuary foreshore, saltmarsh, grassland
Gradients: one fairly gentle hill
Refreshments: tearoom at Caerlaverock Castle
Park: car park at the Wildfowl and Wetlands Trust's East Park Centre at Caerlaverock, signposted off the B725 nine miles (14.5km) south of Dumfries.
Note: entrance fees are charged for entry to the Wildfowl and Wetland Trust facilities and Caerlaverock Castle

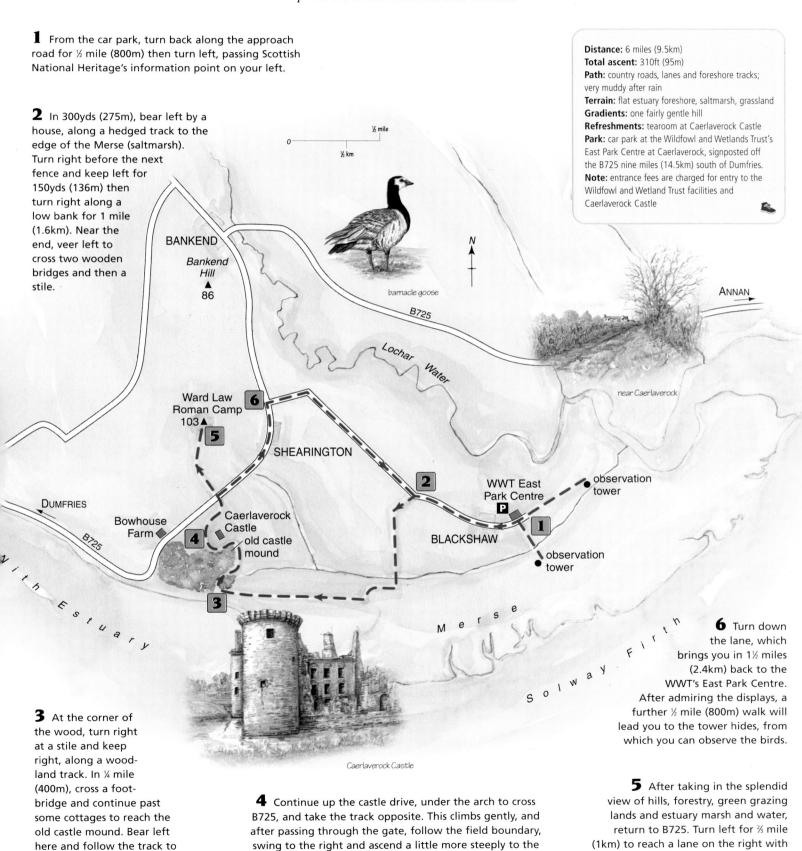

Caerlaverock Castle

3 At the corner of the wood, turn right at a stile and keep right, along a woodland track. In ¼ mile (400m), cross a footbridge and continue past some cottages to reach the old castle mound. Bear left here and follow the track to pass Caerlaverock Castle.

4 Continue up the castle drive, under the arch to cross B725, and take the track opposite. This climbs gently, and after passing through the gate, follow the field boundary, swing to the right and ascend a little more steeply to the ramparts of the roman camp on Ward Law Hill.

5 After taking in the splendid view of hills, forestry, green grazing lands and estuary marsh and water, return to B725. Turn left for ⅔ mile (1km) to reach a lane on the right with a Wildfowl and Wetlands Trust sign.

6 Turn down the lane, which brings you in 1½ miles (2.4km) back to the WWT's East Park Centre. After admiring the displays, a further ½ mile (800m) walk will lead you to the tower hides, from which you can observe the birds.

Four Kingdoms from Criffel

Climb to the top for a view that takes in England, Northern Ireland and the Isle of Man

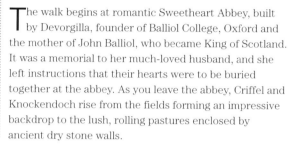

WALK 104

Top right: the distinctive pink sandstone ruins of Sweetheart Abbey

The walk begins at romantic Sweetheart Abbey, built by Devorgilla, founder of Balliol College, Oxford and the mother of John Balliol, who became King of Scotland. It was a memorial to her much-loved husband, and she left instructions that their hearts were to be buried together at the abbey. As you leave the abbey, Criffel and Knockendoch rise from the fields forming an impressive backdrop to the lush, rolling pastures enclosed by ancient dry stone walls.

In the same direction are the massive cooling towers of Chapelcross power station, a jarring dissonance in the rural landscape and visible from miles around. Near by is Gretna Green, famed for centuries as the destination of couples taking advantage of the different marriage laws in Scotland, to be wed, over the anvil, by the village blacksmith. Closer to Criffel is the estuary of the River Nith where the wide, sandy flats of Caerlaverock nature reserve provide a winter home to the Spitsbergen barnacle geese.

Above: the dark moors of Criffel and Knockendoch sweep down to New Abbey in lush Nithsdale

From the summit of Criffel you can look into four kingdoms. The peaks of the Lake District, beyond the Solway, 'mark whaur England's province stands'; to the west lies the Isle of Man; turning further west and north the coast of Antrim is visible, while all around is a part of Scotland steeped in history and legend.

At the mouth of the wide estuary of the Solway is the Mull of Galloway, the southernmost tip of Scotland. Next to that is the Isle of Whithorn, St Ninian's first foothold on Scottish soil, as a Christian missionary over 900 years ago. Kings, courtiers and pious followers made pilgrimage to Whithorn throughout the Middle Ages, ceasing only with the Reformation. Many paths lead through the Galloway hills, marked by pilgrim crosses and even more ancient Celtic stones and runes. Robert the Bruce roamed this land with his followers during the Scottish Wars of Independence, emerging to strike and swiftly disappearing into caves and forests. The cave where Bruce allegedly took instruction from a spider lies east, at Kirkpatrick Fleming.

Along the River Nith lies Dumfries, where Robert Burns worked as an exciseman for the last few years of his life. He rode over 100 miles a week, checking on inns and taverns and hunting the coastline for smugglers. It was down the sands of the River Nith that J M Barrie's 'Lost Boys' first charged imaginary pirate ships, as the young Barrie played at pirates with his schoolfriends, while Captain Hook (his mathematics teacher) corrected their exercises, all unaware of his future role in fiction.

When you descend from the summit of Criffel you will want to spend time exploring in more detail the lovely places you have glimpsed in one of Scotland's best kept secrets: the endless coastline of rocky coves and sandy beaches warmed by the Gulf Stream, the rugged hinterland of the Galloway hills – as challenging as the Lake District but without the crowds – and the tiny hamlets of low stone cottages, nestling in the glens and around picturesque harbours.

Four Kingdoms from Criffel

England, Ireland, Scotland and the Isle of Man are all visible from this looming moorland eminence above the Solway Firth

Distance: 9 miles (14.5km)
Total ascent: 1,867ft (569m)
Paths: mostly good; very boggy in winter and in wet weather
Terrain: road, fields, woodland, heather moorland and farm tracks
Gradients: very steep up Criffel
Refreshments: Abbey Tea Room at car park.
Park: Sweetheart Abbey car park off A710 in New Abbey

8 Go through several gates, cross a burn, then bear right until eventually the track joins the drive to Barbeth Farm. This leads into the village. Follow the road ahead to the main road, emerging at the petrol station. Turn left and follow the road round to the car park at Sweetheart Abbey.

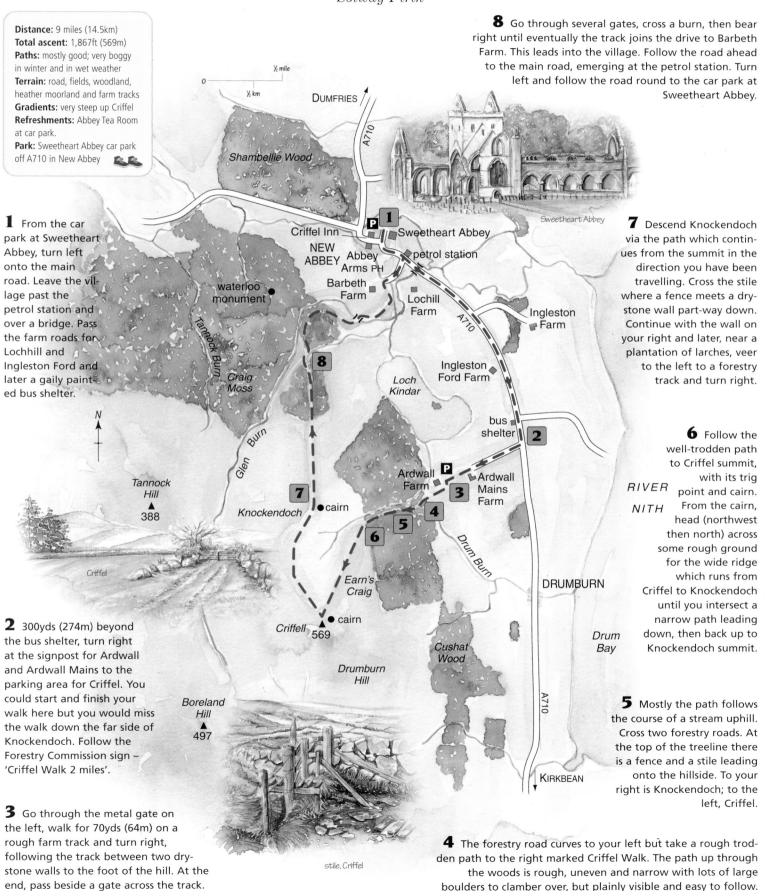

Sweetheart Abbey

stile, Criffel

1 From the car park at Sweetheart Abbey, turn left onto the main road. Leave the village past the petrol station and over a bridge. Pass the farm roads for Lochhill and Ingleston Ford and later a gaily painted bus shelter.

7 Descend Knockendoch via the path which continues from the summit in the direction you have been travelling. Cross the stile where a fence meets a drystone wall part-way down. Continue with the wall on your right and later, near a plantation of larches, veer to the left to a forestry track and turn right.

6 Follow the well-trodden path to Criffel summit, with its trig point and cairn. From the cairn, head (northwest then north) across some rough ground for the wide ridge which runs from Criffel to Knockendoch until you intersect a narrow path leading down, then back up to Knockendoch summit.

2 300yds (274m) beyond the bus shelter, turn right at the signpost for Ardwall and Ardwall Mains to the parking area for Criffel. You could start and finish your walk here but you would miss the walk down the far side of Knockendoch. Follow the Forestry Commission sign – 'Criffel Walk 2 miles'.

3 Go through the metal gate on the left, walk for 70yds (64m) on a rough farm track and turn right, following the track between two drystone walls to the foot of the hill. At the end, pass beside a gate across the track.

5 Mostly the path follows the course of a stream uphill. Cross two forestry roads. At the top of the treeline there is a fence and a stile leading onto the hillside. To your right is Knockendoch; to the left, Criffel.

4 The forestry road curves to your left but take a rough trodden path to the right marked Criffel Walk. The path up through the woods is rough, uneven and narrow with lots of large boulders to clamber over, but plainly visible and easy to follow.

Following St Ninian on the Isle of Whithorn

Much of medieval Whithorn remains intact today, perhaps thanks to a Reformation ban on pilgrimages here

WALK 105

Above right: St Ninian's Priory Church, Whithorn

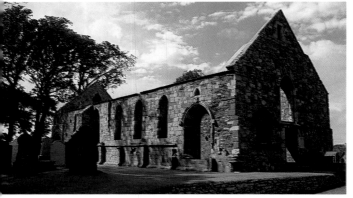

Above: Whithorn Priory, open to the skies

Below: the harbour, Isle of Whithorn

The Isle of Whithorn is situated within a natural harbour where pilgrims from throughout Europe landed en route to the nearby priory at Whithorn. It was also the first stop for pilgrims from more northerly points who were heading for Santiago de Compostello and Rome.

St Ninian's Chapel was built on the island in about  1300 on the site of a much earlier and narrower chapel. Like many early Christian churches, it is surrounded by a wall, and at one time a small cemetery and a priest's house probably also stood within the compound. Local tradition maintains that this was the site of Ninian's first church and it was here that pilgrims, arriving in the small harbour below, would stop to give thanks before continuing on their way to Whithorn Priory.

Sixteen hundred years ago Ninian founded his monastery at Whithorn. Built of white-washed stone, it was originally called Candida Casa, the White House, which 7th century Northumbrians translated into the Old English 'hwit erne'. Ninian was hailed as *Lampada Mundi Luminosa* – the world's bright lamp, although he is now considered a somewhat shadowy figure and few details of his life are known. He was sent to southwest Scotland from Rome to be bishop of the early Christian church in Galloway.

The tomb of St Ninian became a place of pilgrimage for kings, queens and countless crowds of ordinary people. Robert the Bruce and Mary, Queen of Scots visited, and her grandfather, James IV of Scotland, was the most frequent royal visitor. On one occasion, when his queen was sick at childbirth, James set off on foot to Whithorn, and in the Lord High Treasurer's Accounts there is itemised 16 pence paid during that journey for 'soling of one pair schone to the King'. The King and Queen returned to Whithorn later that year to give thanks, and the Accounts give a lively picture of the progress of a royal pilgrimage. There were gifts to singers, pipers, fiddlers and tale-tellers, and payments made when the King lost money at crossbow competitions, cards or nine-pins.

Whithorn was a wealthy and bustling medieval town, reaching the height of its glory in the 15th and 16th centuries, but in 1581 the Reformation dealt it a cruel blow. Pilgrimages were banned by Act of Parliament upon pain of death, and Whithorn went into decline.

Perhaps as a result of that blow to its economic development, much of medieval Whithorn remains today. The basic street plan is still evident, as are the long strips of garden typical of the Middle Ages. The ancient gravestones and crosses in the ruins of the great medieval cathedral bear witness to the fact that this site has been a church since the 5th century. Excavations have revealed the position of one of the earliest buildings, a chapel nearly 1,300 years old, and a massive terrace which was part of the monastery when Viking raiders settled the area. The Viking settlement, and Northumbrian remains below them, have been extensively excavated. The finds are exhibited in the Whithorn Dig and Visitors Centre.

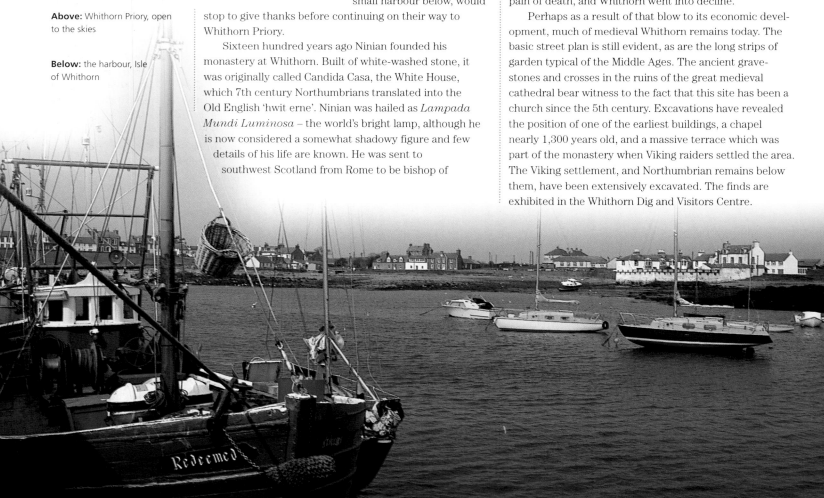

Following St Ninian on the Isle of Whithorn

A coastal walk where St Ninian's early church thrived

2 Follow the path to a large, square, white tower which looks across the Solway to Cumbria. Then enter the chapel grounds via a kissing gate beside a cairn, raised in 1997 to celebrate the foundation of Ninian's church 1600 years earlier.

1 At the harbour, beyond The Steampacket Inn, follow the signpost for St Ninian's Chapel. Follow the track through the children's play area and head for a cairn marking the end of the Pilgrims Way. Look for the chapel to your left.

8 Follow the road past Orfasey Cottage and on until it terminates at a T-junction beside an old barn. Turn right and, at the next junction, turn right again, following the road back round the harbour to your starting point.

7 Nearing a farm, where the path has fallen away, cross the fence into a field. Follow the track in the field through a gate between two drystone walls. Follow the right-hand wall along to another gate then turn left alongside the far wall and over a gate onto the farm road at Morrach and turn right onto a track.

6 The path is easy to follow along the coast, although it may be overgrown at points. Keep close to the barbed-wire fence or cross it temporarily until the obstruction is passed.

3 Retrace your steps, walking round the harbour past the tumbledown red village store, the parish church and the post office. At the Queen's Arms Hotel, turn left into Tonderghie Row, following the sign for Burrow Head Holiday Park past Cutcloy Farm.

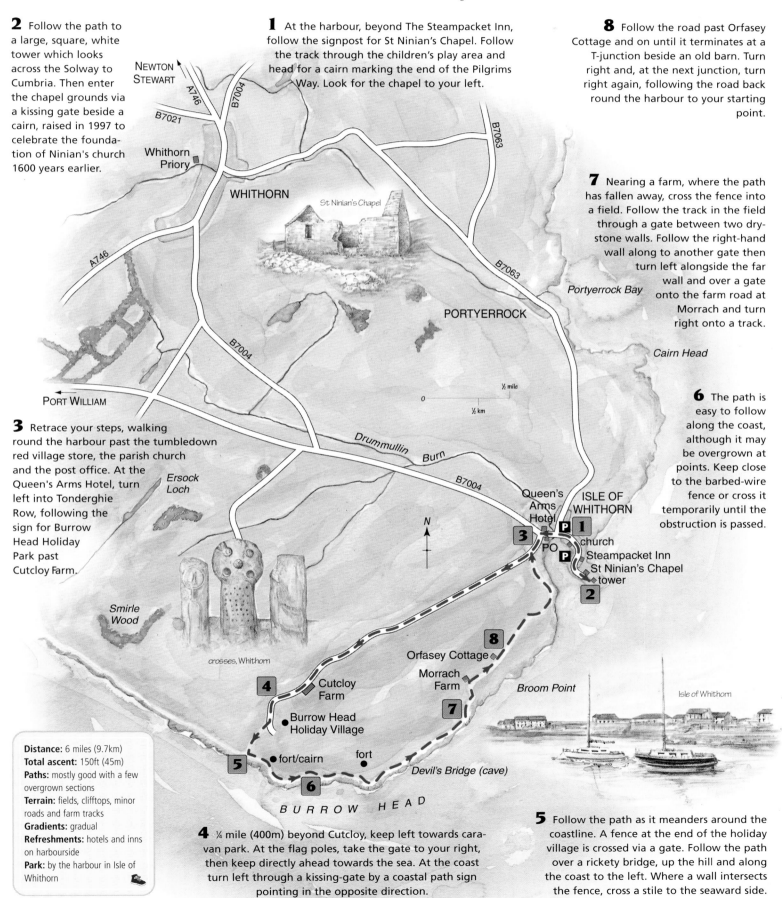

Distance: 6 miles (9.7km)
Total ascent: 150ft (45m)
Paths: mostly good with a few overgrown sections
Terrain: fields, clifftops, minor roads and farm tracks
Gradients: gradual
Refreshments: hotels and inns on harbourside
Park: by the harbour in Isle of Whithorn

4 ¼ mile (400m) beyond Cutcloy, keep left towards caravan park. At the flag poles, take the gate to your right, then keep directly ahead towards the sea. At the coast turn left through a kissing-gate by a coastal path sign pointing in the opposite direction.

5 Follow the path as it meanders around the coastline. A fence at the end of the holiday village is crossed via a gate. Follow the path over a rickety bridge, up the hill and along the coast to the left. Where a wall intersects the fence, cross a stile to the seaward side.

Burns' Alloway and the Brig o' Doon

Follow in the hallowed (but not always sober) footsteps of Scotland's celebrated National Bard

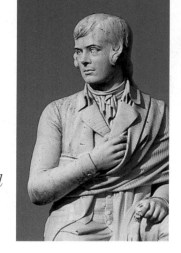

WALK
106

Right: Alloway's favourite son

Above: Robert Burns' birthplace was a humble cottage

Below: the Brig o' Doon, left, and the Burns Monument, seen to the right

The old church at Alloway is the setting for *Tam o' Shanter*, Robert Burns' atmospheric narrative poem of witches discovered by the drunken Tam in the Alloway churchyard, dancing to the frenzied piping of Satan himself. In the half-light in the eerie ruin of the kirk, you can imagine the open coffins and divers malignant tokens confusing Tam's befuddled eyes, and how, beguiled by one comely witch in her short shift, ' Tam tint his reason a thegither, and roars out "Weel done, Cutty-sark!"' Finally, track his last desperate race to the bridge as the 'hellish legion' pours forth 'wi' mony an eldritch skriech and hollo' in fiendish pursuit.

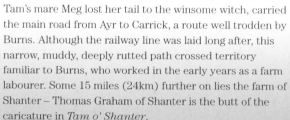

The Brig o' Doon, where Tam's mare Meg lost her tail to the winsome witch, carried the main road from Ayr to Carrick, a route well trodden by Burns. Although the railway line was laid long after, this narrow, muddy, deeply rutted path crossed territory familiar to Burns, who worked in the early years as a farm labourer. Some 15 miles (24km) further on lies the farm of Shanter – Thomas Graham of Shanter is the butt of the caricature in *Tam o' Shanter*.

The walk leads down to the Carrick shore, where many a boat on its way to or from the

Clyde was blown ashore onto the rocks (Tam's favourite witch is blamed for the loss of 'mony a bonie boat'). The path up to the 16th-century castle on Greenan Hill is steep on both sides, and the ruin itself is bricked up. The best view is from the beach, and it would have been a familiar sight to the poet.

Belleisle Country House, now a hotel, was also known to Burns, although not in its present form, since it was extended in 1829. In the main entrance of the hotel there are magnificent carvings of the *Tam o' Shanter* story and other works of Burns. The Victorian glasshouse and walled garden are open from dawn till dusk every day of the year, and the hotel is set in an extensive country park, including a deer park and play areas. These are freely accessible, and surely Burns would have approved of that.

The walk ends where the story started on a bitter January night in 1759, when the gable end of this cottage in Alloway blew in and Robert Burns was born. The cottage, built by Robert's father, is of a type still to be found all over Scotland, with thick stone walls, tiny windows and a thatched roof.

Burns' parents, William and Agnes, are buried in Alloway Kirkyard. Robert moved on to Ellisland in Dumfriesshire, where he farmed and also became an excise man. He died at Dumfries in 1796, at the young age of 37.

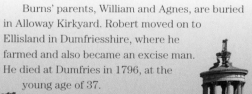

Burns' Alloway and the Brig o' Doon

A landscape much changed, yet still recognisable as the one-time home of Scotland's national poet

Distance: 7 miles (11.3km)
Total ascent: negligible
Paths: good; can be muddy
Terrain: old railway, fields, beach, golf course and woodland
Gradients: some steps
Refreshments: visitor centre at car park
Park: Tam O'Shanter Experience car park, Alloway, near Ayr

1 From Tam O'Shanter Experience, walk to end of car park, furthest from entry road. Go right down path into Burns Monument Gardens. Follow path anti-clockwise around monument then towards Auld Brig (Brig o'Doon) ahead. Visit Statues House, then continue to top of steps down to right. Descend to road, turn right and cross over. Just short of large white hotel, go down steps on left into Riverside Gardens.

2 Walk around gardens by river towards Auld Brig. Leave by steps back up to road, turn right and cross Auld Brig. Continue up path, under old railway bridge to top, swinging right on to main road.

3 Turn right and follow main road back over river. Just over newer bridge, cross over and turn left, up steps, into Auld Alloway Kirkyard (opposite parish church) to Burns' parents' graves.

4 Leaving kirkyard by steps, turn left and go along the road until level with Tam O'Shanter Experience. Cross right into Murdoch's Lone and go left immediately beyond a low white pumping station, steeply down to old railway line. Turn left through two tunnels and beyond.

5 Eventually, emerge on main road at Burton Farm road end. Turn right and follow road over old railway, then turn left on other side into lane, turning back on itself before swinging right towards sea. Continue past estate house on left to cottages at end of track.

6 Go between cottages and leave lane as it swings right, going through gate and down field, through gate to beach. Turn right along beach past Greenan Castle and car park to river mouth.

7 Turn right up road with river to left, to T-junction, opposite garden centre. Turn left over river bridge and cross road, turning right into Greenfield Avenue.

8 As Greenfield Avenue curves, go left through gates by lodge into Belleisle Park. Continue with golf course on right, through trees and then curve off right to pets area. Just before this, turn left into walled garden and carry on into second garden with large greenhouse. Leave by path from far left corner, up to rear of Belleisle House Hotel. Pass in front of golf shop and in 150yds (136m) turn right across golf course, following signs to Practice Area.

9 At path's end, go through green gates to main road and turn right. Follow past Rozelle Park on left and Northpark House Hotel on right, until road curves right into Alloway.

10 In middle of village, pass Burns Cottage on right and continue on main road (B7024) past cricket ground to return to Tam O'Shanter Experience on left.

Greenan Castle

Ayr Bay

Longhill Point

SEAFIELD

Seafield Golf Course

CENTRAL AYR ▲ PRESTWICK

AYR

A719

A79

A713

Belleisle House Hotel

B7024

greenhouse
pets area

9

7

P

8

lodge

Belleisle golf course

Rozelle Park

Greenan Castle

6

cottages

DOONFOOT

N

house and lodge

Doonbank Garden Centre

Northpark House Hotel

Burns Cottage

Rozelle House Galleries

10

P

ALLOWAY

Brig o'Doon

River Doon

4

Parish Church

Ayr By-Pass

A79

FISHERTON

A719

5

Burton Farm

Auld Alloway Kirk

tunnel

Tam O'Shanter Experience

P

1

Burns Monument
Statues House

3

2

Brig O'Doon House

Auld Brig

Newark Castle

Wallace's Stone

B7024

MAYBOLE

A77

MAYBOLE

Burns Cottage

½ mile

0

½ km

Glasgow's Not-so-mean Streets

Ignore the dark past, and marvel instead at this vibrant city's glorious renaissance as a centre of culture and fine architecture

WALK
107

Top right: a decorative window panel, Provand's Lordship

If the rest of Britain needed awakening to the merits of Glasgow, it came in 1990, the year it was designated 'European City of Culture'. Further distinction has come from the Arts Council, which honoured it as '1999 UK City of Architecture and Design'. The sheer energy of the city can be felt as soon as you step into George Square, which is dominated by the Victorian City Chambers, built in the Italian Renaissance style. The roads are busy and traffic flies past until you reach a little square which encircles the beautiful 12th-century cathedral founded by St Mungo, the city's patron saint. Overlooking it are the elaborate Doric columns and neo-classical temples of the cemetery known as the Necropolis, modelled on the Père Lachaise cemetery in Paris.

Close to the cathedral is the gloomy-looking Provand's Lordship, the oldest house in Glasgow, built in 1471. As you walk down the High Street you get the occasional glimpse of skyscrapers in the distance and tall chimneys spouting smoke which mingles gently with the clouds. Eventually you reach the Tolbooth Steeple, built in 1626, which marked the centre of Glasgow until Victorian times. It is the only remnant of a church which was burnt down by drunken members of the local Hell Fire Club.

Once you're in the East End the streets take on a seedy, run-down appearance for a while, but soon you see a large red business centre, built in 1889 as Templeton's Carpet Factory. Its ornate arched windows, turrets and delicate mosaics and tiles make it look more like a palace than a factory – in fact, the architect William Leiper modelled it on the Doge's Palace in Venice. It is bold, generous and uncompromising – just like Glasgow itself.

After admiring this gorgeous building you stroll across Glasgow Green, reputedly the oldest public park in Britain, past the Victorian People's Palace museum. Heading back into town along Trongate, you soon reach the main shopping streets of Argyle Street, Buchanan Street and the stylish Princes Square arcade, where smart and sassy Glaswegians shop for the latest fashions.

A long walk down Sauchiehall Street takes you past the Grecian Chambers built by Alexander 'Greek' Thomson, past Charles Rennie Mackintosh's Willow Tea Rooms and out into the West End. The city's wealthier residents began moving here in the 19th century, when industrialisation brought rapid growth to Glasgow. The streets get quieter and there are elegant terraces, notably the broad white sweep of Royal Crescent.

Just before you reach the large red sandstone Glasgow Art Gallery and Museum, the route takes you over the River Kelvin and gives good views of the Gothic-style university buildings. There are some exquisitely elegant terraces around Park Circus, built for Victorian gentry.

The peace of the West End is left on the other side of the motorway as you walk up a rather scruffy-looking street. You soon appreciate why you are here, however, when you see the Glasgow School of Art, Charles Rennie Mackintosh's most famous piece of work. Simple and elegant, this is art deco at its most striking.

Back in George Square you may conclude that you've only just begun to discover Glasgow's architectural treasures. It's no mean city, that's for certain.

Above: Rennie Mackintosh designed every little detail of the Glasgow School of Art

Right: the magnificent Italianate pile of the City Chambers

Glasgow's Not-so-mean Streets

*Architectural wealth softens the edges of
Scotland's biggest city*

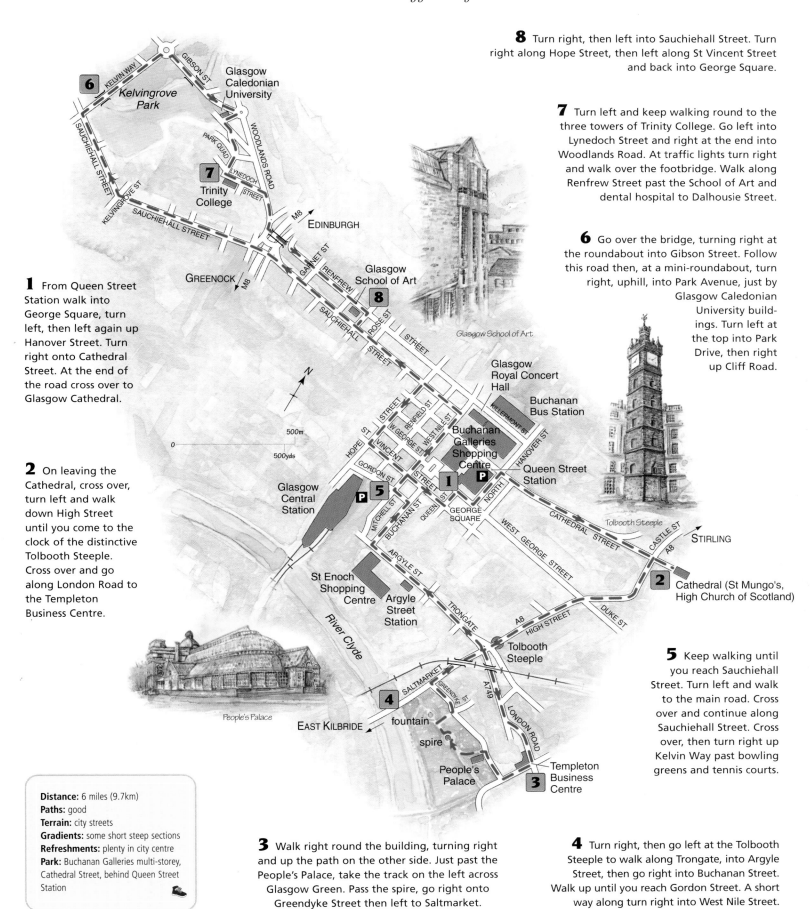

8 Turn right, then left into Sauchiehall Street. Turn right along Hope Street, then left along St Vincent Street and back into George Square.

7 Turn left and keep walking round to the three towers of Trinity College. Go left into Lynedoch Street and right at the end into Woodlands Road. At traffic lights turn right and walk over the footbridge. Walk along Renfrew Street past the School of Art and dental hospital to Dalhousie Street.

6 Go over the bridge, turning right at the roundabout into Gibson Street. Follow this road then, at a mini-roundabout, turn right, uphill, into Park Avenue, just by Glasgow Caledonian University buildings. Turn left at the top into Park Drive, then right up Cliff Road.

1 From Queen Street Station walk into George Square, turn left, then left again up Hanover Street. Turn right onto Cathedral Street. At the end of the road cross over to Glasgow Cathedral.

2 On leaving the Cathedral, cross over, turn left and walk down High Street until you come to the clock of the distinctive Tolbooth Steeple. Cross over and go along London Road to the Templeton Business Centre.

Glasgow School of Art

Tolbooth Steeple

Cathedral (St Mungo's, High Church of Scotland)

5 Keep walking until you reach Sauchiehall Street. Turn left and walk to the main road. Cross over and continue along Sauchiehall Street. Cross over, then turn right up Kelvin Way past bowling greens and tennis courts.

People's Palace

Distance: 6 miles (9.7km)
Paths: good
Terrain: city streets
Gradients: some short steep sections
Refreshments: plenty in city centre
Park: Buchanan Galleries multi-storey, Cathedral Street, behind Queen Street Station

3 Walk right round the building, turning right and up the path on the other side. Just past the People's Palace, take the track on the left across Glasgow Green. Pass the spire, go right onto Greendyke Street then left to Saltmarket.

4 Turn right, then go left at the Tolbooth Steeple to walk along Trongate, into Argyle Street, then go right into Buchanan Street. Walk up until you reach Gordon Street. A short way along turn right into West Nile Street.

Kilmartin Glen, Valley of Ghosts

The mounded cairns of prehistoric burial sites line the floor of a beautiful Argyll valley

Top right: a warrior tombstone in the churchyard

Right: prehistoric burial chambers lie all along this extraordinary valley

Below: the village stands prominently at the heart of the valley

Kilmartin Glen contains one of the most astounding ritual landscapes to be found in Britain, a unique assembly of religious monuments dating from the Stone Age through into Christian times. Neolithic settlers travelling the western sea lanes erected the first shrines and stone alignments when they cleared the land for grazing more than 5,000 years ago. Later generations in the Bronze Age added to the monuments, burying their dead in tombs along the valley floor and etching cup and ring designs on rock faces in the hills above. Iron Age tribesmen ringed the glen with hill forts, and when the Scots arrived from Ireland in the 4th century AD, they chose one of these, Dunadd, as the citadel on which their early kings were crowned. Two centuries later St Columba paid a visit, and his followers are thought to have established Kilmartin church. Walking through Kilmartin Glen you are following in a ghostly procession through incalculable changes in ritual and belief.

Within 100 yards (90m) of the car park, you are standing in an avenue of stones. Are they astronomically aligned, or are they simply pointing up the glen? Your own opinion is as valid as that of any expert. Then you are in Temple Wood Stone Circle and, again, you are presented with the evidence but left to draw your own conclusions. Perhaps, after centuries of use and alteration, even those who used this shrine no longer knew the intentions of its builders. What mattered was a sense of continuity, a link with their ancestors. This clearly also mattered to their own descendants, for, as you continue up the old coach road, you are following a long straight line of tombs that spans at least a thousand years. Each one is subtly different from its predecessor in design, but in essence each is just the same – a final resting place in a homeland under the unchanging hills.

Like the linear cemetery itself, the landscape has developed in the course of the millennia. Over to your right you can see Kilmartin church, where intricately carved medieval tombs lie over prehistoric graves. Then, passing by a quarry, you can see the terrace of a beach, formed after the last Ice Age, which was mined for pebbles by the builders of the cairns. The landmark up ahead is the ruin of Carnasserie Castle, the palatial home built by Bishop Carswell in the 16th century and sacked during Monmouth's rebellion in 1685. In such a haunted landscape, all sense of time becomes confused.

The pine forest is, of course, another recent change, but the dark, dense wood harks back to an older forest

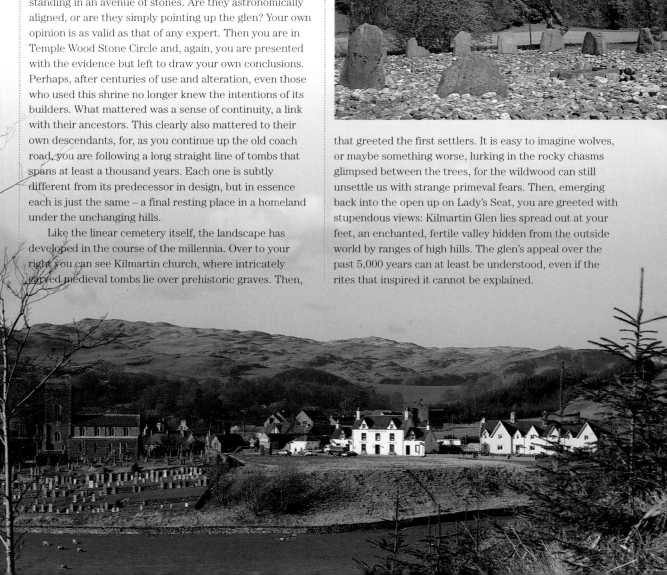

that greeted the first settlers. It is easy to imagine wolves, or maybe something worse, lurking in the rocky chasms glimpsed between the trees, for the wildwood can still unsettle us with strange primeval fears. Then, emerging back into the open up on Lady's Seat, you are greeted with stupendous views: Kilmartin Glen lies spread out at your feet, an enchanted, fertile valley hidden from the outside world by ranges of high hills. The glen's appeal over the past 5,000 years can at least be understood, even if the rites that inspired it cannot be explained.

WALK 108

Kilmartin Glen, Valley of Ghosts

Exploring the glen which may well prove to be the cradle of civilisation in the Highlands

1 Leaving the car park, cross the lane and take the footpath bridge over the stream. Passing Nether Largie Standing Stones, continue on the footpath to a lane beside Temple Wood stone circle.

2 Facing the stone circle, turn right along the lane, passing Nether Largie chambered cairn on your right. At the junction by Kilmartin school, continue straight ahead along a track (old coach road), passing two more cairns that form part of the linear cemetery. After 1 mile (1.6km), as the track crosses the stream, continue across a junction towards the quarry.

Distance: 9 miles (14.5km)
Total ascent: 200ft (61m)
Paths: mostly tracks and forest roads
Terrain: fields and forest
Gradients: moderate
Refreshments: Kilmartin House vistor centre; Kilmartin Hotel
Park: Lady Glassary Wood car park, on junction of A816 and B8025, 1 mile (1.6km) south of Kilmartin

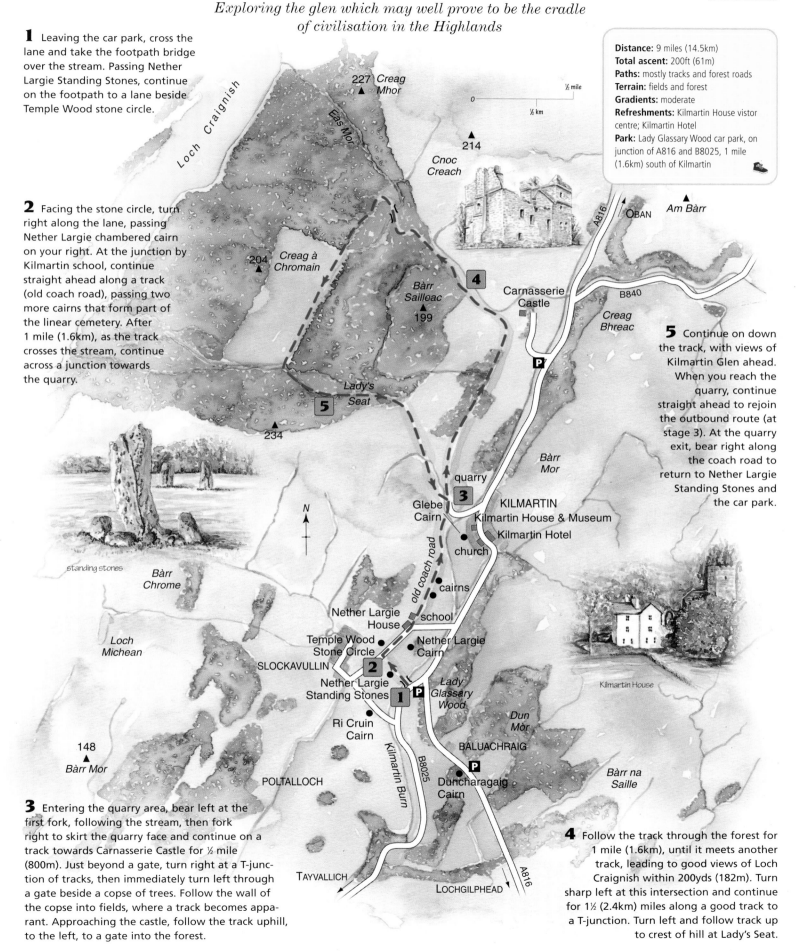

5 Continue on down the track, with views of Kilmartin Glen ahead. When you reach the quarry, continue straight ahead to rejoin the outbound route (at stage 3). At the quarry exit, bear right along the coach road to return to Nether Largie Standing Stones and the car park.

3 Entering the quarry area, bear left at the first fork, following the stream, then fork right to skirt the quarry face and continue on a track towards Carnasserie Castle for ½ mile (800m). Just beyond a gate, turn right at a T-junction of tracks, then immediately turn left through a gate beside a copse of trees. Follow the wall of the copse into fields, where a track becomes apparant. Approaching the castle, follow the track uphill, to the left, to a gate into the forest.

4 Follow the track through the forest for 1 mile (1.6km), until it meets another track, leading to good views of Loch Craignish within 200yds (182m). Turn sharp left at this intersection and continue for 1½ (2.4km) miles along a good track to a T-junction. Turn left and follow track up to crest of hill at Lady's Seat.

Rob Roy and Balquhidder

The walk leads from the old churchyard through Kirkton Glen, home ground to Scotland's most famous outlaw hero

Top right: a heroic depiction of a heroic outlaw

Inset below: Rob Roy lies buried in the churchyard at Balquhidder

Below: the view from the top – Ben More and Stob Binnein

Rob Roy MacGregor lies buried in the old churchyard at Balquhidder, under an ancient 14th-century tombstone depicting a warrior wielding a sword. He is one of the great folk heroes of the Highlands, mythologised by Sir Walter Scott and popularised today in film. Rob was not a great landowner, yet he owned the land as only those who know it by the soles of their feet can. He was a cattle dealer at a time when there was a fine line between legal and illegal dealings, and cattle-raiding was a way of life. As well as requiring knowledge of livestock and good husbandry, cattle-dealing demanded an almost instinctive understanding of the land and climate, adroit commercial dealing and well-honed fighting ability.

It is easy to see the need for all these talents as you head up Kirkton Glen. Due to tree felling, the hillsides are bare once again and you can see the shape of the glen as Rob would have known it. The walk is part of the ancient through-route to Glen Dochart, where Rob had a house at one time. You can imagine the skill required to drive cattle on roads like these, as well as the hardships, particularly when you had to guard the beasts day and night. When he became an outlaw the pass provided an escape route from soldiers who haunted him.

He was not outlawed for his Jacobite sympathies, but because of a bad business deal. His chief drover stole £1,000, which Rob had borrowed from the Duke of Montrose as part of a cattle deal. Montrose tried to use the debt to persuade Rob Roy to give false evidence against the Duke of Argyll. When Rob Roy refused, Montrose had him outlawed, foreclosed the loan and, in terrible weather, evicted Rob's family from their cottage. From then on, Rob waged a fierce war of attrition against Montrose, stealing his cattle and his rents. He even gave the rent money to a tenant who was about to be evicted, and then stole it back again from the factor.

Despite his lawless exploits, Rob Roy died peacefully in his bed. Near the end of the walk you can look up Balquhidder Glen towards his house at Inverlochlarig. It was along the 15-mile (24km) length of this glen that his funeral procession took place on New Year's Day 1735, preceded by the MacGregor pipers.

This rugged, mountainous countryside seems unforgiving to strangers, but would have been a haven of caves, hidden glens and friendly cottages to Rob Roy. It is no wonder that the landed interests, with their militia and laws, failed to capture and hold him. In the early 18th century this land was the start of the Highlands, which the Lowland lairds and burghers were determined to control and profit from. As the 18th century progressed they did indeed tear the heart out of the Highlands, evicting its people to accommodate sheep. Forestation has also altered the landscape, but the land remains untamed and always will be.

Rob Roy and Balquhidder

*Legend and reality merge in the tales of a Highland hero
on the braes of these lovely mountains*

Distance: 7 miles (11km)
Total ascent: 1,750ft (533m)
Paths: good but boggy on hillside
Terrain: mostly forestry roads;
some hillside
Gradients: moderate to steep
Refreshments: Kingshouse Hotel
Park: Balquhidder church,
Balquhidder, off A84 between
Callander and Lochearnhead

8 Eventually this road turns back on itself and goes downhill to join the road beside the burn. Turn left, continuing past the bridge on your right and the water works back to Balquhidder church and the car park.

7 This road is at a higher altitude and will let you see all of the glen before you. After about 1 mile (1.6km) or so look for the magnificent view to your right over Loch Voil and the Braes of Balquhidder.

1 From the church at Balquhidder take the track that goes around to the right, signposted to waterfall. At the back wall of the church there is a stile over a fence and a Forest Enterprise sign for Kirkton Glen.

2 Follow the path uphill, through the woods and past the water works, keeping the burn on your left. A newly made logging road crosses the burn from the left. Continue uphill with burn on the left. There has been a lot of felling work here and it is now possible to see the shape of the Glen.

3 The road follows the line of the burn. It forks after 1½ miles (2.4km) and to your right there is a sign for Glen Dochart Pass. Follow a narrow but well-trodden path going uphill to the left of the sign.

4 Follow the path, crossing the burn at a fence then over the fence at a stile further up, and head for a range of crags as the path becomes indistinct. Follow it as it turns right then curve up to the left through the crags to the Lochan an Eireannaich.

6 Retrace your steps down the hill to rejoin the forestry road. Here you have the choice of three directions. Take the turning to the left and head off down the glen.

5 From here cut across the shoulder of Meall an Fhiodhain, the hill on your right, keeping to the high ground and going through a ruined fence. Your reward is the spectacular view along the course of the Ledcharrie Burn to Glen Dochart.

Meall an Fhiodhain ▲ 778

813 ▲

forestry work

▲ Meall an
851 t-Seallaidh

Meall
Reamhar

Lochan an
Eireannaich

Meall an
Lochan

N

Kirkton Glen

Balquhidder church

Kendrum Burn

Meall
Reamhar

BRAES OF BALQUHIDDER

Auchtoomore
Hill

Gleann Crotha

LOCHEARNHEAD

water
works

church

BALQUHIDDER

AUCHTOO

A84

TULLOCH

Loch Voil

River Balvag

Calair Burn

KINGSHOUSE

0   ½ mile
    ½ km

BALLIMORE

CALLANDER

The Lost Valley of Glen Coe

Surrounded by alpine peaks and accessible only via a tree-lined gorge, this mountain sanctuary was once a hiding place for cattle

WALK
110

Top right: look out for the pink flowers of lousewort

Below: the rocky path down from Allt Coire Gabhail

Below: a sweeping view down Glen Coe, with peaks of the Three Sisters to the left

Think of a glen in Scotland and the chances are that the first to come to mind is Glen Coe. It is notorious for the events of a tragic night in 1692, when a bloody and cowardly massacre of the MacDonalds by the Campbells took place. The road in the glen is constrained on both sides by high mountains, their lingering shadows adding to a sense of foreboding. Even bright summer sunshine cannot entirely dispel the melancholy of a valley which seems to deserve its name – 'Glen of Weeping'. But do not be put off. For dramatic scenery Glen Coe has few equals in mainland Scotland, and there are many opportunities for both high- and low-level walking.

You begin the expedition in the brooding depths of the glen, confronting the towering buttresses of the Three Sisters of Glen Coe at the car park. These three bold spurs present an imposing sight, rising high enough to mask from view Bidean nam Bian, the highest mountain in Argyll. From the footbridge a well-worn but rough path rises up the bolder-strewn gorge between two of the sisters, Beinn Fhada and Gearr Aonach. By limiting grazing, attempts are being made to extend the narrow strip of woodland in the gorge out to the slope above the south bank of the River Coe. The fence-line effect up by the stile is quite pronounced; notice how the heather and scrub birch below the fence, on the protected side, are rapidly becoming re-established.

The gorge of the Allt Coire Gabhail is a green but confined place. On steep riverbanks that are mostly inaccessible to deer and sheep, birch, rowan and hazel are able to grow undisturbed. In spring the floor of this narrow corridor of woodland is speckled with bright yellow primroses and splashed with the white florets of wood anemones. On the wet ground at your feet, look out for the insectivorous butterwort. In early summer this tiny plant flowers a striking purple and its sticky leaves are a deadly trap for small flies.

Leading up to the crossing of the Allt Coire Gabhail there are, in fact, two possible paths to follow. It is a short but steep climb to get up to the higher one above the trees. From here you have a less obscured view back into Glen Coe.

Looking directly behind you, the skyline on the opposite side of the glen is a distinctly jagged one. This infamous ridge of exposed rock is known as the Aonach Eagach (Notched Ridge) and is the preserve of experienced scramblers. Those of you who think you might be up to the challenge would do well to first practice your scrambling technique on the huge boulder just to the right of the path, at the point where it debouches into the Coire Gabhail. Here, quite suddenly it seems, you are overlooking a sanctuary surrounded by the Alpine-like peaks of Bidean nam Bian, Stob Coire Sgreamhach and their projecting spurs. You will appreciate that the name given to this flat-bottomed valley is entirely appropriate and that the Lost Valley is so very well hidden.

For the MacDonalds of Glen Coe, the Lost Valley was a favourite location for hiding stolen cattle. These days it is wild campers who take advantage of the seclusion, and walkers and climbers have replaced Highland cows as the large roaming mammals of the Coire Gabhail. In the skies however, things are much as they were. Keep eyes peeled for golden eagles, for these magnificent and rare birds of prey are frequently seen in the vicinity of Glen Coe.

The Lost Valley of Glen Coe

*Hidden in the mountainous walls of this famous
Highland glen, a hanging valley once sheltered the
Macdonald's cattle from raiders*

1 Start on the path leading down from the car park, to join
the main path through the Pass of Glencoe. Walk down east,
then turn south to cross the footbridge over the River Coe,
located just downstream of the Meeting of Three Waters.
Climb the opposite bank, go through the birch scrub and
up over a ladder stile at fencing.

2 After a further 100yds (91m) or
so, leave the main path and climb a
zigzagging path rising steeply off to
the right. This leads up to the higher
path, the one above the tree-fringed
gorge of the Allt Coire Gabhail. Having enjoyed a
gentle stroll for a while, and just before a large
boulder, descend through the trees to make the
crossing of the river. Take care traversing a few
awkward rocks and roots
on the way down.

> **Distance:** 3½ miles (5.2km)
> **Total ascent:** 855ft (261m)
> **Paths:** rough but clearly defined on ascent; less obvious
> on the short circuit around the Lost Valley
> **Terrain:** confined, steep-sided gorge through woodland
> giving way to more open mountainous aspect at the top
> **Gradients:** short but steep over rocks although no
> serious difficulties
> **Refreshments:** Clachaig Inn, 3 miles (4.8km) west of
> car park
> **Park:** westernmost car park in the Pass of Glencoe on
> A82 between Tyndrum and Ballachulish

3 Stepping stones
make the river cross-
ing easy. Continue the
climb up along the
left bank, clambering
over an outcrop of
rocks before reaching
the point overlook-
ing the distinctively
flat, alluvial plain of
the Coire Gabhail
(Lost Valley).

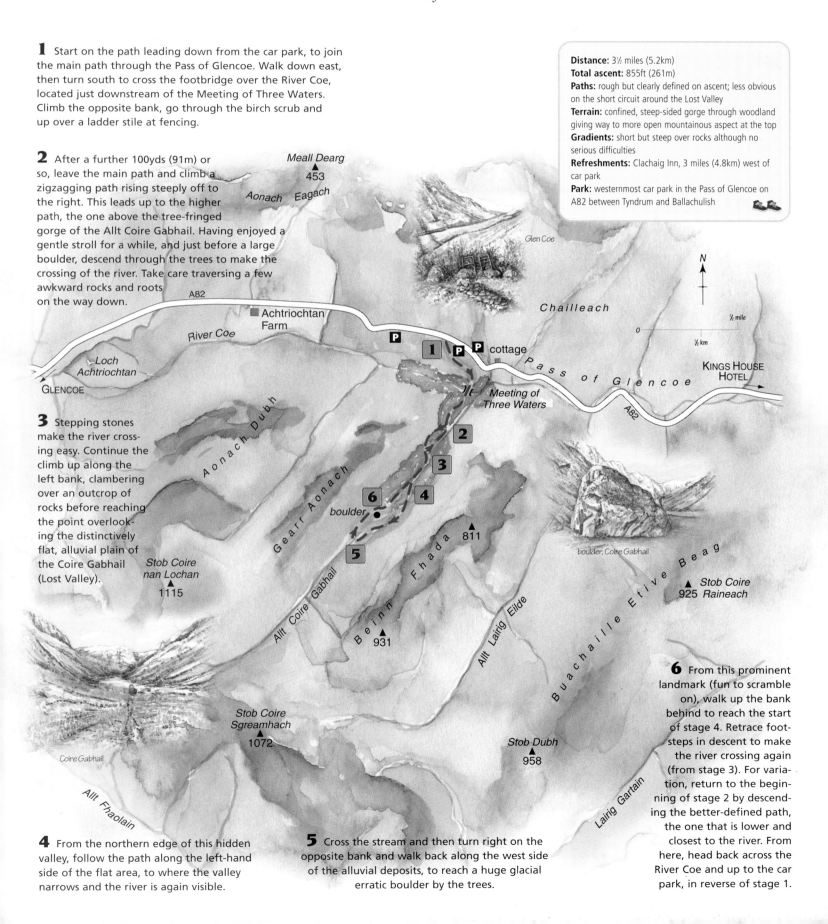

4 From the northern edge of this hidden
valley, follow the path along the left-hand
side of the flat area, to where the valley
narrows and the river is again visible.

5 Cross the stream and then turn right on the
opposite bank and walk back along the west side
of the alluvial deposits, to reach a huge glacial
erratic boulder by the trees.

6 From this prominent
landmark (fun to scramble
on), walk up the bank
behind to reach the start
of stage 4. Retrace foot-
steps in descent to make
the river crossing again
(from stage 3). For variation, return to the beginning of stage 2 by descending the better-defined path,
the one that is lower and
closest to the river. From
here, head back across the
River Coe and up to the car
park, in reverse of stage 1.

Remote Moidart's Citadel

A walk through wild West Highland scenery where idyllic views contrast with reminders of a savage history

Top right: the gaunt ruins of Castle Tioram perch on a rocky mound

Below: red deer haunt these hills

Bottom: looking down to the castle and Loch Moidart

From the 14th century until the Jacobite Rebellion of 1715, the Clanranald chiefs of Castle Tioram ruled as warlords over what amounted to a tribal principality, which extended from South Uist in the Outer Hebrides to the shores of Arisaig and Moidart. Their stronghold on Loch Moidart guarded what were known as the 'Rough Bounds', a wilderness of mountains, moors and labyrinthine sea-lochs where even the most intrepid travellers would seldom dare to venture.

Setting out along the shore from Dorlin, you may feel you are entering a world unaffected by the passage of the centuries. Although the 14th Chief had Castle Tioram burnt when he set off for his final battle, believing that his way of life was doomed, its walls and towers still remain impressively intact. Tioram's strength, however, derived not only from its battlements but from its natural defences. Islands, rocks and tidal reefs shield the castle from the open sea, whilst a tidal sand-bar and high rocky crags protect it from surprise attack from overland. The path, known as the Silver Walk, clings precariously to the cliff through woods and rhododendron thickets, with glittering reflections that sparkle from the sea at every turn.

As you turn inland and climb up to the hills, you will discover an evocative reminder that, although the landscape is now barren, it is not a natural wilderness. High on the plateau, beside a little burn, stand the ruins of a village overgrown with bracken. The families who lived here were evicted from their homes and shipped to Australia in 1853 so that the land they had farmed could be more profitably sold as uninhabited deer forest. With breathtaking views across the loch it is a magical but haunted spot.

Aside from the occasional hillwalker, red deer and birds of prey are now the only living creatures you are likely to encounter as you cross the moor and skirt the waters of a hill-loch. The views stretch far off to the south across the hills of Morvern, but you will not see a wisp of smoke or catch a glimpse of sun reflected off a distant window. Even the most sheltered glens have long been uninhabited and have reverted back to wilderness.

A pass up from the shore of the loch leads to an old reservoir that now makes a delightful spot for a picnic, or perhaps even a refreshing swim. From here the route leads down a wooded glen, with yet more memorable views, this time of the open sea and Hebridean islands. The broken pipeline by the path once provided hydro-electricity to Dorlin House, a mansion that was famed for its Victorian magnificence. You will pass its long-neglected gardens as you return along the road towards the car-park, but the house itself was dynamited in the 1950s by a laird who saw no future for such a relic of a vanished age. Now, half a century later, Castle Tioram is awaiting restoration as a private home. One day even clearance villages may be rebuilt, but, as this walk may well have shown, the Highlands cannot easily be conquered. Whole societies may come and go, but the wilderness remains.

Remote Moidart's Citadel

*By the peaceful lochside at Castle Tioram, once home to a
Clan Ranald chieftain*

**WALK
111**

1 Turn right out of the car
park, passing through a gate to
follow the shoreline path.

5 Cross a field at the
bottom of the valley, go
over a stile and turn right
along the road to return
to the car park.

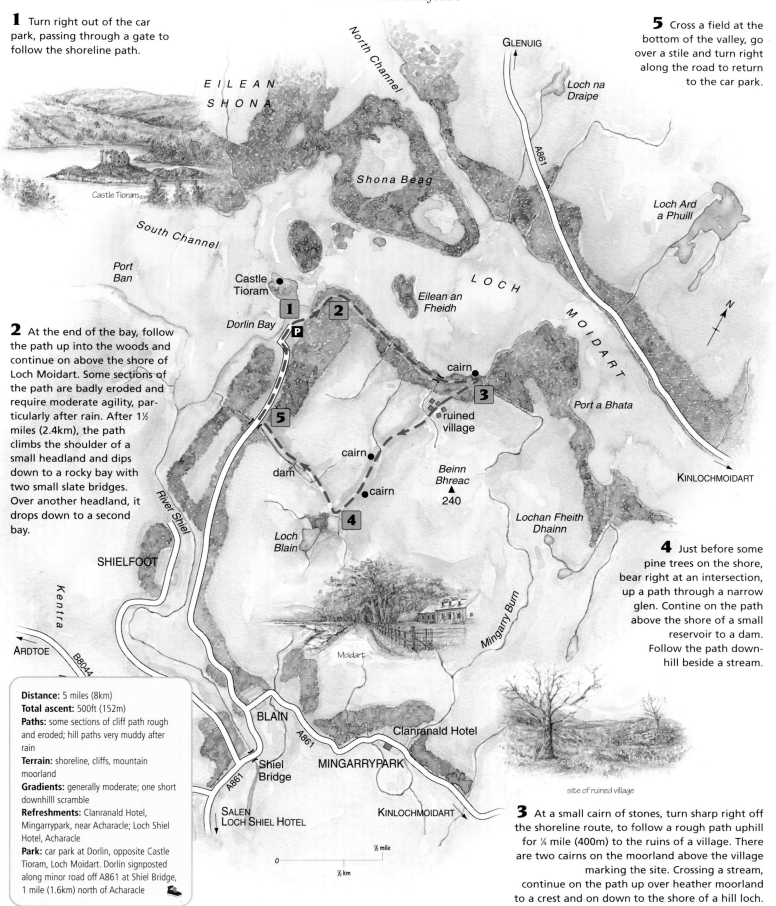

2 At the end of the bay, follow
the path up into the woods and
continue on above the shore of
Loch Moidart. Some sections of
the path are badly eroded and
require moderate agility, particularly after rain. After 1½
miles (2.4km), the path
climbs the shoulder of a
small headland and dips
down to a rocky bay with
two small slate bridges.
Over another headland, it
drops down to a second
bay.

Distance: 5 miles (8km)
Total ascent: 500ft (152m)
Paths: some sections of cliff path rough
and eroded; hill paths very muddy after
rain
Terrain: shoreline, cliffs, mountain
moorland
Gradients: generally moderate; one short
downhilll scramble
Refreshments: Clanranald Hotel,
Mingarrypark, near Acharacle; Loch Shiel
Hotel, Acharacle
Park: car park at Dorlin, opposite Castle
Tioram, Loch Moidart. Dorlin signposted
along minor road off A861 at Shiel Bridge,
1 mile (1.6km) north of Acharacle

site of ruined village

4 Just before some
pine trees on the shore,
bear right at an intersection,
up a path through a narrow
glen. Contine on the path
above the shore of a small
reservoir to a dam.
Follow the path down-
hill beside a stream.

3 At a small cairn of stones, turn sharp right off
the shoreline route, to follow a rough path uphill
for ¼ mile (400m) to the ruins of a village. There
are two cairns on the moorland above the village
marking the site. Crossing a stream,
continue on the path up over heather moorland
to a crest and on down to the shore of a hill loch.

In the Executioner's Shadow, Deep in the Cuillins

Climbing in these rugged mountains is not for the inexperienced, but a walk on the lower slopes rewards the effort

WALK 112

Top right: Alpine lady's mantle grows in the rocky crevices

Walking south from Sligachan, you can feel the adrenaline rise as you approach Sgurr nan Gillean and Am Basteir – 'the Executioner'. Their sharp, distinctive profiles represent the northernmost Munros (mountains over 3,000 feet or 914m) on the most magnificent mountain range in the British Isles, the Cuillin. As with the other 30 or so peaks strung out along this 8 mile (12.8km) arc of bare rock, their summits are mostly out of bounds to all but the most capable scramblers and climbers. However, much of their rugged grandeur can still be enjoyed at close quarters if you explore the more accessible corries of the range. On this walk you will venture up into the Coire a' Bhasteir, a spectacularly impressive ice-scraped hollow.

The walk begins gently enough on a good, well-maintained path. You ascend open moorland across which the view of the Cuillins, from Sligachan, is a much-photographed classic. You will flush grouse from the heather and enjoy some lovely cascades and pools by the banks of the Allt Dearg Beag.

It will soon be obvious that the two main mountain groups of Skye contrast not only in their profiles but also in their colours. To the east rise the rounded pink granite mounds known as the Red Hills or Red Cuillins, whilst to the south, ahead of you, the Black Cuillin skyline of gabbro rock is a sharp and jagged one.

The easy walking comes to an abrupt end at the confined entrance to the corrie, the Bhasteir Gorge. This is a rather forbidding place: vertical walls of rock on both sides cut deep and narrow by the plunging waters of the Allt Dearg Beag. It is a feature made all the more impressive by the dramatic pinnacles of rock (Pinnacle Ridge) soaring skyward behind it. From here on, traversing the hard, rough gabbro up on the steep west side of the gorge is a challenging exercise which requires care, but there are no serious technical difficulties to overcome. The just reward for your efforts and exertions on the final push can be claimed on reaching your objective, the diminutive Loch a' Bhasteir. This tiny body of water is the source of the river which, for the last 1½ miles (2.4km), has never been far from your side. Here you will find yourself in a remarkable location, a wild and remote place surrounded by rugged peaks. Sgurr a' Bhasteir, Am Basteir, the Basteir Tooth and the Pinnacle Ridge of Sgurr nan Gillean offer climbers a paradise, but each peak is a strenuous challenge made all the more difficult in navigation by the compass-deflecting properties of the gabbro.

Your return to Sligachan must be made by retracing footsteps, this time downstream of the Allt Dearg Beag. No viable circuit option exists, unless there are tireless scree-scrambling quadrupeds among you! On descent the view is to the sea. The distant buildings of Portree, the capital of Skye, lie to the north below the great wedge of the Trotternish Ridge. One peculiarly detached pinnacle of rock, the Old Man of Storr, stands out; it is one of Skye's most distinctive landmarks.

If this walk is your first experience of the Cuillins, there is every chance that you will be back, remembering this day as the start of an obsession with a group of mountains that has become, for so many now, something of a Mecca.

Above: the old bridge at Sligachan

Below: the white-painted Sligachan Hotel is dwarfed by the surrounding high peaks

In the Executioner's Shadow, Deep in the Cuillins

Am Bàsteir means 'the Executioner' in Gaelic, but this is a relatively gentle walk beneath its awesome profile

1 From the Sligachan Hotel, walk along the A863 for about 200yds (182m). Take one of the paths on the left, opposite the top of a slip road to the hotel. Most lead across boggy ground to cross the Allt Dearg Mor at the footbridge. Walk south on the gently rising footpath towards Sgurr nan Gillean, the easternmost peak of the mountains seen clearly on the skyline ahead.

2 Do not cross the second footbridge, this time over the Allt Dearg Beag, but instead continue along the right bank of this river. There are many picturesque pools and waterfalls and, higher up, the path traverses rock slabs and a few intervening burns, which are forded easily.

3 The path fades away in the scree below the entrance to the Bhasteir Gorge. Most will be content with the breathtaking views from the mouth of the gorge, both ahead to the towering heights of Am Bàsteir and Sgurr nan Gillean and behind to the wide views of northern Skye. In dry conditions it is worth viewing the gorge itself by descending carefully to the bottom of the ravine. Passage up the gorge, however, is soon blocked by deep pools and precipitous waterfalls. Return to Sligachan by retracing footsteps back down the upward path.

5 The path ends at Loch a' Bhasteir, the tiny body of water held in the secluded recesses of Coire a' Bhasteir, from where you can retrace your steps back to Sligachan. **This upper leg of the walk provides some challenging and exposed walking and should only be attempted by those with experience of walking in the mountains.**

4 Experienced walkers may wish to continue up to the corrie above the gorge by taking a rough path rising to the right of the gorge in steep zigzags over scree. Stay almost directly above the vertiginous sides of the gorge and the stream on the left; do not be tempted to drift too far to the right. The clambering is quite hard going but on approaching a small cave, there is a less steep, better defined path for a while. Beyond the cave, continue the ascent over very rugged terrain, rejoining the uppermost reaches of the Allt Dearg Beag. Follow the stream up to its obvious source in the corrie.

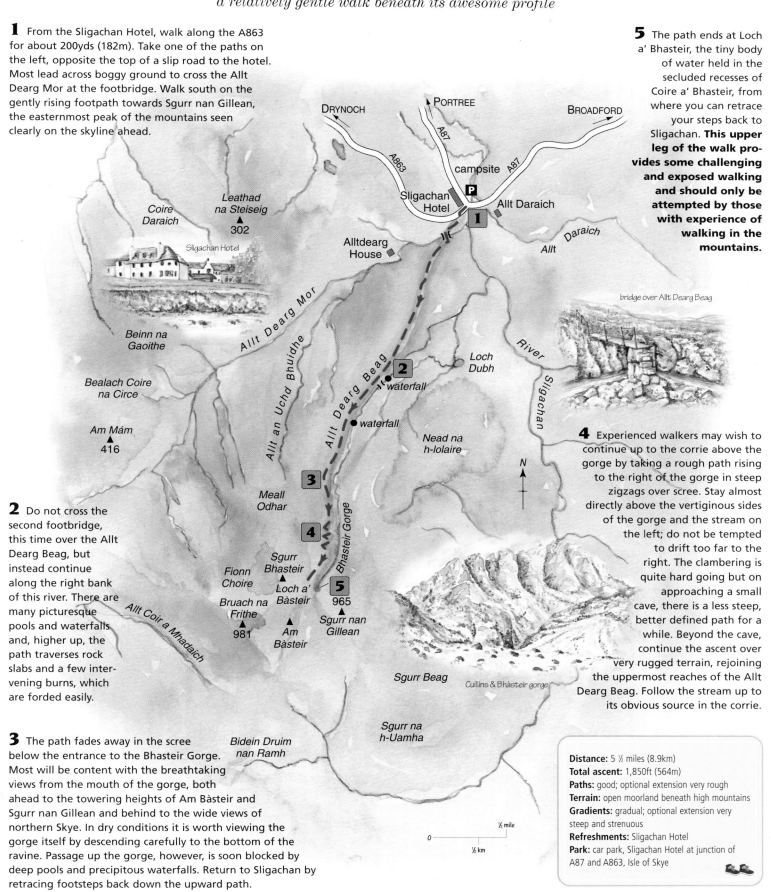

Sligachan Hotel

bridge over Allt Dearg Beag

Cuillins & Bhàsteir gorge

Distance: 5 ½ miles (8.9km)
Total ascent: 1,850ft (564m)
Paths: good; optional extension very rough
Terrain: open moorland beneath high mountains
Gradients: gradual; optional extension very steep and strenuous
Refreshments: Sligachan Hotel
Park: car park, Sligachan Hotel at junction of A87 and A863, Isle of Skye

Ullapool and the Drove Roads

In the days when cattle walked to market, these green tracks were the main highways to the markets of the South

WALK

113

Right: the familiar, shaggy face of a Highland cow

Above: a colourful depiction of drovers with their dog

Below: the neat seafront of Ullapool

A mile-long herd of cattle being driven through a mountain pass is a scene familiar from countless Hollywood films. But instead of endless blue sky and buckskinned cowboys on horseback, picture a grey drizzle and cowboys on foot, clothed in lengths of woollen cloth, kilted round waists and shoulders.

This was the wild west of Scotland 200 years ago, and the cowhands were Highlanders on a drove road. Moving at a rate of 10 miles (16km) a day, the drovers would sleep at night by their beasts, wrapped in their plaids, rising at dawn for another weary day on the road to the great cattle trysts (fairs) of Ardgay, Muir of Ord, Crieff and Falkirk. The trysts were colourful affairs with musicians, beggars, pickpockets and pedlars mingling with the drovers and buyers. Drinking dens in makeshift tents enhanced the merriment, while huge bubbling cauldrons of broth provided a warming change from weeks of oatmeal. The whole event had the atmosphere of a fair or carnival.

Cattle from the Isle of Lewis were regularly ferried across the Minch to Ullapool and then driven through Glen Achall, making for the late autumn sales at Ardgay – a land journey over 150 miles (240km). Although the road along the River Ullapool is now surfaced, the surrounding hills and lochs are unchanging. The drove would have crossed the rivers by the many fords shown on old maps. The ford is quite clear at the second bridge, and in summer you might want to cross by the ford to experience it as a drover would, or just to avoid the rickety bridge with its 'Dangerous Bridge' sign. From Loch Achall the drove road continues for many more miles. The return route over the hill track to Ullapool is not, in fact, a drove road, but recalls better the beaten tracks and rough stony paths the drovers would have known.

Droving in Scotland goes back at least to the 14th century. Meat did not form a substantial part of the Scottish diet, and with no means of sustaining cattle through the harsh winter, the beasts had to be driven south and sold. The drove roads followed the line of least resistance through straths and glens. While some of these ancient tracks are now buried under the tarmac of modern highways, many remain as rights of way.

Droving and linen were the two growth areas of the Scottish economy in the late 17th century. Following the Act of Union, trade with England increased until about the 1830s, when the decline began. Landowners were anxious to stop the passage of droves over their land. Many of the Scottish rights of way were established in the latter half of the 19th century as drovers were driven to litigation to defend their livelihood.

But it was a way of life that was doomed. Improved communications, particularly the coming of steamships and the railway, meant that cattle could be transported without loss of weight. The number of beasts herded in the old way gradually dwindled until, by the end of the century, the Falkirk Tryst was a memory. The last Skye drove was recorded in 1906.

Ullapool and the Drove Roads

*Following the tracks of drovers bringing cattle across
from the isles*

1 From the car park next to Safeway supermarket, exit to Latheron Lane and turn left into Quay Street. At the Riverside Hotel, where the road curves right, turn left into Castle Terrace. Go down the steps to the river on the right and cross a bridge.

2 At the far side, turn right and follow the path along the side of the river. Continue by the riverside to a wooden bridge and up some steps. Turn right at a cattle grid to the main road.

8 The path now winds down the side of the hill, through a kissing gate and out to the main road. Turn left and follow the main road, passing the Far Isles Bar and Restaurant on the right hand side, to the church. Here, turn right and follow the signs back to the car park.

7 When the path forks, go left up the side of the hill. Eventually the track curves to the right. From here the view over Loch Broom, the Summer Isles and Ullapool is breathtaking.

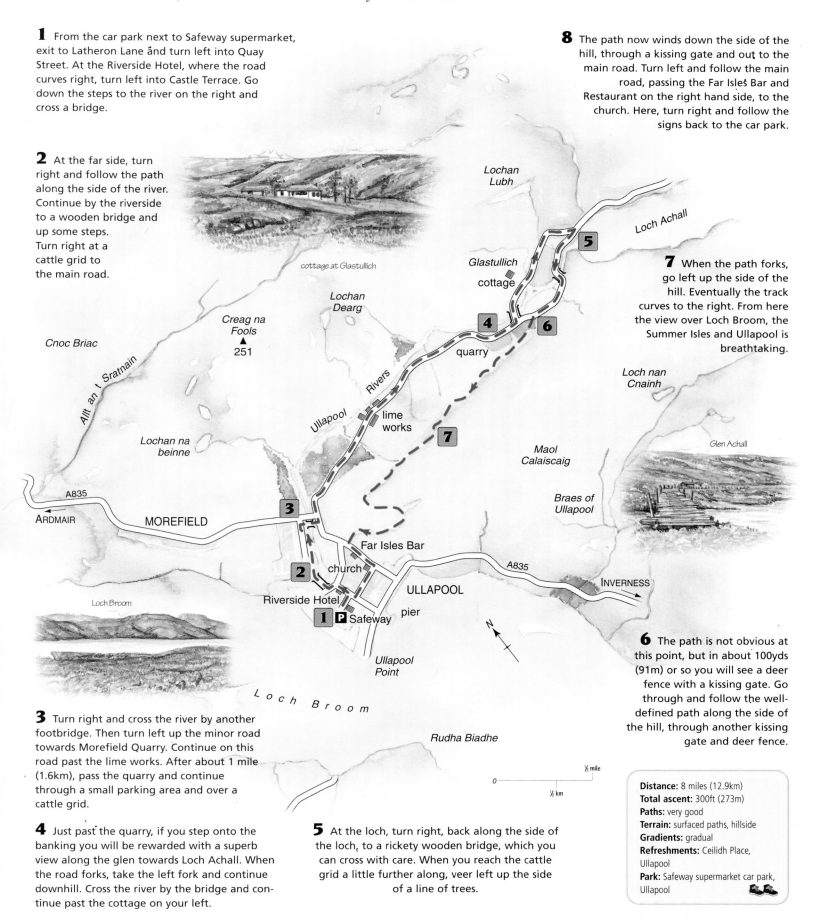

cottage at Glastullich

6 The path is not obvious at this point, but in about 100yds (91m) or so you will see a deer fence with a kissing gate. Go through and follow the well-defined path along the side of the hill, through another kissing gate and deer fence.

3 Turn right and cross the river by another footbridge. Then turn left up the minor road towards Morefield Quarry. Continue on this road past the lime works. After about 1 mile (1.6km), pass the quarry and continue through a small parking area and over a cattle grid.

4 Just past the quarry, if you step onto the banking you will be rewarded with a superb view along the glen towards Loch Achall. When the road forks, take the left fork and continue downhill. Cross the river by the bridge and continue past the cottage on your left.

5 At the loch, turn right, back along the side of the loch, to a rickety wooden bridge, which you can cross with care. When you reach the cattle grid a little further along, veer left up the side of a line of trees.

Distance: 8 miles (12.9km)
Total ascent: 300ft (273m)
Paths: very good
Terrain: surfaced paths, hillside
Gradients: gradual
Refreshments: Ceilidh Place, Ullapool
Park: Safeway supermarket car park, Ullapool

The Flow Country

Explore this unique habitat, where wildlife and bog plants thrive in a remote and very precious wilderness

WALK
114

Bottom: standing water is a vital feature of the boggy Flow Country

Below: peat drying in a stack

The Flow Country of Sutherland and Caithness is one of the last wilderness areas in Britain. The blanket bog lies on flat or gently sloping land surrounded by hills. Climb any of the hills and marvel at the watery wilderness of the peatlands, lochs and small pools. Despite the tales locals tell in the pubs of men, beasts and vehicles disappearing in the bogs, this is relatively safe walking – although a walking pole or stick will prove helpful for checking the firmness of the ground.

It has taken thousands of years for the remains of semi-decomposed plants to form the peat bogs, which are several yards deep in places and amongst the best examples of this habitat in the world. For centuries peat has served as a fuel and provided building materials in the form of peat blocks for walls and roof insulation under the heather thatch. Even roof timbers have come from the bogs: pine trees from the ancient Caledonian Forest can be found perfectly preserved in the lower parts of the bog. These, however, are so rare that it was not unusual for them to be passed down through the generations.

Peat is still used as a fuel, and you will encounter peat cuttings on your walk. From May to June, using traditional tools, locals cut peats from banks and trenches and leave them to dry. Peat is also burnt in the malting process of whisky production, and this combined with the peat content of the water is what gives some Highland malts their unique flavours. Try the ones produced at the distilleries at Clynelish (Brora) and Pultneytown (Wick).

Deep in the wilderness you can scarcely imagine that at one time this land supported a lot of people. The infamous Highland Clearances of the early 19th century saw most of the population moved from the land to make way for sheep. Whole communities were evicted without compensation and their houses burnt. Most emigrated to America, Canada and Australia but some relocated to the barren land round the coast and eked out a living. The fertile farmland found around the coast of Sutherland today is a result of generations of hard work. There remains considerable ill feeling in this area towards the Duke of Sutherland, the biggest landowner.

Although there are few people, there is a lot of life in the peatlands. Red deer are common, and if you are lucky you might see foxes, pine martens, otters, badgers and the shy Scottish wild cat. There is abundant plant life. Look out for bog moss, bog cotton, bog asphodel, bog myrtle, club moss and of course heather.

There is a great variety of insect life including the less desirable Scottish beasties – the cleg (horsefly) and the dreaded midge. Fortunately a remarkable plant called the sundew is common here. Its sticky leaves capture insects, and extract nutrients from them. It is particularly partial to the midge. However take other precautions and use a good insect repellent when walking here in summer and autumn or you'll be eaten alive!

The Flow Country

*A unique landscape of extensive peatlands is glimpsed
from its northern edge*

1 From the lay-by to the southeast of Melvich, cross the road and head up a farm track to the left of a small loch. The track goes through a gate and curves to the left behind a derelict cottage. You will encounter two gates across the track close together.

2 Midway between the two gates, take the rough peat-cutters track that goes uphill on your left. Continue to follow this track, keeping left when it forks, until it disappears. Then continue in this direction heading for the highest point, where you will see Loch Sgiathanach slightly to your left.

3 Head for the left-hand edge of the loch and follow the course of the Allt a Ghlasraich burn, which flows from here to Achridigill Loch.

4 Where the burn meets the loch, turn 90 degrees to the right. You should be heading to the mid-point between two small hills. Loch Baligill lies at the foot of the hills. Follow the shore-line along the right-hand side of the loch.

5 At the end of the loch, turn right and, keeping the hills on your left, head for the highest point in front of you. Climb a short, steep slope and from the top you should see the hill of Cnoc Eipteil ahead of you.

8 If you don't spot it, walk in that direction and eventually you will cut across it. This track will take you back to the main road. Turn right and follow the road through the village and beyond, to where you started.

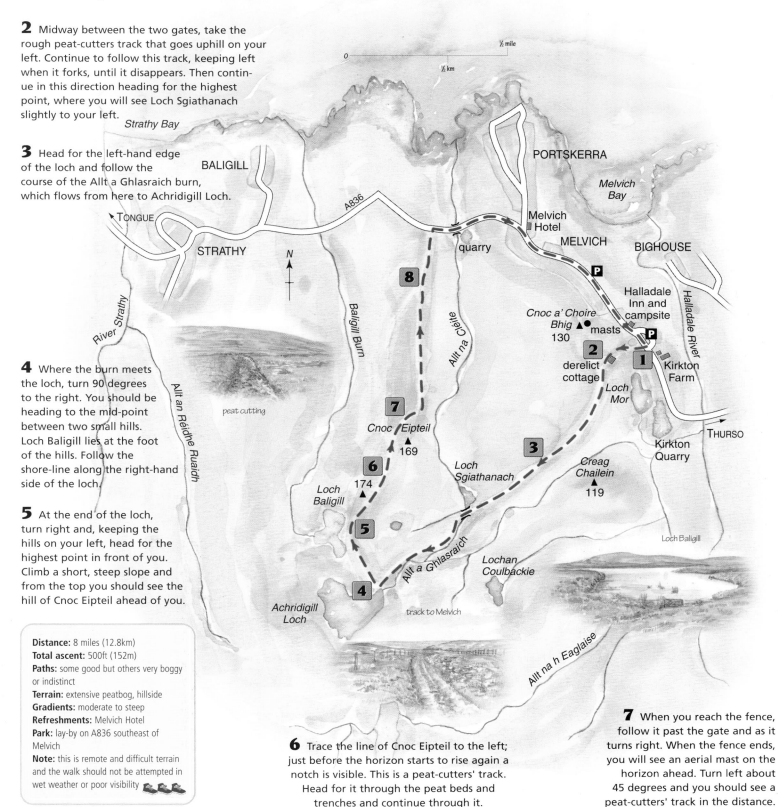

6 Trace the line of Cnoc Eipteil to the left; just before the horizon starts to rise again a notch is visible. This is a peat-cutters' track. Head for it through the peat beds and trenches and continue through it.

7 When you reach the fence, follow it past the gate and as it turns right. When the fence ends, you will see an aerial mast on the horizon ahead. Turn left about 45 degrees and you should see a peat-cutters' track in the distance.

Distance: 8 miles (12.8km)
Total ascent: 500ft (152m)
Paths: some good but others very boggy or indistinct
Terrain: extensive peatbog, hillside
Gradients: moderate to steep
Refreshments: Melvich Hotel
Park: lay-by on A836 southeast of Melvich
Note: this is remote and difficult terrain and the walk should not be attempted in wet weather or poor visibility

The Stuarts' Last Stand at Culloden

This rough moorland was the scene of a major battle in 1746, bringing the Jacobite uprising to a bloody end

WALK
115

Top right: the old cottage on the battle site has been restored, complete with heather thatch

Right: an early depiction of the battle shows a Jacobite charge being met by musket fire, lower right, while dragoons breech their defences to attack the Highland army from the rear, bottom left

Below: a memorial to the fallen

THE BATTLE OF CULLODEN WAS FOUGHT ON THIS MOOR 16TH APRIL 1746. THE GRAVES OF THE GALLANT HIGHLANDERS WHO FOUGHT FOR SCOTLAND & PRINCE CHARLIE ARE MARKED BY THE NAMES OF THEIR CLANS.

As you stroll through the lush pastures and tranquil woodlands surrounding Culloden, it is difficult to imagine the horror of the butchery that took place here. Over the last two and a half centuries the landscape has changed beyond recognition. But step onto the battle site and you are instantly transported to 16 April 1746. This little corner of what was once Drumossie Moor has been restored to the condition in which the opposing sides found it on that day.

The last battle fought on British soil, Culloden was the final clash between the Jacobites, intent on restoring the rightful Stuart line to the throne, and Government troops fighting in support of the Hanoverian monarchy, under the command of the Duke of Cumberland. In less than an hour the Duke had routed the Jacobite army and effectively ended the hopes of the Royal House of Stuart. Wounded Jacobites were slaughtered where they lay. Those who fled were ruthlessly hunted down and killed. Prince Charles Edward Stuart, Bonnie Prince Charlie, escaped from the field and for five months evaded the troops scouring the Highlands for him. Eventually, with a $30,000 price on his head, he escaped to Skye (dressed as Flora McDonald's maid), then on to Italy. Although he would never return to Scotland he would forever be the 'King across the water', subject of more songs than any other character in history.

As you walk around the battlefield, marker boards and flags illustrate the lines of both armies and detail the various clans and regiments who fought here. There were Highland clans on both sides, for this was not a war of Highlander against Lowlander. It was a civil war with religion and politics at its core. The Jacobite Rebellion started with the arrival of Bonnie Prince Charlie and the raising of the Stuart standard at Glenfinnan in 1745. Thereafter the Jacobite army marched south, defeating all who opposed them. They got as far as Derby and were in a position to threaten London when they halted and turned back. By the time they reached Culloden, although weary, hungry and utterly demoralised, they were still a formidable force, their fearsome battle charge legendary for breaking the ranks of their enemies, sending them fleeing before the howling onslaught.

But this time it would be different. From the vantage points behind the Jacobite lines, all you can see across the field of battle is rough, flat, boggy ground. It had been raining heavily and the conditions were not suited to the Jacobite charge. Facing you, between the two flags, would have been the Government's cavalry and artillery, which decimated the Jacobite ranks as they stood awaiting the order to charge. When the charge came it was a ragged, disorganised band that stumbled across the bleak open moor to die in a hail of grapeshot and artillery fire.

Around the field you will find stone memorials to the clans who fought and died here. A thousand fell in a pitiless hour on Drumossie Moor. The atmosphere around the long green barrows of the Jacobite graves is melancholic. Tradition has it that even the birds don't sing here.

The Stuarts' Last Stand at Culloden

*Around the woods and moors of Culloden, where the
Stuart cause died in battle*

1 Turn right onto the B9006, then first left for Balloch, then right onto a forestry road. Turn right at a T-junction, left when you reach a bungalow and complete a circuit returning to the main road and turn left.

2 Return to the visitor centre and enter battlefield site. Turn right at first junction, passing the yellow flag. Go straight on at the junction to a second yellow flag.

3 Turn left towards the red flag. Turn left at the flag, then right at the junction. Turn right at the bench and head for the vantage point for a view over the battlefield.

> **Distance:** 6½ miles (10.5km)
> **Total ascent:** negligible
> **Paths:** mostly good but can be muddy after wet weather
> **Terrain:** moorland, woodland, fields, forestry road and minor roads
> **Gradients:** none .
> **Refreshments:** visitor centre
> **Park:** Culloden battlefield visitor centre car park, off B9006 between Inverness and Croy
> **Note:** the battlefield site is owned by the National Trust for Scotland and an entrance fee is payable

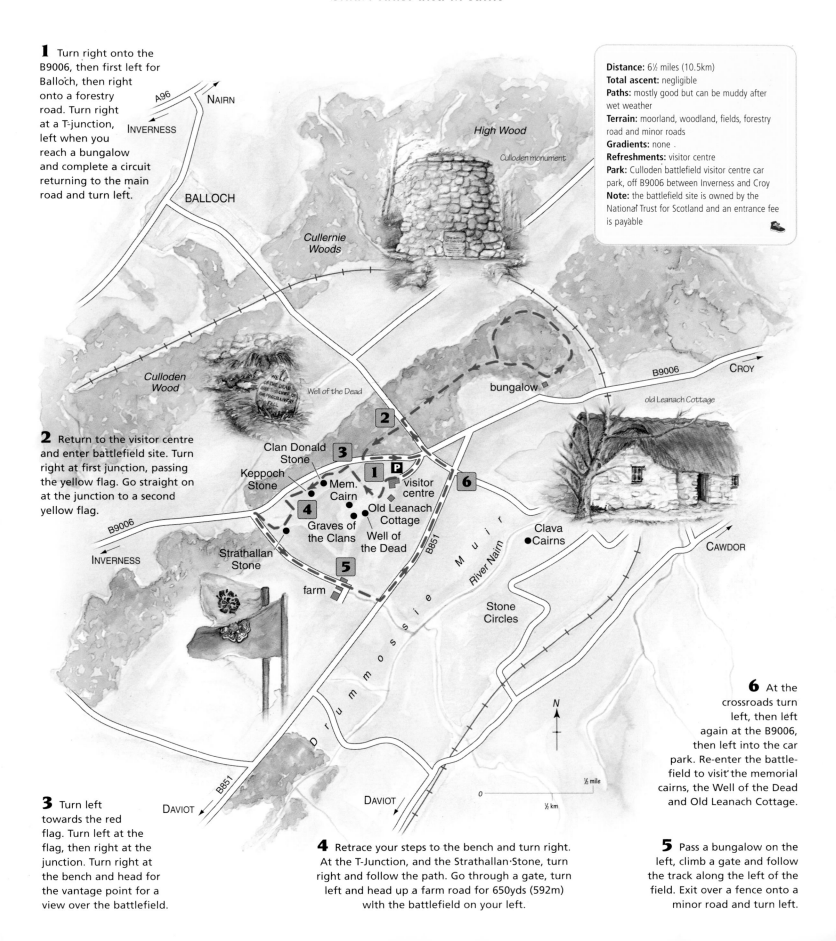

4 Retrace your steps to the bench and turn right. At the T-Junction, and the Strathallan·Stone, turn right and follow the path. Go through a gate, turn left and head up a farm road for 650yds (592m) with the battlefield on your left.

5 Pass a bungalow on the left, climb a gate and follow the track along the left of the field. Exit over a fence onto a minor road and turn left.

6 At the crossroads turn left, then left again at the B9006, then left into the car park. Re-enter the battlefield to visit the memorial cairns, the Well of the Dead and Old Leanach Cottage.

Rothiemurchus – Heart of the Caledonian Pine Forest

A fragment of the past, these ancient woods harbour the very essence of Scotland's natural history

WALK
116

Right: red squirrels maintain their hold here

Up to about 5,000 years ago, over 60 per cent of Scotland was covered in forest. The ancient Caledonian Forest was dominated by the hardy Scots pine with a few deciduous species, such as birch and rowan, mixed in. Then Stone Age settlers began clearing the forest for agriculture and settlement. Man's insatiable demand for timber ever since – for building, for fuel, for shipbuilding and for various war efforts – has, over the centuries, further denuded this precious and irreplaceable resource. Today, less than 1 per cent of that original forest remains, reduced now to just a few fragments scattered across the Highlands. This walk in Rothiemurchus is an exploration of the largest and finest example of surviving native forest.

Clearly marked and well-established tracks and paths lead you through a place of unique biodiversity. Just south of Coylumbridge, beautiful birch trees grow side by side with the old majestic pines. The delicate branches of the deciduous species drip heavy with ragged blue fronds of thick lichen, testimony to the purity of the air. The effect is to exaggerate your sense of being in the midst of a primeval forest.

Along with the desecration of the forest in Scotland has come the extinction of many of its great beasts. Elks, brown bears and wolves once roamed here, making Rothiemurchus today perhaps a safe place for you to walk through, but only because its fragile ecosystem is out of balance. Without predators, deer numbers continue to increase and their grazing has to be carefully managed.

Deer fencing has been erected throughout Rothiemurchus and you will notice that in places it is marked by orange bands. This is to give a warning of its presence to low-flying birds, particularly the very rare capercaillie, a large species of grouse. Rothiemurchus is one of the last strongholds of this 'horse of the woods'. Capercaillie apart, there exist few better opportunities for observing rare Scottish birds, including crested tits and crossbills, but patience is the watchword. If you are out close to dawn or dusk, you may be lucky enough to see a pine martin. Red squirrels, however, are much easier to spot.

Emerging from the forest up near Whitewell croft, you are rewarded by a fantastic view across a vast evergreen canopy with a mountainous backdrop. The true extent of the Cairngorm National Nature Reserve, which includes the mountains and is the largest national nature reserve in Europe, is seen to best effect at the road end above the memorial cairn at Whitewell.

The Cairngorm Mountains make up the highest land mass in Britain, so if you decide to venture up on to the high plateau, be prepared for arctic conditions. In winter the area receives relatively high levels of snow but at any time of year, as you look out east across Rothiemurchus, the ski-worn pistes on the slopes of Cairn Gorm will be clearly evident.

To the southeast you cannot fail to notice the spectacular glacial cutting known as the Lairig Ghru. This most famous of Scottish mountain passes effectively splits the Cairngorm tableland into two. If you are fit and well prepared, you can walk right through, from Speyside to Deeside.

Those with an interest in ancient archaeology can seek out some of the ancient hut circles at Whitewell. These are to be found up off to the right of the road but are actually quite well hidden by the heather.

East of Lochan Deo the forest has a more open aspect. Here, less mature Scots pines and saplings are thriving whereas elsewhere the trees are characteristically more diverse in their age. The forest is dense with fabulously contorted shapes and splashes of salmon-pink bark above a ground layer of bright green juniper and purple heather – a memorable sight. And the telltale heaps of pine needles on the forest floor, most evident between the old trees to the east of the Cairngorm Club Footbridge, betray the presence of those busybodies of the insect world, wood ants. The beauty spot of Loch Morlich bustles with folk in pursuit of water sports and recreation.

Rothiemurchus offers you a unique glimpse of a land of the past. Let us hope that it represents a Scotland of the future too.

Below: sunlight through the pines of Rothiemurchus

Rothiemurchus – Heart of the Caledonian Pine Forest

A memorable ramble through ancient woodland

1 Start on the footpath immediately to the right of the Rothiemurchus Camp and Caravan Park entrance, signposted Public Path to Braemar by the Lairig Ghru. Walk south along the track into the forest, then on through a gate by Lairig Ghru Cottage.

2 Where the track divides take the right fork, signposted for Gleann Einich, passing a large cairn on the left. Soon after, go over a stile at the cattle grid. The track then rises to more open country.

3 Having gained about the highest point along the track, turn sharp right for another track leading up over the heather. Reach a tarmac lane by a cattle grid, turn left and continue to where the lane terminates at Whitewell Croft. From there, bear left down a path for Rothiemurchus footpath. A short deviation leads first to a large memorial cairn on the left.

4 Walk down from the cairn and, on regaining the track for Gleann Einich, turn right for 700 yds (637m) to arrive at a major crossroads of estate tracks. There are fire beaters and signposts here. Follow the Lairig Ghru track to the left, passing pine-fringed Lochan Deo and walking beyond where the other path from Coylumbridge joins from the left. Soon after, reach the Cairngorm Club footbridge over the Allt na Bheinn Mhor.

5 Go over the bridge and turn right on a rough track heading upstream of the river. From where the waters of the Am Beanaidh and the Allt Druidh join forces, veer southeast, passing close to a ruined house on the left before rising gently up to Piccadilly.

6 Piccadilly is the Rothiemurchus Estate name for this other major junction of tracks, a focal point marked by a large cairn. Walk northeast from here, following the Loch Morlich track. Shortly after passing through a stile at Tilhill, turn left joining the track from Rothiemurchus Lodge to Loch Morlich and continue through a further 2 miles (3.2km) of pine forest.

7 Join the road to Glen More and the ski centre by the western shore of Loch Morlich. At certain times of the year the road is served by buses connecting with Aviemore (check with local tourist information), which offers a convenient return; alternatively it is a further 1 hour of walking by the roadside to return to Coylumbridge.

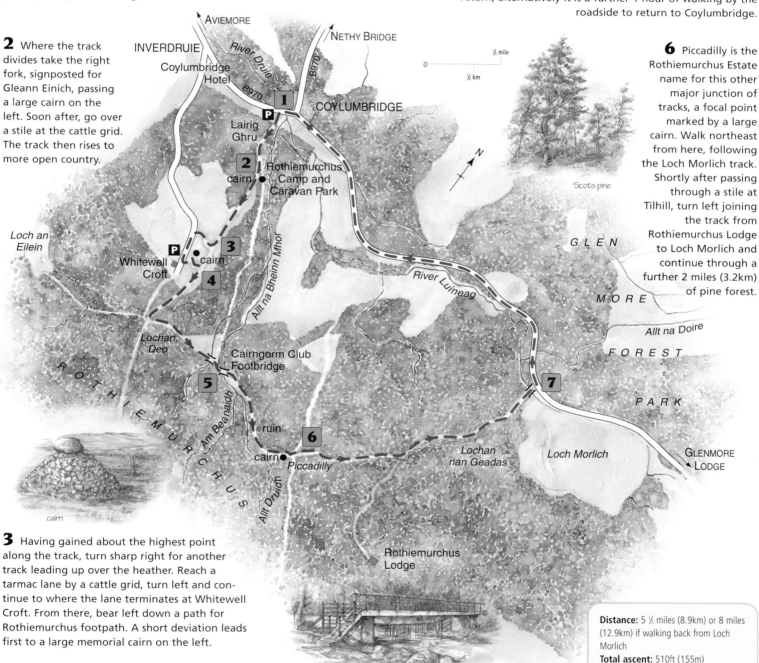

Scots pine

Cairngorm Club footbridge

Distance: 5 ½ miles (8.9km) or 8 miles (12.9km) if walking back from Loch Morlich
Total ascent: 510ft (155m)
Paths: mostly good, level tracks; wet in places after rain
Terrain: pine forest, heather moorland
Gradients: gradual
Refreshments: Coylumbridge Hotel and in Aviemore
Park: by roadside, just west of entrance to Rothiemurchus Camp and Caravan Park, near Coylumbridge, 2 miles (3.2km) southeast of Aviemore

On General Wade's Road

A military road constructed as part of a network to subdue the Highlands provides the starting point of this walk

WALK 117

Top right: reminders of Wade's roads can be found all over the Highlands

Above: it is a tribute to the Highlands' first road builder that successive engineers followed his line

Below: the ruined Ruthven Barracks

In the early part of the 18th century the Highlands of Scotland were wild and inaccessible. Rough drove roads and paths followed the line of glen and river, and most Highlanders lived their entire lives without travelling more than a few miles from home. As the Romans had subdued England by road-building around 1,500 years previously, so His Britannic Majesty's military presence in the Highlands paved his way to dominance.

General George Wade had been sent to Scotland by the Government in 1724 to quell the continuing unrest. His brief was to recommend 'such remedies as may conduce to the quiet of His Majesty's faithful subjects and the good settlement of that part of the Kingdom'. Wade discovered that it was impossible to move troops and supplies efficiently and proposed an intensive programme of road-building. As Military Commander in Scotland, Wade built over 250 miles (400km) of road in the central and western Highlands between 1726 and 1737.

Starting from a well-preserved Wade Bridge, this walk covers a few miles of the surviving fragment to Ruthven Barracks. The construction was back-breaking. First the soldiers would remove the turf and topsoil and dig until they hit rocks and stone. They would then level this by

sledgehammer; if the stones were too big, they would lever them out or blast with gunpowder. Finally, 18 inches (45.7cm) of gravel would be laid on top and compacted by boots and spades. The soil removed was built up as banks, and drainage ditches were dug to keep the surface free from flooding. A soldier would create, on average, a yard and a half (1.4m) per day.

The Highlanders opposed the roads. Clan chiefs saw increased communications as a threat to their power, while others feared the hard surfaces would damage the hooves of their cattle and horses. Ordinary people thought the gravel would cut their bare feet and scorned the use of bridges as feeble. Nevertheless, Bonnie Prince Charlie used Wade's roads to move his army rapidly over long distances during the Jacobite uprising of 1745. Wade, then aged 72, was brought out of retirement to crush the rebels, meriting a jingoistic verse in the National Anthem.

God Grant that Marshall Wade,
May by Thy mighty aid,
Victory bring.
May he sedition hush,
And like a torrent rush,
Rebellious Scots to crush,
God save the King.

The banning of the kilt, tartan and bagpipes, following the defeat of the Jacobite army, could never have been enforced without the accessibility granted by Wade's road network. The subsequent history of the Highlands, including the Clearances can be attributed in some measure to Wade and his roads.

On General Wade's Road

*Discovering a section of the great military occupation
road near Newtonmore*

1 From the visitor centre car park at Ralia turn right and walk 330yds (300m) to the road that runs parallel to the A9. When the A9 exit for Newtonmore joins this road, cross over and take the minor road (signposted to Ralia and Nuide) to the right.

8 Continue on this road towards the A9. Cross the A9 and turn right, then take the first left onto a minor road, signposted from the A9 'Farm Access 200yds'. Continue down this road, past the lane to Nuide Farm, until you return to the car park at Ralia.

2 A short distance along here on the right, at the gap in the trees, climb a gate and follow the track uphill. Cross another gate and turn left onto the A9. About 350yds (320m) further along you reach Ralia Kennels (unmistakable but unsigned).

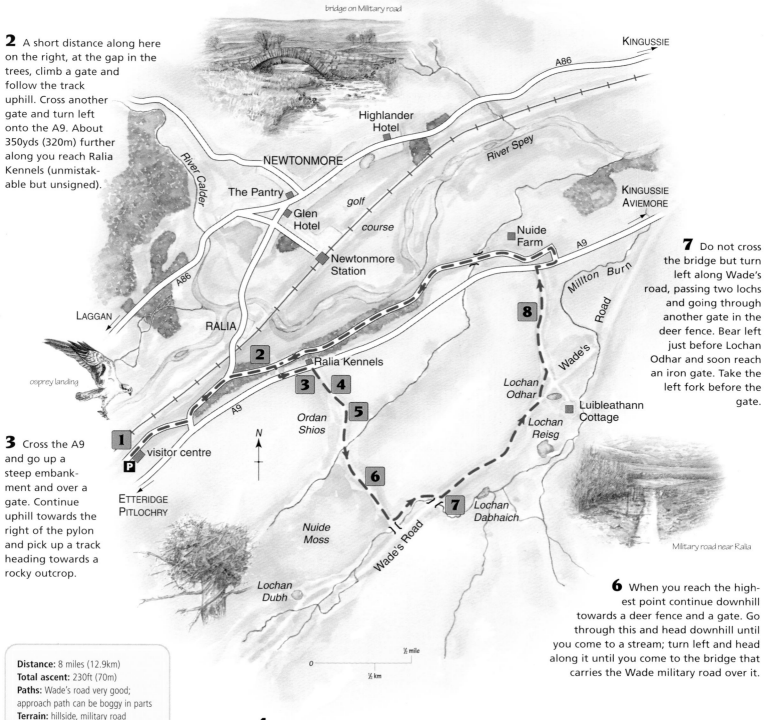

bridge on Military road

Military road near Ralia

3 Cross the A9 and go up a steep embankment and over a gate. Continue uphill towards the right of the pylon and pick up a track heading towards a rocky outcrop.

7 Do not cross the bridge but turn left along Wade's road, passing two lochs and going through another gate in the deer fence. Bear left just before Lochan Odhar and soon reach an iron gate. Take the left fork before the gate.

6 When you reach the highest point continue downhill towards a deer fence and a gate. Go through this and head downhill until you come to a stream; turn left and head along it until you come to the bridge that carries the Wade military road over it.

Distance: 8 miles (12.9km)
Total ascent: 230ft (70m)
Paths: Wade's road very good; approach path can be boggy in parts
Terrain: hillside, military road
Gradients: moderate
Refreshments: visitor centre
Park: Ralia visitor centre, off A9 near Newtonmore

4 Cross a stile at the fence and continue on the track towards the left-hand side of the hill. On a good day it is worth detouring up to the summit to enjoy the panoramic views of the surrounding area.

5 Follow the path round the back of the hill and then turn left. Go downhill and across some boggy ground before rising again to meet a farm track passing in front of you. Cross this and continue on a line uphill.

Great Birnam Wood to Dunkeld

The Birnam Oak, with grand echoes of Macbeth, is the perfect foil to the more modest little town

WALK
118

Top right: the 'little houses' of Dunkeld, cared for by the National Trust for Scotland, are still lived in – so not open to the public

Dunkeld, an ancient cathedral town on the edge of the Highlands, and for centuries a thriving market town, is now a well-preserved historic village lying amidst woods, crags and rivers. The cathedral was an important religious centre from Celtic times to the Reformation. After the Battle of Dunkeld in 1689 the cathedral and most of the houses were razed to the ground. William Cleland, who led the victorious army but was killed in the battle, lies buried in the nave of the cathedral. Ironically, lying next to him is the grandson of Prince Charles Edward Stuart (Bonnie Prince Charlie). Over the centuries the cathedral has been partially restored, and the chapter house contains a small museum.

The little houses built after the town was burned down cluster round the square in the High Street. It would have been a busy place as merchants, millers, cattle-traders and farmers gathered around the old mercat cross, now replaced by a fountain. The bronze ell-measure, which weavers used for measuring cloth (an ell equals 45 inches, or 114cm), is still fixed to the front of the Ell House. St Ninian's Wynd leads to Bakehouse Cottage and the Old Smiddy. The High Street would have been the main thoroughfare before Telford's bridge across the River Tay superseded the ferries. The seven-arched bridge, complete with toll cottage, built in 1809, linked Dunkeld to Birnam. When the railway station was built in Birnam the tolls occasioned great unrest in Dunkeld.

The railways attracted many visitors, including children's writer, Beatrix Potter, who spent her summers in the area. From here she sent letters to Noel Moor, son of her former governess, telling the adventures of Peter Rabbit. The Beatrix Potter Garden has been designed to give an insight into the origins of her stories. There are statues of all her characters, including Mrs Tiggy-winkle, who was based on a Perthshire washerwoman, Kittie MacDonald, 'A comical round little old woman as brown as a berry'.

The rich wildlife and scenery depicted by Beatrix Potter still abounds. The larch wood planted by the third Duke of Atholl harbours many rare species, including red squirrel and capercaillie. The Hermitage woodland walk created in the 18th century has Britain's tallest tree – a 212-foot (65m) Douglas fir – and an enormous cedar of Lebanon 108 feet high (33m). The centrepiece at the Hermitage is a stone summerhouse called Ossian's Hall, built on a rocky outcrop with a dramatic view of the waterfall below. In contrast to the classical lines of Ossian's Hall is Ossian's Cave, where natural rock formations have been built up with stone to form a roofed cell.

Dunkeld and the remarkable woodlands surrounding it are steeped in history. On the riverbank is the massive old Birnam Oak, said to be the last remaining tree from the famous Birnam Wood of the witches' prophecy in Shakespeare's *Macbeth*. Robert Burns visited Dunkeld on his tour of the Highlands, meeting the great Scottish fiddler, Neil Gow. In 1842 Queen Victoria judged the village very, very pretty – and it still is.

Above: the cathedral stands as a reminder that Dunkeld was once an important town

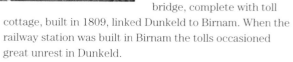

Right: the riverside walk at the Hermitage

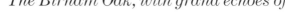

Great Birnam Wood to Dunkeld

With overtones of Macbeth in the wooded Tay Valley

2 Cross the bridge and walk down the steps on the left-hand side of the bridge. At the bottom follow the path to the right, downstream along the river. Just past the Birnam Oak turn up the steps signposted to Birnam, following the path round to the road. Cross to the Beatrix Potter Garden. Leaving there, turn left along the main road.

1 From the car park at Dunkeld walk along Athol Street and turn right into High Street. From the square you can investigate the fountain, rectory, cathedral and surrounding historic buildings. Retrace your steps to Athol Street and turn right.

Distance: 6 miles (9.7km)
Total ascent: 200ft (61m)
Paths: good; can be muddy after rain
Terrain: woodland with some riverbank and pavements
Gradients: gradual
Refreshments: Birnam Hotel, opposite Beatrix Potter Garden
Park: car park at end of Athol Street

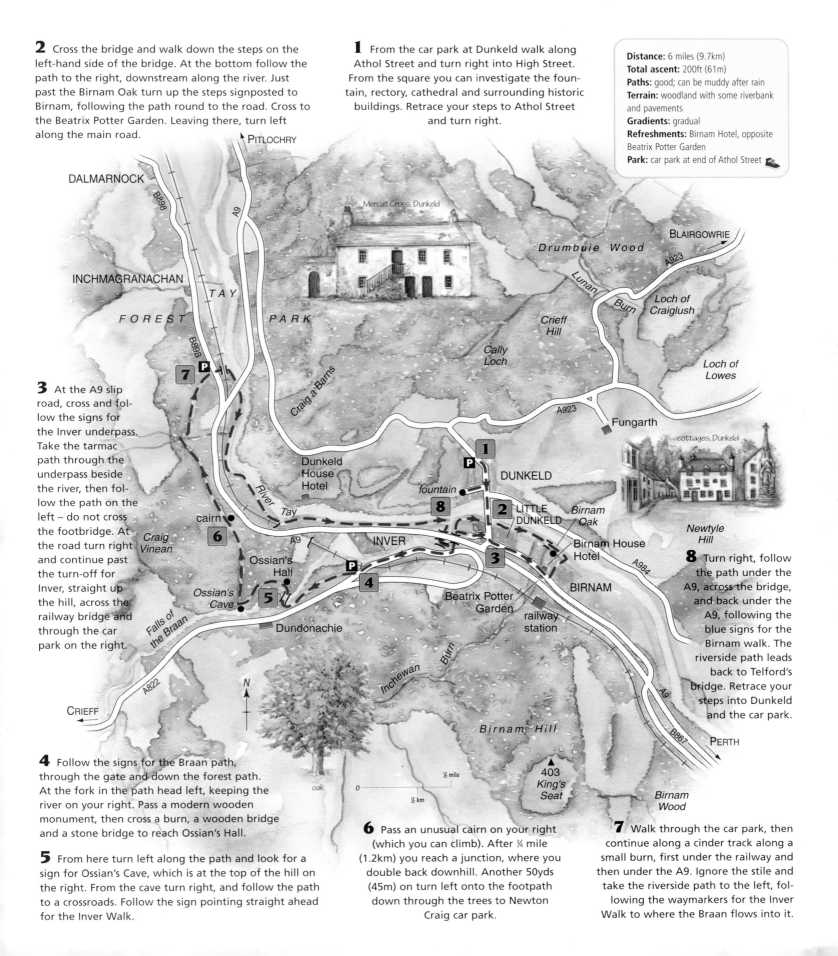

3 At the A9 slip road, cross and follow the signs for the Inver underpass. Take the tarmac path through the underpass beside the river, then follow the path on the left – do not cross the footbridge. At the road turn right and continue past the turn-off for Inver, straight up the hill, across the railway bridge and through the car park on the right.

4 Follow the signs for the Braan path, through the gate and down the forest path. At the fork in the path head left, keeping the river on your right. Pass a modern wooden monument, then cross a burn, a wooden bridge and a stone bridge to reach Ossian's Hall.

5 From here turn left along the path and look for a sign for Ossian's Cave, which is at the top of the hill on the right. From the cave turn right, and follow the path to a crossroads. Follow the sign pointing straight ahead for the Inver Walk.

6 Pass an unusual cairn on your right (which you can climb). After ¾ mile (1.2km) you reach a junction, where you double back downhill. Another 50yds (45m) on turn left onto the footpath down through the trees to Newton Craig car park.

7 Walk through the car park, then continue along a cinder track along a small burn, first under the railway and then under the A9. Ignore the stile and take the riverside path to the left, following the waymarkers for the Inver Walk to where the Braan flows into it.

8 Turn right, follow the path under the A9, across the bridge, and back under the A9, following the blue signs for the Birnam walk. The riverside path leads back to Telford's bridge. Retrace your steps into Dunkeld and the car park.

Stirling, Cockpit of Scottish History

From the heights of Stirling Castle can be seen the sites of many a bitter conflict over the centuries

The rugged volcanic plug beneath Stirling Castle dominates the wide, low-lying plain where standard-bearing knights rode out for honour, greed or power and wild Scots foot soldiers descended on the disciplined English ranks. This stronghold has been the gatekeeper to Scotland since it was settled by the early British Picts. Look over the castle battlements and imagine courtly tournaments and bloody battles. Wander through the great hall, scene of royal banquets, music and feasting over the centuries. The castle became a royal residence in 1226 and continued as a magnificent international medieval court until the time of the Stuarts.

The ladies of the court are said to have used the Ladies' Rock in the cemetery to watch tournaments in the valley below. From this rocky knoll you can see as far as the Trossachs and there is a cairn pointing out all the surrounding battlefields. The two most famous battles fought here were the Battle of Stirling Bridge in 1297, immortalised in the film *Braveheart*, and the Battle of Bannockburn in 1314, when Robert the Bruce defeated the English, and the Scots regained their independence. As well as these you can see the sites of the battles of Falkirk, Sauchieburn and Sherriffmuir, and the tall Wallace Monument, marking where William Wallace camped before the Battle of Stirling Bridge.

The religious wars of the Reformation are commemorated in the cemetery with monuments to the martyrs, the most imposing of which is the incongruous Star Pyramid. A further reminder of the savagery of the age is the Beheading Stone on Gowan Hill. From here you can see the 'auld brig' over the River Forth, a narrow 15th-century stone bridge which replaced the even narrower wooden bridge of the famous battle. The Scots allowed around half the invaders to advance across that earlier Stirling Bridge and then, when the enemy could neither advance nor retreat, William Wallace and the Scots swept forward to an astounding victory over a far superior force.

Further along the river is the 13th-century Cambuskenneth Abbey, which was the site of Bruce's Parliament in 1326. As you return to the castle your walk takes you alongside the old town wall, which held off many attacks over the centuries. The old town was built on this steep approach to the castle and many 16th- and 17th-century buildings survive close by. There is a 17th-century almshouse, called Cowan's Hospital, and the Church of the Holy Rude, where James VI was crowned in 1567. There is also the old high school (now the Royal Highland Hotel), the former Erskine Church (now the youth hostel) and the old town jail, which is open to visitors. Follow the signposts to investigate these and enjoy the ambience of the old town.

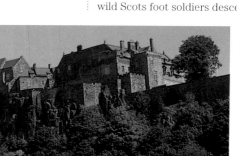

Above: Stirling Castle is set on a crag with an unrivalled view over the plain

Top right: the striking Bannockburn memorial

Below: the Church of the Holy Rude stands within the castle ramparts

Stirling, Cockpit of Scottish History

The history of Scotland has been played out on the streets of this strategic burgh

WALK 119

1 From the castle car park, head downhill, passing the visitor centre on your left. Follow the sign to the right for the Back Walk, passing the old Grammar School, now a hotel called the Portcullis. On the Back Walk, the cemetery is to the left and the Pyramid to the right.

2 Turn into the cemetery by the iron gates opposite the Pyramid. Climb the Ladies' Rock for a view over the historic sites of Stirling and the Forth Valley and exit by the back gate. Turn right and continue until you see a fork to the left.

3 Ignore the steps to the left and take the path alongside as far as a narrow tarmac road. Cross the road via two kissing gates and continue on the path, ignoring two forks to the left and passing Gowan Hill with a pair of cannons on top.

4 Continue on the path, ignoring a right uphill fork. At the houses turn left down a lane with the Wallace Monument ahead in the distance. At the T-junction bear left on a lane, then take the narrow, grassy track on your left up to Gowan Hill.

5 Return to the lane and continue to the main road. Cross and turn left, heading through the pedestrian underpass. Old Stirling Bridge is to your left and accessible through the hospital grounds. Retrace your steps from the bridge and turn left into an underpass to the centre of the roundabout. Turn left again through another underpass which exits beyond the road bridge.

6 Follow the riverside path under the railway bridge and continue until the river begins to bend left. Take the path on the right behind the bowling club and follow the riverside path again to the footbridge to Cambuskenneth. Cross the bridge, head up the street and turn right at the T-junction to reach Cambuskenneth Abbey. Retrace your steps back over the bridge and turn left, then right to continue along Abbey Road towards the town.

7 At the station, cross the railway bridge and take the underpass to Maxwell Place. Follow the curve of the street to the left to the post office. Cross into Friars Street. At the end turn left and follow the road up and around to the right, to Corn Exchange Road on the left.

8 On Corn Exchange Road, beyond the Municipal Building and opposite the library, take the cobbled lane to the right signposted Upper Back Walk. Head uphill, with the old town walls on your right. You can investigate the Old Town as you ascend, finally arriving back at the castle car park.

Distance: 5 miles (8km)
Total ascent: 100ft (30m)
Paths: good; mostly paved but some dirt tracks
Terrain: town trail and riverside
Gradients: gentle, one short steep section
Refreshments: Castle Tea Room
Park: car park, Castle Esplanade, Stirling

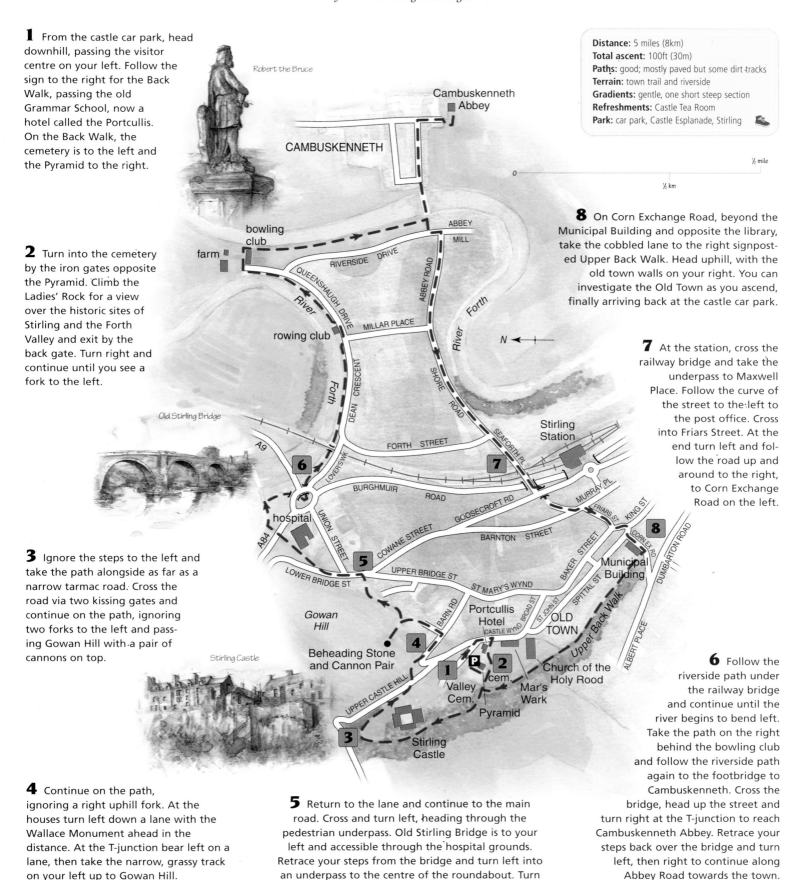

Robert the Bruce

Cambuskenneth Abbey

CAMBUSKENNETH

bowling club

farm

RIVERSIDE DRIVE

QUEENSHAUGH DRIVE

River Forth

rowing club

MILLAR PLACE

DEAN CRESCENT

ABBEY ROAD

MILL

ABBEY

SHORE ROAD

River Forth

SEAFORTH PL

N

Old Stirling Bridge

A9

FORTH STREET

LOVER'S WK

BURGHMUIR ROAD

GOOSECROFT RD

6

hospital

A84

UNION STREET

COWANE STREET

BARNTON STREET

Stirling Station

7

MURRAY PL

FRIARS ST

KING ST

BAKER STREET

8

CORN EX RD

Municipal Building

DUMBARTON ROAD

5

UPPER BRIDGE ST

LOWER BRIDGE ST

ST MARY'S WYND

BARN RD

ST JOHN ST

BROAD ST

SPITTAL ST

Upper Back Walk

ALBERT PLACE

Gowan Hill

4

Beheading Stone and Cannon Pair

Stirling Castle

Portcullis Hotel

CASTLE WYND

1

P

Valley Cem.

2

cem.

Mar's Wark

Pyramid

Church of the Holy Rood

OLD TOWN

3

UPPER CASTLE HILL

Stirling Castle

The Lomond Hills of Fife

Some of the finest views and best wildlife in Fife may be enjoyed on this magnificent hill walk

WALK
120

Top right: the delicate flowers of grass-of-parnassus may be seen here

Below: looking eastwards from the summit of West Lomond hill

Inset below: a venerable boundary marker

If the thought of struggling up Munros (mountains over 3,000 feet or 914m) makes you break out in a cold sweat yet you would still like to view Scotland's scenery from a decent vantage point, this walk is for you. You can enjoy the two finest views over the Kingdom of Fife and a lively nature ramble between them, for a modest expenditure of energy.

The path to West Lomond crosses open heather-clad moorland. Three hundred million years ago this was an active volcano. The hard rock produced by the two volcanoes protected the softer stone underneath from erosion, leaving the Lomonds the highest points in Fife. The slopes of the hills were once cloaked by an ancient forest of oak, ash and elm that has long since vanished as the land was cleared for farming. To the right is the valley of the Howe of Fife, where an Iron Age people, the Venicones, built a fort at Maiden Castle and another on the top of East Lomond. You can still make out the rings of the fortification ditches. You may come across stones with 'W R 1818' carved on them, which are boundary markers from the enclosures when, by Act of Parliament, the common grazings were removed from the people and given to local landowners, overseen by the king's commissioner, Sir William Rae.

This moorland is one of the last remaining expanses of heather in Fife, providing a habitat for animals and birds that need open spaces. Look out for grouse and listen for the haunting cry of the curlew. Short-eared owls hunt here in daylight, flying low, swooping back and forth with military precision until they plunge for the kill. There are also pheasants, and in the forested areas woodpigeons and roe deer. Away from the heather you may come

across wild orchids, particularly the heath spotted orchid. Forestry development has altered the landscape but is not new to the Lomonds: early in the 19th century the laird of Falkland Estate, Onesiphorus Tyndall Bruce, planted thousands of trees, many of which are still standing. Look out for the clusters of old Scots pine that can be seen from many points of this walk.

From the summit of West Lomond the Kingdom of Fife unfolds like a huge patchwork. The villages of Falkland, Strathmiglo and Auchtermuchty stretch out along the Howe. The north side is bordered by the tail end of the Ochils and, beyond, Dundee and the River Tay are clearly visible. Looking back towards East Lomond the entire panorama of the day's walk is spread before you to trace the paths and tracks from start to finish. To get the best from this walk head up West Lomond early in the day, then spend the remaining hours meandering across moorland, through forest and by water. Finally climb East Lomond for a glorious skyline as the sun sets across the Howe of Fife and West Lomond.

The Lomond Hills of Fife

*Topping out on the highest point of the
ancient Kingdom of Fife*

2 Follow the diversion signs to the right of the hill and part-way round turn left up a narrow path to the summit. Retrace your steps to the diversion sign and continue round the front of the hill.

1 Follow the sign to West Lomond. Go up some steps, cross a stile and turn left. At the top of the field go through a gap in the wall, turn right, through another wall, and turn left onto the path to West Lomond.

3 Follow the track as it bears away from the hill to a stile where three fences meet. Cross this and head downhill beside the cut of the stream. Cross a plank bridge and another stile on your right then turn left following the line of the wall.

4 At the bottom of the field go left through a kissing-gate and follow the path towards the edge of the wood. A kissing-gate on the right leads you across a bridge and to a road through the wood.

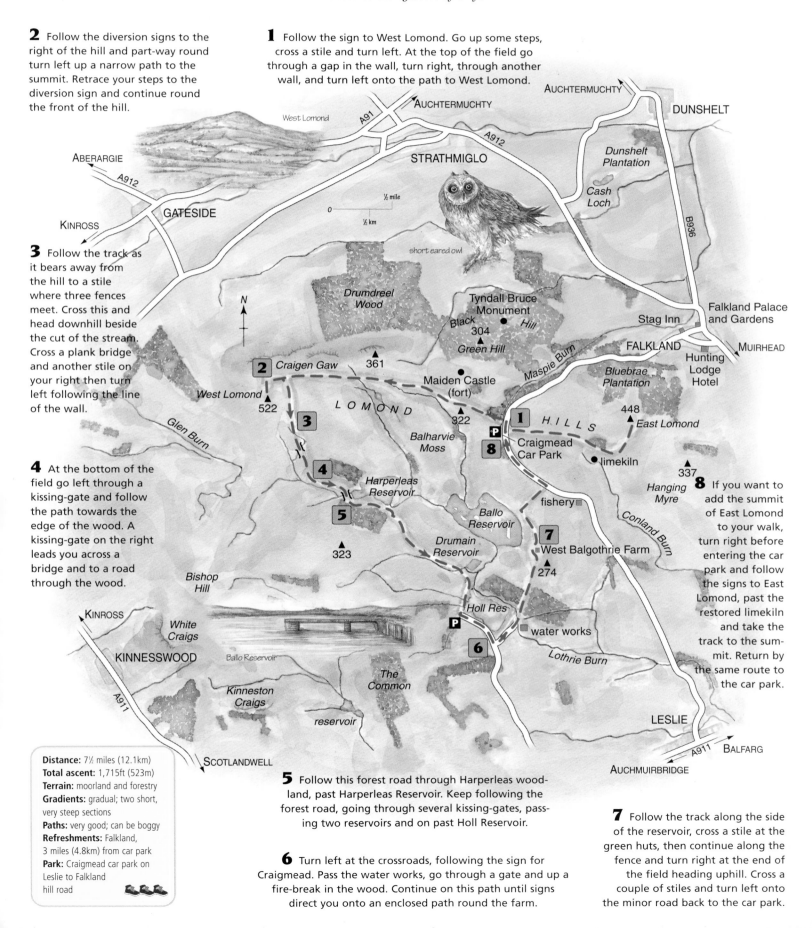

8 If you want to add the summit of East Lomond to your walk, turn right before entering the car park and follow the signs to East Lomond, past the restored limekiln and take the track to the summit. Return by the same route to the car park.

Distance: 7½ miles (12.1km)
Total ascent: 1,715ft (523m)
Terrain: moorland and forestry
Gradients: gradual; two short, very steep sections
Paths: very good; can be boggy
Refreshments: Falkland, 3 miles (4.8km) from car park
Park: Craigmead car park on Leslie to Falkland hill road

5 Follow this forest road through Harperleas woodland, past Harperleas Reservoir. Keep following the forest road, going through several kissing-gates, passing two reservoirs and on past Holl Reservoir.

6 Turn left at the crossroads, following the sign for Craigmead. Pass the water works, go through a gate and up a fire-break in the wood. Continue on this path until signs direct you onto an enclosed path round the farm.

7 Follow the track along the side of the reservoir, cross a stile at the green huts, then continue along the fence and turn right at the end of the field heading uphill. Cross a couple of stiles and turn left onto the minor road back to the car park.

Index

Acknowledgements

Walks written and compiled by: Chris Bagshaw, Nick Channer, Paddy Dillon, Martin Dunning, Rebecca Ford, John Gillham, David Hancock, Alison Layland, Lawrence Main, Terry Marsh, Julie Meech, John Morrison, Brian Pearce, Richard Sale, Hamish Scott, Roly Smith, Christopher Somerville, Hugh Taylor and Moira McCrossan, Hilary Weston, Stephen Whitehorne, Angela Wigglesworth, Nia Williams, David Winpenny.

Map illustrations: Chris Orr and Associates

Page layout: Graham Dudley

We would like to thank Janet Tabinski and Nick Reynolds for their editorial input, and Jenny Gill of Skelley Cartographic Services for compiling the maps.

Photographs
The Automobile Association would like to thank the following establishments, libraries and photographers for their assistance in the compilation of this book: ARCAID 92c; CHRIS BONNINGTON PICTURE LIBRARY 156c; BRADFORD COUNCIL REGENERATION MARKETING 180c; EA BOWNESS 1b ,150b,152a 156b, 158a, 158b, 158c, 160; BROXTOWE BOROUGH COUNCIL DH LAWRENCE HERITAGE 130b; K CARROLL f/c, b/c, 1, 2 leaf; BRUCE COLEMAN COLLECTION 30a, 32a, 38b, 40a, 40b, 50a, 72a, 72b, 138b, 150a, 154a, 170b, 206a, 234a, 276a, 266b, 276b; STEVE DAY 6b, 46b, 46c; ET ARCHIVE 204b, 274b; MARY EVANS PICTURE LIBRARY 12, 16b, 56, 68a 86a, 92a, 96a, 102, 112b, 132b, 164b, 174a, 174b, 186a, 190a, 238, 242a, 262a, 270b; DEREK FORSS 24b, 38c, 48c, 50c, 54/5, 74a, 84a, 84b, 90c, 160c, 182b; FOTOMAS INDEX 60a, 126a, 136a, 136b, 248a; JOHN GILLHAM 190c, 216b, 218c, 220a; HULTON GETTY PICTURE COLLECTION 94a 144, 180a, 278b; IMAGES COLOUR LIBRARY 142/3, 192/3; IMPERIAL WAR MUSEUM 24a; INTERNATIONAL PHOTOBANK 195, 196/7; IRONBRIDGE GORGE MUSEUM TRUST 106a; LAST INVASION CENTRE FISHGUARD 210b (tapestry design Elizabeth Cramp, photo Mirander Walker);
LEICESTERSHIRE COUNTY COUNCIL 101a, 132a; LAURENCE MAIN 210c, 214a, 214b, 214c, 224a; TERRY MARSH 120a, 154b, 232a, 232b, 232c, 234b, 234c; JULIE MEECH 7a, 52c, 108b, 114a, 114b, 114c, 124b, 198a, 198b, 204a, 270a; JOHN MILLER 8/9; JOHN MORRISON 180b, 186b; JOHN MOTTISHAW 126b; EDMUND NAGELE f/c f; NATIONAL PORTRAIT GALLERY 78b, 148a; NATIONAL TRUST PHOTO LIBRARY © 1d, 7b, 62a, 62b, 110 (Jo Corish), 1a (D Sellman), 6a (Chris Warren), 126 (Geoff Morgan), 152, 222a (William R Davis), 272 (Kevin J Richardson); NATURE PHOTOGRAPHERS 152b, 216a, (R Bush) 176a, 246a, 284a, 286b (P R Sterry), 218a (P Newman) 222b, (A J Cleave) 264a, 250a (E A Janes) 268a; TONY OLIVER 230a, 230b, 230c; BRIAN PEARCE 1c, 2, 34a, 36a, 36c; PHOTO LIBRARY OF WALES 193, 206b, 206c, 212a, 212c, 224c, 228a, 228b, 228c; PICTURES COLOUR LIBRARY 60b; P RAMM 94c; JOHN PRINGLE 244a, 246b, 248b, 248c, 264b, 284b, 284c; R G SALE 20a, 42a, 42b, 50b, 176b; SCOTLAND IN FOCUS 252b; SPECTRUM COLOUR LIBRARY 11, 16c, 32c, 46a, 74b, 74c, 86c, 186c, 252a, 274a; STILL MOVING PICTURE COMPANY 262b; DAVID TARN 143, 172B; UNIVERSITEIT GENT 52b; VIEWFINDERS (W Voysey) 18a, 18ca, 34b, 44c, 64b, 80a, 80c, 82c, 90a, 90b; H WEBSTER SHPL 266c; WELSH TOURIST BOARD 208b; WILDFOWL & WETLANDS TRUST 250b; STEVE WHITEHORN 246c; G WILLIAMS f/c d; WORLD PICTURES 40c.

The following photographs are taken from the Association's own Picture Library, with contributions from: M Alexander f/c e, 239, 244b, 244c, 250c, 256a; M Alward-Copin 204c; P Athie 220c; A Baker 98a, 98b, 106b, 106c, 278c; P Baker 12/13, 20b, 22b, 22c, 66b, 76c, 100/1, 136c; V Bates 88a; J Beazley 168a, 168b, 182a, 254a, 254b, 254c, 260a; A Besley 28a, 28b; M Birkitt 94b, 94d, 104/5, 116a, 118b, 118c, 122a, 122b, 128a, 128b, 128d, 130a, 130c,132c, 134a, 134c, 138a, 138c, 140a, 140b; E A Bowness f/c a, 156a; I Burgum 208a, 210a, 216c, 224b; J Carnie 241, 262b, 278a; R Czaja 18b; D Corrance 240/1; S Day 14/15, 15, 48a, 48b, 144/5, 145, 148b, 237, 238/a, 280a, 280c, 282a, 282c; R Eames 220b; E Ellington 272b; R Elliott 242b, 268c, 270c; P Enticnap 82, 82b; R Fletcher 80b; D Forss 55, 58, 72c, 86b, 96b, 96c, 260b; S Gibson 258a, 258b, 258c; D Hardley 260c; J Henderson 264c, 268b; A J Hopkins 103, 120b, 122c, 124c, 194/5; C Jones 52a, 102/3, 112a, 112c, 226a, 226b; A Lawson 13, 22a, 32b, 34c; C Lees 147, 164a, 164c, 166b, 166c; S & O Matthews 16a, 56/7, 76a, 76b, 98c, 108a, 146/7; J Miller 57, 64b, 66a, 68a, 68c, 70a, 70b, 70c; C Molyneau 202b, 202c; J Morrison 162b, 170c; R Moss 26a, 26b, 30a, 30c, 44b; R Newton 44a, 118a, 128c, 134b, 172a, 188b; K Patterson 256b, 266a; N Ray 10/11; P Sharpe 236/7, 256c, 282b; T Souter 58/9, 78a; R Strange 202a; D Tarn 143, 172b, 162a, 174c, 178b, 178c; M Taylor 272a; M Trelawny 78c; A Tryner 116b, 116c; W Voysey 38a, 59, 92b, 176c, 190b; R Weir 274c; J Welsh 110a, 110c, 112c; L Whitwam 184a, 184b, 188b; H Williams 36b, 178a, 200b, 208c, 218b; P Wilson 176c, 190b; AA 170a, 200a, 212b, 280b.